THE MUTE STONES SPEAK

THE
MUTE
STONES
SPEAK

THE STORY
OF
ARCHAEOLOGY
IN
ITALY
SECOND EDITION

PAUL MacKENDRICK

W · W · NORTON & COMPANY · NEW YORK · LONDON

To My Wife

Copyright © 1983, 1960 by Paul MacKendrick
All rights reserved.
Printed in the United States of America.
Library of Congress Cataloging in Publication Data
MacKendrick, Paul Lachlan, 1914–
      The mute stones speak, Second Edition
      Bibliography: p.
      Includes index.
      1.   Italy—Antiquities.   I.   Title.
DG77.M27   1983   937   82–14154

ISBN 0-393-30119-2

W. W. Norton & Company, Inc., 500 Fifth Avenue, New York, NY 10110
W. W. Norton & Company Ltd., 10 Coptic Street, London WC1A 1PU

   3 4 5 6 7 8 9 0

CONTENTS

List of Illustrations   xi

Sources of Illustrations   xviii

Preface to the Second Edition   xix

1. Prehistoric Italy: 1

Neolithic sites in Puglia, Liguria; Val Camonica, Monte Circeio, Belverde, Scoglio del Tonno, Novilara—The Terremare: Molino del Ledro—Sardinian *nuraghi*—The early Iron Age: Villanovan and Siculan cultures

2. The Etruscans: 28

Introduction—Origins—Etruscan cities—Political organization—Language: the Pyrgi inscriptions—Religion—Creative arts—Life and customs

3. Early Rome and Latium: 71

The Sant' Omobono area—Decima, Alban Hills, Latial sites—The Palatine hut—The Forum and Esquiline necropoleis—Rome of the Kings—The burial place of the Scipios—Lavinium: altars and heroön—The "Servian" Wall—Largo Argentina temples—The third and second centuries B.C.

4. Roman Colonies in Italy: 113

Ostia—Alba Fucens—Cosa—centuriation—Exploiting a frontier

5. Nabobs as Builders: Sulla, Pompey, Caesar: 141

The Sanctuary of Fortune at Praeneste—Pompey's Theater and Portico—Caesar's Forum—Second and first century monuments and works of art

6. Augustus: Buildings as Propaganda: 178

Propaganda in temples, theaters, houses, villas, statues—Augustus's Forum—The Arch of Augustus—The Mausoleum—the Gemma Augustea—The Altar of Peace

7. Hypocrite, Madman, Fool, and Knave: 216

The Cave "of Tiberius" at Sperlonga; Domus Tiberiana, Palatina; villa, Capri—The ships of Lake Nemi—The Tomb of Eurysaces and subterranean basilica at the Porta Maggiore—Nero's Golden House and Anzio villa

8. The Victims of Vesuvius: 244

Introduction—Pompeii's town plan—Public life—Private life in town and country houses—Trade and tradesmen—Religion—Art

9. Flavian Rome: 282

Temples of Claudius and Vespasian—The Forum of Peace—The Colosseum—The Arch of Titus—The Tomb of the Haterii—The Cancelleria reliefs—The *Forum Transitorium*—Domitian's palace, villa, and stadium

10. Trajan: Port, Forum, Market, Baths, and Column: 314

Ostia: its town plan—Municipal life and amenities—*Insulae*—The harbors—Trade—Religion; Rome: Trajan's Forum, Market, Baths, and Column

11. An Emperor-Architect: Hadrian: 342

The villa near Tivoli—The "Teatro Marittimo"—"Stadium"—The Temple of Venus and Rome—The Pantheon—The Piazza d'Oro —Small Baths—Hadrian's Mausoleum—The Canopus—The end of an era

12. Antonines through Constantine (A.D. 138–337):   374

Sette Bassi—Antonine column, temples, arch—M. Aurelius: equestrian statue—Capitoline *insula*—M. Aurelius: column—Palatine: Severan buildings—Vesta—Aqueducts—Severan arches—Baths of Caracalla—Roads—Amphitheatrum Castrense—Aurelian's Wall—Baths of Diocletian—Curia—Maxentian buildings—Constantine: arch—"Janus Quadrifrons"—"Minerva Medica"—Circus Maximus

13. Caesar and Christ: 420

The Imperial Villa at Piazza Armerina: its plan and mosaics—The Vatican cemetery and the shrine of St. Peter—Catacombs

Abbreviations Used in the Bibliography: 446

Bibliography: 448

Index   473

List of Illustrations

FIG.	PAGE	
1.1	3	Prehistoric sites in Italy (map)
1.2	4	Passo di Corvo, a prehistoric site in Puglia: air photograph
1.3	8	Comparative table of early cultures
1.4	9	Val Camonica cave art
1.5	12	Terramara at Castellazzo di Fontanellato, Pigorini's plan
1.6	14	Molina di Ledro, lakeside settlement
1.7	17	Su Nuraxi, a Sardinian *nuraghe*
1.8	17	Cremating and inhumating peoples of prehistoric Italy (map)
1.9	22	Villanovan artifacts
1.10	22	A hut-urn
1.11	25	The Certosa *situla*
1.12	25	Picene tomb furniture from Fabriano
1.13	25	The Warrior of Capestrano
2.1	31	Lemnos, inscription in local dialect, similar to Etruscan
2.2	31	Vetulonia, Avele Feluske stele
2.3	33	Early Italy, to illustrate Etruscan and other sites. Inset: early Rome (map)
2.4	34	Marzabotto, grid plan
2.5	37	Spina, plan
2.6	39	Spina, grid plan, air photograph

FIG.   PAGE

2.7   39   Vetulonia, fasces from the Tomb of the Lictor
2.8   43   Etruscan alphabet
2.9   43   Tarquinia, Tomb of Orcus, inscription
2.10   46   Chiusi, possible tomb of Lars Porsenna, plan
2.11   49   Piacenza, bronze model of sheep's liver
2.12   50   Piacenza liver, schematic representation
2.13   52   Potentiometer profile, revealing tomb chambers under-
                ground
2.14   53   Tarquinia, Tomb of Hunting and Fishing (painting)
2.15   55   Tarquinia, Tomb of Orcus, portrait of the lady Velcha
2.16   56   Tarquinia, Tomb of Orcus, the demon Charun
2.17   59   Rome, Conservatori "Brutus," *ca.* 300 B.C.
2.18   61   Veii, Apollo (terracotta) from Portonaccio temple
2.19   61   Satricum terracotta antefix, satyr and nymph
2.20   63   Tarquinia, Museum: winged horses (terracotta) from
                Ara della Regina
2.21   63   Cerveteri, Tomb of the Reliefs, interior
2.22   67   Cerveteri, gold pectoral from Regolini-Galassi tomb

3.1   73   Chronological table, 1400–500 B.C.
3.2   80   Rome, Esquiline fresco
3.3   84   Rome, Palatine, prehistoric hut, reconstruction
3.4   84   Rome, Forum necropolis, cremation and inhumation
                graves
3.5   88   Rome, Forum, strata at Equus Domitiani, photograph
3.6   88   Rome, Forum, strata at Equus Domitiani, schematic
                drawing
3.7   93   Rome, Forum, *lapis niger* stele
3.8   96   Rome, Forum, Rostra, third phase
3.9   96   Rome, Forum, Rostra, fifth phase
3.10   97   Early Latium (map)
3.11   98   Lavinium, altars
3.12   99   Veii, Aeneas-Anchises, terracotta statuette
3.13   100   Rome, Republican Forum, plan
3.14   107   Rome, "Servian" Wall at Termini Station
3.15   109   Rome, Largo Argentina, temples, plan

4.1   114   Roman colonization (map)
4.2   116   Ostia, *castrum,* plan
4.3   118   Alba Fucens, plan
4.4   125   Cosa, *arx,* plan

FIG.	PAGE	
4.5	126	Cosa, plan
4.6	129	Cosa, Capitolium, view
4.7	130	Cosa, Capitolium, reconstruction drawing
4.8	132	Cosa, Comitium, plan
4.9	135	Alba Fucens, centuriation
4.10	136	Cosa, centuriation
4.11	138	Paestum, Roman grid of streets: air photograph
5.1	144	Palestrina, Museum: Barberini mosaic
5.2	146	Palestrina, Sanctuary of Fortune, reconstruction
5.3	146	Palestrina, Sanctuary of Fortune, inclined column capitals
5.4	150	Palestrina, Sanctuary of Fortune, buttresses and ramp (model)
5.5	153	Palestrina, Sanctuary of Fortune, model
5.6	156	Kos, Sanctuary of Asclepius, reconstruction
5.7	156	Tarracina, view toward Circeii from Temple of Jupiter Anxoranus
5.8	159	Tarracina, Temple of Jupiter Anxoranus, reconstruction
5.9	160	Rome, Tabularium
5.10	162	Tivoli, Temple of Hercules Victor, reconstruction
5.11	164	Republican Rome (map)
5.12	165	Rome, Pompey's theater and portico, from *Forma Urbis*
5.13	168	Rome, Via dell' Impero, inaugurated by Mussolini, 1932
5.14	168	Rome, Imperial Fora, plan
5.15	170	Rome, Forum of Caesar, photograph
5.16	171	Rome, Pons Fabricius
5.17	172	Rome, Forum Boarium, round temple
5.18	173	Rome, Palatine antiquarium, large cubiculum from Casa dei Grifi
5.19	175	Boston, Museum of Fine Arts, "Domitius Ahenobarbus"
5.20	176	Rabat, Museum, bronze bust of Cato the Younger from Volubilis
6.1	180	Rome, Temple of Palatine Apollo, Hercules revetment plaque
6.2	181	Rome, Temple of the Deified Julius, model
6.3	184	Rome, Villa under Farnesina, girl decanting perfume (Terme)
6.4	185	Prima Porta, Villa of Livia, garden fresco (Terme)
6.5	187	Rome, Vatican, Prima Porta Augusta
6.6	190	Rome, Forum of Augustus, model

FIG.	PAGE	
6.7	192	Rome, Forum of Augustus, colossal footprint
6.8	196	Rome, Forum: Arch of Augustus, reconstruction
6.9	198	Rome, Mausoleum of Augustus
6.10	199	Vienna, Kunsthistorisches Museum, Gemma Augustea
6.11	200	Family tree of the Julio-Claudians
6.12	203	Rome, Altar of Peace, plan of freezing apparatus
6.13	205	Rome, Altar of Peace, fragments known up to 1935, plan
6.14	205	Rome, Altar of Peace, results of Moretti's excavation, plan
6.15	207	Rome, Altar of Peace, reconstruction
6.16	207	Rome, Altar of Peace: Augustus
6.17	209	Rome, Altar of Peace: family group of Julio-Claudians
6.18	209	Rome, Altar of Peace: Agrippa, Julia, and Livia
6.19	213	Rome, Altar of Peace: Aeneas
6.20	213	Rome, Altar of Peace: Tellus or Italia
7.1	218	Sperlonga, Cave of Tiberius
7.2	218	Sperlonga, Cave of Tiberius, reconstruction
7.3	221	Sperlonga, Cave of Tiberius, Polyphemus group, reconstruction
7.4	223	Sperlonga, Cave of Tiberius, archaic head of Athena
7.5	223	Nemi, Borghi finds (1895) from ships
7.6	226	Nemi, ship in museum before German destruction
7.7	226	Nemi, ship, elevation
7.8	226	Nemi, ship, imaginative reconstruction
7.9	229	Rome, tomb of baker Eurysaces at Porta Maggiore
7.10	231	Rome, subterranean basilica at Porta Maggiore
7.11	232	Rome, subterranean basilica, plan
7.12	234	Rome, subterranean basilica, apse
7.13	238	Rome, Golden House, west wing, plan
7.14	238	Rome, Golden House, east wing, plan
7.15	241	Rome, Golden House, reconstruction drawing of whole area
7.16	241	Rome, the Neronian Sacra Via, plan
8.1	246	Pompeii, victims of Vesuvius, from House of Cryptoporticus
8.2	247	Pompeii, air view
8.3	247	Pompeii, plan
8.4	251	Pompeii, House of Tragic Poet, cutaway model, from EUR

FIG.	PAGE	
8.5	253	Pompeii, House of the Moralist, plan
8.6	253	Pompeii, House of the Moralist, reconstruction
8.7	254	Pompeii, House of the Moralist, triclinium
8.8	256	Pompeii, Villa of the Mysteries, plan
8.9	258	Pompeii, Villa of the Mysteries, reconstruction
8.10	258	Pompeii, Villa of the Mysteries, statue of Livia as found
8.11	259	Pompeii, Villa of the Mysteries: winepress, reconstructed
8.12	261	Malibu Beach, Calif., Getty Museum, replica of Herculaneum villa, peristyle with statues
8.13	262	Torre Annunziata, peacock fresco, detail
8.14	265	Pompeii, *thermopolium* or bar
8.15	265	Pompeii, bronze bust of Caecilius Jucundus
8.16	265	Pompeii, House of D. Octavius Quartio, garden, reconstruction
8.17	271	Pompeii, House of D. Octavius Quartio, garden, with trellis
8.18	274	Pompeii, House of Caecilius Jucundus, earthquake reliefs
8.19	280	Pompeii, Villa of the Mysteries, fresco: woman being scourged
9.1	283	Rome, Temple of Claudius, west terrace wall
9.2	285	Rome, Palatine, model, showing Domitianic buildings
9.3	286	Rome, Forum of Peace, reconstruction from *Forma Urbis*
9.4	288	Rome, *Forum Transitorium, Colonnacce* before excavation
9.5	288	Rome *Forum Transitorium, Colonnacce* after excavation
9.6	290	Rome, Imperial Fora, model
9.7	294	Rome, Colosseum, beast elevator, elevation
9.8	295	Rome, Colosseum and environs, model
9.9	297	Rome, Arch of Titus
9.10	299	Rome, Vatican: Tomb of Haterii, relief of Domitianic buildings
9.11	299	Rome, Vatican: Tomb of Haterii, relief with treadmill-operated crane
9.12	302	Vatican City, Cancelleria reliefs, procession of Domitian, greeting by Vespasian
9.13	303	Vatican City, Cancelleria relief, head of Vespasian
9.14	303	Vatican City, Cancelleria reliefs, Domitian transformed into Nerva
9.15	307	Rome, Palatine: Palace of Domitian, plan
9.16	307	Rome, Palatine: Palace of Domitian, reconstruction

FIG.	PAGE	
9.17	311	Rome, Piazza Navona, air view
9.18	312	Rome, Stadium of Domitian, plan
9.19	312	Rome, Stadium of Domitian, model
10.1	317	Ostia, Museum, bust, possibly of Plotinus
10.2	318	Ostia, plan
10.3	318	Ostia, air view
10.4	324	Ostia, Casa dei Dipinti, reconstruction
10.5	325	Ostia, harbors, plan
10.6	325	Ostia, harbors, air view
10.7	325	Ostia, harbor of Trajan, model
10.8	329	Ostia, Mithraeum of Felicissimus, plan
10.9	334	Rome, Trajan's Market
10.10	337	Rome, Baths of Trajan, plan
10.11	340	Rome, Trajan's Column, detail
11.1	343	Tivoli, Hadrian's Villa, Serapeum at Canopus, "pumpkin" vaults
11.2	344	Tivoli, Hadrian's Villa, plan
11.3	345	Tivoli, Hadrian's Villa, model
11.4	346	Tivoli, Hadrian's Villa, Teatro Marittimo, air view
11.5	350	Tivoli, Hadrian's Villa, "Stadium," model
11.6	351	Tivoli, Hadrian's Villa, "Stadium," plan
11.7	354	Rome, Temple of Venus and Rome, model
11.8	354	Rome, Temple of Venus and Rome, plan
11.9	355	Rome, Temple of Venus and Rome, apse with scale figure
11.10	355	Antinous
11.11	357	Rome, Pantheon, reconstruction
11.12	359	Rome, Pantheon, plan
11.13	360	Rome, Pantheon, interior, reconstruction
11.14	363	Tivoli, Hadrian's Villa, Piazza d'Oro, plan
11.15	365	Rome, Arch of Constantine, Hadrianic medallion, dedication to Apollo
11.16	366	Tivoli, Hadrian's Villa, Piazza d'Oro, reconstruction
11.17	369	Tivoli, Hadrian's Villa, Small Baths, plan
11.18	369	Tivoli, Hadrian's Villa, Small Baths, axonometric reconstruction
11.19	370	Rome, Hadrian's Mausoleum, reconstruction
11.20	371	Tivoli, Hadrian's Villa, Canopus
12.1	376	Sette Bassi, villa, model

FIG. PAGE

12.2 378 Rome, Temple of Antoninus and Faustina

12.3 379 Rome, Hadrianeum, province panels

12.4 381 Vatican, Column of Antoninus Pius, base

12.5 384 Rome, equestrian statue of M. Aurelius

12.6 386 Rome, Column of M. Aurelius, three spirals

12.7 388 Rome, Palatine, model, showing Septizodium

12.8 390 Rome and environs: aqueducts (map)

12.9 392 Aqueducts near Capannelle, painting

12.10 397 Rome, Severan arch, northwest panel

12.11 398 Rome, Arch of Argentarii, panel

12.12 401 Rome, Baths of Caracalla, air view

12.13 401 Rome, Baths of Caracalla, Great Hall, reconstruction drawing

12.14 404 Roman road construction

12.15 406 Rome, Aurelian's Wall

12.16 407 Rome, Aurelian's Wall and major monuments, plan

12.17 411 Rome, Baths of Diocletian, air view

12.18 414 Rome, Circus of Maxentius, air view

12.19 415 Rome, Basilica of Maxentius

12.20 417 Rome, Arch of Constantine, *allocutio* panel

12.21 418 Rome, "Minerva Medica"

13.1 421 Piazza Armerina, Imperial Villa, "Bikini girls" mosaic

13.2 422-23 Piazza Armerina, Imperial Villa, reconstruction

13.3 427 Piazza Armerina, Imperial Villa, Circus Maximus mosaic

13.4 427 Piazza Armerina, Imperial Villa, small hunting scene, mosaic

13.5 431 Piazza Amerina, Imperial Villa, large hunting scene, mosaic

13.6 431 Piazza Armerina, Imperial Villa, Labors of Hercules mosaic, detail

13.7 437 Vatican City, excavations under St. Peter's, west end, plan

13.8 437 Vatican City, excavations under St. Peter's, Mausoleum F, stuccoes

13.9 440 Vatican City, excavations under St. Peter's, Campo P, plan

13.10 442 Vatican City, excavations under St. Peter's, Aedicula, reconstruction

Sources of Illustrations

Preface to the Second Edition

This book owes much to many: to the Hays Fund of the American Philosophical Society, the Trustees of the American Academy in Rome, the John Simon Guggenheim Memorial Foundation, and the Research Committee of the University of Wisconsin Graduate School, for giving me the opportunity to spend over three years in Italy; to Laurence and Isabel Roberts, for hospitality and moral support; to the late Axel Boëthius, for friendship and instruction; to the late Ernest Nash, for photographs and advice; to Mrs. Inez Longobardi, the best and most helpful of librarians and friends; to Ferdinando Castagnoli, for sharing with me his incomparable knowledge of the topography of Rome and Latium; to R. I. W. Westgate and Alston Chase, who taught me Latin at Harvard and have been my friends for fifty years; to Professor Ann Laidlaw, kind friend and severe critic, who is not responsible where I did not heed; and to Frank E. Brown, who introduced me to archaeology and is hereby absolved from responsibility for all untoward results of the introduction. My overarching debt is acknowledged in the dedication.

THE MUTE STONES SPEAK

1

Prehistoric Italy

In May of 1945 two young British Army officers, John Bradford and Peter Williams-Hunt, based with the R.A.F. at
Foggia in the province of Puglia, near the heel of Italy,
found that the World War II armistice left them with time
on their hands. Both trained archaeologists, they readily prevailed upon the R.A.F. to combine routine training flights
with pushing back the frontiers of science. The result of
their air reconnaissance was to change profoundly the
archaeological map of Italy.

The value of air photography for archaeology had long
been known; as early as 1909, pictures taken from a balloon
had revealed the plan of Ostia, the port of ancient Rome.
But the English, especially such pioneers as Major G. W. G.
Allen and O. G. S. Crawford, early took the lead in interpreting, on photographs taken usually for military purposes,
vegetation marks showing the presence and plan of ancient
sites buried beneath the soil—invisible to the groundling's
eye. Where the subsoil has been disturbed in antiquity by
the digging of a ditch, the increased depth of soil will produce more luxuriant crops or weeds; where soil depth is de-
creased by the presence of ancient foundations, walls, floors,

or roads, the crop will be thin, stunted, and lighter in color. Air photographs taken in raking light, just after sunrise or just before sunset in a dry season, especially over grassland, will highlight these buried landscapes. The Tavoliere, the great prairie where Foggia lies, thirty by fifty-five miles in extent, suits these conditions admirably; its mean annual rainfall is only 18.6 inches (0.6 in July) or half that of Rome, and Rome is a dry place, at least in summer. So Bradford and Williams-Hunt had high hopes for their project.

In a Fairchild high-wing monoplane, in which the position of struts and nacelles does not interfere with the operation of a hand-held camera, they took oblique shots at 1,000 feet with an air camera of 8-inch focal length. For vertical shots they used, at 10,000 feet, air cameras of 20-inch focal length, mounted tandem to produce overlap for stereoscopic examination, which makes pictures three-dimensional. The thousands of resulting photographs were at a scale of about 1:6,000, or ten inches to the mile, over four times as large as the best available ground maps (the 1:25,000 series of the Italian Istituto Geografico Militare).

Bradford, realizing the archaeological value of the millions of air photographs taken during the war by the British and American Strategic Air Commands, prevailed upon the authorities to deposit prints, giving complete coverage for Italy, in Rome (with the British and Swedish Schools and the American Academy). The initiative of Prof. Kirk H. Stone procured a similar set for the University of Wisconsin. The stereoscopic study of these collections will mean great strides in Italian archaeology. The accuracy of the data obtained is amazing: ditches estimated from the photographs with a good micrometer scale to be four feet wide proved when measured on the ground to be precisely that.

What the photographs revealed were over 2000 settlements, scattered over the 1650 square miles of the Tavoliere, some up to 800 yards across, and surrounded by one to eight

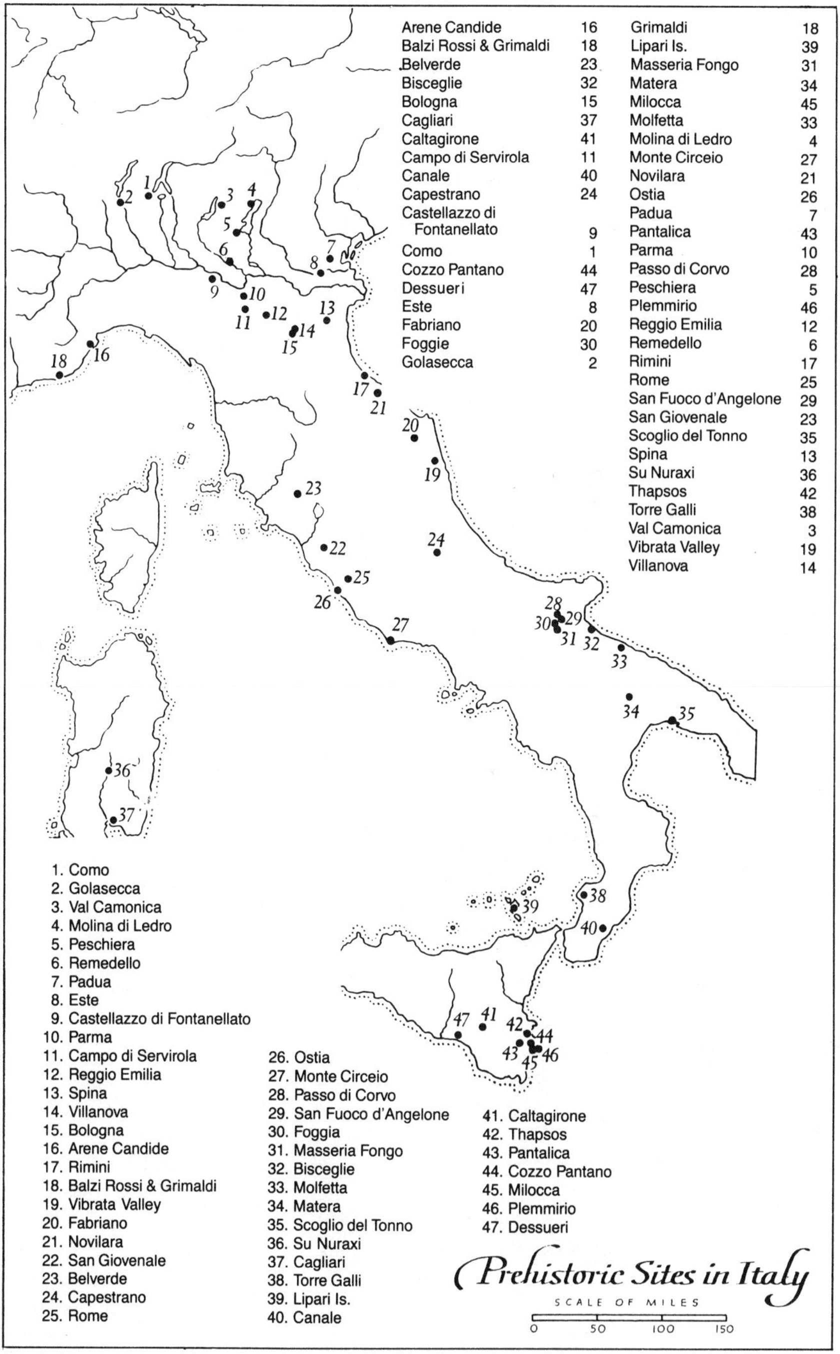

Arene Candide	16	Grimaldi	18
Balzi Rossi & Grimaldi	18	Lipari Is.	39
Belverde	23	Masseria Fongo	31
Bisceglie	32	Matera	34
Bologna	15	Milocca	45
Cagliari	37	Molfetta	33
Caltagirone	41	Molina di Ledro	4
Campo di Servirola	11	Monte Circeio	27
Canale	40	Novilara	21
Capestrano	24	Ostia	26
Castellazzo di Fontanellato	9	Padua	7
		Pantalica	43
Como	1	Parma	10
Cozzo Pantano	44	Passo di Corvo	28
Dessueri	47	Peschiera	5
Este	8	Plemmirio	46
Fabriano	20	Reggio Emilia	12
Foggia	30	Remedello	6
Golasecca	2	Rimini	17
		Rome	25
		San Fuoco d'Angelone	29
		San Giovenale	23
		Scoglio del Tonno	35
		Spina	13
		Su Nuraxi	36
		Thapsos	42
		Torre Galli	38
		Val Camonica	3
		Vibrata Valley	19
		Villanova	14

1. Como
2. Golasecca
3. Val Camonica
4. Molina di Ledro
5. Peschiera
6. Remedello
7. Padua
8. Este
9. Castellazzo di Fontanellato
10. Parma
11. Campo di Servirola
12. Reggio Emilia
13. Spina
14. Villanova
15. Bologna
16. Arene Candide
17. Rimini
18. Balzi Rossi & Grimaldi
19. Vibrata Valley
20. Fabriano
21. Novilara
22. San Giovenale
23. Belverde
24. Capestrano
25. Rome
26. Ostia
27. Monte Circeio
28. Passo di Corvo
29. San Fuoco d'Angelone
30. Foggia
31. Masseria Fongo
32. Bisceglie
33. Molfetta
34. Matera
35. Scoglio del Tonno
36. Su Nuraxi
37. Cagliari
38. Torre Galli
39. Lipari Is.
40. Canale
41. Caltagirone
42. Thapsos
43. Pantalica
44. Cozzo Pantano
45. Milocca
46. Plemmirio
47. Dessueri

Prehistoric Sites in Italy

SCALE OF MILES

0   50   100   150

Fig. 1.1   Prehistoric sites in Italy.

ditches. Within the ditched area, and approached by in-turned, tunnel-shaped entrances, were smaller, circular patches, which looked like hut enclosures, or "compounds." Three examples of the sites photographed will illustrate typical settlements. At a site identified on the map (Fig. 1.1) as San Fuoco d'Angelone, eight miles northeast of Foggia, the photographs showed a ditch-enclosed oval measuring 500 x 400 feet and an inner circle 260 feet across, with what proved to be the characteristic funnel-shaped opening. At Masseria Fongo, four miles south of Foggia, the oval was estimated at 480 yards long, with a 12-foot entrance and 12-foot ditches. At Passo di Corvo (Fig. 1.2), eight miles northeast of Foggia, the enclosure measured 800 x 500 yards, and the details were revealed by masses of flowers, yellow wild cabbage, mauve wild mint, and white cow parsley.

So much for results from the study of photographs. The next step for Bradford was to spend a fruitful season in the study. Archaeology is a comparative science: to know one site is to know nothing; to know a thousand is to see some factors unifying all. Thus the settlement shapes of the Tavoliere are reminiscent of the fortified stronghold of

FIG. 1.2   Passo di Corvo, low, oblique air photo (May 1945, by John Bradford) across the Neolithic settlement, 7 miles N.E. of Foggia. Crop marks revealed the parallel lines of sur-rounding ditches (in foreground and back-ground), with many enclosures inside.

Dimini in Thessaly, dated by its excavation in the late neolithic age, which in Greece means about 2650 B.C. They also look like the fortified site of Altheim near Munich, also late neolithic, which in Germany means about 1900 B.C. Culture in Europe moved from east to west; in general the farther west the site, the later it reached its successive levels of culture. The Tavoliere sites, lying geographically between Dimini and Altheim, might well be intermediate in date also; by their shape, at any rate, they are almost certainly to be dated sometime in the neolithic period. So much can be guessed before the indispensable next step is taken. The next step is excavation.

Modern archaeological excavation is neither haphazard nor a treasure hunt. It is a scientific business, preceded by careful survey, conducted with minute attention to levels and strata (the level in which an object is found determines its relative date; comparison with similar objects found elsewhere which can be dated determines its absolute date), and followed by scrupulous recording and publication of the evidence. A dig is not a treasure hunt. Naturally an archaeologist is pleased if he turns up gold or precious stones, but he knows in advance that an Old Stone Age site will produce neither—rather, something infinitely more valuable: an intimate knowledge of man's past, gained from ordinary humble objects of daily household use. To find these was Bradford's object when he began to dig. (Williams-Hunt had meanwhile been posted to the Far East.) And he found them. Passo di Corvo, for example, yielded typical neolithic artifacts: stone axes, querns (handmills for grinding grain), bone points, stone sickles, pendants, spindle whorls, and, best of all, vast quantities of potsherds, over 4,000 found in fourteen days. The potsherd is the archaeologist's best friend. Pots are virtually indestructible; they turn up everywhere, and comparison with pots of similar shape and decoration, found elsewhere, yields precious information about dates, imports, exports, trade routes, and the aesthetic taste of the pot's maker and user.

S. Fuoco d'Angelone, for example, yielded typical neolithic pottery: rich brown or glossy black burnished ware, undecorated but thin-walled, symmetrical, and well-made (by hand, not on a potter's wheel; sooner or later the use of the wheel produces shoddy commercialism). Together with it were found shreds of a fine-textured buff ware, painted with wide bands (*fasce larghe*) of tomato red. There were also very thin, burnished bowls in cream and gray.

After excavation, the archaeologist must return to the study and to the comparative method—an exacting and exciting pursuit of parallels, especially for the pottery, in the hope of dating it and tracking down its origins. The facts are recorded in technical excavation reports, often buried in obscure or local journals. Oftener, the results of excavation are unpublished (it is always more fun to dig than to write.) In that case, the facts are treasured up in the notes or the memories of the excavator, often a local archaeologist. He belongs to a splendid breed, burning with enthusiasm, brimful of knowledge, and eager to share what he knows, in conversation if not in print.

So Bradford read and talked and found his parallels. The wares he had excavated were familiar; they had been found elsewhere in the heel of Italy, especially opposite or in Matera, in Lucania, and Molfetta, in Puglia, between Barletta and Bari, in contexts dated 2600–2500 B.C. And this pottery proves to have affinities, too, with that of Thessalian Sesklo, a neolithic site not far from Dimini. This same type of pottery can be traced across the Balkans into Illyricum, and thence across the Adriatic to Bradford's sites, giving in the process a glimpse of neolithic man as a more daring seafarer than had previously been thought.

And so, by patient, detailed work like Bradford's, the newly discovered sites are fitted into and enrich the pattern of the neolithic world. The total mapping fills a huge gap in the picture of the findspots of neolithic sites in Italy. Before 1945, some 170 were known; now the Tavoliere alone makes up more than that number. And Passo di Corvo becomes the largest known neolithic site in Europe.

The things the archaeologists did not find are instructive, too. No weapons were found: the inference is that the Tavoliere folk were unwarlike. There is no evidence that the sites survived into the Bronze Age: it looks as though, as with unwarlike peoples all too often elsewhere, they were wiped out in an invasion.

It is clear from the artifacts and the site plans that neolithic man on the Tavoliere lived like neolithic man elsewhere in Italy, and that the culture was on the whole uniform. He lived in a wattle-and-daub hut with a sunken floor, a central hearth, and a smokehole—the remote and primitive predecessor of the atrium-and-impluvium house of historic Roman times, whose central apartment had a hole in the roof with a pool below to catch rain water. Fortunately for us, his wife was a slovenly housekeeper, and from her rubbish we can reconstruct her way of life. In his enclosures neolithic man penned the animals he had domesticated: other Italian sites have yielded the bones of the sheep, goat, horse, ox, ass, and pig. The dog has not yet become man's best friend in the neolithic Tavoliere. Primitive man in Italy had a rudimentary religion: the Ligurian caves of Arene Candide and Grimaldi have yielded statuettes of big-breasted, pregnant women, which probably had something to do with a fertility cult. In another Ligurian cave, Balzi Rossi, over 200,000 stone implements have been found. Not far along the Adriatic coast from Foggia, in the Vibrata Valley, lie the foundations of 336 neolithic huts. We know something, too, of neolithic man's burial customs, and macabre enough they seem: skulls have been found smeared with red ochre; apparently the flesh was stripped from the corpse—a practice called in Italian *scarnitura*—and the stain applied to the bared bone. At Arene Candide was found a rich burial of about 8000 B.C.: a young man dressed in skins, supine on a bed of red ochre, and provided, for the after life, with a *baton de commandement*, a flint knife, and a cap decorated with shells. A child buried at Arene Candide wore a necklace or cape of squirrels' tails and had pebbles and shells for toys in the hereafter. At Remedello, in the Po Valley south of Lake Garda, a cemetery of the Chalcolithic Age (transitional between neolithic and Bronze) contained 119 burials, furnished with daggers, arrows, and axes; nearby Villafranca yielded a fine silver pectoral. All this suggests a level of culture far below that which the Near East was enjoying at the same time: Passo di Corvo's mud huts are contemporary with the Great Pyramid of Egypt and with palaces and temples in Mesopotamia (see table in Fig. 1.3). But there is no evidence that neolithic man in Italy was priest-ridden or tyrannized, as the Egyptians and Akkadians were; he is rather to be thought of as the ancestor of the

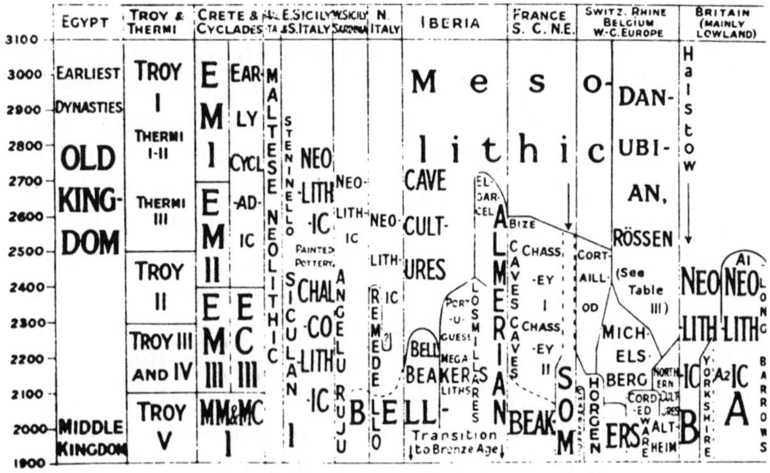

FIG. 1.3 Comparative table of early cultures.
(C. F. C. Hawkes, *The Prehistoric Foundations of Europe*, Table IV)

sturdy peasant stock that was to form the backbone of
Roman Italy.

The most famous center of Italian prehistoric art is in the
Val Camonica Caves, between Lakes Como and Garda. The
drawings are incised and painted bright red and yellow. The
subjects include fields and houses (Fig. 1.4), men dancing
and brandishing axes; oxen, horses (the date is 1090–1020
B.C.); and the sundisk, for the valley seems to have been a
religious center.

In South Italy, one of the oldest sites is Monte Circeio, a
peninsula halfway between Rome and Naples, where caves
yielded skulls like those of Neanderthal man (100,000 B.C.),
the "cave man" of popular belief. At Belverde, in southern
Tuscany, a Bronze Age village (Carbon-14 date 1245 ± 80
B.C.) possesses unique rock cuttings: the "Amphitheater" has
what might be seats round an apron stage, used for pag-
eantry, political or religious; the "Observatory" is perched on
an isolated crag.

FIG. 1.4   Val Camonica, cave art: houses and fields. (© 1971 by
Centro Camuno di Studi Preistorici, 25044 Capo di Ponte, Italy)

Scoglio del Tonno (Tuna Reef), forming one arm of Taranto Harbor, is chiefly noteworthy for the evidence it provides (pottery, figurines) of continuous contact with Aegean Greece, especially Mycenae, from 1400 through Sub-Mycenaean and into Protogeometric times. Bisceglie, near Bari, has a late Bronze Age dolmen or gallery grave of 1000–900 B.C., containing a collective burial (eleven skeletons). An important Picene Iron Age site is Novilara, south of Pèsaro; a rich woman's grave from here, now in Rome's Pigorini Museum, is dated by *fibulae* (the ancient safety pin, which appears with changed shapes at datable intervals) to the seventh century B.C. It contained, besides the fibulae, pottery, beads, pendants, and large disk earrings of Baltic amber.

Bradford's methods are scientific, but archaeology has not always been the exact science it is today. Americans may be proud that the first recorded scientific excavation took place in Indian mounds in Virginia. The date was 1784, and the excavator was Thomas Jefferson. But thereafter archaeological progress was sporadic, and relapse accompanied advance. In the mid-nineteenth century most excavations in Italy were more like rape than science, their aim being to dredge up treasures for the nobility and the art dealers.

Thus when in 1889 the distinguished Italian anthropologist Luigi Pigorini excavated the site of Castellazzo di Fontanellato, twelve miles northwest of Parma, in the Po Valley, there was no absolute guarantee that the dig would be scientific. Yet Pigorini's announced results have colored the whole picture of the Bronze Age in Italy, and it is only recently that they have been doubted. The story of his announced results, the growing skepticism, the reexamination of the ground, and the present state of the question is an illuminating, if sobering, one.

What Pigorini was after was the evidence for the prehistoric settlements, which have come to be called *terremare*. They owe their discovery, their name, and their destruction to the fertilizing quality of the earth of which they are composed. *Terra marna* is the name in the dialect of Emilia for the compost heaps formed by the decay of organic matter in certain mounds of ancient date, mostly south of the Po. Farmers repeatedly found potsherds and other artifacts, often of bronze, in these mounds, and Pigorini determined to examine them before all the evidence should be dispersed. Castellazzo di Fontanellato is the most famous of his efforts.

He found clear, though meager, evidence in pottery and metal artifacts (axes, daggers, pins, razors) of a Bronze Age culture, but no report of the levels in which he found these objects survives. Indeed, in this as in most *terremare* the farmer's shovel has completely upset the levels. Roman terracotta, medieval pottery, and prehistoric bronze axeheads jostle one another in confusion. Besides, the prehistoric site has been continuously inhabited, and, in consequence the soil continuously turned over, ever since Roman times.

Pigorini apparently dug isolated, random trenches rather than the continuous ones that would have enabled him to trace a ground plan securely. It is hard to see, without more evidence that he supplies, how the grandiose grid of his ultimate plan (Fig. 1.5) could be deduced from the disconnected series of trenches figured on his earliest one. Though he had to contend with the most vexatious swampy conditions, working in the midst of constant seepage and ubiquitous mud, in which a rectangular grid could hardly have survived, he was nevertheless able to persuade himself, at Castellazzo, of the existence of a ditch and a rampart, reinforced by wooden piling. (Postholes and piles he certainly found, and photographed.)

By 1892 he had convinced himself that his site had a trapezoidal plan, surrounded by a ramparted ditch thirty yards wide and ten feet deep. (Some of his dimensions suggest a prehistoric unit of measure in multiples of five; others, a foreshadowing of the Roman foot of twenty-nine centi-

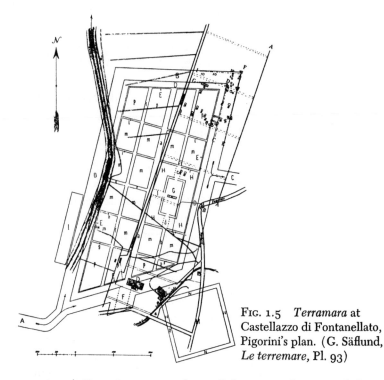

FIG. 1.5   *Terramara* at
Castellazzo di Fontanellato,
Pigorini's plan. (G. Säflund,
Le terremare, Pl. 93)

meters.) Running water derived from a tributary of the Po
supplied the hypothetical ditch, which was crossed on the
south by a wooden drawbridge thirty yards wide and sixty
yards long. South of the site, Pigorini claimed to have found
a cemetery (*M*) perfectly square in plan, for cremation-urn
burials, and westward another, rectangular one.

In 1893 he announced the discovery, within the rampart,
halfway along its east side, of a mound in a reserved area
or *templum* (*G*), surrounded by its own ditch; in 1894 this
templum became the *arx*, or citadel of the settlement, having
in its midst a sacrificial trench (*mundus*) containing in its
floor, for the deposit of the sacrificial fruits, five sinkholes
each equipped with a wooden cover.

In 1895 and 1896 he published claims to have found within the rampart a grid of streets (*cardines* and *decumani*), which he held to be the ancestor of the grid in Roman camps and Roman colonies. The total plan was alleged to resemble that of primitive Rome (Roma Quadrata), and the wooden bridge was compared to Rome's early wooden one across the Tiber, the Pons Sublicius. At another site one of Pigorini's pupils claimed to have found traces of a ritual furrow like that with which hundreds of years later the Romans were to mark the line of the future walls of a colony. For Pigorini and his school regarded the *terremare* folk as the ancestors of an Iron Age people called Villanovans, and ultimately of the Romans of historical times.

Since Pigorini's death in 1920 other archaeologists have been moved to go over the ground again, revising his findings and his inferences. Having excogitated his grid plan for Castellazzo di Fontanellato, Pigorini seems to have generalized from it rather more widely than the evidence warranted. While rectangular or square plans are not denied for some *terremare* (modern investigators enumerate ten), many sites are oval, not unlike Bradford's Tavoliere hut settlements. In fact the *terremare* plan varies more than Pigorini was willing to admit. Furthermore, parallel in date to the *terremare* are unmoated hut villages and true lake dwellings. (The *terremare* are lake dwellings without the lake, presumably a reminiscence in the minds of immigrants from beyond the Alps of their primordial homes.)

But while we must grant to his critics that Pigorini had, to say the least, a strong imagination, we need not go so far as one of his detractors who argued that the *terremare* are Bronze Age pigsties. One site has an area of thirty-five acres, which is a bit large for a pigsty.

A more scientifically excavated lake-dwellers' village (Fig. 1.6) is at Molina di Ledro, on a pond off the north end of Lake Garda. Here was found the plank flooring of houses, some of them perhaps projecting over the water; firmly inset beams suggest sturdy rectangular structures. The lake dwellers hunted (bows were found) and fished from dugout canoes. They ate masses of wild cherries, baked bread, and ate pasta, very like the *gnocchi* of their modern descendants. Their women wove linen: balls of flax thread were found, along with bits of patterned cloth, spindle whorls, and loomweights. They also smelted bronze (the date of the settlement is early Bronze Age, about 1800 B.C.); the evidence is the clay nozzles of bellows. Another, later Bronze Age site (of about 1150 B.C.) at Peschiera, on the southeast shore of Lake Garda, under a nineteenth-century Austrian fortress, yielded over two thousand artifacts, in bronze, bone, and pottery.

Fig. 1.6   Molina di Ledro, early Bronze Age lakeside settlement. (© 1971 by Centro Camuno di Studi Preistorici, 25044 Capo di Ponte, Italy)

The *terremare* are important: they preserve the memory of an immigrant population, distinct in culture from the aborigines. The distinguishing marks of this new culture are knowledge of metalworking, a pottery identifiable by its exaggerated half-moon handles, and the practice of cremation rather than inhumation. On the evidence, we must suppose that this new culture emerged about 1500 B.C. as a fusion of indigenous hut dwellers and immigrant lake dwellers. Bronze bits found in their settlements show that they had domesticated the horse, and there is some evidence, outside the *terremare*, for dogs as well, described by Randall-MacIver as "doubtless good woolly animals of a fair size."

In fact the Bronze Age in Italy of which the *terremare* are a part represents a considerable cultural development beyond the level of the neolithic Tavoliere folk. Cave dwellings from Liguria show a people using wagons and ox-drawn plows. Chemical analysis of their copper shows that some of it comes from central Germany, though a copper ingot from Sardinia betrays by its impressed double-ax trademark some connection with Minoan Crete. (The *terremare* are contemporary with Grave Circle A at Mycenae.) Bronze Age women wore jewelry: jadeite arm rings, necklaces of pierced red coral, bored stones, or clamshells. Curious stamps called *pintaderas* were used to impress a pattern in color on the body. A horned mannikin, with penis erect, from Campo di Servirola, now in the museum of Reggio Emilia, may be evidence for a fertility cult, like the neolithic female idols from the Ligurian caves.

Since Säflund * wrote (1939), the term *terremare* has come to be applied to a smaller area, confined to the central Po Valley, and the Italian Bronze and early Iron Age culture is now called Apennine. Its characteristics are cave settlements or hut villages (usually unfortified; Pianello, near

* Relevant articles by scholars mentioned in the text are listed in the bibliography.

Ancona, is an exception) and burnished ware decorated with spirals of meanders. Urn-field sites like Bismantova, west of Bologna, and Pianello show invasion, about 1000 B.C. or a little later, by a cremating people. Some scholars call Bismantova "Proto-Villanovan."

The Po Valley in the Bronze Age was a melting pot in which a variety of cultures, indigenous and immigrant, mingled. What is to be read from the excavations is almost a recapitulation of this early period, in terms of creative imitation of imported and native forms and ideas, of the whole cultural history of Rome. To our knowledge of this culture, and to our appreciation of the importance of scrupulous archaeological recording, the curious story of Pigorini's *terremare* contributed not a little.

The island of Sardinia to the archaeologist is a fascinating curiosity, isolated, until recently, by its unhealthy climate and its odd dialect. In prehistoric times, however, while Sardinia's development does not parallel that of the mainland, its level of culture appears from archaeological finds and monuments to have been higher, not lower, than that of Italy proper. This superior level seems to have been due to Sardinia's richness in metals. To protect the wealth, the prehistoric islanders built enormous watchtowers, called *nuraghi*, which developed into veritable feudal castles with villages nestling at their feet.

Recent excavations (1951–56) by Professor Giovanni Lilliu of the University of Cagliari have cast clearer light on Sardinia's culture. He excavated the huge *nuraghe* of Su Nuraxi, at Barumini, 38 miles north of Cagliari. Su Nuraxi was a small hill covered with ruins, earth, and scrub. Now six campaigns have revealed a truncated conical tower (Fig. 1.7) built, without mortar, of huge many-sided blocks of basalt. Clustered about the tower he found a small village; the whole complex—tower plus village—is surrounded by

FIG. 1.7 Su Nuraxi, a Sardinian *nuraghe*. (*Illustrated London News*)

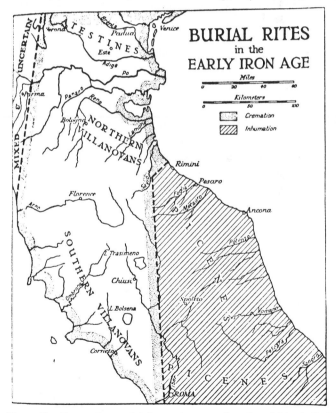

FIG. 1.8 Cremating and inhumating peoples of prehistoric Italy.
(D. Randall-MacIver, *Italy before the Romans*, p. 45)

other *nuraghi* on neighboring hills. To the original single tower four others, with upper courses of dressed stone, were added (early eighth century) in a cloverleaf pattern, linked by a curtain wall enclosing a court sixty feet deep, with a reservoir fifteen feet deep for drinking water. The central tower is three stories high, with a corbeled or false-vaulted roof built of gradually converging horizontal courses. The upper stories were reached by a spiral stair in the thickness of the wall. Lilliu meticulously observed stratigraphy; for dating, he submitted samples of carbonized matter from the towers to laboratories in Milan and was told that the Carbon 14 process dates his remains as 1270 B.C. $\pm$ 200 years.

The C^{14} method of dating, an American device discovered and perfected by Professor W. F. Libby and his associates at the University of Chicago Institute of Nuclear Studies, is sufficiently new to deserve a word of explanation here. All living matter has a uniform radioactivity associated with its carbon content. The supply of the radioactive isotope C^{14} ceases when living matter, wood, foliage, and so forth dies. Scientists can calculate the time elapsed since death by counting the residual radioactivity of C^{14} in the organic specimen, since the rate of decay can be described by specifying how long it takes for half the number of atoms in a given sample to disintegrate. For C^{14} this period, called its "half life," is 5700 years. If the present assay of a specimen of organic matter, for instance, is 12.5 C^{14} explosions per minute per gram of carbon, an ancient organic sample assaying at 6.25 would be 5700 years old (the half life of C^{14}). Checking with samples of known date has proved the method accurate within 200 years either way. For most classical objects found in association with organic matter this is valueless, since a trained archaeologist can date a pot, an inscription, or an architectural block by eye within fifty years or less. But the method is invaluable for making more precise the great sweeps of time in prehistory. Thus the lowest C^{14} date for Su Nuraxi, 1070 B.C., would take it almost into the Iron Age in Italy; at this date culture on the mainland was much more primitive.

Lilliu calls the period of the four added towers Lower Nuragic I and dates it 800–750 B.C. These smaller towers each contain a single cell with two rows of loopholes. They are guard posts and are equipped with speaking tubes for the guard to use when challenging.

In the next period, Upper Nuragic I, dated by Lilliu 750–500 B.C., the earth having subsided, the four towers and the walls were reinforced. The ground-level entrance was blocked and replaced by a new entrance twenty-one feet higher, accessible only by ladder. Battlements now replaced the loopholes. Stone balls found in the excavations were apparently the projectiles hurled from these battlements. From a watchtower added to the central *nuraghe* come conch shells, perhaps intended to be sounded like trumpets.

The surrounding village, of 200 or 300 huts, separated by narrow labyrinthine passages, housed the troops; the chief lived in the tower. The village, hard hit when the Carthaginians sacked it late in the sixth century B.C., survived in decadence till the late first century B.C. The typical oval or rectangular plan of an early Su Nuraxi village hut resembles that of the Bronze Age in Sicily or Cyprus. One contained a pit for votive offerings. Sixty round huts, with lower courses in stone, have been dated in Upper Nuragic I. They would have been roofed, like shepherd huts in Sardinia to this day, with logs and branches weighted by stones. One larger circle has seats around its inner perimeter. It was equipped with shelves, a niche, a stone basin, and a sacred stone (a model of a *nuraghe*). Lilliu thinks this must have been the warriors' council chamber.

Su Nuraxi yielded artifacts in stone, terracotta, bronze, iron, lead, and amber, the latter showing connections with trade routes to the Baltic. Lilliu found axes, millstones,

pestles, and bronze votive statuettes. Pottery and fibulae suggest connections with Phoenicia—via Carthage—and Etruria,
whose rich and, in certain respects, mysterious culture is discussed in the next chapter.

In a later phase, after the Carthaginian invasion, the huts
have fan-shaped rooms, each devoted to a specialized occupation: baking, oil pressing, stone-tool making. A pair of
stone boot trees, or shoe lasts, presumably from a cobbler's
shop, was one of the more curious finds. Gewgaws in glass
paste, poor, decadent, commercialized, but traditional in
design, testify to the material and aesthetic poverty of this
period. Only the last phase yielded tombs, but a huge stele
with a curved top may have marked the entrance to what
the peasants call a Giant's Grave, a Stone Age slab-edged
tomb, forming a corridor sometimes as much as twenty yards
along, from which two wings branch off to form a semicircular approach.

This scientific dig provides a fixed foundation for future
research into earlier ages on Sardinia. Lilliu is understand-
ably excited about the "dynamic spirit" revealed by the
creators of this amazingly early massiveness, but like all
massiveness, whether of pyramid, ziggurat, or Roman Imperial palace, it undoubtedly justifies the unhappy inference
that with all this grandeur went autocracy.

Perhaps the mainland political system in the early Iron
Age was less rigid; at any rate it can boast no architectural
remains as sophisticated as the Sardinian *nuraghi*. But the
artifacts, especially from graves, are more numerous than
for the Bronze or Neolithic Ages, and the graves show that
roughly speaking* the peninsula was divided in the early
Iron Age between two cultures (Fig. 1.8): the folk west of a

* Since Randall-MacIver wrote (1928), further tomb discoveries have
shown that the line between cremation and inhumation cannot be drawn so
sharply: there is evidence for cremation in Etruria as late as the end of the
seventh century B.C.

line drawn from Rome to Rimini cremated their dead; those east of that line inhumed them. In and near Rome the two burial rites are mingled: the significant inference from this fact will be explained later. Because the finds are so much more numerous on the mainland, the resulting inferences involve a much more complex subdivision into cultures and periods. We may single out three sets of inferences, based primarily on three major archaeological efforts. The first is Pericle Ducati's work at Bologna, which distinguished four cultural phases, named from Villanova, the village where a major cemetery was found, and from the Benacci and Arno-aldi estates, whence key finds come. The second centers at Este, near Padua, famous for its bronze *situle* or buckets finely decorated by punching from the back, in the technique called *repoussé*. The third is Paolo Orsi's exemplary work in Sicily and South Italy. The complex chronology is best set out in a tabular view (see chart, p. 23).

The cremation cemetery excavated as early as 1853 at Villanova, near Bologna, produced artifacts (ossuary urns, fibulae, razors, hairpins, distaffs, bracelets, fish hooks, tweezers, *repoussé* bronze belts, dated about 700 B.C. [Fig. 1.9], which match objects found later at other sites farther south, in Latium and Etruria; for example, the village excavated (1956–65) at San Giovenale, near Bieda, by the late King Gustav VI of Sweden. Here Proto-Villanovan huts survive down into the Etruscan seventh century B.C. Sherds show that nearby Luni sul Mignone, a Villanovan village, traded with Mycenae. It had a citadel, circuit walls, and a monumental cult center. Like San Giovenale, it was later occupied by Etruscans. Thus the inference is warranted that this whole area was inhabited in the early Iron Age by a people unified in culture. Since the Villanovans, unlike the aborigines, cremated their dead, we infer that they were foreigners, probably invaders; that they descended from the *terremare* folk is not proven. That they lived in wattle-and-daub huts roofed

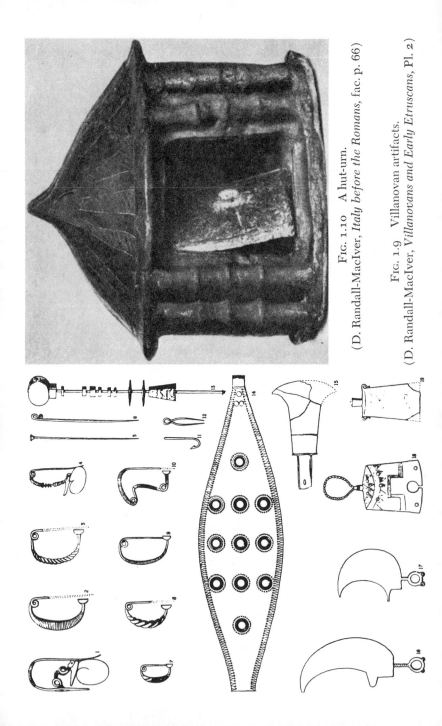

FIG. 1.10 A hut-urn.
(D. Randall-MacIver, *Italy before the Romans*, fac. p. 66)

FIG. 1.9 Villanovan artifacts.
(D. Randall-MacIver, *Villanovans and Early Etruscans*, Pl. 2)

THE IRON AGE

DATES	ITALY			SICILY	GREECE & AEGAEAN
	North	*Central*	*South*		
900	Proto-Villanovan		Torre Galli, Canale	Siculan III	Troy VIII Geometric pottery
850	Benacci I				
800		Early Etruscans			
750	Benacci II	Alban & Forum graves	Pantalica South		
700				Gk. col., Syracuse	Oriental-izing pottery
650		Etruscan tombs			
600	Arnoaldi			Rise of Carth. Empire	
550					
500	Marzabotto	Roman republic. Cape-strano warrior			Black-figure ware Troy IX
450					Red-figure ware
400	La Tène Culture				

with carved beams is inferred from the hut urns (Fig. 1.10) in which the Southern Villanovans (in Rome and Latium) placed the ashes of their dead. Though these huts show no great advance over those of the Tavoliere or *terremare* folk, the people who lived in them were skilled artisans, producing fine bronze work. The finest example, from the late Arnoaldi period in Bologna (*ca.* 550–525 B.C.) is the Certosa *situla* (Fig. 1.11), where the scenes portrayed are so vivid that even a funeral comes to life. In one band is a vignette of rustic festival, where a slave drags a pig by the hind leg, a piper plays, and the lord of the manor ladles his wine while he waits for a dinner of venison. The deer is being brought on a pole by two slaves, while a curly-tailed dog marches beneath.

Three other areas of Iron Age digs are worthy of mention. One is Este, whose culture in general resembles Bologna's, with fine bronze buckets, belts, and pendants. A second is Golasecca, near Lago Maggiore, where, as at Como, the finds reveal a people making a living as transport agents, forwarding artifacts back and forth between the Transalpine country, Etruria, and the Balkans. The graves yield safety pins, bronze buckets, small jewelry of bronze, iron, amber and glass, horse bits, chariot parts, helmets, spears, and swords. A third is the territory of Picenum, on the central Adriatic coast; here the tombs are filled (Fig. 1.12) with maces, greaves, breastplates, even chariots, as might be expected from the ancestors of those thorns in Rome's flesh, the warlike Samnites (Fig. 1.13). The Warrior of Capestrano (550–500 B.C.), found in Picenum, has Etruscan parallels for the apron and the sandaled feet; it has been plausibly interpreted as an image of one who has survived intended self-sacrifice for victory in battle. It stands over seven Roman feet high; the feather headdress is detachable; the side supports bear an undeciphered Picene inscription and representations of spears. Celtic parallels have been noted: see the

FIG. 1.12 Picene tomb furniture from Fabriano. (F. von Duhn and F. Messerschmidt, *Italische Gräberkunde*, 2, Pl. 31)

FIG. 1.11 The Certosa *situla*. (Bologna, Museo Civico)

FIG. 1.13 Chieti, Museum. The Warrior of Capestrano. (Italian Ministry of Public Instruction)

head from Entremont (*Roman France,* Fig. 1.15).

Finally, a brief word about Sicily in prehistory. Incised cave drawings (Carbon-14 date *ca.* 10,000 B.C.) from Levanzo Island, off Trapani, and Addaura, near Palermo show lively human and animal figures. The neolithic type-site, Stentinello near Syracuse, dated *ca.* 4000 B.C., has a rock-cut ditch surrounding an oval area measuring 600 by 700 feet. The acropolis on the volcanic island of Lipari, off Sicily's northeast corner, shows a remarkable continuity from the neolithic to the Iron Age. The settlement owed its prosperity to exploiting and exporting obsidian, a glasslike product of volcanic action, which splits into razor-sharp blades. The dwellers in the plain below the acropolis felt so secure that they left their village unwalled. Recent excavations of over 400 graves in the Lipari Islands, and of a Siculan village near Lentini, whose huts have front porches and otherwise resemble those of Latium, has established closer connections with the mainland than used to be thought possible. But our main knowledge of Siculan culture results from the earlier excavations of Paolo Orsi, near Syracuse, and on either side of the toe of Italy, at Torre Galli and Canale. These provided a model of archaeological method. The table opposite, resulting from Orsi's careful observation of both the strata in which pots of various fabrics were found in his digs near Syracuse and the frequency of their distribution within levels, shows how division into archaeological periods is arrived at. The Geometric ware (the latest) is characteristic of the period he called Siculan III, contemporary with Villanovan of the eighth century B.C. Orsi's sites at Torre Galli and Canale are urn fields, dated by the Geometric pottery (meander and swastika patterns, the latter perhaps to insure good luck) in the eighth century. They show a trade with Greece 150 years before the first Greek colony was founded in South Italy.

Site	Yellow surface ware	Fine gray ware	Myce- naean ware	Red polished ware	Feather- pattern	Geo- metric	Siculan Period
Milocca	+ +		−				Early II
Plemmirio		+					Early II
Cozzo Pantano	+	+	−		=		II
Thapsos	−	+ +	+ +				II
Pantalica, N.		=		+ +		−	II
Caltagirone		=		+	=	+	Late II
Dessueri		= .		−	−		Late II
Pantalica, S.				+	+ +	+	Early III

(= signifies very rare; −, not common; +, not unusual; + +, very common)

If the prehistoric folk who lived on the Tavoliere—in the *terremare* and around the *nuraghi*—and the later Villanovans and Siculans have any reality for us, we owe our insights into their culture to the patience, critical spirit, and intelligence of Bradford, Pigorini's critics, Lilliu, Ducati, Orsi, and other archaeologists. Their work has pushed back the frontiers of Italian history nearly two millennia and revealed to us how the energy and capacity for creative borrowing of provincial Italians contributed to the ultimate strength and coherence of the Roman state, or how the Italians fought the Romans when they proved high-handed. To Roman culture of historical times another great contribution was made by the Etruscans.

2

The Etruscans

Between Tiber and Arno there flourished, while Rome was still a collection of mud huts above the Tiber ford, a rich, energetic, and mysterious people, the Etruscans, whose civilization was to influence Rome profoundly. Their riches have been known to the modern world ever since the systematic looting of the fabulous wealth of their underground tombs began, as early as 1489. Visitors to the Vatican and Villa Giulia Museums in Rome and, better still, the Archaeological Museum in Florence can marvel at the splendid weapons, rich gold work, and handsome vases with which more or less scientific grave robbers have enriched the collections in the last hundred years. Travelers to Tarquinia, on the Tuscan seaboard, can wonder at the strange, vivid paintings and seemingly indecipherable inscriptions on the walls of mysterious and intricate underground chambers. Etruscan bronze work inspired the sculptors of the Renaissance; Etruscan tombs were drawn by the pen of the great engraver Piranesi; Etruscan cities and cemeteries were described by perhaps the most interesting author, certainly the best stylist, who ever wrote on archaeology: the Englishman George Dennis.

Dennis's *Cities and Cemeteries of Etruria,* though its last edition appeared in 1883, is still the best general introduction to Etruscology. His achievement is the more remarkable in the light of the conditions under which he worked: execrable roads, worse lodging, and malaria stalking the whole countryside. In his day Etruscan tombs were exploited exclusively in the interest of the art dealers—with methods utterly unscientific. Artifacts without commercial value were ruthlessly destroyed: it is heart-rending to read Dennis's account of the rape of Vulci.

> Our astonishment was only equalled by our indignation when we saw the labourers dash [coarse pottery of unfigured and . . . unvarnished ware, and a variety of small articles in black clay] to the ground as they drew them forth, and crush them beneath their feet as things "cheaper than seaweed." In vain I pleaded to save some from destruction; for though of no remarkable worth, they were often of curious and elegant forms, and valuable as relics of the olden time, not to be replaced; but no, it was all *roba di schiocchezza*—"foolish stuff"—the [foreman] was inexorable; his orders were to destroy immediately whatever was of no pecuniary value, and he could not allow me to carry away one of these relics which he so despised.

Unfortunately, looting of this kind produced much of the material in our museums, whose precise "findspots" (from the German *Fundort*, the precise place where an archaeologically significant object was found) are consequently often not known. On the other hand, scientific excavation, when it came, in the mid-nineteenth century, found some tombs still unplundered.

Our knowledge of Etruscan civilization is almost entirely a triumph of this modern scientific archaeology, since written Etruscan, with no known affinities, is still largely undeciphered, though scientific methods have made large strides possible. In the last three generations archaeologists have attacked and in great measure solved the problem of the origin of the Etruscans, the nature of their cities, their political organization, their religious beliefs and practices, the degree of originality in their creative arts, their life and customs. The result is a composite picture of the greatest people to dominate the Italian peninsula before the Romans.

As to origins, the Etruscans might have been indigenous, or come down over the Alps, or, as most of the ancients believed, have come by sea from Asia Minor. The difference of their burial customs and, probably, their language from those of their neighbors makes it unlikely that their ruling class was native like, for example, the Villanovans; the archaeological evidence for their links with the North is very late, and the Northern theory has tended to fall along with the discrediting of Pigorini's notions (based, as we saw, on unwarranted reconstruction of the *terremare*) about a single line of descent for Etruscan and Italic peoples. There remains the theory of Near Eastern origin, first stated in the fifth century B.C. by the Greek historian Herodotus and recently (in the 1930s) given some slight support by Italian excavators' discovery of an inscription dated about 600 B.C. on the island of Lemnos, off the coast of Asia Minor opposite Troy. Though the Lemnian dialect is non-Indo-European and, therefore, like Etruscan, cannot be read, its archaic letters can be transliterated. Beginning with the bottom center line (Fig. 2.1), continuing with the line on the far left, and reading *boustrophedon* (alternately from right to left and from left to right, like an ox plowing), it reads *evistho zeronaith zivai/ sialchveiz aviz/ maraz mav/ vanalasial zeronai morinail/ aker tavarzio/ holaiez naphoth ziazi.* The resemblance to the alphabet and the art forms of the Avele Feluske stele from Etruscan Vetulonia (Fig. 2.2) is obvious. The particular letter form transcribed as *th* occurs elsewhere

FIG. 2.1
Lemnos. Inscription in local
dialect, similar to Etruscan.
(M. Pallottino, *Etruscologia*, Pl. 4)

FIG. 2.2
Vetulonia. Avele Feluske stele.
(M. Pallotino, *Etruscologia*,
Pl. 21)

only in Phrygia in Asia Minor. The very words and word endings of the Lemnian stele can be found on Etruscan inscriptions. Thus the inscription shows at the very least that on an island "geographically intermediate between Asia Minor and Italy a language very similar to Etruscan was employed by some persons." The ancient tradition localizing the original home of the Etruscans somewhere in or near northwest Asia Minor receives here some archaeological support.

But the important thing is not where they came from, but how their culture was formed. The archaeological evidence justifies the hypothesis that they were a small but vigorous military aristocracy from the eastern Mediterranean, established in central Italy, where they built, by borrowing and merging, upon a structure created by the Villanovans. For example, at Tarquinia there are two Villanovan phases (1000–700 B.C.) before Etruscan begins. Certainly the Etruscans did not come bag and baggage into an empty land. A new approach, the analysis of bones from Etruscan tombs to ascertain the blood types of their ancient occupants, may, by comparison with the persistent blood types of modern Tuscans, enable the archaeologist to determine what proportion of the ancient population was native and what intrusive.

Archaeology tells us, too, that Etruscan civilization is a culture of cities. Ancient literary sources speak of a league of twelve Etruscan places (Fig. 2.3), most of which have yielded important archaeological material: from Veii, the great terracotta Apollo; at Cerveteri, Vetulonia, Orvieto, and Perugia, the remarkable rock-cut tombs; at Tarquinia, Vulci, and Chiusi, strikingly vivid tomb paintings; at Bolsena, Roselle, and Volterra, mighty fortification walls; at Populonia, the slag heaps from the iron works which made Etruria prosperous. At Populonia, the weight of the slag has crushed some of the tumuli which cover rich seventh- and sixth-century

FIG. 2.3   Early Italy, to illustrate Etruscan and other sites. Inset: early Rome. (V. Scramuzza and P. MacKendrick, *The Ancient World*, Fig. 32a)

graves. But the most interesting, and some of the latest, evidence for Etruscan city planning and fortifications comes from three sites, two in the northern Etruscan sphere of influence—Marzabotto on the River Reno, fifteen miles south of Bologna; Spina, near one of the seven mouths of the Po—and one in northern Etruria itself, Bolsena, ancient Volsinii.

The first recorded excavations at Marzabotto date from the 1860s, but the ruins had been known since 1550. The striking discovery at Marzabotto was that the site (dated by pottery in its necropolis to the late sixth or early fifth centuries B.C.) had a regular, oriented, rectangular grid of streets (Fig. 2.4), enclosing house blocks (*insulae*) averaging 165 by 35 yards. The main north-south street, or *cardo,* and the main east-west street, or *decumanus*, were each over forty-eight feet wide, the minor streets one-third as broad. The

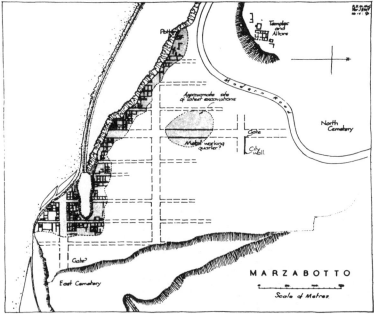

FIG. 2.4   Marzabotto: grid plan.
(J. B. Ward Perkins, "Early Roman Towns in Italy," Fig. 5)

streets were paved, as they were not in Rome until 350 years later. Drains ran beneath all the streets except the reserved area (the Romans were to call it the *pomerium*) just inside the circuit wall. The house plans resemble closely the fourth-century ones discovered in the 1930s at Olynthus, on the Chalcidice Peninsula in Greece, by an American expedition. The house doors had locks and keys. A number of the buildings were recognizable as shops, with back rooms for living quarters.

Bearing in mind the sobering experience of Pigorini's unwarranted claims about a grid plan for the *terremare,* we might be tempted to skepticism about Marzabotto, except for two facts: Brizio, the excavator, himself expressed doubts, as early as 1891, about Pigorini's reconstruction; furthermore, a re-examination of the site in 1953 confirmed the authenticity of Brizio's findings.

The city is dominated, on the high ground to the northwest, by an *arx,* with the same orientation as the city grid. It bears the footings, some of considerable size with impressive moldings, of five structures, temples or altars. One of them, facing south and divided at the back into three *cellae,* is the prototype of the Roman Capitolium, decorated by an Etruscan artist and dedicated to the triad Jupiter, Juno, and Minerva (in Etruscan, Tin, Uni, and Menerva). Until World War II, when they were wantonly destroyed, the finds in terracotta from the arx were preserved in the local museum. There were revetments, plaques forming a thin veneer of fired clay, with nail holes for affixing them to the wooden frame of a typical Tuscan temple. They included archaic antefixes: ornamental terracotta caps to mask the unsightly ends of half-round roof tiles. Terracotta revetments like these, for wooden construction, continue to be canonical in Roman temples down to the first century B.C.; marble as a building material does not come into use until after the middle of the second century B.C. But recent excavation has turned up the head of a marble kouros of *ca.* 500 B.C.; both city and necropolis yielded Attic vases of 550 to 450 and votive small bronzes. The city was an industrial center: it had smithies, tile works, and potteries. Under the lee of the arx was a necropolis with contents like those found in Gallic graves, mute evidence of the occupation of Marzabotto by the wave of Gauls which brought terror into Italy early in the fourth century B.C. In sum, Marzabotto is so perfect an example of an Etruscan town site that it merits the name of the Etruscan Pompeii.

Marzabotto remained for many years the only known Etruscan site with a grid plan. Lying as it does outside Etruria proper, it was clearly the product of Etruscan expansion northward. Since 1922, reclamation by drainage canals has revealed the necropolis of another northern outpost, Spina, near one of the mouths of the Po. Working under the greatest difficulties from mud and seepage, archaeologists have unearthed the contents of no less than 1213 tombs, often finding golden earrings and diadems gleaming in the mud against the skulls in the burials. These precious ornaments, together with necklaces of northern amber, perfume bottles in glass paste and alabaster from Egypt, and Greek black- and red-figured vases, are now the pride of the Ferrara Museum. Though the vases are Greek, both Etruscans and Greeks lived in the site together, as is proved by *graffiti* in both languages scratched on the pottery. The spot, commanding the Adriatic, would be the ideal port of entry for foreign luxury goods imported to satisfy the taste for display of wealthy Etruscans. Wealthy as they were, they were all equal in the sight of Charun: the skeletons were regularly found with small change, to pay the infernal ferryman, clutched in the bony fingers of their right hands. Pathetic graves of children contained jointed dolls and game counters.

This rich and crowded cemetery was all that was known of Etruscan Spina until further drainage operations in 1953, in the Pega Valley, south of the original site (Fig. 2.5),

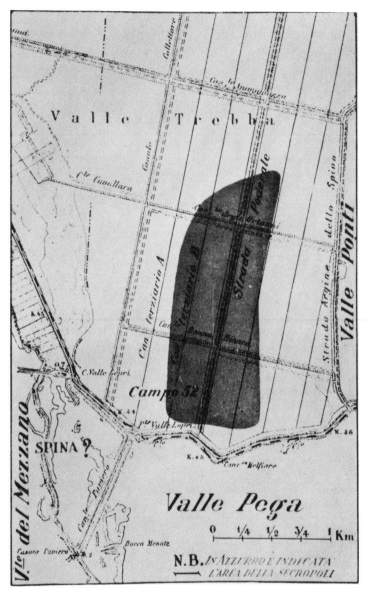

FIG. 2.5 Spina, plan.
(S. Aurigemma, *Il R. Museo di Spina in Ferrara*, Pl. 4)

brought to light not only 2398 new tombs, but also further surprises. In October 1956, an air photograph in color revealed beneath the modern irrigation canals the grid plan (Fig. 2.6), resembling Marzabotto's, of the port area of the ancient Etruscan city. This time the *decumanus* is a canal, sixty-six feet wide, and the marshy site is revealed as a sort of Etruscan Venice. Later air photographs showed evidence of habitation over an area of 741 acres, large enough for a population of half a million. Since the artifacts of this vast city are a little later in style than those of Marzabotto, we assume that Spina flourished a little later. Almost no weapons were found in the graves: Spina apparently felt secure on her landlocked lagoon, but she reckoned without attacks from the landward side. Few vases datable later than the late fifth century are found in the graves: the inference is that Spina fell, about 390 B.C., before the same Gallic invasion that despoiled Marzabotto. The two sites together reinforce each other in giving evidence for the use by Etruscan city planners of the kind of square or rectangular grid of streets later made famous by Roman colonies and Roman camps; unfortunately the question is still open whether the Etruscans invented the grid used in Italy or whether it was a Greek import.

Archaeology tells us something about Etruscan fortifications, too, not least important being some recent negative evidence: many polygonal walls in Etruria and Latium, formerly believed Etruscan, are now proved to be of Roman date. But there are Etruscan circuit walls at Castel d'Asso (Axia, a grid-planned city five and a half miles west of Viterbo), Roselle (Rusellae, near Grosseto), and Volterra (Volaterrae, thirty miles southeast of Leghorn). And excavations conducted since 1947 at Bolsena by the French school in Rome have unearthed walls that seem genuinely Etruscan, surrounding an Etruscan site and having Etruscan letters hacked on the blocks. The marks, concentrated on strategic sections of the wall, were probably apotropaic, intended to

FIG. 2.6   Spina: grid plan, air photograph.
(ENIT, *Italy's Life*, p. 91)

FIG. 2.7   Vetulonia: fasces from the Tomb of the Lictor.
(M. Pallottino, *Etruscologia*, Pl. 22)

work as magic charms against the enemy. One section of the wall was only one block thick. It could not have been self-standing; it must have been intended as the spine of an *agger* or earthwork. Just such a spine was a part of Rome's earliest walls, and a similar technique is to be seen in early earthworks at Anzio and Ardea. The discovery of these walls has suggested the identification of Bolsena with Etruscan Volsinii, one of the twelve cities, and the scene of regular meetings of the Etruscan League. On the same site were found some temple foundations and a grid plan, but the amphitheater, theater, odeon, and baths identified within the walls are Roman. Orvieto, some ten miles northeast and now known to have Etruscan walls, is a strong rival for identification as Volsinii. Wherever the Etruscan city was, when the Romans sacked it in 264 B.C., two thousand statues were among the booty.

Grid plans suggest a sophisticated, if rigid, political organization for Etruscan cities. Evidence for the political life of a civilization normally comes from literature and inscriptions, very little from artifacts. Yet the Avele Feluske stele from Vetulonia, already mentioned, shows a figure carrying a double-headed ax. Later, axes were carried by the consul's twelve bodyguards, whom the Romans called lictors. There seems to be a connection between the number twelve and the twelve cities of the Etruscan confederacy. Vetulonia, another grid-planned city, has yielded another object of importance for understanding Etruscan political organization and Rome's debt to it. In the Tomb of the Lictor was found, besides a chariot and a metal coffer containing gold objects wrapped in gold leaf, a double-headed iron ax (Fig. 2.7) hafted on to an iron rod surrounded by eight others. This is the prototype of the Roman *fasces,* and indeed Silius Italicus, epic poet of the Silver Age, assigns the origin of the fasces to Vetulonia. Such artifacts suggest that the ruler of an Etruscan city, whether king or aristocrat, was surrounded by considerable pomp: in Vetulonia's case, supported by wealth from the exploitation of mines.

Etruscan political organization, Romans believed, at one stage embraced Rome: an Etruscan inscription on a shiny black *bucchero* dish in Rome confirms this. More impressive confirmation comes from a mid-third-century frescoed Etruscan tomb in Vulci, discovered by A. François in 1857. The fresco is part myth, part history; both parts are sanguinary. The dominant mythological theme is the Trojan War: Achilles, for example, strikes down a Trojan prisoner, while a winged Etruscan death goddess, labeled Vanth, and a hook-nosed Charun carrying his hammer and painted a ghastly blue, look on. One panel shows Vel Saties, who commissioned the tomb, in an elaborately embroidered robe, and his dwarf Arnaz with a falcon perched on his hand. The major historical scene portrays bloody duels of Etruscan leaders (dramatic date *ca.* 500 B.C.) and one Caile Vipinas (Latin Caelius Vibenna), freed by Macstrna (magister). In another panel Marce Camitlnas (M. Camillus) inflicts a death blow upon Cneve Tarchunies Rumach (Cn. Tarquinius Romanus), of the family of the Etruscan kings of Rome. Seventeen more Etruscan inscriptions, and six Latin, were found in the Tomba delle Iscrizioni in 1959. An Avile Vipina occurs in a votive inscription, from a context dated in the sixth century B.C., found at Veii on a *bucchero* sherd. The conclusion is inescapable that A. and C. Vibenna were actual historical figures, Etruscan leaders involved in a political struggle for the domination of Rome, Macstrna is identified in Roman tradition with Servius Tullius, a good king whose rule falls, according to the literary tradition, between the tyrannical reigns of the two Tarquins. The fresco may represent an episode in Servius Tullius' life unknown to the Roman tradition, before he became king in Rome; he is represented rescuing C. Vibenna from the Romans and killing Tarquin. Thus archaeology here not only confirms the literary tradi-

tion of Rome's Etruscan kings; it suggests something about
the internal policy of sixth-century Etruscan cities: existing
in them, perhaps by a constitutional transformation from an
archaic kingship, was a strong military authority, like that of
the *magister populi* or dictator of the later Roman Republic.
Etruscan tomb inscriptions, with their many personal names,
show that official Etruscan nomenclature included—as did
the later Roman—the name of the clan. Clan organization
is in origin aristocratic. As later in Rome aristocrats with a
clan organization overthrew the original monarchy, so too,
we may suppose, the clans operated in Etruria.

In the example just cited, light is thrown on Etruscan
political organization by the inscriptions on the fresco, and
it is in fact to inscriptions in the Etruscan alphabet (Fig.
2.8) that we owe most of what we know about Etruscan
politics. For, paradoxically, though Etruscan, as a non-Indo-
European language, is technically indecipherable (in the
sense that the longest inscriptions in it cannot be entirely
translated), valid inferences can be made about some of the
short ones. For example, one of the inscriptions on the wall
of the Tomb of Orcus at Tarquinia, discovered in 1868 (Fig.
2.9), reads in part *zilath : amce : mechl : rasnal,* at first sight
a most unlikely combination of letters. Another Tarquinian
inscription, this time from a sarcophagus in the local museum (splendidly installed in the fifteenth-century Vitelleschi
palace) reads in part *zilath rasnas.* If we extrapolate from
the Roman practice of recording on funerary monuments the
official career (*cursus honorum*) of the deceased (beginning
with the highest offices held), it appears likely that the term
zilath refers to a magistracy. It occurs often, and when it
occurs in a series, it occurs early; this warrants the inference
that it refers to an important magistracy. Certain late Latin
inscriptions from Etruria refer to a *praetor Etruriae.* Might
not the *zilath* be the Etruscan official corresponding to the
Roman praetor? This is the more likely since the words

Typical Letterings	Archaic Letterings (vii–v cent.)	Late Letterings (iv–i cent.)	Modern Equivalents	Typical Letterings	Archaic Letterings (vii–v cent.)	Late Letterings (iv–i cent.)	Modern Equivalents
A	A	A	a	⊞			(s)
B			(b)	O			(o)
ꓶ	�283	Ɔ	c(k)	ꓶ	ꓶ	ꓶ	p
ꓷ			(d)	M	M	M	ś
ꓱ	ꓱ	ꓱ	c	Q	Q		q
ꓱ	ꓱ	ꓱ	v	ꓷ	ꓷ	ꓷ	r
I	I	ꓕ	z	ꓵ	ꓵ	ꓵ	s
目	日	日	h	T	T	ꓔ	t
⊗	⊗	⊙	δ (th)	Y	Y	V	u
I	I	I	i	X	X, +		ṡ
ꓘ	ꓘ		k	Φ		Φ	φ (ph)
ꓦ	ꓦ	ꓦ	l	ꓦ		ꓦ	X (ch)
M	M	m	m		8	8	f
ꓨ	ꓨ	n	n				

FIG. 2.8 Etruscan alphabet. (M. Pallottino, *The Etruscans*, p. 259)

FIG. 2.9   Tarquinia: Tomb of Orcus, inscription.
(*Corpus Inscriptionum Etruscarum*, no. 5360)

rasnal, rasnas closely resemble the word *Rasenna,* which a Greek historian tells us is what the Etruscans called themselves in their own language. There remains the word *mechl.* A similar word, *methlum,* occurs next to the word *spur* in a curious text, the longest we have in Etruscan, written on the cloth of a mummy wrapping now preserved in the museum of Zagreb, in Yugoslavia. The context appears to list the institutions for whose benefit certain religious ceremonies were performed. Several names of offices are accompanied, and probably modified, by the words *spureni, spurana.* It looks as if the word means "city." Suppose the other institution, the *methlum,* mentioned next to the *spur,* were of larger size. Might it not be the Etruscan for "League"? The Tomb of Orcus inscription, then, might mean, "He was the chief magistrate of the Etruscan League." It is by inferences like these that we force a language technically indecipherable to tell us something about the political organization of the mysterious people who spoke and wrote it.

Another example comes from a long inscription on a scroll held in the hands of a sculptured figure on another sarcophagus in the Tarquinia museum. It contains the word *lucairce.* In the text of the Zagreb mummy wrapping, mention is made of ceremonies celebrated *lauchumneti,* presumably a noun with an ending showing a place relation and obviously related in root to *lucairce.* And both seem connected with the word *lucumo,* used in Latin to refer to Etruscan chiefs or kings. *Lucairce* contains the ending *-ce,* which we interpreted on the Tomb of Orcus inscription as verbal; it might mean "was king (or chief)." In that case *lauchumneti,* with its locative ending, might mean "in the [priest]-king's house" (Latin *Regia*). Thus by reasoning from the known to the unknown we can find evidence from the Etruscans themselves that at some stage they were ruled by kings. Since the Tarquinia sarcophagus with the scroll is on the evidence of artistic techniques dated late (second century B.C., a date at which the Roman Republic fully controlled Etruria), we must suppose that by that date the *lucumo* had been reduced to a mere priestly function, much as in Rome itself the priest who in Republican times discharged the sacred duties once performed by Rome's kings (*reges*) was still called the *rex sacrorum*.

A final example. On Etruscan inscriptions occurs a root *purth-*, with by-forms *purthne, purtsvana, eprthne, eprthni,* and *eprthnevc*. This looks like the root which occurs in the name of the king of Clusium, in Latin Lars Porsenna: he who in the *Lays of Ancient Rome* swore by the Nine Gods. Legend made of his tomb at Clusium (modern Chiusi, map, Fig. 2.3) an elaborate affair of superimposed pyramids, with a labyrinth beneath. A labyrinth 900 feet around, of tunnels and rock-cut burial chambers arranged in tiers, exists at Poggio Gaiella, about three miles north-northeast of Chiusi: Fig. 2.10 reproduces Dennis's entrancing plan. The root *purth-* probably occurs in the Greek *prytanis*, which means something like "senator." Clearly another official of importance is referred to here.

In sum, archaeologists looking for evidence of Etruscan political organization have found such outward signs of pomp as fasces, plus evidence for magistrates resembling the later Roman dictator, praetor, priest-king, senator, and for cities probably combined into a league.

If inscriptions can be made to yield this kind of evidence, what can we say about the state of our knowledge about the Etruscan language in general? The same kind of combinatory method applied to other inscriptions yields with patience results justifying the statement that progress, though agonizingly slow, is being made. Many short inscriptions can be read entire: they are usually funerary, and give the names, filiation and age of the deceased. An example (p. 47), from yet another sarcophagus in the Tarquinia museum:

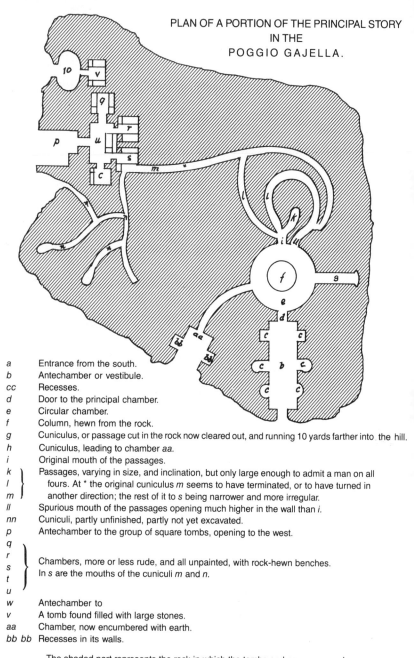

PLAN OF A PORTION OF THE PRINCIPAL STORY
IN THE
POGGIO GAJELLA.

a   Entrance from the south.
b   Antechamber or vestibule.
cc   Recesses.
d   Door to the principal chamber.
e   Circular chamber.
f   Column, hewn from the rock.
g   Cuniculus, or passage cut in the rock now cleared out, and running 10 yards farther into the hill.
h   Cuniculus, leading to chamber aa.
i   Original mouth of the passages.
k ⎫
l   Passages, varying in size, and inclination, but only large enough to admit a man on all
m ⎭   fours. At * the original cuniculus m seems to have terminated, or to have turned in
     another direction; the rest of it to s being narrower and more irregular.
ll   Spurious mouth of the passages opening much higher in the wall than i.
nn   Cuniculi, partly unfinished, partly not yet excavated.
p   Antechamber to the group of square tombs, opening to the west.
q ⎫
r ⎪
s ⎬   Chambers, more or less rude, and all unpainted, with rock-hewn benches.
t ⎪   In s are the mouths of the cuniculi m and n.
u ⎭
w   Antechamber to
v   A tomb found filled with large stones.
aa   Chamber, now encumbered with earth.
bb bb Recesses in its walls.

     The shaded part represents the rock in which the tombs and passages are hewn.

FIG. 2.10   Chiusi, possible tomb of Lars Porsenna (Dennis).

partunus vel velthurus   *satlnal-c*   *ramthas clan*
"Partuni Vel of Velthur and of Satlnei Ramtha the son,
avils   *XXIIX lupu*
of years 28,   dead."

Here for translation one assumes that Etruscan, while not
Indo-European in its roots, is an inflected language, where
an -*s* or -*l* ending shows possession, and the enclitic -*c*, like
the Latin -*que*, means "and." Another example shows similar
case endings, uses vocabulary we have seen before, and adds
a place name:

Alethnas Arnth   *Larisal*   *zilath Tarchnalthi amce*
"Alethna Arnth (son) of Laris praetor at Tarquinia was."

Altogether some 10,000 Etruscan inscriptions are known.
Of these only three are of any length: the Zagreb mummy
wrapping, a tile from Capua, and the previously mentioned
scroll from Tarquinia. The next seven taken together total
less than 100 words. Given this material, there is some bitter
truth in the statement that if we could unlock the secret of
Etruscan, we would have the key to an empty room. But
whole cities in Etruria remain to be dug; there is no knowing
what new inscriptions excavations now in progress at Vulci,
Roselle, or Santa Severa may turn up, including perhaps a
bilingual, where identical texts in Etruscan and a known
language like Latin may solve the puzzle, as the Greek of
the Rosetta Stone made possible the deciphering of Egyptian
hieroglyphs. At Pyrgi, the port of Caere, a discovery in
1964 bade fair to solve the problem: three rectangular sheets
of gold leaf, dated about 500 B.C., one in Phoenician, two in
Etruscan, on the same subject. But, alas, the one is not a
translation of the others. The purport is that the Etruscan
ruler of Caere makes a dedication to Punic Astarte and prescribes annual rites. The date is close to that of Rome's 509
treaty with Punic Carthage, made when Rome was still
under, or just freeing herself from, an Etruscan dynasty. A

fragmentary bronze plaque, slightly earlier in date, mentions Uni (Etruscan equivalent of Astarte) three times; she shared the cult with Tinia (equated with Jupiter). An antiquarium on the site houses terracotta revetments from the temples and pottery from the dig, together with copies of the plaques; the originals are inaccessible.

Etruscan loan words in Latin tell us something: *antemna,* "yardarm"; *histrio,* "actor"; *atrium,* "patio"; *groma,* "plane table"—all suggest Etruscan predominance on the sea and the stage, in domestic architecture and surveying. But we know more than loanwords: the known vocabulary in Etruscan amounts now to 122 words, in seven categories, including time words (*e.g.,* the names of several months), the limited political vocabulary already discussed, names for family relationships, some three dozen verbs and nouns, and the same number of words from the field of religion.

It is about Etruscan religion, and especially funerary rites, that we are best informed. The Etruscans had the reputation of being the most addicted to religious ceremonial of any people of antiquity, and we learn much about Etruscans living from Etruscans dead. We know what sort of documentation to expect on religious matters from an Etruscan tomb, by extrapolating back from rites which the Romans believed they had inherited from Etruria, especially in the area of foretelling the future by examining the livers of animals (hepatoscopy) or observing the flights of birds (augury). One of the most curious surviving documents of Etruscan superstition is the bronze model of a sheep's liver (Fig. 2.11) found in 1877 near Piacenza, on the upper Po, and now in the Civic Museum there. The liver is split in two lengthwise. From the plane surface thus provided, three lobes project; over each lobe various gods preside. The total is 24. The border of the plane surface is subdivided into sixteen compartments (Fig. 2.12); also over each of these a god presides.

FIG. 2.11 Piacenza, Civic Museum. Bronze model of sheep's liver, used in foretelling the future. (ENIT, *Italy's Life*, p. 37)

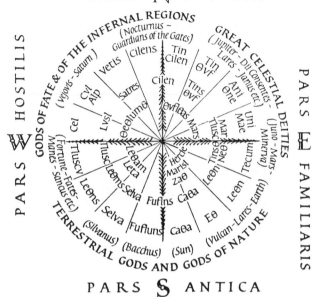

FIG. 2.12   Piacenza liver, schematic representation.
(M. Pallottino, *The Etruscans*, p. 165)

The same sixteen subdivisions were used in the imaginary partition of the sky for augury, and the same principle governed the layout and orientation of cities like Marzabotto and probably Spina. The same superstition found in Babylonia directs our attention once more to the probable Near Eastern origin of the Etruscan ruling class. The priest would take his position at the crosspoint of the intended *cardo* and *decumanus* of the city, facing south (we recall that the three-celled temple on the *arx* at Marzabotto faces south). The half of the city behind him was called in Latin the *pars postica* (posterior part); the part in front of him, the *pars antica* (anterior part); on his left was the *pars familiaris* (the lucky side; hence thunder on the left was a good omen); on his right, the *pars hostilis* (unlucky). To the sub-division of the earth below corresponded a similar subdivision of the sky above; either was called in Latin (using a concept clearly derived from Etruscan practice) a *templum*, "part cut off," a sacred precinct, terrestrial or celestial. From the Piacenza liver and the orientation of Marzabotto we can deduce both the orderliness of the Etruscan mind and the ease with which it degenerated into rigidity and superstition. For this deadly heritage the Etruscans apparently found in the Romans willing recipients; often, but not always, for old Cato said, "I cannot see how one liver-diviner can meet another without laughing in his face."

The vast number of Etruscan tombs and the richness of their decoration and furnishings tell us much about another aspect of the Etruscans' religion: their view of the afterlife. About this the fabulous painted tombs of Tarquinia tell us most and bid fair to tell us more as new methods are applied to their discovery and exploration. The ubiquitous Bradford has been at work in Etruria too; his quick eye has detected on air photographs over 800 new tomb mounds at Tarquinia alone, and new methods of ground exploration, worked out by the dedicated Italian engineer C.M. Lerici, have enormously speeded the work of exploration. Electrical-resistivity surveying with a potentiometer, sensitive to the difference between solid earth and empty subterranean space, makes possible the rapid tracing of a profile showing where the hollows of Etruscan tombs exist underground (Fig. 2.13). A hole is then drilled large enough to admit a periscope; if the periscope shows painted walls or pottery, a camera can be attached to make a 360-degree photograph. By this method Lerici reports exploring 450 tombs in 120 days. In one of these, the Tomba della Nave, dated 460/50, the ship is probably symbolic, ready for the journey to the other world. This work, rapid as it is, is being done none too soon: land redistribution schemes, good for the farmer, bad for the archae-

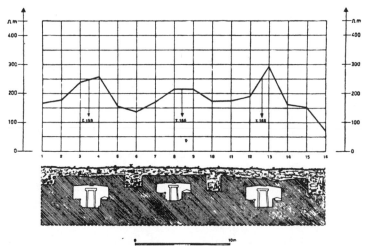

Fig. 2.13   Potentiometer profile. The high points on the graph show
where hollowed tomb chambers exist under ground. (ENIT, *Italy's
Life*, p. 106)

ologist, are changing the face of south Etruria day by day;
deep plowing and the planting of vines and fruit trees are
destroying or obscuring the archaeological picture.

Dennis would hardly lament the passing of the conditions
he so graphically describes: "Among the half-destroyed tumuli of the Montarozzi [at Tarquinia] is a pit, six or eight
feet deep, overgrown by lentiscus; and at the bottom is a
hole, barely large enough for a man to squeeze himself
through, and which no one would care to enter unless aware
of something within to repay him for the trouble, and the
filth unavoidably contracted. Having wormed myself through
this aperture, I found myself in a dark, damp chamber, half-
choked with the *debris* of the walls and ceiling. Yet the walls
have not wholly fallen in, for when my eyes were somewhat
accustomed to the gloom, I perceived them to be painted,
and the taper's light disclosed on the inner wall a banquet in
the open air." Modern gadgetry like Lerici's has destroyed

some of the romance; there is something graphic about descriptions like Mengarelli's of opening a tomb at Cerveteri in
1910, in the presence of the local and neighboring landlords,
the Prince and Princess Ruspoli and the Marchese Guglielmi.
As the blocks of the entrance were removed one by one and
sunlight was reflected into the tomb by mirrors, there were
to be seen against the black earth objects of gleaming gold
and priceless proto-Corinthian vases resting on shreds of de-
composed wood, which were all that was left of the funeral
bed, while other vases were to be seen fixed to the wall with
nails.

The Tomb of Hunting and Fishing at Tarquinia, discovered in 1873, gives us our most attractive picture (Fig. 2.14)
of how Etruscans in their palmiest days viewed the next
world. The tomb is dated by the black-figured Attic vases
it contained in the decade 520–510 B.C., when the Etruscan
ruling class was still prosperous. A more charming invitation
to the brainless life could hardly be imagined. The most

FIG. 2.14   Tarquinia: Tomb of Hunting and Fishing, painting.
(M. Pallottino, *Etruscan Painting*, p. 51)

vivid scene is on the walls of the tomb's inner room, which are conceived as opening out into a breezy seascape, with a lively population of bright birds in blue, red, and yellow, frisky dolphins, and boys, friskier still, at play. Up a steep rock striped in clay-red and grass-green clambers a sunburnt boy in a blue tunic, who appears to have just pushed another boy who is diving, with beautiful form, into the hazy, wine-dark sea. On a nearby rock stands another boy firing at the birds with a slingshot. Below him is a boat with an eye painted on the prow (to ward off the evil eye; fishing boats are still so painted in Portugal). Of the boat's four passengers, one is fishing over the side with a flimsy handline, while beside the boat a fat dolphin turns a mocking somersault. All is life, action, humor, vitality, color; such is the notion of blessed immortality entertained by a people for whom God's in his heaven, all's right with the world.

A quarter of a century or so after the Tomb of Hunting and Fishing was painted, the Etruscans suffered a major naval defeat at the hands of Greeks off Cumae. Rome, expanding, eventually took over the iron mines of Elba and the ironworks of Populonia, and Etruscan prosperity declined agonizingly to its end. Let us look again at a Tarquinian tomb of the period of the decadence, the Tomb of Orcus. There, beside one of the loveliest faces ever painted by an ancient artist (Fig. 2.15), is portrayed one of the most hair-raising demons a depressed imagination could conceive (Fig. 2.16). Its flesh is a weird bluish-green, as though it were putrefying. Its nose is the hooked beak of a bird of prey. The fiend has asses' ears; its hair is a tangled mass of snakes. Beside its monstrous wings rises a huge crested serpent, horribly mottled. In its left hand the demon holds a hammer handle. An inscription identifies him as Charun, the ferry-man of the dead; it is to pay this monster that the skeletons of Spina clutch their bronze small change in their right hands. The contrast between the gaiety of the scenes in the Tomb

FIG. 2.15   Tarquinia: Tomb of Orcus, portrait of the lady Velcha.
(MPI)

of Hunting and the gloomy prospect of the lovely lady—her
family name is Velcha—in the clutches of this grisly demon
has been held to epitomize the contrast between the views of
an afterlife entertained by a prosperous and by an economi-
cally depressed people.

Other noteworthy necropoleis are at Norchia, twelve miles
northeast of Tarquinia; Castel d'Asso; and Orvieto. Norchia,
presenting one of the most romantic and attractive landscapes in all Etruria, is a cliff-tomb city, of deep wooded

FIG. 2.16   Tarquinia: Tomb of Orcus, the demon Charun. (MPI)

glens: "ever wrapt in gloom," says Dennis, apparently feeling, in the teeth of the evidence, that cemeteries should be lugubrious. The visitor sees an amphitheater of rock-cut tombs, two of which (fourth century B.C.) have templelike façades, where the pediments portray gladiatorial contests (an Etruscan invention) and either the fight over Patroclus' body or mourning for Niobe's daughters. On the steep slope of a newly cleared glen, opposite the acropolis, is a panorama of 50 to 70 tombs, in two tiers. Many have porticoes; their façades have false doors, symbolic entrances to the underworld. The real entrances are below these, hidden by tangles of brush and vines. The rock-cut exteriors are cubical, with flat roofs and outside stairs, like Mediterranean houses today. Besides the rock-cut tombs at Castel d'Asso, there are many at Blera (Bieda), near San Giovenale. Under the lee of Orvieto, the necropolis of Crocefisso del Tufo arranges 318 tombs in a grid of streets, a town of the dead. Numerous inscriptions here record non-Etruscan names, showing absorption of resident aliens. The frescoes of a late fourth-century tomb called Golini I, from nearby Poggio Settecamini, now reconstructed in the Archaeological Museum in Florence, show an underworld banquet and, adjoining, an underworld larder hung with sides of beef, fowl, a fawn, and a hare.

Other finds cast further light. The Capua tile prescribes funerary offerings to the gods of the underworld. An inscribed lead plaque from near Populonia is a curse tablet, in which a woman urges Charun or another infernal deity, Tuchulcha, to bring his gruesome horrors to bear on members of her family whose death she ardently desires. Bronze statuettes give details of priestly dress (conical cap tied under the chin, fringed cloak) or show Hermes, Escorter of Souls, going arm-in-arm with the deceased to the world below. The total picture is one of a deeply religious, even superstitious people, attaching particular importance to the formalities of their ritual relations with their gods and obsessed with the afterlife, of which they take a progressively gloomier view as their material prosperity declines.

What can archaeology tell us about Etruscan cultural life? Of art for art's sake there seems to have been very little, of literature none, except for liturgical texts. The Etruscans excelled in fine large-scale bronze work, like the famous Capitoline Wolf who suckled Romulus and Remus, a fifth-century work; the Chimaera of Arezzo, now in Florence, a mythological monster, part lion, part goat, part snake; the "Mars" of Todi, another fourth-century work, now in the Vatican, portraying a heroized young warrior in armor; the Conservatori "Brutus" (Fig. 2.17), a splendid bearded head of 300 or a little later, which might well express how Romans wanted the first consul of their new Republic to look; and the Arringatore (Orator), in Florence (90–50 B.C.), an Etruscan, Avle Metele, with a Roman name, symbolizing how Rome absorbed Etruscans, who became Roman citizens and behaved like Romans. But their minor masterpieces in bronze deserve mention also, especially the engraved mirrors—the cylindrical cosmetic boxes called *ciste*—for example, the Ficoroni cista (late fourth century), from Praeneste, in the Villa Giulia. It is incised with an Argonautic adventure and inscribed with the names of maker, buyer, and eventual recipient: "Novios Plautios med Romae fecid; Dindia Macolnia fileai dedit." E. M. Forster has made a charming imaginative essay called "Macolnia Shops" out of this inscription. There are also statuettes whose attenuated bodies appeal strongly to modern taste. Etruscan painting at its best shows in its economy of line how intelligently they borrowed from the Greeks, in its realism how sturdily they maintained their own individuality. In architecture, Etruscan temples, having been made of wood, do not survive above their foundation courses. But recent discoveries of terracotta temple models at Vulci tell us something about their appearance, and masses of their

FIG. 2.17 Rome, Conservatori "Brutus," *ca.* 300 B.C. (DAI)

terracotta revetment survive. There are brightly painted geometric, vegetable, or mythological motifs: designs to cover beams, to mask the ends of half-round roof tiles, or (in pierced patterns called *à jour* crestings) to follow the slope of a gable roof. Made from molds, the motifs could be infinitely repeated at small expense, an aspect of Etruscan practicality which was to appeal strongly to the Romans.

But the Etruscans' artistic genius shows at the best in their architectural sculpture in painted terracotta, freestanding or in high relief. Their best-known masterpiece in this genre is the Apollo of Veii (Fig. 2.18), designed for the ridgepole of an archaic temple. Discovered in 1916, it is now in the Villa Giulia Museum in Rome. The stylized treatment of the ringlets, the almond eyes, the fixed smile are all characteristic of archaic Greek art, and the fine edges of the profile, lips, and eyebrows suggest an original in bronze. But this is no mere copy. It is the work of a great original artist, probably the same Vulca of Veii who was commissioned in the late sixth century B.C. to do the terracottas for the Capitoline temple in Rome. The sculptor is telling the story of the struggle between Apollo and Hercules for the Hind of Ceryneia: the god is shown as he tenses himself to spring upon his opponent; the anatomical knowledge, the expression of mass in motion, and the craftsmanship required to cast a life-size terracotta (a feat which even now presents the greatest technical difficulties) are all alike remarkable.

From a temple at Pyrgi beside which the famous inscribed gold plaques were found comes an elaborate pedimental terracotta of *ca.* 510–485, showing Athena involved with some of the Seven against Thebes. She carries a pot of the ointment that conferred immortality. At her feet, to her horror, her favorite—the Argive Tydeus—cannibalizes the Theban Melanippus. Also present is Capaneus, about to be thunderstruck for trying to overthrow the Zeus-protected walls of Thebes. From various temples at Falerii Veteres

Fig. 2.18 Rome, Villa Giulia
Museum. Apollo of Veii,
terracotta. (MPI)

Fig. 2.19 Rome, Villa Giulia Museum. Terracotta antefix
of satyr and nymph, from Satricum. (MPI)

(Civita Castellana, eighteen miles southeast of Viterbo) come other architectural terracottas now in the Villa Giulia: the Hellenistic warriors-acroterion from the Mercury temple at Sassi Caduti; the fine fifth-century head of Zeus; and the Alexander-like Apollo of about 300 from Lo Scasato. When the Romans transplanted the citizens in 241, worship continued at the old site.

A set of antefixes (used, as we have seen, to cover the ends of half-round roof tiles), of 500–490, from the archaic temple at Satricum in Latium and in the same museum, are noteworthy for their humor. They represent a series of nymphs pursued by satyrs. The satyrs are clearly not quite sober, and the nymphs are far from reluctant. In a particularly fine piece (Fig. 2.19) the satyr frightens the nymph with a snake which he holds in his left hand, while he slips his right hand over her shoulder to caress her breast. Her gestures are almost certainly not those of a maiden who would repel a man's advances.

A third Etruscan masterpiece in terracotta, of later date, but still showing the same striking vitality as the two pieces just described, is the pair of winged horses in high relief (Fig. 2.20), first published in 1948. They come probably from the pediment of the temple called the Ara della Regina, on the site of the Etruscan city (as opposed to the necropolis) of Tarquinia, and now in the Tarquinia Museum. The proud arching of the horses' necks, their slim legs, and their rippling muscles are rendered to make them the quintessence of the thoroughbred, so that we forget that the delicate wings would scarcely lift their sturdy bodies off the ground. In these three masterpieces art is none the less vibrant for being at the service of religion. Here is created a new Italic expressionistic style, so admirable that many would hold that Italian art did not reach this level again until the Renaissance.

We must mention in passing the remarkable collection of over six hundred alabaster ash urns in the museum at Vol-

FIG. 2.20   Tarquinia, Museum. Winged horses, terracotta
relief, from Ara della Regina. (MPI)

FIG. 2.21   Cerveteri: Tomb of the Reliefs, interior. (MPI)

terra (Volaterrae, see map, Fig. 2.3). Since they average only thirty inches long, the recumbent figures on the lids receive Procrustean treatment, but the reliefs on the sides interestingly combine Greek myth and local color: a boar hunt, circus games, processions with lictors, fasces, and curule chair, triumphs, sacrifices (including human), school scenes, banquets, and deathbeds.

Just as archaeology's finds can convince us of the vitality of Etruscan art, so they can bring to life ancient Etruscan life and customs. Most illuminating in this area are two tombs from Cerveteri, ancient Caere, one of the great cities of the Etruscan dodecapolis—only twenty-five miles up the coast road from Rome, and close, too, in cultural relations. Here again Bradford has been at work, spotting over six hundred new tombs, but the one that tells us most about Etruscan everyday life has been known since 1850. It is the early third-century Tomb of the Reliefs (Fig. 2.21), with places for over forty bodies. The front and back walls of this tomb, and two pillars in the middle, are covered with representations in low relief of Etruscan weapons and objects in daily use; here, as elsewhere in Etruscan tombs but in far more detail, the tomb chamber reproduces the look of a room in an Etruscan house. Such chambers served again as shelters in modern times—against bombs in World War II. In the central recess in the farthest wall is a bed for a noble couple. It is flanked by pilasters bearing medallions of husband (on the left) and wife (on the right). On the husband's side appears the end of a locked strongbox, covered with raised studs or bosses, with a garment lying folded on top. On the wife's side is a sturdy knotted walking staff, a garland, necklaces, and a feather fan. The couch has lathe-turned legs; it is decorated with a relief of Charun and the three-headed dog Cerberus, with a serpent's tail. The couch rests on a step on which a pair of wooden clogs awaits their master's need.

Above the couch, and continuing all the way around the room, is a frieze of military millinery: helmets with visors, helmets with cheekpieces, the felt cap worn under the helmet to keep the metal from chafing, swords, shields, greaves or shin guards, and a pile of round objects variously interpreted as missiles, decorations for valor, or balls of horse dung. The central pilasters, with typical Etruscan economy, are decorated only on the sides visible from the door. What is represented is the whole contents of an Etruscan kitchen. Identifiable objects include a sieve, a set of spits for roasting, a knife rack, an inkpot, a dinner gong, a game board (not unlike those provided in English pubs for shove-ha'penny) with a bag for the counters, and folding handles; a ladle, mixing spoons, an egg beater, pincers, a duck, a tortoise, a cat with a ribbon around its neck, playing with a lizard; a belt, a pitcher, a long thin rolling pin for making macaroni, a pickaxe, a machete, a coil of rope, a pet weasel teasing a black mouse, a *lituus* (the augur's curved staff), a wine flask of the familiar Chianti shape, a knapsack, and a canteen. Over and flanking the door are *bucrania* (ox skulls), wide, shallow sacrificial basins, and a curved war trumpet or hunting horn. Surely never a household embarked better equipped for the next world. This tomb is as good as a documentary film; nothing ever found by archaeology brings Etruscan daily life more vividly before our eyes.

While the Tomb of the Reliefs is full of homely details of Etruscan life, the Regolini-Galassi tomb, also at Cerveteri, was crammed with objects of conspicuous consumption and conspicuous waste. The tomb is named for its discoverers, General Alessandro Regolini and Fr. Vincenzo Galassi, archpriest of Cerveteri in 1836. Its contents are datable in the eighth or seventh century B.C. It consists of a long narrow entranceway or *dromos,* two oval side chambers, and a long, narrow main tomb chamber roofed with a false vault—"now," says Dennis, "containing nothing but slime and serpents."

When it was entered through a hole in the roof on April 21, 1836, an incredible treasure of gold, silver, bronze, and ceramics, over 650 objects in all, burst upon the workmen's gaze. All was cleared with feverish haste in less than twenty-four hours, and no detailed inventory was compiled until seventy years later. The riches are fabulous; to quote Dennis again, "here the youth, the fop, the warrior, the senator, the priest, the belle, might all suit their taste for decoration—in truth a modern fair one need not disdain to heighten her charms with these relics of a long past world." In those days, Etruscan objects were not allowed to languish in a museum. A report of 1839 states, "a few winters ago the Princess of Canino [wife of Lucien Bonaparte] appeared at some of the [British] ambassador's fêtes with a *parure* of Etruscan jewellery which was the envy of the society, and excelled the *chefs-d'oeuvre* of Paris or Vienna." Though the contents of the tomb have been now for many years the pride of the Gregorian Museum in the Vatican, the definitive publication did not appear until 1947.

The tomb contained three burials, including one of a woman of princess's rank. With one of the males was buried his chariot (which was first dismantled and its wooden parts ceremoniously burned); his funeral car, plated with bronze in a swordlike leaf design; and his bronze bier, with a raised place for the head and a latticework of twenty-nine thin bronze bars. With the woman was buried a priceless treasure of gold, of baroque barbarity: a magnificent golden fibula; a great gold pectoral (Fig. 2.22) decorated in *repoussé* with twelve bands of animal figures (this, one would like to think, was what the Princess of Canino wore to the ambassador's party); gold and amber necklaces; massive gold bracelets and earrings to match the pectoral; silver bracelets, rings, pins, a spindle, and buckets, the latter decorated with fantastic animals; ivory dice; a bronze wine bowl, with a beautiful green patina, decorated with six heads of lions and

FIG. 2.22   Vatican City, Vatican Museum: gold pectoral from the
Regolini-Galassi tomb, Cerveteri. (Musei Vaticani)

griffins, turned inward; and (reconstructed) a great bronze-plated chair of state with footstool, the whole ornamented with vegetable and animal motifs; the arms end in horses' heads; the back legs, in cows' hoofs. To the second male burial belonged a set of splendid bronze parade shields; a bronze incense burner on wheels, with a rim of lotus flowers in bronze; a bronze vase stand, with a conical base surmounted by two superimposed oblate spheroids, supporting a bronze container for the vase, the whole ornamented in *repoussé* with bulls and both winged and wingless lions; bowls in silver and silver gilt, decorated with horsemen, footsoldiers, archers, lancers, chariots, lions, dogs, bulls, vultures, and palm trees, in a style that might be Egyptian, Cypriote, or Syrian. Such of the treasure as is imported from the Near East bespeaks the wealth of Etruscan overlords; such as is of local manufacture bespeaks the skill of Etruscan craftsmen.

Two other princely tombs, the Barberini and the Bernardini, at Praeneste, twenty-odd miles east of Rome, vie with the Regolini-Galassi in the richness of their contents, on view in the Villa Giulia. They are in the same orientalizing style, and of nearly the same date (640–20 B.C.). The material is gold, silver gilt, bronze, ivory, amber; the artifacts are plaques, vases, tripods, an incense burner on wheels, shields, a throne. The decoration portrays humans (hunting, dancing, riding, driving chariots) and flowers; it shows a strong preference for animals mythological or real: chimaeras, griffins, sphinxes, centaurs, sirens; leopards, stags, lions (very numerous), dogs, an ostrich. Two gold brooches are particularly striking: they measure eight by five inches and are adorned with rows of animals in fine granulated work, totaling 130 or 131 on each. Though the inspiration is Near Eastern, the workmanship, as often, is Etruscan, perhaps from workshops at Caere.

From other places come other clues to Etruscan life and customs. We may end with two observations, both taken from tombs in Tarquinia: Etruscan women were treated on a par with men; Etruscan sports were sometimes of barbaric cruelty. The tomb of the Leopards (fifth century B.C.) shows women (with dyed hair) reclining on the same dining couch with men; later (Tomb of the Shields, third century B.C.), women sat at meals, while men reclined, but the sexes dined together; there was no Oriental seclusion. The Tomb of the Chariots shows women along with men watching athletic events: horse racing, pole vaulting, boxing, wrestling, discus throwing, running. A fifth-century tomb discovered by Lerici just in time to be restored for the 1960 Olympic Games in Rome is called the Tomb of the Olympic Victors, and shows similar events, including a chariot race with an overturned car.

But Etruscan spectator sports were not always so innocent. On the right wall of the Tomb of the Augurs (540/30 B.C.) in Tarquinia, a masked figure, in false beard, blood-red tunic, and conical cap, is shown inciting a fierce hound to attack a hairy-chested figure, nude but for a loincloth and carrying a club; his eyes are blinded by a sack tied over his head, and his movements are impeded by a cord held by a bystander. The victim is already bleeding from several savage bites. Unless, handicapped as he is, he can club the dog to death, he will surely be torn to bits. Perhaps this sanguinary and savage scene represents human sacrifice (and, if so, it is none the less forbidding), but it is a tempting hypothesis that what we have pictured here is real men representing ghosts, or a mythological mime, of Hercules after the hellhound Cerberus, or a predecessor of the kind of spectacle the Romans later enjoyed in their amphitheaters, when gladiators fought to the death. Gladiatorial contests were, in fact, traditionally of Etruscan origin, first imported from Etruria for certain funeral games in 264 B.C.

We end, then, where we began, with archaeological evidence for Etruscan influence, for good or for ill, upon Rome. As with the story of prehistoric man in Italy, the Etruscan story is one of influences in part originating in the Near East and in part indigenous, creating a civilization with durable elements that could be and were transmitted, playing a predominant rôle in forming the culture of ancient Italy. The Etruscans are important in themselves, of course, but it is a mistake to assume, because their language, unique on the Italian peninsula, is non-Indo-European, that their culture is isolated, too. As a culture of cities, Etruria must have had its effect, not without cross-fertilization from Greek practice, upon Roman town planning. Etruscan political forms and practice recur in Roman usage. The language claims our attention for the light it throws, however dimly, on Etruscan politics, religion, and family life, and for the challenge it has presented to modern scientific scholarship to penetrate its mystery. Etruscan religion, as illuminated by archaeological finds, has its own fascination, foreshadows Roman formalism, and is noteworthy for changing, under the stress of political and economic decline, from an optimistic to a pessimistic view of the afterlife. Etruscan art, especially terracotta sculpture, shows a striking vitality, humor, and independence; Etruscan architecture makes its impact upon Roman. Finally, the evidence of artifacts as to Etruscan daily life shows a standard of material comfort, and even of luxury, not to be achieved again on the peninsula for two hundred years. Etruscan equality of sexes foreshadows the independence of Roman women; the brutality of Etruscan games is to strike an answering chord in sadistic Roman breasts. Etruria has its own intrinsic fascination, yet for the Western world its major interest must lie in its legacy to Rome. When Etruscan culture was at its brilliant, golden height, Rome was a primitive village of wattle-and-daub huts. Archaeology has been able to trace the metamorphosis of those huts into palaces, with all the concomitant story of grandeur and barbarity; to that metamorphosis the rest of this book will be devoted.

3

Early Rome and Latium

Since the first edition of this book, in 1960, the archaeology of no period has been so vigorously pursued as that of archaic Rome and Latium (ninth to sixth centuries B.C.). The energetic younger generation of Italian archaeologists is mostly Marxist and tends to stress material culture, in contrast to what it views as the fascist emphasis on the grandiose buildings of the high Empire.

Everyone remembers that Augustus left Rome a city of marble, but too few people recall that he found it a city of brick. The picture of Rome in most people's minds is of a marble metropolis, proud mistress of a Mediterranean Empire. This to be sure she eventually became, but the archaeological evidence is that until the end of the third century B.C. Rome looked tawdry, with patched temples and winding, unpaved streets. To trace the development is fascinating, and archaeology is our chief guide, though there is also literary, linguistic, and religious evidence.

The traditional date of Rome's founding is 753 B.C.—specifically, April 21, on which day modern Rome celebrates her birthday. But the archaeological evidence is not of a founding in a single act but of an ongoing process, beginning far

earlier than 753. In 1959 Gjerstad discovered in the Sant'
Omobono area, under the south slope of the Capitoline Hill,
sherds of a Proto-Villanovan and Apennine culture which push
the date of earliest Rome back at least into the twelfth or
thirteenth century B.C. (see chronological table, Fig. 3.1), a
date which fits the myth of the arrival here of refugees from
the Trojan War. Though Rome at its beginnings was just
another Latial village (by no means paramount, as later
Romans believed), it had a promising location—at a crossroads and a ford, with water and protection (the Palatine
Hill) for flocks and herds.

The Sant' Omobono area remained sacred down into historical times: potsherds (some from Ischia, in the Bay of
Naples, others from Corinth, Sparta, and Athens) and terracotta revetments and pedimental sculpture date an archaic
temple in or not long after the reign of Servius Tullius (traditional dates, 578–534). A later phase was dedicated (264
B.C.) by M. Fulvius Flaccus, the greedy conqueror of Volsinii,
from which, as we saw, he took as spoils two thousand statues. In Phase V (212 B.C.), twin temples, to Fortuna and
Mater Matuta, were built on a stone platform adjoining the
present church; it was from the fill of this platform that the
Proto-Villanovan sherds came.

Across the street from the Sant' Omobono temples, in the
Forum Holitorium (vegetable market), the church of San
Nicola in Carcere encloses a temple to Juno Sospita, of 197–
194. On either side of it, temples to the two-headed Janus
and to Spes (Hope) date from Rome's First Punic War
(264–241).

Another relevant site lies in the Alban Hills—extinct vol-
canoes in the Roman Campagna, sixteen miles southeast of
Rome, close to Castel Gandolfo, the lovely lakeside spot
where nowadays the Pope has his summer palace. Here, in
a pastureland called the Pascolare di Castello, some peasants
in 1817 were cutting trenches for planting vineyards. Under

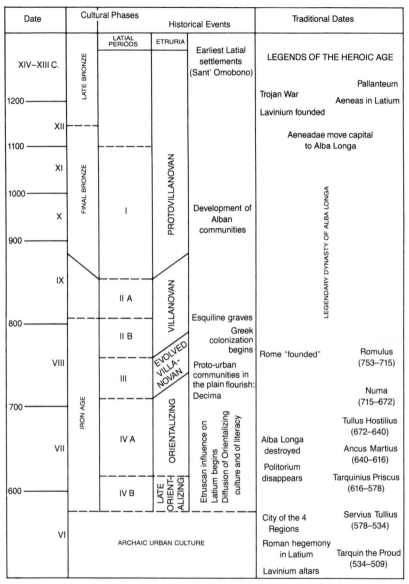

FIG. 3.1 Chronological Table, 1400–500 B.C. (After *Civiltà del Lazio Primitivo*, p. 56.) The chronology of this period is in a state of flux. M. Torelli prefers the following: Phase I, 10th c. (Veii, Alban Hills); IIA, 900–850 (Alban Hills); IIB, 850–770 (Rome, Lavinium, Ficana, Gabii); III, 770–720 (Decima); IVA, 720–630 (Esquiline, Satricum); IVB, 630–580 (Vulci, Ardea, Rome: Forum, Regia, Comitium, Curia, Vesta; Satricum: Valerius). (L. Quilici)

the topsoil of the Alban Hills is a thick bed of solid lava, called tufa, which seals in a layer of ashes. In digging their trench the peasants cut through the lava seal and revealed large *dolia,* jars of rough clay, each of which contained, in an urn shaped like a miniature oval hut, the ashes of a cremation burial, together with fibulae, objects in amber and bronze, and numerous vases. It was not until fifty years later that a committee of experts, including the same Pigorini who afterward overstepped his evidence about the *terremare,* first connected the burials with the city of Alba Longa, traditionally founded in the mists of prehistory by the son of Aeneas.

Road building since 1953 and excavation since 1971 have revealed—at Castel di Decima (see map, Fig. 3.9: possibly ancient Politorium, and not Laurentum, as Miss Tilly thought) ten miles south of Rome on the road to Lavinium—a rich five-acre necropolis, containing 350 tombs, grouped by families and dated between 725 and 600 B.C. The female burials are especially opulent, with jewelry in gold, silver, and amber, gold hair-spirals, and a dress of silver scales with amber and faience (glass paste) appliqués. There were five chariot burials and many finds of weapons, armor, and bronze tripods. The pottery showed contacts with Etruria, Magna Graecia, and mainland Greece; scarabs showed trade with Egypt. There were violin bow, bloodsucker, serpentine, and boat fibulae. To the east, virtually unexplored, is an acropolis, with earthwork, retaining wall, and huts of the ninth-century building. Tombs of the same range of dates in the Alban Hills area yielded similar finds, though with less evidence of wealth.

At Osteria dell' Osa, near Gabii (Fig. 3.9) at the twelfth milestone on the Via Praenestina, 194 tombs have been excavated; they range in date from the tenth to the sixth century. Worth special mention are 40 bronze votive statuettes and 600 bronze cut-out figurines. As in the Forum necropolis,

there are both cremation and inhumation graves; as at Alba
Longa, and in the Forum, there are hut urns—one, an 18½-
by 21-inch monster. The urns are buried in subgroups, indicating separate clans. There is evidence for a primitive village
of about one hundred inhabitants, but the grave goods are
far from primitive; they show a growing cosmopolitanism,
with prestige goods that reveal increasing conspicuous consumption and cleavage between haves and have-nots. The
necropolis adjoins the well-known Gabine temple of Juno.

Just short of two miles northwest of Gabii is the probable
site of Collatia, at modern Lunghezza, commanding a cross-
ing of the Anio River, and the Veii-Gabii road. Here, the
castle has yielded bits and pieces, including a lovely late
sixth-century female head from a terracotta cornice. Collatia
plays an important part in sixth-century Roman legend: it
was here that the son of the last Tarquin allegedly raped the
chaste matron Lucretia, precipitating the fall of the Etruscan
dynasty and the founding of the Republic.

Antemnae (Fig. 3.9), at the confluence of the Tiber and
the Anio, west of the Via Salaria, flourished from the seventh
to the fifth century, and had an archaic temple with terracotta antefixes and revetment plaques like those at Falerii
Veteres. There was a circuit wall of the late sixth or early
fifth century. A fine fourth- to third-century terracotta head
of a youth in the Villa Giulia (Helbig[4] 2841) comes from
here.

Ficana (Fig. 3.9), near Acilia, and two-and-a-half miles
northwest of Decima, has Proto-Villanovan remains of the
tenth century: child burials under hut floors. An earthwork
protected the place; its necropolis is dated 650–600 (reign
of Ancus Martius, when the town was allegedly destroyed):
its tomb furniture has parallels in the Esquiline necropolis in
Rome and at Decima. A substantial building with cut tufa
foundations, of the late six century, has terracotta revetments, as at Acquarossa and in the Regia: they show chariots

and warriors. The excavator attributes to a change in ideology an early fourth-century decline in the quality of grave goods: it now became fashionable to spend accumulated wealth another way—on public buildings, sanctuaries, and temples, whose foundation deposits show that they were richly accoutered.

Crustumerium (Fig. 3.9), across the Tiber from the Prima Porta villa of the Empress Livia, was defended by earthwork and ditch; it yielded finds (of the late sixth to the early fifth century) like those from the other Latial sites we have been discussing. Its defenses were no proof against the Romans, who in 495 made of its territory the "tribe" (voting district) Clustumina. Some of the Sabine women who were Rome's first wives and mothers came from here. The site lies near the Allia River, where Roman troops based on Crustumerium were disastrously beaten by the Gauls in 387 (traditional date, 390).

At Satricum (Fig. 3.9), in the Pontine Marshes, when Dutch archaeologists re-examined the foundations of the temple of Mater Matuta (550–500)—whose amusing terracotta revetments are in the Villa Giulia—they found an archaic inscription. One of Rome's oldest, it is a dedication to the Roman popular hero Valerius Poplicola by a sodality of worshipers of Mars. This discovery sharply reduces the suspicion in which Poplicola's existence had been held because of the reputation for lying of the historian Valerius Antias, who claimed descent from him.

At Acqua Acetosa (Fig. 3.9), five miles south of Rome on the Via Laurentina, recent excavation (the results of which were published in 1978) has revealed a village and necropolis of the eighth through the sixth centuries. The village, sited by a mineral spring, has a ditch and an earthwork strengthened by tufa spalls, as at Decima, Satricum, and Ardea. The necropolis, though much destroyed by the quarrying of pozzolana, yielded 150 archaic burials, in groups marked off by circles cut in the tufa. Some of the tombs were as princely as those of Decima, containing a chariot (in a female tomb), shields, bronze and iron weapons, incense trolleys, ivory, amber, silver, gold, and bronze tripods and *ciste* (chests); also fine pottery, Phoenician amphoras, Greek vases with griffin *protomai* (heads projecting from the rim), and gleaming black Etruscan bucchero.

Thus archaeology reveals a uniform culture in Latium at this time, with Rome as but one of many sites.

In 1902, in cremation graves from a necropolis to which we shall return, on the edge of the Roman Forum itself, hut urns and artifacts were found so similar to those from the Pascolare in the Alban Hills that the inference of cultural connection was inescapable. Whether Alba Longa was the metropolis and Rome the colony, as stated by the literary sources, or the other way about, was not evident from the artifacts.

A necropolis, or graveyard, implies an inhabited site. The inhabited site of Alba Longa was destroyed by the Romans about 650 B.C. Where was the inhabited site that used the Forum in Rome as a necropolis? It could hardly have been the Forum itself, which was a swamp not drained and fit for habitation until about 575 B.C., a date which, as we shall see, marks the end of the necropolis. Could it have been the Palatine Hill, which rises from the south side of the Forum? At first sight it seemed unlikely that any evidence for pre-historic habitation could be found on the Palatine, since the hill was covered with the substructures of Imperial palaces. But beneath these, as early as 1724, were found the remains of the mansions of Republican nabobs (recorded in literature, too, as having lived here), and beneath these in turn why should there not lie the traces of even earlier dwellings? Vergil had pictured Aeneas humbly entertained on the Palatine by Evander, and lodged in a hut with swallows under the eaves. The great Italian archaeologist G. Boni (who lived in a villa on the Palatine and whose memorial bust appropriately adorns the Farnese Gardens there) found under the Flavian Palace, and published in 1906, traces of huts containing artifacts matching those found in the Forum necropolis.

These artifacts fell into two phases. The first included the rough handmade pottery called *impasto,* which we have already seen to be characteristic of Villanovan sites; serpentine fibulae (which match those found in the First Benacci period at Bologna); ware incised with a clamshell in dogtooth, meander, and swastika patterns, or with a ropelike clay *appliqué;* pierced beads, spools, and a curious kind of Dutch oven with a perforated top, examples of which were known from the Forum necropolis and the Alban Hills but not elsewhere. Artifacts of a different and more developed type, belonging, therefore, to a second phase, included pots with thinner walls, sharper profiles (as seen in elevation drawings), and more complicated handles; they are decorated with spirals and semicircles, apparently compass-drawn. There was even a miniature clay sheepdog, his curly coat represented by circles impressed with a metal tube or a hollow reed. Such artifacts match those found in the evolved Villanovan culture, dated in the first half of the sixth century B.C. This culture is contemporary with a rich, sophisticated one in Etruria, but the techniques in Rome and its vicinity are much more primitive than in Etruria. We conclude that the Palatine village was infinitely less prosperous than, say, the contemporary Etruscan cities of Caere or Tarquinia. But equally primitive artifacts are found in the Alban Hills burials, certain tombs on the Quirinal and Esquiline Hills in Rome (discovered when the city expanded after Italy's unification in the 1870s), and in burials in hollowed-out tree trunks from the Forum necropolis, the latter now on display in the Forum Antiquarium.

The Esquiline necropolis, dated by pottery in the early

eighth century, contains inhumations, not cremations, and belonged to the Sabines, who according to legend (the Rape of the Sabine Women) coalesced with the Palatine Latins, who cremated their dead and buried them in the Forum necropolis (discussed below) beside the later Temple of Antoninus and Faustina. The Esquiline tomb furniture shows new vase shapes, bloodsucker and serpentine fibulae, pectorals, shields, and chariots, the latter an evidence of the rise of social distinctions—between those who could afford expensive horse-rearing and those who could not. There is much imported ware, from both Etruria and Magna Graecia, whose trade routes converged on Rome.

The most famous Esquiline find is a tomb fresco, now in the Conservatori Museum (Fig. 3.2); it dates from Rome's Second Samnite War (322–295) and probably celebrates the exploits of Q. Fabius Rullianus, five times consul, whose name appears in its third register. In the second register, in front of a battlemented wall, a figure in a loincloth, greaves, and plumed helmet, wearing a goatskin mantle and carrying an oval shield, extends his hand in friendship to a man in a toga who carries a spear. The third register portrays and names a Fannius (Samnite) and Fabius, both in armor, the latter with a retinue. In the bottom register is a battle scene.

In 1907 D. Vaglieri began excavations in the southwest corner of the Palatine which revealed cuttings in the rock. These were actually, though Vaglieri did not recognize them as such, cuttings for early Iron Age huts, the date being an inference from the artifacts, whose stratification Vaglieri did not record. After a sharp controversy with Pigorini (whose prestige, because of public interest in the *terremare*, was then at its height), the dig was suspended, leaving one hut half-excavated. Here, in this intact area, excavations were resumed in 1948 by a younger specialist in the prehistoric archaeology of Italy, S. M. Puglisi. This time, the methods were rigorously scientific, and the cultural strata were ob-

FIG. 3.2   Rome, Esquiline fresco. (Bull. Comm. 1889)

served and recorded with meticulous care. Puglisi recognized that a scientific dig requires the constant presence on the site during working hours of a competent archaeologist; no precise results can ever be obtained by an excavation director who visits his site only a couple of times a week, since unsupervised workmen can hardly be expected to respect levels of stratification, preserve the right artifacts, or keep accurate excavation notebooks, without which, of course, no scientifically valid conclusions can be drawn.

In the area left undug by Vaglieri, Puglisi was able to distinguish five levels, which have been schematically reproduced on the walls of the Palatine Antiquarium. The top level consisted of nine feet of ancient dump. But the four levels beneath the dump amounted to six and a half feet of compact, undisturbed strata, of which the bottom eight inches represented what had collected on the hut floor while it was still in use. Here the sherds were very tiny, for they had been walked on, it being the regular practice of Iron Age man—and woman—to live comfortably in the midst of their own debris. The hearth (one of the Dutch ovens was discovered in fragments *in situ*) was near the center of the hut, very close to a cutting for a central supporting post—the first evidence ever found for such construction. But there was no danger of setting the central post on fire, since the cooking flame was entirely enclosed within the clay of the oven. Bits of fallen wattle and daub revealed the wall construction. There were animal bones and impasto sherds bearing the marks of fire, but no *bucchero* (the best examples of which are rarely found in Rome in contexts earlier than 700 B.C.) and no painted ware. This level, then, belonged to the first phase of the Iron Age, dated, by parallels with the finds from beneath the Flavian Palace, about 800–700 B.C. A child's grave from here is dated by pottery between 640 and 625 and matches in contents the burials at Decima (p. 74). The lowest level being so shallow, and the sherds showing the

marks of fire, the inference is that the hut had not been occupied very long before it was burned down.

The contents of the next superimposed level, two feet
deep, show that the site was next used as a kitchen midden
or refuse heap. Here the deposits resemble those from a well
(dug long ago but never described in a detailed scientific
article), in the sanctuary of Vesta in the Forum, which is
dated in the second phase of the Iron Age (700–550 B.C.),
corresponding in the tradition to the reigns of the five Roman
Kings from Numa to Servius Tullius (see Fig. 3.1 for dates).
These finds include polished *impasto*, with high or twisted
handles and out-turned rims; slat-smoothed ware covered
with a thin coating or engobe of reddish clay, ornamented
with double spirals and palmettes, and of a size to fit on the
Dutch ovens; sherds of fine *bucchero* (the first evidence of
imports from Etruria), and of a coarser gray local imitation;
painted ware, of the style known as sub-Geometric, imported from south Italy, and also some local imitations identified by their cruder technique.

The next higher level shows fat-bodied "bloodsucker"
fibulae, and flanged tiles, some with horses molded in low
relief, betraying a completely different and more sophisticated building technique, like that used in Etruscan temples.
The artifacts matched those found in the level under the
late Republican House of the Griffins and under the "House
of Livia" on the Palatine, and in the upper strata of the shrine
of Vesta well; they are associated with the huts built in the
Forum after it was drained; that is, with a transitional period
after about 575 B.C. The lower date suggested by the archaeological finds for this second phase corresponds to the dates
assigned by the literary tradition to Rome's Etruscan kings,
Tarquin I, Servius Tullius, and Tarquin the Proud.

The hut itself (Fig. 3.3) was a large one (12 by 16 feet),
sunk about a yard into the tufa of the hill, with six cuttings
for the perimetral posts, two for a front porch, and one for

the central support. The cuttings, averaging fifteen inches in diameter, are wider than is necessary for posts to support so flimsy a structure; the logs were probably held upright by wooden or stone wedges. The hut, reconstructed, represents a historical fact very much like what Vergil had in mind when he described the sleeping quarters assigned by Evander to Aeneas, and such *capanne* can be found in out-of-the-way places of the countryside near Rome even today. Lucretius, Vergil, and Livy all knew what a Bronze and an Iron Age meant; their generation venerated a replica of the "Hut of Romulus" on the Palatine. It suited Augustus's propaganda purpose to stress Rome's rise from humble origins; so, too, to us, archaeology's picture of Rome's primitive beginnings may well make the story of her later expansion seem more impressive, and her domination of subject peoples less overbearing.

Archaeology's second major contribution to our knowledge of early Rome is provided by Boni's excavation of the Forum necropolis (Fig. 3.4), the results of which are displayed with great clarity in the Forum Antiquarium, installed in the cloister of the church of S. Francesca Romana in the Forum itself. The surviving part of the necropolis stretches between the Temple of Antoninus and Faustina, on the north side of the Forum, and a late Republican structure to the east which was pretty certainly (to judge from the built-in beds, the narrow rooms, and the analogy with a building similar in plan at Pompeii, certainly identified by its erotic pictures) a house of ill-fame. The original extent west and southward was probably much greater. The graves have now been filled in, but their sites are marked by plots of grass, round for cremation graves, oblong for inhumation ones. The two types sometimes cut into each other; what inferences are warranted by this fact are better postponed until we have discussed the grave contents.

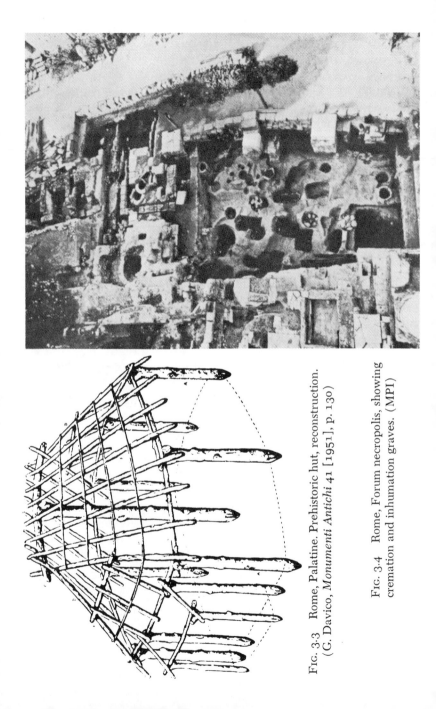

FIG. 3.3 Rome, Palatine. Prehistoric hut, reconstruction. (G. Davico, *Monumenti Antichi* 41 [1951], p. 130)

FIG. 3.4 Rome, Forum necropolis, showing cremation and inhumation graves. (MPI)

The Forum nowadays is an austere, even at first sight a forbidding place. It looks much more attractive in a painting by Claude Lorraine or a print by Piranesi, with a double row of olives planted down the middle, romantic broken columns, oxen and peasants scattered about the flowered greensward in picturesque confusion, and the Arch of Septimius Severus buried up to its middle. But picturesqueness is not everything. The Forum is history, stark history; every stone is soaked in blood. To understand that history, mere picturesqueness had to be sacrificed; Boni's graves are not picturesque; they are informative. From them the historical imagination can create a picture of Rome's beginnings which no Piranesi print could rival.

Sixteen feet of picturesqueness had to be cleared before Boni could reach the necropolis level. The cremation tombs are small circular wells, most of them containing, as in the Alban Hills tombs, a *dolium* or large jar, covered by tufa slabs. In the *dolia* were found ash containers, often in the shape of miniatures of huts like the full-sized ones on the Palatine. The oblong graves contained rough sarcophagi of tufa, or coffins made of hollowed-out oak logs. Both types of tomb contained, intact on discovery, tomb furniture not differing much between the types, and not differing much from the finds in the bottom two levels of Puglisi's Palatine hut; *i.e.*, rough *impasto*, decorated with incised spirals, parallel lines (done with a comb) or zigzags; *bucchero*, some fibulae inlaid with amber, glass beads, tiny enamel plaques, remains of funeral offerings of food. It is all very humble, a far cry from the Regolini-Galassi treasure, though some of the tombs are of the same date. The finds show that the necropolis was in use from the ninth to the sixth centuries B.C. The site was, as we saw, on the edge of a swamp; when the swamp was drained, the cemetery went out of use, and huts, of which more later, were built over it.

In the necropolis, sometimes inhumation graves cut into

cremation ones, sometimes vice versa. There is thus no ground for assuming that the cremation graves are older, especially as the grave contents of the two types are so similar. The difference is not one of time but of funeral practice, as today; it suggests two different populations living peacefully together. The cremators were related to the people whose graves were found so long ago in the Alban Hills, and, as we have seen, to the Palatine hut-dwellers. Who were the inhumers? We know that other Roman hills than the Palatine were inhabited from very early times, though the natural features of the Palatine seem to give it priority: plenty of fodder, abundant water within easy reach, a retreat made safe at night by the hill and the river for the people and their livestock.

But habitation of the Esquiline and Quirinal Hills in the sixth century is attested by a number of tombs from a total of 164 found there in the 1870s. The finds from these were never scientifically recorded, and they have never been published, but it is noteworthy that they include weapons, which are absent from the cremation graves in the Forum. It looks as though the Esquiline folk were invaders, with a more warlike tradition than the Palatine hut-dwellers. The Esquiline folk might earlier have used the Forum necropolis for inhumation. We know that the Sabines buried their dead. Literary tradition records that the early Romans got their wives from among the Sabines. Numa Pompilius, the second of the legendary Roman kings, bears a Sabine name. Though a few scholars oppose the idea of an equation between nationality and funeral rite, might not the two types of graves in the Forum necropolis represent the peaceful fusion of cremating Latins and inhuming Sabines who had laid aside their warlike ways?

On top of the Forum necropolis, when the swamp was drained, huts were built, and burials, except for infants,

ceased. The archaeological evidence for this phase was provided by Boni's stratigraphic excavation (recently confirmed
by Gjerstad) to the northwest of the site of the equestrian
statue of the Emperor Domitian in the middle of the Forum.
Gjerstad dug a trench sixteen feet long and eleven feet wide,
down to virgin soil, which he found nineteen feet below the
present Forum level. On the earth wall of the trench the story
of the centuries could be read in the successive levels (Figs.
3.5 and 3.6). Between levels three and nineteen, six pavements could be counted, but level nineteen takes us, to judge
by the pots found in it, only back to about 450 B.C. In layers
twenty to twenty-two, Gjerstad found three pebble pavements, which he dates about 575 B.C. If he is right in assign-
ing to this date the beginning of monarchic Rome, he has
pushed its date down in our direction over 150 years from
the traditional 753 B.C. But there is more history below this.
Strata twenty-three to twenty-eight are remains of huts,
similar to but (pottery again) later than the ones in the
Palatine. Gjerstad dates them in two phases: 650–625 and
625–575 B.C. Rather than push the traditional date down so
far, it seems plausible to suppose that these huts represent
the period assigned by the literary tradition to the early kings
and to argue that the sophisticated period, symbolized by
the Forum's earliest pebble pavement, was inaugurated by
Rome's earliest Etruscan king, Tarquin I.

These other huts confirm the other archaeological data,
which show that what later was unified into urban Rome
was originally a group of simple hut villages clustered on
various hills, the Forum huts having spilled down, as it were,
from the village on the Palatine. The huts in the level just
above the Forum necropolis represent a still earlier stage of
this spillover; they antedate the earliest huts in Gjerstad's
twenty-nine levels. By the date of Gjerstad's earliest pebble
pavements, the huts in the necropolis area have been replaced by a more developed domestic architecture, perhaps

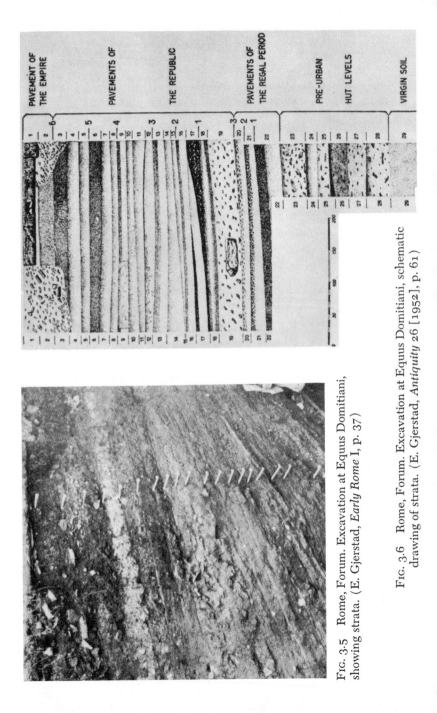

Fig. 3·5   Rome, Forum. Excavation at Equus Domitiani, showing strata. (E. Gjerstad, *Early Rome* I, p. 37)

Fig. 3·6   Rome, Forum. Excavation at Equus Domitiani, schematic drawing of strata. (E. Gjerstad, *Antiquity* 26 [1952], p. 61)

with rooms opening on a central court. These houses have rectangular plans, mud-brick, wood-braced walls, and tufa foundations. At the spillover stage, the villagers from the various hills formed some kind of confederation symbolized archaeologically by the two types of graves in the Forum necropolis, and in literature by the tradition of the joint religious festival called the Septimontium.

The period of the first pebble pavement (575 B.C.) is one of major change, from village to urban life, to a city now for the first time boasting a civic center, destined to become the world's most famous public square, the Roman Forum. Of the same date are the earliest remains on the Capitoline Hill, which was to be the *arx* or citadel of historic Rome, and a phase of the Regia, which later generations revered as the palace of the kings. About this complex we now have much more accurate knowledge, thanks to American excavations under F. E. Brown. The Regia of the handbooks, which looks like a Mycenaean megaron house, divided into porch, vestibule, and main chamber, proves to be the last of five phases. Before the first phase (*i.e.*, before 616–578 B.C.), the area contained a cobbled road, eleven huts (like those on the Palatine), and two infant burials. Regia Phase III had terracotta revetments, including one of the Minotaur. Since recent excavations at Acquarossa and elsewhere have shown that such revetments also adorned private houses, Regia I-IV may have been in fact the king's "palace," which would include cults; *e.g.*, of Mars and Ops. The final phase was not a dwelling but a sanctuary set up in a house with a trapezoidal courtyard. On the walls of its west room were hung spears (*ancilia*), which quivered at the approach of war; in the east, a sanctuary of Ops, Rome's tutelary goddess; between, a vestibule. In the courtyard, a well, an altar, and a portico: here there were sacrifices to Jupiter and Janus. At the Regia occurred the concluding phase of one of Roman religion's most curious rites: the sacrifice of the "October horse." The right-hand horse of the winning team in an October chariot race was sacrificed, his tail cut off and conveyed at speed to the shrine of Vesta, his blood allowed to drip into the ashes of the hearth, then collected as paste and stored for purification rites the following spring. The head also was cut off and fought over by factions: the winner hung it in the Regia.

Of the same date as the Regia is a sophisticated phase of the round shrine of Vesta, which encircled the sacred flame, symbol of the city's continuity. The literary tradition would date the last two earlier, at least to Numa's reign. However no architectural remains have so far been discovered which associate them with the earlier date.

In his interpretation of the archaeological evidence about the date of the beginning of the Roman Republic, Gjerstad is just as iconoclastic as about the dating of the kings. His argument, more ingenious than convincing, is that an event as important politically as a change from a monarchy to a republic should be reflected in the artifacts, changing from richer to poorer, whereas no such objective evidence of a cultural break is visible in the levels dated by him (perhaps more closely than the facts warrant) at 509 B.C. Such a cultural break does not come until some fifty years later, when Etruscan imports cease. There are grave difficulties in pushing the date of the Roman Republic's beginning down so far, of which the chief is a list (the *Fasti*) of pairs of consuls 509–450 B.C. where many names are too obscure to have been invented. Gjerstad's excavation, in sum, is important as confirming the accuracy of Boni's methods, and as telling us much about the village stage of Rome, but the absolute chronology cannot be said to be as yet firmly fixed, nor the traditional one definitely upset.

Apart from absolute chronology, what unequivocal evidence can archaeology provide that early Rome was ruled by kings? The ideal evidence would be an inscription, and one was discovered in 1899 in the Forum near the Comitium, where, in the open air in front of the Senate House, the popular assembly met. The inscription is called the *lapis niger* stele, because it lies under a later pavement of black marble (*lapis niger*), now preserved under a deplorable corrugated iron roof. But the stone on which it is carved is not marble but tufa, identified as having come from the quarries of Grotta Oscura in the territory of Veii, some nine miles north of Rome.

On the various kinds of tufa or volcanic stone in use in early Rome there hangs a tale. In 1924 an American, Tenney Frank, published an epoch-making study of Roman building materials in which he put the dating of Roman monuments on a firmer basis by distinguishing several different kinds of tufa used by Roman builders at successive dates. Subsequent studies have blurred the dividing lines and shown the possibility of overlap, but Frank's nice eye for discriminating tufas has revolutionized the architectural history of the Roman Republic. The following table illustrates Frank's methods:

Type	Characteristics	Quarries	Where used
Cappellaccio	flaky dark gray ash	Rome	Capitoline temple (509 B.C.)
Grotta Oscura	friable grayish yellow	2½ mi. N. of Prima Porta	Forum stele, "Servian" Wall, Tullianum (prison)
Fidenae	flecked black fragments (scoriae)	Castel Giubileo, 5 mi. N. of Rome	Castrum, Ostia (338 B.C.) Argentina Temple A (ca. 200 B.C.)

(continued on following page)

Type	Characteristics	Quarries	Where used
peperino	peppered; can be carved	Marino (Alban Hills 11 mi. SE)	Tomb of Scipios (early 3rd cent.) * Altar, Argentina C (ca. 186 B.C.)
sperone	coarse-grained brown	Gabii (12 mi. E)	Milvian Bridge (109 B.C.)
Monteverde	reddish, olive streaks	Across Tiber	Sullan pavement nr. *Lapis niger*
Anio	brown	Cervara (35 mi. ENE)	Tomb of Bibulus (before 50 B.C.)

* The burial place of the Scipios, between the Via Appia and the Via Latina, just outside the Servian Wall, is cut into the tufa, with a mid-second century façade consisting of semi-pilasters on a rock-cut dado, with inset panels for inscriptions and, originally, statues in rectangular niches above arched openings into the burial place itself. The Scipios *buried* their dead; other clans cremated theirs. The sarcophagus chamber was roughly square, with passages on the periphery and across the middle. Nine important sarcophagi symbolize the role of this aristocratic clan in politics, war, and religion. The most important, now in the Vatican (cast *in situ*), is of Lucius Cornelius Scipio Barbatus, consul 298. It has a Doric frieze with varied rosettes in metopes; its lid had volutes at either end; and it bears two inscriptions, the later incised, in Saturnians—the meter of "The queen was in the parlor, eating bread and honey." It praises the deceased for his strength, practical wisdom, good looks, courage, offices held, and conquests made. This monument has recently been interpreted as an altar for the cult of Barbatus as his clan's founding father. Of the other sarcophagi, the latest is dated about 135 B.C. They record the careers of consuls, praetors, aediles, quaestors, a flamen Dialis (a priest of Jupiter whose arcane duties were so exacting that the office was sometimes used to reform ne'er-do-wells). These men captured islands (Corsica), subjected kings (Antiochus III of Syria), were prolific, virtuous, upholders of the family reputation (*laus maiorum*), and in three cases died young. One woman is among them; of her nothing is recorded save her husband's name. The most illustrious Scipio of all, Africanus, conqueror of Hannibal (202) is not here: he died in self-imposed exile at Liternum in Campania (184/3). But the discovery of what may have been his townhouse was reported in 1961 under the Basilica Julia in the Roman Forum.

The *lapis niger* stele, inscribed on tufa of the second type in this series, could be of the very late sixth century B.C., and this date is borne out by the very archaic letter styles (Fig. 3.7), which resemble those on the Avele Feluske stele from Etruscan Vetulonia. Interpreting what the stone says is not made easier by the fact that the top is cut off and the lines are inscribed *boustrophedon* (like the Lemnian stele among other examples), so that in successive lines the beginning and the end are alternately missing. To the left below is printed a text of the letters as they appear on the stele; to the right, a translation into classical Latin; below, a translation into English. Though the gaps are perhaps too boldly filled, the sense arrived at is plausible.

Obviously the inscription, thus restored and interpreted,

Fig. 3.7 Rome, Forum: *lapis niger* stele. Note the word RECEI, which may be evidence for the historicity of Rome's kings. (P. Goidanich, *Mem. Acc. It.* 7.3 [1943], Pl. 9)

QVOI HOI	QVI · HV[nc locum violaverit,
SAKROS ᠄ ESE	manibus] SACER · SIT;
ED SORD	ET SORD [ibus qui haec contam-
OKAFHAS	inet l]OCA, FAS
RECEI ᠄ IO	REGI, IV[dicio ei hab-
EVAM	ito, adimere rem pr]EVAM ·
QVOS ᠄ RE	QVOS · RE[x per hanc senserit
M ᠄ KALATO	vehi via]M, KALATO-
REM HAB	REM, HAB[enis eorum, iubeto
TOD ᠄ IOVXMEN	ilic]O · IVMEN-
TA ᠄ KAPIA ᠄ DOTAV	TA · CAPIAT, VT · A V°[ia stati-
M ᠄ I ᠄ TER PE	M · ITER PE[r aversum locum
M ᠄ QVOI HA	pergant puru]M · QVI HA[c]
VELOD ᠄ NEQV	VOLET, NEQV[e per purum
IOD ᠄ IOVESTOD	perget, iudic]IO, IVSTA
LOIVQVIOD QO ᠄	LICITATIONE, CO[ndemnetur].

"Whosoever defiles this spot, let him be forfeit to the shades of the underworld, and whosoever contaminates this spot with refuse, it is right for the king after due process of law, to confiscate his property. Whatsoever persons the king shall discover passing on this road, let him order the summoner to seize their draft animals° by the reins, that they may turn out of the road forthwith and take the proper detour. Whosoever persists in traveling this road, and fails to take the proper detour, by due process of law let him be sold to the highest bidder."

° If DVO TAV[r is the right reading, it prescribes a fine of two cows.

marks a spot which is taboo, its ill-omened nature being further emphasized by the later black marble pavement, which was fenced off by a balustrade of thin white marble slabs set on edge. Beside the stele is a U-shaped shrine or altar,* on a higher level and therefore of a later date than the inscription. Archaeology provides no clue to the purpose of this structure, but learned Romans believed it marked the tomb of Romulus, their first king. This would be a sacred spot indeed, not to be profaned by the feet of men or animals. From one edge of the shrine run the remains of a semicircular platform with steps (Figs. 3.8 and 3.9), also later in date than the inscription. The platform was the Rostra, so called because of its decoration, after 338 B.C., with the

---

* Professor Ferdinando Castagnoli and Dr. Lucos Cozza reported in 1959 the discovery, at Pratica di Mare, ancient Lavinium, sixteen miles south of Rome (Fig. 3.10), of a series of thirteen such altars (Fig. 3.11), together with an inscription on bronze, with lettering like that of the *lapis niger* stele. They date their finds in the late sixth century B.C. The inscription is to Castor and Pollux, the Great Twin Brethren, who, the Romans believed, brought them divine aid at the battle of Lake Regillus (495). A roof now protects the altars from the elements. They mark the site as Latium's federal sanctuary. A hundred meters southeast, a seventh-century tumulus and a fourth-century shrine with a square cella and pronaos and a monumental tufa door mark the heroön of Aeneas. A statuette from Veii of the same date shows him carrying his father Anchises on his shoulder (Fig. 3.12). The heroön reflects his importance in Rome's foundation legend: the acroteria of Veii's Portonaccio temple may represent him with wife and child. His legend competes with the myth of the twins Romulus and Remus, which is very old, reflecting a pastoral society with dual origins (Palatine and Quirinal), and anticipating the two consuls of the Republic. Tomb furniture from the heroön includes a bronze lance, an antenna sword (with horns branching from the hilt), and Proto-Corinthian ware of 675/50 with parallels from Ischia, Cumae, and Tarquinia. A sixth-century wall surrounded the site. Other tombs yielded miniature weapons, silver hair-spirals, a torque (metal neckband) inset with amber, silver bloodsucker fibulae, and a bronze fibula with amber pendants. In 1977 was announced the finding of a cache of 60 life-size terracotta statues, of the sixth to fourth century; one of them, over six feet tall, represents Minerva in combat; she has sword, shield, and snake. The others are of women bringing offerings (dove, rabbit, pomegranate). Minerva, important in Rome as a member of the Capitoline triad, and figured with Hercules in a statue from the sanctuary of Fortune in the Forum Boarium, now seems to derive from Latium and not Etruria.

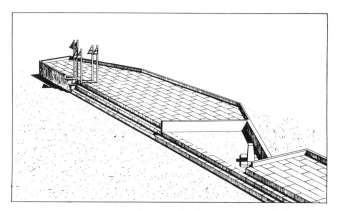

FIG. 3.8   Rome, Forum. Rostra, third phase (fourth-third century B.C.). (E. Gjerstad, *Skrifter* 5 [1944], p. 142)

FIG. 3.9   Rome, Forum. Rostra, fifth phase (Sullan).
(E. Gjerstad, *op. cit.*, p. 143)

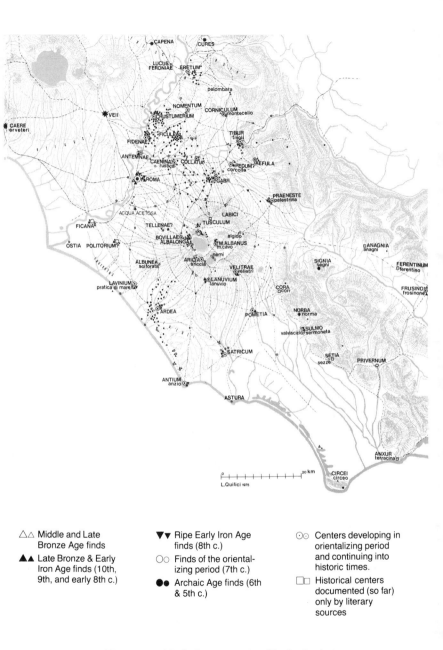

△△ Middle and Late
   Bronze Age finds

▲▲ Late Bronze & Early
   Iron Age finds (10th,
   9th, and early 8th c.)

▼▼ Ripe Early Iron Age
   finds (8th c.)

○○ Finds of the oriental-
   izing period (7th c.)

●● Archaic Age finds (6th
   & 5th c.)

⊙○ Centers developing in
   orientalizing period
   and continuing into
   historic times.

□□ Historical centers
   documented (so far)
   only by literary
   sources

FIG. 3.10   Early Latium, map (L. Quilici)

bronze *rostra* or ramming beaks of captured enemy war galleys. The Rostra was in historical times the speakers' platform; from it in one of its phases resounded the sonorous oratory of Cicero. But it was also the spot from which traditionally funeral orations were delivered, while modern men wearing, according to Roman custom, the death masks of their ancestors sat behind the orators in curule chairs on the platform. To the logical Roman mind a platform beside the tomb of the first king would seem the appropriate place for funeral speeches.

Since American excavations at Rome's Latin colony of Cosa in 1953 identified as a Comitium a circular, step-surrounded space in front of the local Senate House, it appears that the semicircular steps leading to the platform in Rome were Rome's Comitium, and new excavations to prove or disprove this were started in 1957.

Careful equations between the fifteen levels in the Comitium and the twenty-nine levels near the equestrian statue of Domitian prove the Comitium a monument of the Roman Republic: the first phase coincides with the first Tarquin,

FIG. 3.11   Lavinium, altars. (Fototeca)

and its last two with Caesar and Augustus, in the late first century B.C., when the Republic ends. Thereafter freedom of speech, and an arena for it, were but a memory. But the first Rostra was built where it was because the founders of the Roman Republic associated it with the first of Rome's kings.

The *lapis niger* inscription, which refers twice to a king, rests on a base which cannot be older than the sack of Rome by the Gauls in 387 B.C. (for the base is on the same level as the second of the Comitium pavements, laid over traces of a major fire; the Gauls had set Rome on fire). But an inscription of course is a movable monument, and the present location of the stele may not be where it was originally set up. Furthermore, letter styles so archaic are probably older than 387 B.C.: the alternatives, then, are either that the stele,

FIG. 3.12   Veii, Aeneas-Anchises, terracotta statuette. (B. Bini)

of venerable antiquity, was reset, on a new platform, as a part of rearrangements after the fire, or that it is a deliberately archaizing copy of a much older original. The theory that the king (*rex*) referred to is not the temporal monarch but the *rex sacrorum,* a Republican priest of later Republican times who inherited the king's religious functions, is virtually ruled out by the letter styles.

The *lapis niger* stele presents one aspect of primitive Roman religion under the kings: the taboo. Another is the pious tending of the sacred flame on the public hearth, a rite performed in historical times by the Vestal Virgins in Vesta's shrine at the east end of the Forum. The superstructure of the shrine as now restored there yielded no remains earlier than the Gallic fire, but the round plan must reflect the shape of a primitive straw hut of the Palatine type, with central

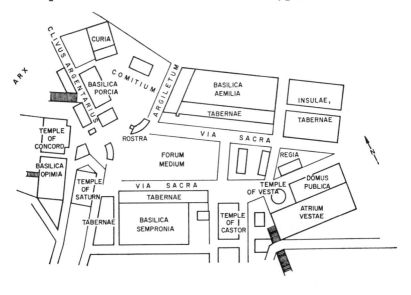

FIG. 3.13   Rome, Republican Forum, plan.
(J. Russell, *Phoenix* 22 [1968] 311, Fig. 3)

hearth and smoke hole, and the earliest artifacts, from the previously mentioned well there, are dated in the seventh and sixth centuries B.C. The shrine of Vesta, then, preserves another memory of Rome of the kings.

Kings, like ordinary mortals, need a dwelling place. Traditionally in Rome, this was the Regia (related in root to *rex*, "king"), on the trapezoidal plot between the Forum necropolis and Vesta's shrine (see plan, Fig. 3.13). Romans believed its first occupant was the Sabine Numa, the second and most pious of the kings, but no archaeological remains confirm so early a date (traditionally 716–672 B.C.). It seems unlikely that the king could have dwelt there before the necropolis was closed, for the king was a priest, and it was unlucky for a priest to look upon a cadaver, or upon death. The earliest datable masonry remains are a foundation in *cappellaccio* of about 387 B.C., another evidence of rebuilding after the Gallic fire. But there might well have been, before the fire, a more primitive structure in wood, revetted in terracotta; indeed, fragments of terracotta revetment, some of a late sixth or early fifth century style and some even earlier, were found there, as well as a gray *bucchero* sherd scratched with the word *rex* in archaic letters. The Regia, as it stands, is the result of at least three rebuildings, the last in 36 B.C. It still has an old-fashioned air: ancient, straggling, intractable, very holy: the shape of its ground plan never changing from beginning to end. In keeping with the Etruscan tradition—as at Marzabotto—the building is oriented north and south. Its south side as a dwelling, later the office of the Pontifex Maximus; among the great Romans who worked in this building was Julius Caesar. The rest of the Regia was an area partly unroofed. It was a shrine of Mars, hung with shields and the magic lance that quivered at the threat of war. The Pontifex Maximus recorded yearly, day by day, on a whitened board in the Regia, events in which he and his fellow priests had a profesisonal interest:

temple dedications, religious festivals, triumphs, eclipses, famines, rains of blood, births of two-headed calves, and other prodigies. Fragments of this lost archaeological record, piously kept by the pontiffs, turn up in extant Roman history: Livy often refers to them at the end of his account of a year, particularly an unlucky year.

Orientation like the Regia's is an Etruscan practice, and it is with domination by the Etruscans that we should expect Rome's primitive simplicity to evolve into something more like grandeur. The literary tradition ascribed to the Etruscan, Tarquin the First (616–578), a great Temple of Jupiter on the Capitoline Hill, built by the forced labor of Roman citizens and decorated by Etruscan artisans like Vulca of Veii, the sculptor of the Apollo (page 60). But since Vulca was not at work until the end of the century, Brendel has tried to explain the discrepancy by supposing that the footings were laid under the first Tarquin, and the superstructure built by his grandson, Tarquin the Proud. Andrén has ingeniously used coins (of 83 B.C.) to suggest what the cult statue of Jupiter looked like: bearded, austere, and with the hair wound into hair-spirals such as have been found in Etruscan tombs. World War I confirmed the literary tradition archaeologically. The Italians, on the Allied side in that war, ousted the Germans from their embassy, splendidly situated on the Capitoline Hill in the Palazzo Caffarelli, and remodeled the palace into a museum. In the process was revealed a massive podium, sixteen feet high, built without mortar of blocks of *cappellaccio*, the oldest of Rome's building stones. Fortunately, diagonally opposite corners were found, making it possible to establish how impressive were the podium's dimensions: roughly 120 by 180 feet. Three corners of the podium having been isolated, archaeologists were able to fit into the plan the remains of a substructure which had been found in 1865 under the Palace of the Conservatori. This substructure, now built impressively into a corridor of the Conservatori Museum, proved to be the support for columns. The platform as a whole, then, was the podium of a temple, the largest of its time, over twice the size, for example, of the one at Marzabotto. Traces of the settings for the columns proved them to be placed too wide apart to be connected by architraves in stone; they must instead have been great wooden beams. The wood would have been revetted or faced with terracotta, and in fact enough fragments of terracotta revetments were found on the site to establish this temple as decorated in the typical Etruscan style. If its sculptures were as striking as the Apollo of Veii, they were masterpieces indeed. The temple, repeatedly and ever more grandiosely rebuilt—in one phase it was roofed with gilded bronze, and the cult statue was gold and ivory—was the center and symbol of Rome's religious life. Here the triumphal processions ended. Here the triumphing general, surrounded by his spoils of victory, descended from his chariot drawn by four white horses and passed through the open doors and the clouds of incense to give thanks to Jupiter the Best and Greatest for his victory. From the cliff behind the temple, the Tarpeian rock, traitors were thrown to their deaths; here, in 133 B.C., Tiberius Gracchus, the friend of the people, was murdered. Religion, dignity, pride, greed, pomp, tragedy: all are the stuff of Roman history; all are here, and archaeology illumines their story. Horace boasted that his poetry would endure "so long as, with the mute Vestal, the pontifex climbs up to the Capitoline Temple." For him as for us Rome was the Eternal City, and the Capitoline was the symbol of its permanence. Through the assaults of riot, fire, earthquake, poverty, popes, barbarians, limekilns, wind, rain, and earth, the foundations have endured.

The literary tradition tells us how Rome's Etruscan monarchy fell: of Tarquin's despotism and his son's rape of

Lucrece, daughter of a Roman aristocrat, whose husband avenged her and allegedly became one of Rome's first pair of consuls. It tells us how the Roman nobles rose, drove out the Tarquins, and founded the Roman Republic. Archaeology cannot confirm the traditional date (indeed the founding of temples, Etruscan style, continues, as we saw, for half a century after 509). But about the middle of the fifth century the contents of the tombs on the Esquiline begin to grow mean and shabby. Contact with Etruria has been cut off, and the Romans make a virtue of necessity, pass sumptuary laws against excessive display, and practice simplicity and frugality. The late fifth century B.C. in Rome, as archaeology reveals it, is a period of isolation, stagnation, and retrenchment.

Hardly had the new Roman Republic rallied to conquer Veii (traditionally in 396 B.C., after a ten-year siege, like Troy's), when the Gauls descended from the north with fire and sword. Rome bought them off and, resisting the temptation to move to Veii, fell to rebuilding, mindful of how its ancestors had built their city up out of forest and swamp— in love with their protecting hills, their fruitful open spaces, their busy river. The building was done planlessly; the main concern was to strengthen defenses.

The primitive Rome of separate villages on the hills had been defended, at most, by separate palisades and ditches. It is with King Servius that literature associated the Rome of impressive buildings and a beetling wall, of squared stone, sturdy enough to repel all invaders. With how much justification Roman historians called the wall "Servian," we are now to learn. The tradition associates Rome's earliest wall with Servius Tullius, who falls between the two Tarquins, and certain surviving traces of earthwork and masonry, plus the Cloaca Maxima, or Great Drain through the Forum, are assigned by some archaeologists to the sixth century. Indeed until 1932 most scholars accepted the sixth-century date for

the whole early circuit. But in that year the Swedish archaeologist Gösta Säflund (who seven years later was to
explode Pigorini's myth about the *terremare*) published the
results of some painstaking fieldwork which radically changed
the picture.

Beginning with the Palatine and working counter-clock-
wise, Säflund examined every inch of the surviving eleven-
kilometer circuit ascribed to Servius (Fig. 2.3). Considerable
structures had been torn down during Rome's great expansion in the 1870s after she became the capital of a United
Italy. For these, he had access to unpublished notes and
sketches by Boni and another great nineteenth-century Italian archaeologist, Rodolfo Lanciani. Everywhere he paid
careful attention to materials, techniques, dimensions, mason's marks, the relation of the wall to terrain, neighboring
tombs, and ancient artifacts found in its context. It was
chiefly from the building material that Säflund drew his conclusions.

The stone was in the main Grotta Oscura tufa, which he
knew from Tenney Frank's studies to have been in use in
the year (378 B.C.) in which Livy says the censors contracted
to have a wall built of squared stone. Furthermore, some of
the Esquiline tombs already mentioned, containing mid-
fourth-century artifacts, were outside the line of the Grotta
Oscura wall, while some of the tombs containing archaic
artifacts were inside. The Romans rarely buried their dead
within a city wall: the inference is that at the date of the
earlier tombs, Rome had no proper ring wall, while by the
date of the later (fourth-century) tombs a circuit wall had
been built. The Great Drain through the Forum is also of
Grotta Oscura, and is therefore probably to be dated in 378,
like the wall—though some feeder lines are in *cappellaccio,*
which, as we have seen, was the earliest volcanic stone the
Romans used, and we know (because we know the Forum
swamp was drained by 575 B.C.) that there must have been

some sort of drainage system, possibly open ditches, earlier than 378.

But Säflund found Fidenae tufa also. This he knew, again from Frank's study, to have been in use from about 338 B.C. down into the second century. It had been used to patch the wall in places. What more appropriate time for such repairs than when Hannibal was threatening the city, in 217 B.C.? Thereafter, Roman and Latin colonies, advanced bases, served her in the office of a wall, and her own fortifications were allowed to fall into disrepair.

But there are places in Rome's wall where Monteverde stone has been used for arches, rising from footings set in concrete; in other places the wall has a concrete core faced with Anio tufa. Säflund knew that concrete was little in use in Roman building before 150 B.C., and that it had become a favorite material by Sulla's time (see p. 155). Sulla had marched on Rome in 88 B.C. and taken it; he must have reinforced the wall to keep his enemy Marius from duplicating his own feat. And Sulla included the bridgehead on the far side of the Tiber in his circuit, reinforced the Aventine Hill, and added *ballistae* (great catapults for shooting stones) in arched casemates flanking the main gates.

Thus Säflund distinguished three building periods for the so-called Servian Wall, though none as early as King Servius Tullius. One section of earthwork, or *agger,* on the Quirinal Hill, faced in part with small blocks of *cappellaccio,* looked older than 378 B.C., and Säflund knew from observations at Ardea, Cerveteri (and, as we now know, Anzio), that the use of the earthwork was standard in the sixth century to reinforce weak places on hilly sites. Some early sixth-century sherds, but none later, were found *under* the agger. This helps to confirm that the agger was a part of Rome's sixth-century, genuinely Servian defenses, never a complete ring wall, but an adjustment and reinforcement of natural defenses, later incorporated into the circuit wall of 378 B.C.

A splendid stretch of the facing of this reinforced agger, 100 yards, survives today by the Termini railroad station (Fig. 3.14).

But Säflund's careful observations did more than redate the wall in its several phases. By comparison of the mason's marks, hacked in Greek letters on the heads of the Grotta Oscura blocks only, with similar marks found on the blocks of the fortifications of the Euryalus above Syracuse, in Sicily (built in the late fifth century B.C. by Dionysius I), Säflund was able to demonstrate that Rome's wall was built by Sicilian workmen, Rome not having the manpower or the skill at the time. (Dionysius for his wall had employed 6000 men and 500 yoke of oxen.)

The wall of 378 B.C. is evidence that Rome had emerged

FIG. 3.14   Rome, "Servian" Wall of 378 B.C., surviving stretch beside Termini railway station. (Author)

from the doldrums into which the Republic had begun to
sink. Before 387 B.C. she had depended on men, not walls.
The Gallic sack had proved her not invincible, and had also,
as war emergencies will, produced a new sense of solidarity.
The wall symbolizes it, and so does the bill passed in 367 B.C.
(while the wall was still under construction), opening the
highest office in the Republic to plebeians. Thus a reinforced
oligarchy was formed, which by 338 B.C. could beat its once
powerful enemies, the neighboring settlements linked in the
Latin League; proudly (even arrogantly) mount the beaks
of enemy ships on the new Rostra; and embark upon a career
of Manifest Destiny in Italy. The Republic had reached
adulthood.

There were other outward and visible signs of the Republic's new maturity and prosperity. The gods deserve their
reward for fighting on the side of the biggest battalions, and
so the expanding Republic built temples. In another age of
arrogant expansion, in 1926, not long before Säflund began
his work on the walls, slum clearance in front of the Argentina theater (on the site of the portico of Pompey's theater,
where Caesar· was murdered) revealed the foundations of
four Republican temples (Fig. 3.15), nowadays the haunt
of countless tomcats. The temples (north to south) may have
been dedicated to Juno Curritis, Fortuna huiusque diei (the
Luck of the day), the Italic agricultural goddess Feronia,
and the Lares Permarini, but since these identifications are
uncertain, the temples are called, with proper archaeological
sobriety, Temples *A, B, C,* and *D.* The foundations of Temple
C (Feronia's?), the third from the north, are the deepest; it
is therefore the oldest. It is set in the Italic manner at the
back of a high podium, built of Grotta Oscura tufa; its mason's marks match those of the "Servian" wall. Clearly it was
built by the same masons or in the same tradition. The
podium carries the distinction of being the oldest surviving
datable public building in Rome. Terracotta revetments

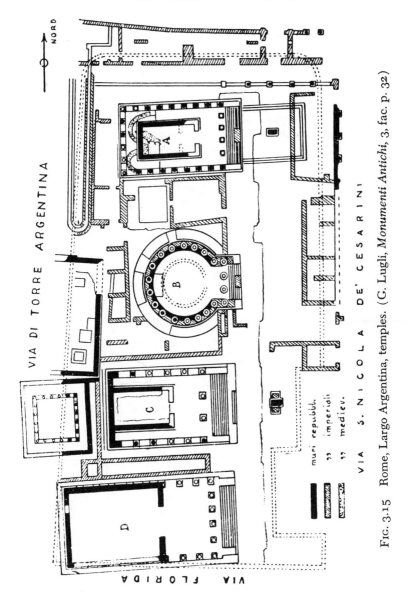

FIG. 3.15 Rome, Largo Argentina, temples. (G. Lugli, *Monumenti Antichi*, 3, fac. p. 32)

found in excavating are of fourth century type. Besides
meanders, the so-called Greek frets or key design, an angular
pattern of lines winding in and out, their decorative motifs
include strigil patterns: parallel troughs, made by the workman's thumbs in the wet clay and then painted in contrast-
ing colors. The strong curve of the profile resembles that of
the strigil or scraper used by athletes in the gymnasium to
remove caked oil and dirt from their bodies; hence the
name. The roof's peak and corner ornaments, called *acroteria,*
have spikes set in the clay to discourage birds from perching
and committing nuisances. Temple A (Juno's?) is of the third
century B.C.; D (of the Lares Permarini, household gods
deemed responsible for a naval victory) is early second; B
(Fortuna's?) is of 101. Perhaps from here came, from a
statue six meters high, a colossal head now in the Conservatori Braccio Nuovo: it has pierced ears and originally
wore a diadem and veil. A portico on the north is Severan;
the Republican Porticus Minucia, shown on the Severan
Marble Plan of Rome, stretched away to the east. After a
fire in 111 B.C. the whole area was paved with tufa and
porticoed. Below this level, in front of Temple C, is the inscribed altar of A. Postumius Albinus (consul 180); *on* the
tufa pavement is a later altar at right angles to Postumius's.
Above the tufa pavement is one in travertine, dating from
after Nero's fire of A.D. 64. The new higher level involved
reducing the number of steps to Temple A from nine to six,
raising C's level by two meters, and building new steps to D.
At the same time, the circular Temple B was widened. Behind the temples are two latrines of Imperial date, one of
them a splendid 32-seater. Abutting the sacred area on the
west is the room in the portico of Pompey's theater where
the Senate was meeting on the Ides of March, 44 B.C., when
Julius Caesar was assassinated. A glass plate in the wall of
the pedestrian subway under the southwest corner of the
sacred area permits a view into the underpinnings of the site.

Finally, brief notice should be taken of five third- and second-century buildings or complexes, which illustrate Rome's increasing sophistication (for good or ill). Two are temples to Greek divinities: the sanctuary of Aesculapius on the Tiber island and the temple of Magna Mater on the Palatine. Aesculapius' temple lay under the church of San Bartolomeo; a modern hospital on the island testifies to the healing cult's longevity. At the island's eastern tip a travertine revetment was carved into the shape of a ship's prow, bearing a relief of Aesculapius' serpent, to commemorate the import hither in 293 B.C., after a plague, of a ship bearing his snake from Greek Epidaurus. The other Greek temple, of 191, belonged to the Magna Mater, the Romans' name for Cybele, an Anatolian fertility goddess. Her priests, following the example of her votary Attis, emasculated themselves in her honor; a number of Attis statuettes were found on the site. Reliefs in the Villa Medici, across Rome, now the seat of the French Academy, probably depict its exotic architectural sculpture: Phrygian dancers, the lions who drew the goddess' chariot, her eunuchs, and her throne, supporting a turreted crown. The surviving podium belongs to the original temple; opus quasi-reticulatum is said to mark a rebuilding after a fire in 111 B.C.; the tufa columns lying beside the podium are Augustan. In a theatral area in front of the temple were held the Ludi Megalenses, at which the plays of Plautus and Terence were performed.

Just west of the Forum, under a sixteenth-century church, lies Rome's prison, the Tullianum, small because it was illegal to incarcerate Roman citizens. It consists of a trapezoidal upper room, in Monteverde and Anio tufa, once beehive shaped; a terrible oubliette, into which convicted enemies of the state—the Numidian resistance-leader Jugurtha, the Catilinarian conspirators, the Gallic resistance-leader Vercingetorix—were dropped to be strangled. St. Peter is said to have been imprisoned here and to have caused a spring to well up, in the waters of which he baptized his jailer. The oubliette is in peperino and may date from the third century B.C.

A recently discovered piece of the Marble Plan of Rome definitively locates the Circus of Flaminius (221 B.C.) west of Augustus's Tiber-side Theater of Marcellus. And, downstream, under the lee of the Aventine Hill, quays and a warehouse, the Emporium and the Porticus Aemilia, were constructed in 193 B.C., reflecting Rome's expanding commerce.

All this is still a long way from the grandiose marble and gold of the Augustan Age, but it is an equally long way from the primitive wattle-and-daub huts of the Palatine village. It marks a stage in the painstakingly unraveled archaeological story of Rome's expansion, which we shall follow at various sites in Italy.

4

Roman Colonies in Italy

Rome's wall begun in 378 B.C. took twenty-five years to build. However secure she might feel behind it, immediately beyond the gates lurked enemies. To the north the Gauls, to the east and south, Italic tribes (whom Rome successively feared, rivaled, dominated, and invited to partnership; of these the Samnites were the most fearsome), on the seas the Syracusan and Carthaginian navies—all represented a clear and present danger. Rome's population being inadequate to keep legions in the field, much less a fleet at sea, against all these threats at once, she evolved a system of advanced bases, called Latin colonies (Fig. 4.1), manned partly with trustworthy local non-Romans, though with a hard core of Roman legionaries. This avoided undue drain on the Roman manpower, and placed the responsibility for frontier defense upon frontiersmen who had the greatest interest in their own security.

During the last thirty years the efforts of archaeologists of several nations (for example, Italians at Ostia, Belgians at Alba Fucens, Americans at Cosa) have added much to the sum of our knowledge of these frontier outposts: their fortifications, street plans, public buildings, housing arrange-

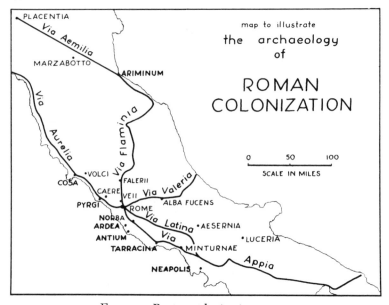

FIG. 4.1 Roman colonization, map
(P. MacKendrick, *Archaeology* 9 [1955], p. 127)

ments, and the surveyed ("centuriated") quarter-sections of land (allotments) stretching away from the walls into the countryside round about. From these brute facts inferences can be drawn—about what prompted the founding of these outposts (was the motive always military?), about relations with neighbors and with Rome, about communications, about economic, social, and cultural life.

At Ostia, at the Tiber's mouth, historical tradition said that there had been Romans settled since the days of King Ancus Marcius, and that, even earlier, Aeneas had landed there and built a camp.

Recent excavation under the Hadrianic Baths of Neptune has allegedly brought to light earlier material, late Bronze Age or Proto-Villanovan. In 1938 the great Italian archaeologist Guido Calza began soundings to ascertain the date of the oldest surviving stratum. The area he chose was beneath Ostia's Imperial Forum, where the two main streets, the *cardo* and the *decumanus,* crossed. (The Via Ostiensis, from Rome to the river mouth, determined the line of the *decumanus.*) What he found (Fig. 4.2) was a set of walls enclosing a rectangle 627 feet long and 406 feet wide. The wall was built of roughly squared blocks of tufa in a technique not unlike that of Rome's wall of 378 B.C., but since there was Fidenae stone in it, Calza dated the wall somewhat later than 378. The wall was pierced by four gates of two rooms each, with portcullis. The south gate was demolished in the early Empire to provide space for a temple of Rome and Augustus; the north gate gave way under Hadrian to the massive podium of a Capitolium, but the footings of the east and west gates survive, well below the level of the Imperial pavement. Calza found drains within the walls and traces of four other streets (unpaved) besides the *cardo* and *decumanus,* but no identifiable buildings. Some terracotta revetments found in the area suggest an unidentified temple of the third century B.C.

What Calza found at Ostia was a coastguard station, or *castrum,* planted by the Romans at the river's mouth once their control of the sea was established by their victory over Antium's navy (which produced the bronze beaks on the Rostra). The normal complement of such a station was 300 men. A contingent of that size could have manned Ostia's *castrum* wall with one soldier every six feet. Thus the prime motive of the founding was military, and the *castrum* plan is like the familiar and standard plan of a Roman army camp. But the civilian plan antedated the military: Polybius in his description of the Roman camp of about 150 B.C. says that it was planned *like a town* (*i.e.,* with a rectangular grid like Marzabotto). And Ostia's function must from the beginning, or soon after, have been commercial as well as military. Its site at the river mouth was as ideal for collect-

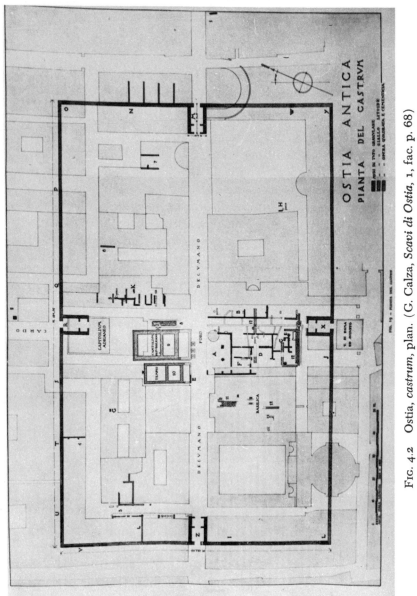

FIG. 4.2   Ostia, *castrum*, plan. (G. Calza, *Scavi di Ostia*, 1, fac. p. 68)

ing the customs as for guarding the coast. Grain from Egypt and Sicily to feed Rome may from the earliest days have been landed here and stored in warehouses for later shipment upriver by barge. At all events history records the appointment as early as 267 B.C. of a special finance officer or *quaestor* for Ostia, and Calza found the footings of warehouses of Republican date. The terracotta revetments mentioned above date from this period. The houses and shops remained humble for seven generations, but those generations saw the departure of many a fleet, and the arrival of many a consignment of grain. An inscription dated in 171 B.C. marking the limits of public land in Ostia shows that by then it had expanded far beyond the *castrum* walls. But the story of Ostia's development, her new wall under Sulla, new theater under Augustus, new port under Claudius, new garden apartment houses under Trajan, and the rest, belong to later chapters.

In the last half of the fourth century Rome fought two wars against the Samnites. Alba Fucens (Fig. 4.3) in the Abruzzi, one of her advanced bases in the Second Samnite War, has been explored since 1949 by the Belgians. It lies 3,315 feet above sea level, on the Via Valeria sixty-eight miles east-northeast of Rome. (The sixty-eighth milestone of the Valeria was found *in situ* inside the colony wall.) Alba's site dominates five valleys. The Latin colony of 6,000 planted here in 303 B.C. assured Rome's communications on two sides of Samnium, eastward to the Adriatic and southeastward through the Liris Valley.

The pride of Alba is its walls, nearly two miles of them, surrounding the three hills on which the colony lies. The material is limestone, which breaks at the quarry into irregular, polygonal blocks. These are set without mortar. The excavators distinguished four different building techniques in the wall. They assumed that the roughest sectors, built of

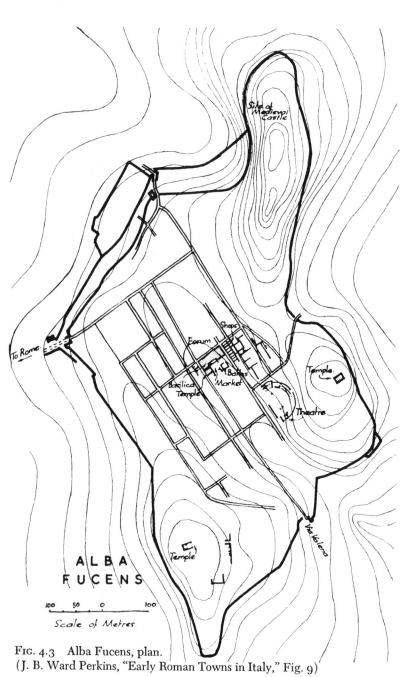

Site of
Medieval
Castle

To Rome.

Forum

Shops

Basilica
Temple

Baths

Market

Temple.

Theatre

Via Valeria

Temple

A L B A
F U C E N S

100   50   0   100

Scale of Metres.

FIG. 4.3   Alba Fucens, plan.
(J. B. Ward Perkins, "Early Roman Towns in Italy," Fig. 9)

enormous blocks, were the oldest, coeval with the foundation
of the colony. These polygonal walls, common all over central Italy, used to be called Pelasgian or Cyclopean, and were
formerly assumed to be of immemorial antiquity, but recent
archaeological work has pushed the dates of most of them
down into the late fourth century or later. At Alba, where the
excavators date the wall about 250 B.C., the techniques involve the use of smaller blocks and more careful workmanship in successive phases, until finally with the use of cement
we reach the 80s B.C. and the age of Sulla. On the northwest,
where the hill has the gentlest slope, the circuit is triple, and
the outermost is the latest. The loop to the north was the
arx; it was destroyed by an earthquake in 1915. The wall is
pierced by four gates, some with portcullis and bastions. The
Via Valeria entered at the northwest, made a right-angled
turn, passed the civic center, and emerged at the southeast;
that is, it was made to conform to a grid plan within the
colony, a grid plan laid down despite the hilly terrain, which
made terracing necessary.

Excavating Alba's civic center, the Belgians found a Forum,
with curia, comitium (at the other end of the Forum, opposite the basilica), altar and miniature temple, buried under
many feet of earth. The basilica (a rectangular, roofed hall
with nave and two side aisles, used as a law court and commercial center), presents its long side, with three entrances,
to a portico facing the Forum. Beside the basilica is a market, with baths on one side and a temple on the other, with
early revetments, repeatedly restored; also, a sanctuary of
Hercules, with a large, double-porticoed courtyard. An adjoining street, parallel to the Valeria, was lined with shops,
including a fuller's drycleaning establishment and at least
one wineshop. The doorsills still show slots for the shutters.
In front of the shops ran a portico supported on high pilasters.
Drilled through the curb were holes through which customers might tie their mules. At the corner of the *decumanus,*
the excavators found charming statuettes of elephants, used

as street signs. Under the market were revealed subterranean chambers accessible only by manholes; the excavators suggest that these are the very dungeons, dark underground *oubliettes,* where prisoners of state like King Syphax of Numidia in 203 B.C., King Perseus of Macedonia in 167, the Gallic chief Bituitus in 121 were incarcerated, for the Romans often used their colonies as detention points.

Archaeologists, taking account of levels, construction techniques, and artifacts, have assigned various dates to these buildings, but their earliest phases fall in the Republican period, in the age of Sulla or earlier. To the age of Sulla belongs also a handsome rock-cut theater. There is an amphitheater of the early Empire; as we know from a new inscription, its donor was Macro, the notorious informer under the Emperor Tiberius, who brought about the fall of the Emperor's ambitious and scheming favorite, Sejanus. On the hill in the southern sector, under the fine Romanesque church of S. Pietro, lay a temple of Apollo, of the second century A.D. From a Domitianic villa in the environs comes a statue of Polyphemus like the one in Sperlonga (see chapter 7). The finds of statuary from the site (a Venus, a Hercules, portrait busts) are in the Chieti Museum, forty miles northeast.

Walls, grid, civic center, public buildings: these made of Alba a smaller and more orderly replica of Rome. The general layout is repeated so often in so many places that it suggests a master plan made in the censor's office in Rome. By the time Cosa was founded, in 273 B.C., the Romans already could draw on the experience of founding at least eighteen colonies.

Cosa, where the writer did his first excavating, may be used to supply a little more detail on materials and methods in field archaeology. A number of eight-week spring seasons of excavation there (1948–54; 1965–71), modestly intended as laboratory training for young American classicists, have in fact resulted in a remarkably complete picture of an old-style Latin colony. The site was chosen for excavating because it looked attractive from air photographs, because it was convenient to Rome (ninety miles up the Via Aurelia on the Tyrrhenian Sea), and because its walls were almost perfectly preserved, great gray masses of polygonal limestone looming up as high as a four-story building on a 370-foot hill that rises out of the reclaimed swamplands of the Tuscan Maremma. For Cosa was planted, carved out of the territory of the once proud Etruscan city of Vulci, to mount guard over Rome's newly acquired marches, and to affirm Rome's name and supremacy in a restive neighborhood.

A large assortment of gear is necessary for a modern scientific dig, even a modest one: for surveying and leveling, clinometer (which measures slopes), plane table (which measures angles), alidade (which shows degree of arc), prismatic compass with front and back sights (for taking accurate bearings—the prism brings the object being sighted, the hair-line of the front sight, and the reading on the compass card all in a vertical line together)—leveling staves marked in centimeters (for measuring elevations); templates for recording the curves of moldings; brooms, brushes, and mason's tools for cleaning the architectural finds; zinc plates and sodium hydroxide pencils for electrolysis of coins; measuring tapes of all sizes, mechanical drawing instruments, trowels, marking pegs, cord, squared paper, large sheets of filter paper for taking "squeezes" of inscriptions, catalogue cards, India ink, shellac, wooden boxes, small plastic bags, labels, journal books, field notebooks, and a small library of technical manuals. The gear was divided between the villa where the staff lived and an abandoned Italian anti-aircraft observation post on the site itself, whose concrete gunmounts made excellent drying floors for freshly washed potsherds.

Ambitious excavations use a light railway for carting earth to the dump, but at Cosa, which ran on a shoestring budget

($5,000 for eight weeks), the vehicle was the wheelbarrow, the track a set of boards bound at the ends with iron to keep them from splitting. Twenty of the local unemployed formed the corps of workmen. The foreman, in better times a master carpenter, used a pick with all the delicacy of a surgeon with a scalpel.

The first step in excavating a site is to lay down a grid—fifty-meter squares are convenient—marked with wooden stakes set in cement and leveled. During the ten months of the year when there was no digging and Cosa was abandoned to the shepherds, they operated on the conviction that the stakes marked the spot where the treasure lay buried. They would overturn them and dig like badgers, and each new season would have to begin with a partial re-survey.

A typical excavating day would begin with the removal of surface earth in wheelbarrows. As large objects came to light—bits of amphora, roof tile, terracotta revetments—they were placed in shallow yard-square wooden boxes called *barrelle*, equipped fore and aft with carrying shafts, and labeled accurately with the precise designation of the area from which the finds came: Capitolium Exterior South, Level I; Arx North Slope, Surface, and the like. Small objects—bone *styli*, small sherds, loomweights (pierced terracotta parallelepipeds, whose weight held the threads hanging straight down on an ancient vertical loom), lamps, fragments of inscriptions—went into separate, marked cloth bags. Thus the horizontal and vertical findspot of each object was precisely known, so that when a dated or datable object was found in a level, the whole level could be automatically dated, and so the whole mosaic painstakingly put together and the history of the site analyzed, or, as the archaeologist says, "read." The meanest potsherd, accurately defining a context, thus becomes more valuable historically than a whole museum shelf full of gold jewelry from an unstratified dig.

When a *barrella* and a set of cardboard boxes had been

filled, they were carried to the excavation shack and sorted. Objects that could not be "read"—shapeless bits of rubble, parts of coarse pots without profile of base or rim—were discarded, the rest sent to be washed. After washing and drying, cataloguing began. Every object was painted with a small square of shellac, on which its catalogue number was written in India ink and then shellacked over to preserve it. A letter indicated the dig, another the season, a number showed the place of the object in the chronological sequence of finds. A typical entry might read like the card shown below. Leica or plate photographs were taken of all important

---

CC 1487   Capitolium Exterior South
                 Level I
Moulded terra-cotta revetment
Width 0.17 (centimeters)
Height 0.14
Thickness 0.03
   Pale pink terra-cotta, much pozzolana. All edges preserved, slight crack lower right corner. Nail holes each corner. Strigillated cornice moulding above, finishing in a half-round moulding, enriched thunderbolt pattern in field. Thunderbolt runs from upper left to lower right, tapering to points at ends, hand grip in center; enriched on either side of hand grip with seven-point sword-and-sickle palmettes. Photograph.

---

finds and separately indexed for ready reference in the final publication.

After the workmen's day (7:00 A.M. to 4:30 P.M., with a half-hour for lunch) was over, there was still much for the staff to do. Pottery, spread out on trestle tables, had to be examined, joins made where possible, types distinguished. (Careful attention at Cosa to plain Roman black glaze has led to an arrangement of types in a dated series which will be useful for future dating on other sites.) Evenings were devoted to writing up the journal, studying the manuals, making drawings, planning the next day's dig, and shop talk. The results of a typical season's work in 1950, on the *arx* at Cosa (Fig. 4.4), were to isolate a second temple at right angles to the Capitolium, restore on paper the design of several sets of terracotta revetments, follow the line of the Via Sacra from the *arx* gate to the Capitolium, clear the *arx* wall, get down to bedrock beside the Capitolium, discover a terracotta warrior who was part of the pedimental sculpture of an older temple under the excavation shack, and in general get a pretty clear idea of the religious center of the colony as it was, perhaps, in the time of the elder Cato, in the early second century B.C.

In the two seasons preceding the discoveries on the *arx* just described, much work had been done. In the survey to set up the fifty-meter grid, Cosa's own ancient rectangular grid of streets, with pomerial street running just inside the wall as at Marzabotto, came out clear enough to be plotted on the plan (Fig. 4.5)—together with the standard blocks of housing, like the identical "ribbon-development" apartment blocks of a welfare state, which compensated the pioneers for whatever fleshpots they had given up in the metropolis or elsewhere. Housing was found to occupy two-thirds of Cosa's thirty-three acres, while public buildings took just over 20 percent, and streets the rest. The site, which is waterless, was found to be honey-combed with cisterns: over sixty-five were plotted. The mile and a half of walls, with their eighteen towers, spaced an effective bowshot apart, had been closely examined. In technique they closely resemble those of nearby Orbetello, which may have been Cosa's Etruscan predecessor. They were found to be built with two faces and a rubble fill. The outer face was handsomely finished, with tight mortarless joints, and sloped seven degrees back—this is called "batter"—from the perpendicular; the inner face was left rough. Potsherds of the Etrusco-Campanian style found in the fill just within the walls were

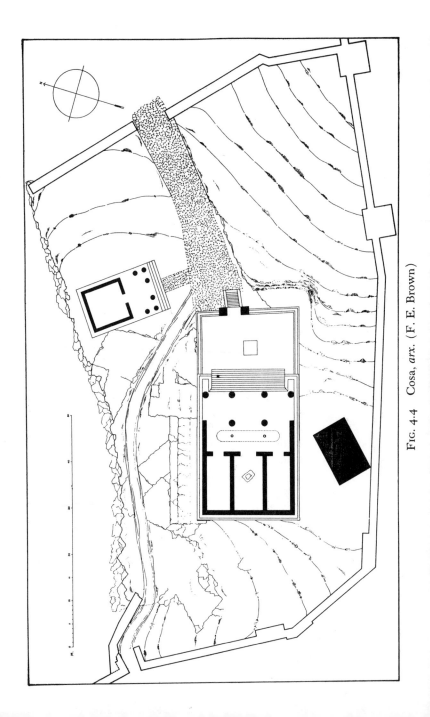

Fig. 4.4 Cosa, *arx.* (F. E. Brown)

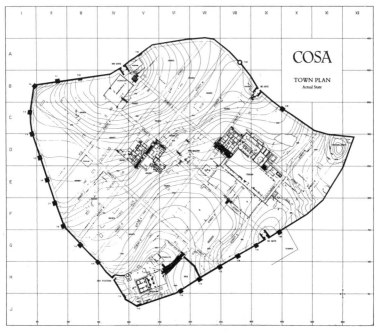

FIG. 4.5   Cosa, plan.
(F. E. Brown, 1980, by permission of U. of Michigan Press)

of a period matching Livy's date of 273 B.C. for the colony.*
It was clear that the walls, which show throughout no difference in technique, were built all at one go, at the time the
colony was founded. Those impatient of the Roman reputation for perfect engineering will be pleased to know that the
ancient craftsmen, when they came to close the ring of the
wall, found they had made an error of from two to four

---

* The dating of Italian black-glaze pottery had long been despaired of
because, being unfigured, it provided no chronology derived from style. But
the Cosan black-glaze, in the late Doris Taylor's landmark publication, *was*
accurately dated, because serious attention was paid to stratigraphy, in five
deposits, at the Capitolium, cella and south side; the Forum, basilica and
atrium publicum; and a spot outside the walls between towers eight and
nine.

Roman feet. (The Roman foot approximately equals the English.) The three gates were examined and found to be of two rooms, with the main gate grooved on its inner walls with slots for the rise and fall of the portcullis as at Alba. Bordering the roads leading from the gates were tombs.

The director of the excavations and, later, Anna Marguerite McCann and her associates used skindiving* to examine the outworks of the port (built to prevent silting) and established them as Roman. There was a jetty 360 feet long, supported on huge piers measuring twenty by thirty Roman feet, and forty-five Roman feet apart. Beyond the jetty was a series of breakwaters; between the harbor and the lagoon was the emporium, for imports and exports; at the south end of the lagoon, fishtraps and fish farms.

Fifteen miles out to sea southwest of the port, the islet of Giannutri has a mole and seaside portico, of Flavian date, serving a charming villa with its architectural members in mint-fresh condition, though it was in use till the middle of

* Undersea exploration is one of the most fascinating branches of archaeology. This is a convenient place to report a 1950 Italian operation off Albenga, on the Ligurian coast between Genoa and the French border. Along this stretch of the Italian Riviera fishermen's nets had frequently brought up amphoras, presumably from an ancient wreck, which was soon located in twenty fathoms. The use of an iron grab damaged the sunken hull, but an impressive number and variety of objects were recovered. The ship yielded over 700 more-or-less intact cork-sealed, pitch-lined amphoras, from a cargo of perhaps thrice that number; their shape was that current in the second and first centuries B.C. Some had contained wine, others still held hazel nuts. Campanian black-glaze pottery, of a type datable in the last half of the second century B.C., was found in sufficient quantity to enable Professor Nino Lamboglia, who was in charge of the operation, to set up a whole typology of black-glaze ware, based on types, fabrics, and glaze. It is a typology which proved a useful check for dating Cosan pottery, and for which the Cosan results have provided some corrections. Lead pipes and lead sheathing resembled those found in the ships from Lake Nemi (see chapter 7), and a stone crucible with molten lead in the bottom suggested that running repairs could be carried out at sea. Fragments of three helmets, of unusual design, may have been intended for Marius' army, which was campaigning in the north against Germanic tribes in the late second century B.C. The finds are on display in the Albenga Museum (see N. Lamboglia, "Il Museo Navale Romano di Albenga," *Rivista Ingauna e Intemilia* [1950] Nos. 3 and 4).

the third century. Its grounds were terraced; it had cisterns, master's and servants' quarters, baths, and a dolphin mosaic. Its column shafts were of granite from the nearby island of Giglio; the capitals were marble.

The Capitolium (Figs. 4.6 and 4.7) was situated so that its central *cella* lay over a cleft in the rock, a sacred pit in which ritual vessels from the temple's predecessor were buried. Between porch and *cellae,* running the width of the building, was a cistern lined with the waterproof cement called *opus signinum,* made of lime, sand, and pounded bits of terracotta. The temple walls, which stand on the south to an impressive height, visible far out to sea, were built of bricklike slabs of the local calcareous sandstone, set in mortar. On the north, the line worn in the rock by water dripping gives mute evidence of the wide overhang of the roof, Etrusco-Italic style. Some of the terracotta revetments belonged to the older, wooden temple. It must have made a brave show when it was new, covered with brightly painted tiles, its pediment and roof ornaments glittering in the sun. Just northeast of the Capitolium lies the small temple of Mater Matuta, goddess of growth, whose worship was conducted by women, as Cosan inscriptions confirm. Its revetments were made (200–175 B.C.) from molds brought from Rome. A pedimental terracotta warrior, half life-size, may belong to a depiction of the battle of Telamon, fought against the Gauls in 225 B.C. a dozen miles up the coast. A twin to this temple overlooked the port.

Further campaigns of digging attacked the Forum area, thickly overgrown with asphodel, acanthus, and thistles. Here lay the remains of an ungainly but monumental triple arch of about 150 B.C., the oldest dated arch in Italy. It had a central roadway for wheeled traffic, two side arches for pedestrians, and a stone bench attached to the outer face where old men could sit in the sun and gossip. There was a basilica (of 150 to 125 B.C.), as big as a New England town

FIG. 4.6   Cosa, Capitolium. (Fototeca)

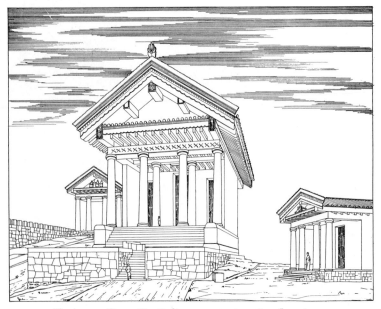

FIG. 4.7   Cosa, Capitolium, reconstruction drawing.
(F. E. Brown)

hall, like Alba's. It presented its long side to the Forum, had
a nave and two side aisles, and a tribune for the presiding
judge at the back, with a vaulted cell, perhaps the local
lock-up, beneath it. At some time in the early Empire the
basilica was abandoned as a legal center and restored as a
galleried festival hall, or intimate theater, with clerestory
and timber truss. The forum was porticoed, with shops on its
southwest and south sides. Midway of the southwest side a
mall with a bulletin board beside it (175–150 B.C.) led to the
fish market. (The structure by the northwest gate was probably the cattle or vegetable market.) Trees, for which planting holes were provided, shaded the forum's south half;
put-holes between were for posts that kept the citizens in
orderly lines at voting time.

Other buildings held fascinating secrets. A complex beside the basilica turned out to be an Atrium Publicum (of 240–220 B.C.), a public hall in the form of the central unit of an Italic house, which was rebuilt as an inn for the patrons of the adjoining festival hall. When, about A.D. 35 (on the evidence of pottery—the Arretine ware characteristic of the period), the basilica wall collapsed, it crushed and entombed in place the inn's complete furnishings and equipment. The excavators suddenly found their hands full of tableware, kitchen crockery, and all sorts of household gear, in metal, glass, and stone; decorative pieces, including a lively marble statuette of Marsyas; and objects of personal adornment, including a fine engraved amethyst. For the first time outside of Pompeii an ancient building had yielded not only its structure but its contents.

On the other side of the basilica, excavation of what had been called Building C brought further surprises. When the workmen had stripped the surface humus off the area of the forecourt, the excavators found themselves looking at a perfect circle of dark earth enclosed by a sandy yellow fill. Further digging established this as a circular, theaterlike structure, big enough to hold 600 people. There was an altar in the middle. This must have been the Comitium, the colony's assembly place (Fig. 4.8). Building C, behind it, must have been the Curia, or Senate House. The undisturbed fill under the Curia floor proved completely sterile; hence the curia must have been built at a date near the foundation of the colony. At this stage both Curia and Comitium were apparently of wood, replaced in a second phase, before the end of the third century B.C., with purple tufa from nearby Vulci. The building just southeast of the Curia was dedicated to Concord, as an inscription testifies; its revetment molds came from Tarquinia.

In the fourth or fifth Christian centuries (dates from coins), a shrine or clubhouse of devotees of Bacchus was

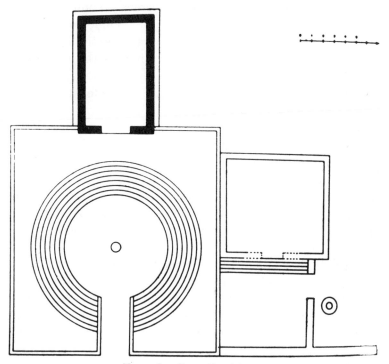

FIG. 4.8   Cosa, Comitium.
(L. Richardson, Jr., *Archaeology* 10 [1957], p. 50)

built over the Forum's southeast entrance. Since it contained statues of other gods, it may have provided a sym-
pathetic roof for them in a time of Christian ascendancy. A
miscellany of drinking vessels and lamps suggests Bacchic
revels in the evening. (Cosan utilitarian pottery shows closer
relations to Rome, Ostia, and coastal colonies than to southern Etruria.)

A healthy site, an orderly plan, a water supply, strong
walls, housing, provision for political and religious needs:
the basic necessities are all here, at Cosa, and all as early as
the founding of the colony. By hard work, painstaking accu-

racy, and intelligent inference, Brown and Richardson, the excavators of Cosa, have given us the clearest possible picture of the physical structure of a Roman colony well on in the first intense period of history in the planting of advanced bases. Cosa is clearly the fruit of long practice and Etrusco-Italic tradition, little touched by Hellenism (except for some recent Greek innovations in the gates) or by new-fangled techniques (no brick or concrete in the early phases). When we carry down Cosa's architectural history to the early Empire, we infer the death of freedom of speech from the remodeling of the basilica into a theater. And when freedom of speech and public life died, the colony lost its sense of community. Its thirty-three acres held, in the first draft of settlers numbering probably 2,500 families, perhaps 9,000 souls. (We infer families, not soldiers only, from the discovery of loom-weights, hardly appropriate for Roman legionaries.) Those who lived within the walls had government housing, uniform without, altered within to suit individual tastes or needs. The plans, without atrium or peristyle, included a garden, cistern, cesspool, and perhaps a stable for the family donkey. One house, restored as a site museum and workshop, had a charming garden, now planted with the shrubs and flowers that grew there originally. From a nearby house came a hoard of two thousand silver denarii, the latest of 71/0 B.C. At this date a catastrophe, probably a pirate incursion, overwhelmed the colony, so thoroughly that it was not resettled for forty years. Some must have lived well outside the colony; only those whose four-acre centuriated allotments, explained below, lay nearest the walls would have lived in the colony proper. Of 130 sites identified outside the walls, perhaps 15 percent were modest estates. One, the Villa delle Sette Finestre, had a turreted wall like a toy fort, a cryptoporticus, simple mosaic floors, and brick columns stuccoed over to look like marble, but its decor included revetment plaques and antefixes like those usually associated with

temples. The villa's estate comprised 1,250 acres, about half
of which would have been devoted to vineyards, producing,
during the first Christian century, wine for the overseas
market. The villa may have been one of several granted by
Sulla to his partisans. Inscriptions confirm that among Cosan
estate owners were the Domitii Ahenobarbi, ancestors of
Nero; and the gens Tongilia, which was wealthy enough to
donate a stone basin on the *arx,* and had one member who
was a Catilinarian conspirator. The estate of the Domitii may
have been absorbed into imperial property. In the second
century, cereals and sheep farming replaced viticulture. The
holders of more distant plots would come to town only for
market, worship, litigation (as long as the basilica lasted),
or refuge from raiding parties of Gauls or other enemies. And
so, under despotism, the community disintegrated. The temples held on longest. "Only the gods, in the end," writes Professor Brown, "held steadfastly to their ancient seats."

By derivation, a *colonia* is a place where men till the soil.
Colonists were assigned centuriated allotments. Since traces
of centuriation have been found both at Alba Fucens and
at Cosa (Figs. 4.9 and 4.10), as well as at nearly fifty other
certain and half as many possible sites in Italy, this seems
an appropriate place to discuss the subject. Wherever colonies were planted, wherever land was captured, confiscated,
redistributed to the poor or to veterans, the surveyor with
his *groma,* or plane table, was on hand. Air photography is
a great help in revealing traces of the Roman surveyor at
work, for modern land use has often overlaid the ancient
traces, leaving ancient crop marks as the only clue. The
standard surveyor's unit was the *centuria* of 200 *iugera* (the
iugerum, five-eighths of an acre, being the area an ox could
plow in a day), and a side of twenty *actus* (776 yards), its
corners marked by boundary stones, some of which survive.
There has been too little digging to confirm the results of

FIG. 4.9   Alba Fucens, centuriation.
(F. Castagnoli, *Bull. Mus. Civiltà Rom.* 18 [1953–1955], p. 5)

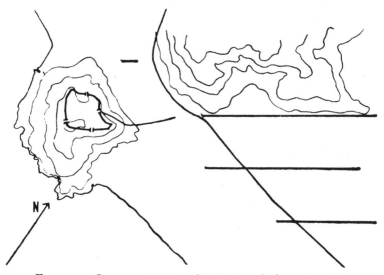

FIG. 4.10   Cosa, centuriation. (F. Castagnoli, *loc. cit.*, p. 6)

air reconnaissance, but it seems clear that some centuriation goes back to the late third century B.C. Prof. Ferdinando Castagnoli, the Italian expert, is inclined to date that of Alba and Cosa, as well as large stretches in the fertile Campanian plain northwest of Naples, at least this early.

The surveyor liked to link up his centuriated grid with a colony plan. Thus at Cosa the *groma,* for siting the allotments, could have been set up in the Porta Romana (the northeast gate), and at Alba the line of the Via Valeria inside the walls, if projected, would cut the lines of centuriation at right angles. The four sides of the *centuria* were usually marked by roads, the inner subdivisions by narrower roads, trees, hedges, or drainage or irrigation ditches. Modern land use often follows the line of the ancient: one stretch recently laid out and now in use at Sesto, west of Florence, deliberately follows the traces of Roman centuriation, restored by a classically trained engineer for modern man to admire. As with the grid inside a colony wall, the centuriated grid of allotments was laid out from a basic *cardo* and *decumanus*. The Roman surveyors were balked by no natural barriers. Bradford cites one line of centuriation running as high as 1,600 feet above sea level (though within the *centuriae* the furrows might follow the contours), and another, in Dalmatia, continues from a peninsula across to the mainland, spanning an arm of the Adriatic Sea three miles wide. In north Italy, where the flatlands of the Po Valley made the survey easy, one can ride from Turin (Roman Augusta Taurinorum) to Trieste (Roman Tergeste), three hundred miles, through centuriated systems all the way. The same air photographs which revealed neolithic sites to Bradford in Apulia showed Roman centuriation, too, and subsequent digging turned up pottery of Gracchan date (about 133–122 B.C.). A particularly extensive stretch, outside of Italy, is found in Tunisia. It has been traced from the air 175 miles from Bizerta to Sfax, and southwestward from Cape Bon for 100 miles inland. Some of it goes back to ambitious plans of Gaius Gracchus, about 122 B.C., to resettle Rome's urban proletariat (see *North African Stones Speak*, 30–33. Figs. 2.2 and 2.4).

The examples of colonized and centuriated sites mentioned here hardly even scratch the surface of the subject. Dozens of others remain to be explored, on hilltops and headlands, by rivers and crossroads, the length and breadth of Italy. Recent excavation at the Latin colony of Paestum, on the coast fifty miles southeast of Naples, has traced the Roman grid (Fig. 4.11), identified yet another Comitium, and produced over a million small finds. And still other colonial sites lie under populous modern towns and cities: examples, in chronological order of planting, are Anzio, Rimini, Benevento, Brindisi, Spoleto, Cremona, Piacenza, Pozzuoli, Salerno, Vibo Valentia, Bologna, Pèsaro, Parma, Modena, and Òsimo. Their foundation dates span the years

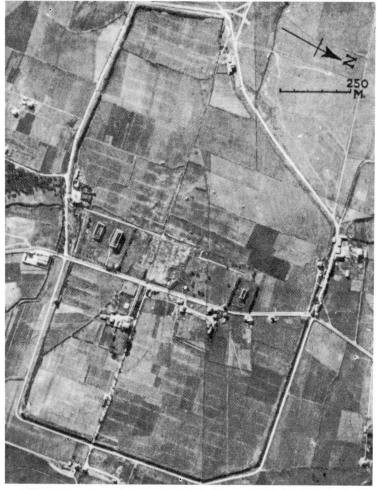

FIG. 4.11   Paestum: Roman grid of streets (air photograph).
(Italian Ministry of Aeronautics)

from about 338 to 158 B.C., the expanding years of the
Roman Republic, the years of "Manifest Destiny." Their continued existence compliments the Roman founders' nice eye
for a promising site, but makes large-scale investigation of

Roman levels difficult or impossible, for residents of flourishing modern cities naturally resist resettlement in the interests of archaeology. Excavation in these populated areas must wait upon repair of earthquake damage, urban improvements (as when laying new sewer mains reveals Roman ones that follow the grid of the Roman streets), or new building to bring new facts to light. For example, at Lucus Feroniae, eighteen miles north and slightly east of Rome, building the Rome-Florence autostrada revealed a luxurious late Republican and early imperial villa, with sixty rooms, spacious peristyle, mosaics, statuary (Hercules, Euripides, Menander, Hadrian's wife Sabina), and a family shrine of the Volusii. The villa, which was sited to command a view of the Sabine Hills, has been tastefully restored.

No colony has been completely excavated. At least 40 percent of ancient Ostia and Pompeii remains to be dug. But generations of archaeologists of many nations have dealt patiently and intelligently with the evidence. Perhaps, considering the long span of two and a half millennia since the earliest tradition of the planting of Roman colonies, the wonder is not that we know so little but that we know so much.

What archaeology has revealed is the story of the exploitation of a frontier, with much that is exciting and much that is sordid. There are many points of resemblance to the history of the American West, though two differences should be emphasized: the Romans often planted their outposts in the territory not of savages but of their cultural equals, and the Roman frontier was settled not by private but by government enterprise. But the likenesses are striking. Centuriation produces something like quarter sections; land grants to veterans resemble grants under the Homestead Act; the Roman grid town plans were reproduced in our Spanish settlements of the Southwest. And perhaps, on the Roman as on the American frontier, the atmosphere was less democratic than Frederick Jackson Turner thought.

What archaeology digs up in the colonies is material remains, brute facts, but what it infers is men; men marching out in serried ranks under their standards for the formal act of founding (*deductio*); Romans and local Italians living side by side with some degree of amity and equality; Romans impressing their ways and speech on the peoples round about; Roman slum dwellers given a new chance in the new territory; large estates broken up to give land to the landless; grizzled veterans settled in the quiet countryside after a lifetime of hard campaigning; Romans homesick in strange places, undergoing the rigors of frontier existence, subject to the ferment of success and failure, forging a cultural life (the epic poet Ennius, the dramatist Pacuvius, the satirist Lucilius, all came from Roman colonies).

The grid plans, in town and country, as Bradford has pointed out, show, if not genius, then strong determination and great powers of organization. The grids are, like the Romans themselves, methodical, self-assured, technically competent. They are also regimented, arbitrary, doctrinaire, and opportunist. This was the price the Mediterranean world had to pay for the security of the Roman peace.

But before that peace-without-freedom could be enjoyed, the Roman Republic was to suffer its death throes. That blood path was the work of the nabobs of the last century before Christ, who left their stamp, as nabobs will, on the buildings they erected to testify to their glory.

5

Nabobs as Builders: Sulla, Pompey, Caesar

The aftermath of Sulla's second march on Rome in 83 B.C.
was a spate of political murders and confiscations. The profits
were enormous, and Sulla used them for the most ambitious
building program in the history of the Republic. His motive
was in part the desire to rival what he had seen in the cities
of the Greek East, in part his understanding that massive
building projects are the outward and visible sign of princely
power. And so he monumentalized the same Forum in which
he displayed the severed heads of his enemies, planning, in
the Tabularium, or Records Office, a theatrical backdrop for
the tragedy which in the ensuing years was to be played below. He settled 100,000 of his veterans in colonies in central
and south Italy. He built or reinforced walls in Rome, Ostia,
and Alba Fucens; theaters in Pompeii, Alba, Bovianum Vetus,
and Faesulae; he built temples in Tibur, Cora, Tarracina,
Pompeii and Paestum. And this is only a sample of his prodigious building activity. But by all odds the most grandiose
of his completed projects took shape at Praeneste (nowadays Palestrina)—a little over twenty miles east of Rome,
where he sacked the town to punish it for taking the side of
his enemy Marius. He then built or restored there the great,

axially symmetrical, terraced Sanctuary of Fortune, the most splendid monument in Italy of the Roman Republic.

In 1944 allied bombing sheared off the houses from the steep south-facing slope where the medieval and modern town was built, and revealed the plan of the Sanctuary. Now, after fourteen years of excavation and restoring (reinforcement with steel beams, injecting liquid concrete, loving reproduction of the craft of ancient masons), the plan is clearer than it has been at any time since antiquity. The finds are displayed to advantage in the Barberini Palace at the top of the Sanctuary, splendidly reconstructed as a museum. The site repays a visit perhaps more than any other in Latium.

The archaeological zone of Palestrina falls into an upper and a lower part. In the lower area exciting discoveries were made in 1958. Its southernmost retaining wall, and the monumental ramped entrance, the Propylaea—enlivened in antiquity with jets of water playing—was cleared. Between it and the buildings of the lower zone, excavation seventy years before had shown traces of pools and shaded porticoes. In 1958, also, the façade was removed from the cathedral in the center of the lower zone, revealing behind it an imposing Roman temple with a lofty arched entrance, its *cella* corresponding to the forward (south) part of the nave of the present church. To the left rear (northwest) of this temple was a natural cave, long known as the Antro delle Sorti, where, according to time-honored local lore, the lots were cast which gave this sanctuary of Luck its fame. The cave, the excavators discovered, had been monumentalized into the apse of a building (not shown in the plan), its floor paved with a mosaic representing the sea off Alexandria. The mosaic was sunk a couple of inches below floor level and sloped forward to allow a thin film of water to play over it, which brightens the colors and makes the mosaic fish extraordinarily realistic. The mosaic also portrays architectural elements

—an altar, column, and capital—in what corresponds to the so-called Second Style at Pompeii, dated in the first half of the first century B.C.

Opposite this building in the plan is another with a grotto much like the natural cave on the left. It was from this apse, again at a level a couple of inches below the rest of the floor, that the famous Barberini mosaic (Fig. 5.1) came, a late Hellenistic copy of an original of the early Ptolemaic age in Egypt. It is now handsomely restored and displayed in the museum at the top of the Upper Sanctuary. The mosaic combines a zoological picturebook of the Egyptian Sudan—its real and fabulous monsters labeled in Greek—with a spirited scene of the Nile in flood, with farmhouse, dove cote, a shipload of soldiers, crocodiles, hippopotamuses, an elegant awninged pavilion, a towered villa in a garden, a group of soldiers feasting in mixed company (after them, the deluge), more wine, women and song in an arbor nearby, behind the pavilion a temple with statues of Egyptian gods in front, before them a man riding, his servant following afoot with baggage; behind the arbor a straw hut, with ibises in flight above it; in the flood waters, canoes (one loaded with lotus blossoms) and two large Nile river craft with curving prows —altogether the most spirited essay which has come down to us in the art of the mosaic. Interest in Egypt is a striking feature of both Pompeian and Roman wall painting of the last half-century of the Republic and the early Empire. Examples are the scene from Pompeii of pygmies fighting a rhinoceros and a crocodile, now in the Naples Museum, the cult scenes from the Hall of Isis under the Flavian Palace on the Palatine, and the frescoes of the Pharaoh Bocchoris in the Terme Museum from the villa under the Farnesina. Alexandria was then the intellectual and artistic capital of the world. The Lucullus who founded the Sullan colony at Praeneste appears from an inscription found in the lower area to be not the famous *bon vivant* (who had been in Alexandria,

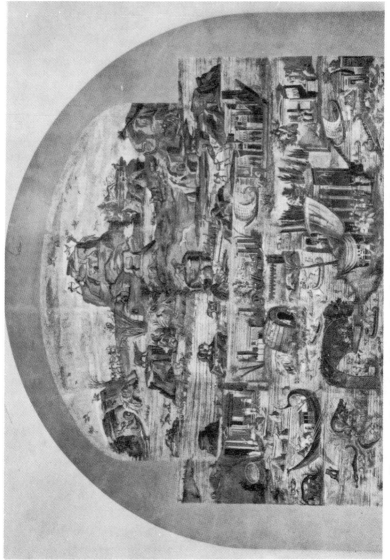

Fig. 5.1   Palestrina, Museum. Barberini mosaic. (Museum photo)

the first foreign general ever to be entertained by a Ptolemy in the palace) but his brother Marcus. Nevertheless, the two brothers were very close, and the more famous of them may have supplied the mosaic, the mosaic maker, or the idea of using Egyptian motifs.

M. Lucullus's name was carved on a fallen epistyle, a marble block intended to connect two columns. Where did the block belong? Gullini, the excavator, connected it with a building which ran between the two apsidal halls in the lower area. What survives is a back wall, built in the technique called *opus incertum,* a strong lime and rubble wall, studded externally with fist-sized stones of irregular shape. This technique was standard in the age of Sulla, though not confined to that period. The wall was decorated at regular intervals with two stories of half-columns, ingeniously combining function with decoration: they mask drainage conduits. The pavement in front of the wall shows the marks of two column bases in two different rows, enough to justify restoring on paper a whole forest of twenty-four columns. Two dimensions are known: the diameter of the bases and the height of the half-columns on the wall behind. Their proportionate relation is appropriate to Corinthian columns, and some Corinthian capitals of a size to fit were found in the area. Working from these finds, the architect Fasolo could restore on paper a two-story basilica (Fig. 5.2, bottom) between the two apsidal halls (only one hall is shown in the reconstruction). The basilica is on a higher level than the newly isolated temple to the south of it. The difference in level is made most clearly visible by sets of superimposed columns on the southwest side of the basilica (where the lower columns are below the basilica pavement level), by the pavement below the *piazza* of the modern town, and in the façade of the right-hand (eastern) apsidal hall, which is in *opus incertum.* Its lower level, the colony's *aerarium* or treasury, heavily built of tufa blocks, had the difference in construction hidden by a portico with Doric columns.

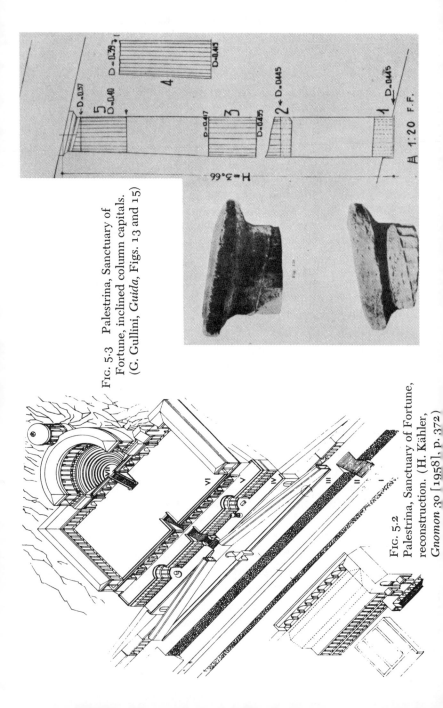

FIG. 5.3 Palestrina, Sanctuary of Fortune, inclined column capitals. (G. Gullini, *Guida*, Figs. 13 and 15)

FIG. 5.2 Palestrina, Sanctuary of Fortune, reconstruction. (H. Kähler, *Gnomon* 30 [1958], p. 372)

The terrace marking the transition between the lower area and the Upper Sanctuary used to be covered by houses and shops, all damaged or destroyed by the 1944 bombing. When the debris was cleared away, it was found that the modern buildings had rested on a two-level terrace (I and II in the reconstruction) and had backed against and protected from centuries of weathering 325 magnificent feet of polygonal wall. The wall gives an architectonic front to the cliff and is at the same time functional. Its top was the architect's base line; on it he built his complex, a splendid series of superimposed terraces, which, now that the rubble from the bombing has been cleared away, is revealed in all its magnificence, of ramps (III), Hemicycle Terrace (IV), Terrace of Arches with Half-columns (V), and Cortina Terrace (VI), all leading up to the final stepped hemicycle (VII) with the circular *tholos* for the cult statue at the very top. A draped torso in blue Rhodian marble (now in the museum), of a size to fit the *tholos*—whose dimensions are preserved in the fabric of the Barberini Palace—may be the cult statue of the goddess Fortune: Lady Luck herself.

The next level is approached by a pair of imposing ramps running east and west, converging on an axis. Fasolo and Gullini found that the ramps were supported by a series of concrete vaults, concealed, all but one, by a facing of *opus incertum* (see p. 145). The exception is the central vault, which was left open, lined with waterproof concrete, and made into a fountain house. The terrace in front of the ramps is beautifully paved with polygonal blocks. A room— perhaps priests' quarters—at the bottom of the left ramp is decorated in the Pompeian First Style—embossed polychrome squares, red, buff, and green, with dado. Houses at Pompeii thus decorated are dated between 150 and 80 B.C. The decorated room is paved with waterproof cement with bits of white limestone imbedded in it. The technique, called *lithostroton*, was in vogue in Sulla's time.

On the ramps were found three curious column capitals, which at first puzzled the excavators, and then gave the clue to the whole complex on top of the ramps. What is odd about the capitals is that they incline (Fig. 5.3) twenty-two degrees with respect to the axis of the columns. Since this slant corresponds to the grade of the ramp, the columns must have been intended to bear an inclined architrave or beam of stone. This poses a difficult problem in statics; that Sulla's architect solved it is the wonder of his modern successors. The roadway up the ramp shows, on the outboard (south) side of a drain running up its middle, a stylobate (course of masonry on which columns rested) with cuttings for column bases. Reading these stones, Fasolo and Gullini concluded that the outboard half of the roadway up the ramp was roofed, while the inboard half was open to the sky. On the extreme outboard edge of the roadway are preserved the remains, about a yard high, of a wall in *opus incertum,* with the bottoms of half-columns, their fluting laid on in stucco, mortised into it at intervals corresponding to the cuttings in the stylobate. The half-round profile at the bottom of the wall suggests projecting the same profile all the way up. This involves restoring a blank windowless wall (windows would make it too weak to bear the weight of the roof) closing the entire south side of the porticoed roadway, blocking the breathtaking view across Latium to the sea and forcing the eye upward to the top of the ramp. Architectural members designed to be clamped together in pairs, of a size to fit the tops of the inclined capitals, gave the answer to the question how the portico was roofed. One of the pairs supported a barrel vault, the other a vertical masonry wall designed to mask the spring of the vault. Other architectural members, with an oblique chamfer, found at the top and the bottom of the ramp, suggest that the ends of the vaults were masked with a pediment or gable end, and therefore that the whole vault was covered with a pitch roof. The two ramps debouch at the top in an open space paved in herringbone brick, a sort of balcony with—at last—a splendid view southward. To the north a stair led to the next level, the level of the Hemicycle Terrace.

The Hemicycle Terrace (IV) is planned, Fasolo and Gullini discovered, symmetrically to the axis of the whole composition, at this level marked by a central stair which has suffered a good deal from having had a modern house built on top of it. One can make out, however, that the stair was narrowed at one point (where there may have been a gate) by fountain niches on either side. At the gate, pilgrims may have paid admission fees. A great sanctuary like this profited from the sale of votive offerings (sold in the stalls on Terrace V), from tourist business, tithes, and loans: temples were often banks. The play of water is important at every level of the Sanctuary. Under the stair passes a vaulted corridor connecting the two axially symmetrical halves of the terrace. Closest to the stair on each side are four arches; beyond these, the monumental hemicycles, which are the architectonic center of each wing. They have vaulted, coffered ceilings and a concentric colonnade with Ionic-Italic (four-voluted) columns. Before they were restored, these were badly corroded and covered with verdigris from the acid of the coppersmith's shop which occupied the spot before the bombing. The epistyle carries an inscription, almost illegible, but apparently referring to building and restoring done on the initiative of the local Senate, presumably after the Sullan sack. The outer surface or extrados of the vaults is concealed—as it was on the porticoed ramp—by a story called an attic, in *opus incertum*, divided into rectangular panels by engaged columns with semicircular drums in tufa. At the back of each hemicycle runs a platform approached by two steps, with consoles on which planks could be placed to make more room; this suggests that it was intended for spectators to stand on. The pavement, as in the room at the foot of the ramp, is *litho-*

stroton; the likeness in the paving justifies the inference that the two terraces (III and IV) were built about the same time. On the far side of each hemicycle are four more arches. In front of the right-hand (eastern) hemicycle is a wishing well, with footings round it from which Fasolo and Gullini have been able to restore to the last detail, with the help of some architectural fragments, a small, round well house, with a high grille above its balustrade, now to be seen in the museum. Coins found in the well, whose heaviest concentration is in the mid-second century A.D., suggest that the well house is much later in date than the terrace on which it stands. But the well house stands on the central terrace of seven; it may have been the spot where, in the early days of the Sanctuary, the lots were cast. From either end of the Hemicycle Terrace ramps (Fig. 5.4) ascended to the Cortina Terrace (VI), the next but one above.

The stair which divides the Hemicycle Terrace leads to the

Fig. 5.4   Palestrina, Sanctuary of Fortune. Model from southwest, showing buttresses, and ramp from Hemicycle Terrace to Cortina Terrace. (H. Kähler, *Ann. Univ. Saraviensis* 7 [1958], Pl. 39)

Terrace of the Arches with Half-columns (V), also symmetrically planned on the axis of the stair. There are nine deep
arches on either side of the stair. Possibly these were stalls
for the various guilds—wine merchants, wagoners, cooks,
weavers, garland makers, second-hand dealers, money-chang-
ers—who, as we know from inscriptions, made dedications to
Fortune and had a financial interest in her Sanctuary. Here
again close observation has enabled the excavators to tell
exactly how the façade of this terrace looked when it was
new. The even-numbered arches are narrower and lower than
the odd-numbered ones, are left rough within, and are floored
with a pebble fill, from all of which it is inferred that they
were not meant to be seen. Sills found *in situ,* and uprights,
cornices, and volutes, found on the Hemicycle Terrace, where
they do not fit into the architecture and therefore must have
fallen from above, can be restored as blind doors set in the
walls which closed the even-numbered arches. Small travertine panels, with a molded surround and a cornice above,
found on this terrace, will have been set into the wall on either
side of the blind doors, at lintel level. The same decorative
motif was found in place on the back wall of the basilica area
in the lower zone. The repetition of motif makes an aesthetic
link between the two levels. The odd-numbered arches are
mosaic paved and plastered, and were therefore meant to be
visible. Enough remains in place to show that the profile of
the arch was set with tufa blocks supported on pilasters.
These alternating open arches framed with pilasters and
closed arches with blind doors all supported an epistyle and
cornice which in turn supported the parapet of the Cortina
Terrace above.

The Cortina Terrace (VI), nearly 400 feet deep, was a
hollow square, open to the south except for a balustrade,
closed to the east and west by a three-columned portico,
connected at the back (north) with a *lithostroton*-paved
vaulted corridor, called a cryptoporticus, which runs under

the stair to the semicircular Terrace VII. Again, similarity of plan and décor ties the whole ensemble together. (Nowadays, the approach to Terrace VII is by a double-access stair, but this is of the seventeenth century.) At the back of the terrace, six arches, three on either side of the central stair, gave access to the cryptoporticus. At either end of the three-arch sequence is an arched projecting fountain house in appearance not unlike a Roman triumphal arch, with a pair of narrow windows in its back wall, opening on the cryptoporticus. Heavy deposits of lime on the back wall suggest an arrangement whereby persons passing through the cryptoporticus could look out through a thin sheet of water onto the Cortina Terrace. Enough traces remain to restore on paper the three-columned portico on the east and west. It was roofed with a pair of barrel vaults, coffered like the ones in the hemicycles of Terrace IV (another aesthetic link), and roofed like the great east-west ramps which connect Terraces III and IV. The portico's outer walls were buttressed, and the north-south ramps from the Hemicycle Terrace also helped to counter the outward thrust.

And so we come to the exedra, the seventh of the superimposed terrace levels, a most holy place, where the priests could appear and offer sacrifice on an altar in full view of the faithful assembled on the semicircular steps. At the top of the exedra there now rises the splendid semicircle of the Barberini Palace, but plate glass let into the museum's ground floor paving shows the tufa footings of a semicircular series of columns, which must have been the middle set of another double portico answering to the one on the Cortina Terrace below, and, like it, double-barrel-vaulted and pitch-roofed, but of course semicircular in plan instead of U-shaped. Access to the porticoes was not on the central axis of the whole complex, but by a short narrow stair at either end of the exedra. (We shall see how Hadrian, too, centuries later, liked these split-access arrangements.) But, though there is no direct approach, the distance between the columns on either side of the main axis is extra wide, to give a better view of the circular building (*tholos*) above and behind, the culminating point of the whole plan, where the cult statue was placed.

Such is the careful plan of the complex, justifying this detailed treatment because it is a turning point in the history of Roman architecture, perhaps the most seminal architectural complex in the whole Roman world. Everything (Fig. 5.5) centers on an axis, everything rises, aspires to the apex at the cult statue, embracing a superb and at each level more extensive view of the plain stretching away southward to the sea. The materials and technique with which this form is realized and supported are interesting in themselves and for what they contribute to the dating of the Sanctuary. The basic materials are tufa, limestone, and concrete; no marble is used except in statuary. Limestone, which in Roman architecture comes to predominance later than tufa, is used for the facing of polygonal walls and *opus incertum*, for décor (*e.g.*,

Fig. 5.5   Palestrina, Museum. Sanctuary of Fortune, model.
(J. Felbermeyer photo)

the Corinthian capitals of tufa columns), for pavements. The limestone spalls or chips left over from the facing of *opus incertum* were used in concrete cores and for fill. Tufa is used for footings, structure in squared blocks (*e.g.*, caissons for concrete), the voussoirs, or wedge-shaped blocks, of arches, column drums, the core of stuccoed decorative elements, cornices, corners. Both materials are subordinate to concrete.

The use of concrete at Palestrina amounts to an architectural revolution, and, as often, the revolution in taste is combined with a revolution in materials and methods. This strong, cheap, immensely tough material enabled the architect to enclose space in any shape; henceforward architects could concentrate on interiors, and the day of the boxlike temple was over. The architectural history that culminates in the Pantheon begins here. The architect was clearly more expert in the use of concrete than in the use of stone. Palestrina concrete is hydraulic, a combination of limestone chips and mortar made of *pozzolana* (volcanic sand) and lime. Concrete footings, Fasolo and Gullini found, go down to bedrock everywhere; *e.g.*, each of the three rows of columns of the Cortina Terrace portico rests on a foundation wall of concrete based on bedrock, while the space between is hollow, to relieve weight. For the same reason, the whole hollow square of the Cortina Terrace rests on a series of rectangular concrete coffers with a stone fill. The result of this use of concrete is that the whole Upper Sanctuary is structurally a single unit. Each level is planned as a step toward, and a retaining wall of, the level next above. The stresses, Fasolo reports, are never more than about three pounds per square yard for walls and eight pounds per square yard for columns; this in a structure which is in effect a skyscraper 400 feet high. There is repetition of motif throughout, not from paucity of imagination, or because it is the easy way, but of set aesthetic purpose, to emphasize the concealed structural unity and to use the functional parts of the complex to give architectonic unity to the

whole. Thus the upper hemicycle stair repeats the two hemicycles of the lower terrace, and the relation between them is
a triangle, which repeats in a different plane the triangle of
the double converging ramp. The arches are treated as beams
to bear the weight of stone construction, and the stone construction is a caisson for the concrete.

Fasolo and Gullini argue ingeniously for a date earlier than
Sulla for the Sanctuary, but, though there is epigraphic evidence that the Upper Sanctuary existed in some form before
82 B.C., their arguments have not found general favor. The
most that can be said is that certain inscriptions mentioning
restoration, reconstruction, or dedications to Fortune earlier
than 80 B.C. imply a previously existing and probably much
simpler structure, centering on the east half of the Hemicycle
Terrace. Sulla's vengeance upon Praeneste, which had taken
Marius's side in the civil war, was murderous: most of the
important families were wiped out. It follows that inscriptions connected with the Sanctuary which bear the old names
are likely to be pre-Sullan, and so is some phase of the Sanctuary. This is Degrassi's argument: he dates the pre-Sullan
phase 110–100, and Gullini now accepts this.

In materials and methods, in massiveness and axial symmetry, the Sanctuary of Fortune bears a Roman stamp. But
when we recall the experience of Sulla and his lieutenants,
the Luculli, in the Greek East, Greek influence is very likely.
Of the many Hellenistic Greek complexes available for comparison, the closest in spirit to Palestrina is the Sanctuary of
Asclepius on the island of Kos in the Dodacanese, in the
southeast Aegean Sea, where the major temple, built in the
mid-second century B.C., is the focal point of a grandiose composition (Fig. 5.6). Placed on the highest of three terraces, it
is framed by a three-sided colonnade like the Cortina Terrace
at Palestrina, and approached by three successive monumental stairways leading up the lower terraces, which are arched
as at Palestrina. A few standard architectural ingredients,

FIG. 5.6   Kos, Sanctuary of Asclepius, reconstruction.
(R. Herzog and P. Schatzmann, *Kos* 1, Pl. 40)

FIG. 5.7   Tarracina. View toward Circeii from Temple of Jupiter
Anxoranus. (H. Kähler, *Rom und seine Welt*, Pl. 49)

arches, colonnades, monumental stairways, are grouped as a clearly defined composition, easy to grasp, simple, bold, plastic, the few standard elements firmly juxtaposed. Contrasts of scale, an elevated and central position, an axial approach, all make of the temple the focal, culminating point of the composition. It is exactly so at Palestrina, and in scores of other Hellenistic sanctuaries. Also noteworthy in both places is "the same outspoken taste for vista. Not only is the triple-terraced sanctuary visible from afar, not only is the crowning element, a temple, a beacon toward which visitor and worshipper alike are drawn by the now familiar devices of setting, frontality and access, but again, once we have reached the summit, a scene of breathtaking beauty, of unexpected amplitude, of mountain, sea and plain confronts us." The words are those of Phyllis Lehmann, from whom the description of the site at Kos draws heavily, and they were reinforced by a visit made by the present writer to the island in September 1956, expressly to compare the site with Palestrina. Mrs. Lehmann goes on, "Although many factors, notably the sanctity of a cult spot, were involved in the choice of such sites, their architectural treatment attests a keen awareness of landscape setting as a prime aesthetic ingredient in the total effect." The unknown architect-genius who planned Palestrina probably knew the Greek Sanctuary at Kos; he was certainly in touch with the main movement of mind of his age. But the final impression of this dynamic, utterly functional, axially symmetric complex is not Greek but Roman, a great memorial façade to celebrate the end of a Civil War. Italy as well as Greece can provide ground plans by which parts of the Sanctuary at Palestrina might have been inspired, notably one in Cagliari in Sardinia and another at Gabii, near Rome.

This Roman classical masterpiece has, then, ancestors; what about its descendants? They are many: from the Sanctuary of Fortune contemporary and later architects learned much. An example of this influence is the Temple of Jupiter Anxoranus at Terracina, above the Via Appia where it touches the coast sixty-seven miles south of Rome. Here the use of concrete, of arch and vault, of setting and landscape, is in the unmistakable idiom of Sulla's architect. It is an architectural complex and a seascape which mediates, as Palestrina does, between man and nature. It is designed to capture attention from the colony below, to become more impressive as one approaches, and to give a gradually widening view of the sea as one ascends. The temple was oriented north and south, with a portico behind (Fig. 5.8). It is set at an angle upon a tremendous concrete podium, with arched cryptoporticus as at Palestrina. On the seaward side the play of light and shadow on the podium arches is enormously impressive; on the side toward Sperlonga the sturdy blind buttress arches are again strongly reminiscent of what we have seen on the Terrace of the Half-columns. Within the cryptoporticus (the vaults under the temple platform) the play of light and shadow is again very satisfying, and yet the structure is functional as well: the cryptoporticus lightens the huge weight of the concrete, and the sturdy concrete construction has stood the test of time.

Another Sullan descendant is the Tabularium (Public Records Office) in Rome (Fig. 5.9), finished in 78 B.C. by Quintus Lutatius Catulus, to whom Sulla's veterans transferred their allegiance after Sulla's death. It was a part of Sulla's plan for monumentalizing the Forum, to provide, as it were, a scenic backdrop for it, which serves at the same time as a terrace level to give order to the Capitoline Hill above.

There is a re-entrant angle at its southwest corner, to leave room for a temple of Veiovis (a youthful Jupiter). Tunnel building in 1939 disclosed the temple. Though lack of light and space made excavation difficult, the archaeologists were able to ascertain that the visible phase of the temple, wider

FIG. 5.8   Tarracina. Temple of Jupiter Anxoranus, reconstruction.
(F. Fasolo and G. Gullini, *Il Santuario di Fortuna Primigenia*, Pl. 25)

than it was deep, with a travertine podium and a lithostroton
pavement in the cella, was contemporary with the Tabularium itself. The earliest phase, in lithoid tufa, dates from
the original foundation in 192 B.C. At some time in the Dark
Ages, a part of the Tabularium wall fell, concealing and protecting the cult statue and altar. The statue, which is head-
less, was originally over eleven feet tall.

FIG. 5.9   Rome, Tabularium. (Fototeca)

The Tabularium's plan, its frontality, and its use of arch, vault, and concrete is in the Palestrina tradition. There is a cryptoporticus in concrete, fronted by arches framed in half-columns placed at points in the wall which required extra strength. The upper levels of the Tabularium were removed by Michelangelo when he designed the Palazzo del Senatore, Rome's city hall. Perhaps this may be taken as a symbol of the extent and the limits of the influence of Palestrina's architect on Renaissance masters. One archaeologist, Heinz Kähler, has argued, ingeniously but without carrying conviction, for an influence of the Cortina Terrace and the exedra above it upon the design of Pompey's theater in Rome: one nabob borrowing architectural effects from another.

Finally, about the time of Cicero's consulship (63 B.C.), Palestrina influenced the Sanctuary of Hercules Victor at Tivoli, well-known to many from Piranesi's etching as the Villa of Maecenas. Like Kos and Palestrina (Cortina Terrace), it had a portico on three sides and a temple against the back wall. Once it housed a paper mill; now it is expropriated, uncluttered, and virtually inaccessible. There was an approach by ramp and semicircular stair (Fig. 5.10), very theatrical, like Palestrina and the Tabularium; the material is again concrete faced with *opus incertum*. The podium is again supported on concrete vaults and lightened by a complicated arrangement of subterranean rooms. A vast cryptoporticus pierces the whole podium to carry the Via Tiburtina, the main road from Rome to Tivoli. The famous terraced gardens of the Villa d'Este nearby, with their plays of water, felt the inspiration of Palestrina; their architect, Pirro Ligorio, has left sketches of our site made by him on the spot. Pietro da Cortona, Bramante, Raphael, Palladio, and Bernini also knew and sketched Palestrina. Another successful terrace plan inspired by Palestrina is Valadier's treatment in the 19th century of the steep slope up the Pincio from the Piazza del Popolo in Rome.

FIG. 5.10   Tivoli, Temple of Hercules Victor, reconstruction.
(Fasolo and Gullini, *op. cit.*, Pl. 27)

Palestrina inspired the architects of the Roman Empire, too: for example—one among many—it influenced to some extent (see also p. 334) the architect of Trajan's Market in Rome, who uses terracing, concrete, and framed arches (but the arches are flat, the framing is pilasters instead of half-columns, and the façade is brick instead of *opus incertum*). The inspiration does not stop here: it is to be found on the Palatine, in Hadrian's villa near Tivoli, Diocletian's Baths in Rome, and his palace at Spalato, and the Basilica of Maxentius in the Roman Forum.

From his building, from which the history of Roman architecture really begins, we can reconstruct the personality of the architect. It makes the whole history of Roman architecture come alive, when we really know one complex. The architect was a master of the manipulation of surface, of light and shade, of counterthrust, controlled views, the unitary plan, of space both full and empty. For him, organic function is also decorative; the stylistic fact is the constructive solution; his organization is clear; his use of the classical "orders" of Graeco-Roman architecture, Tuscan and Ionic, in stone as bearing walls is classical in its combination of beauty and function. The plan of his Sanctuary imposed itself as well on the secular plan of the colony below. He is a real genius, one of the greatest architects of all time. He achieves his magnificent results by creative imitation of earlier models, and in this he is Roman. Because his imitation is creative, it does not peter out in formalism, but has a seminal effect upon other architects of the Republic, the Empire, the Renaissance. A detailed study of his masterpiece not only leaves us profoundly impressed with the patience, thoroughness, and imagination of Italian archaeologists; it reinforces again the lesson of the continuity of history and the cultural importance for the whole Western world of the Roman Republic.

Sulla went into voluntary retirement and—a rare archievement in his time—died in bed. The next nabob to equal him in stature, violence, and unconstitutionality was a man who had begun his career as Sulla's lieutenant, Pompey the Great. Victories in Sicily and Africa, against slaves, pirates, and Mithridates, brought him enormous spoils; he too turned his mind to buildings to monumentalize his glory. The result was Rome's first stone theater (Fig. 5.11), in the Campus Martius, dedicated in his third consulship (52 B.C.) but begun in his second (55 B.C.), in a great show involving 500 lions and 17 to 20 elephants. What survives of it is little more than a curve in a Roman street, some blocks of tufa beneath

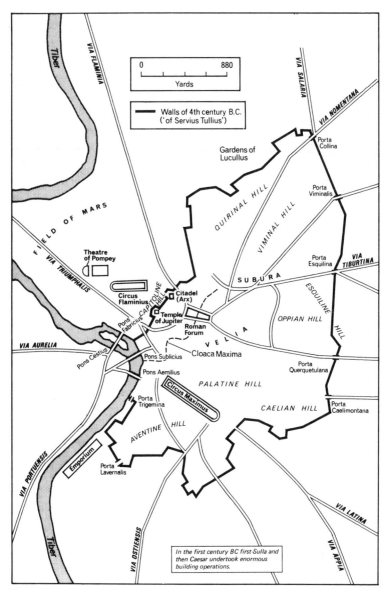

Fig. 5.11 Republican Rome, map. (M. Grant, *Ancient History Atlas*
© Weidenfeld and Nicholson, London, 1971; Macmillan & Co., New
York, 1972)

a Roman square, and a memory. Beneath the curve of the Via di Grotta Pinta, which perpetuates the outline of its *cavea,* one may visit today, in the lower regions of a Roman restaurant, the underpinnings of the great building, which once held 12,000 spectators. The technique of these vaults, a development of *incertum* called *opus reticulatum,* involves setting pyramidal bricks, point inward, in a lozenge pattern into a cement core. But though the entire superstructure has disappeared, an ancient plan survives. In the late second century A.D. the Emperor Septimus Severus caused to be placed on the wall of the library in Vespasian's Forum of Peace a marble Plan of Rome, the *Forma Urbis,* which has come down to us in over 1,000 fragments. The ingenuity with which these have been pieced together; *e.g.,* the identification of the Theater of Balbus and the Circus of Flaminius, would make a story in itself, but for our present purpose only four fragments (Fig. 5.12) are relevant. The two parallel walls to the right (which is west; north is at the bottom) give a fascinating insight into the puritanical Roman mind at work.

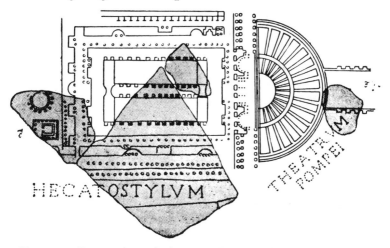

Fig. 5.12   Rome, Pompey's theater and portico, from *Forma Urbis.*
(G. Lugli, *Mon. Ant.,* 3, p. 79)

Straitlaced Romans objected to theaters as immoral.* Pompey's architect therefore designed at the top of the theater's *cavea* a temple of Venus Victrix, represented by the two parallel walls in the plan. The theater seats might then pass as a hemicycle approach to a temple (compare the hemicycle approach to the *tholos* at Palestrina). Puritanism was appeased.

Behind the stage the marble plan shows a great rectangular portico, with a double garden plot in the middle, where we may restore in imagination trees planted, fountains playing, and works of art displayed, perhaps including the powerfully contorted Belvedere torso now in the Vatican. At a Senate meeting in a building associated with the portico, on the Ides of March, 44 B.C., Caesar fell at the base of Pompey's statue, pierced by twenty-three daggers. (The tufa blocks visible today through a sheet of plate glass in the pedestrian underpass at the southwest corner of the Argentina temple area are part either of the portico or of a building at the back of Temple *D*. Temples *A* and *B* of the Largo Argentina appear to the left in the plan.)

Caesar was a greater man than Pompey. His spoils of victory, after eight years in Gaul, were richer, and so was his building program. The most impressive surviving evidence of it is the ground plan of his basilica, the Basilica Julia in the Republican Forum, and, north of the old Forum (which Rome and his own grandeur had outgrown), a grandiose new one—the prototype of an Imperial series.

The Basilica Julia was planned and executed at Caesar's direction between 54 and 46 B.C., to balance the second-century Basilica Aemilia across the Forum. (Some twenty to forty years later, the Basilica Aemilia was adorned with a frieze of scenes from early Roman history, such as the rape

---

* There is reason to believe that Roman authorities deliberately delayed building structures in which crowds might gather, so as to minimize opportunities for riotous demonstrations.

of the Sabines and the punishment of the traitress Tarpeia. Casts of these have been set up in the basilica; the originals are on display in the Forum Antiquarium, in the ex-church of S. Francesca Romana.) All that remains is pavement and piers, but the size of the piers is enough to show that the building had two stories, presumably with a balcony to afford a view of spectacles in the open space of the Forum below. Time and man have dealt harshly with the basilica. When it was excavated, in the 1840s, a medieval limekiln was found on the pavement. This, plus the knowledge that its stone was sold by the oxcart load in the Middle Ages for the benefit of a hospital which rose on the site, explains what happened to the superstructure. Scratched on the pavement are rough sketches, done by ancient idlers, of statues which once adorned the building or the Forum adjacent, and over eighty "gaming-boards," scratched circles divided into six segments on which dice were thrown and counters moved. Lawyers' speeches apparently did not always hold the full attention of the Forum hangers-on. The basilica is vast: 328 by 159 feet, thrice the size of Cosa's. Excavation under the nave has revealed the remains of a house which might be that of Scipio Africanus, conqueror of Hannibal and hero of the Second Punic War.

Caesar's Forum has left more impressive remains. It cost him a fortune, since his enemies, owners of the expropriated houses, charged him 100,000,000 sesterces, five million uninflated dollars, for the land. Its excavation was begun in 1930 and finished in three years, by Corrado Ricci, as a part of Mussolini's (Fig. 5.13) grandiose plan for systematizing the center of the city and restoring the ancient dictator's Forum to set off a modern dictator's monument, a new street, the Via dell'Impero, driven through slums and ancient monuments to connect the Colosseum with his headquarters in the Palazzo Venezia. The excavation exposed the southern two-thirds of Caesar's Forum (Fig. 5.14); the rest lies under the

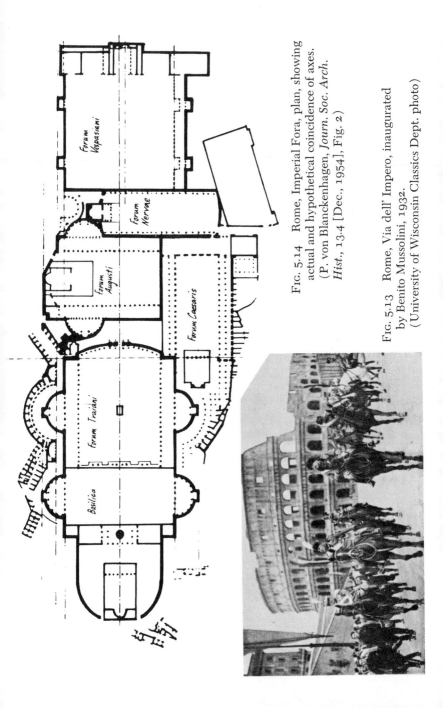

Fig. 5.14 Rome, Imperial Fora, plan, showing actual and hypothetical coincidence of axes. (P. von Blanckenhagen, *Journ. Soc. Arch. Hist.*, 13.4 [Dec., 1954]. Fig. 2)

Fig. 5.13 Rome, Via dell' Impero, inaugurated by Benito Mussolini, 1932. (University of Wisconsin Classics Dept. photo)

new street. The Forum as revealed by Ricci is another example of axial symmetry, a narrow porticoed rectangle, over twice as long as it was wide, with a temple set in the Italic fashion on a high podium at the back. Working with great patience and delicacy, Ricci set up three of the temple's fallen columns (Fig. 5.15), with their architrave, frieze, and cornice. Some of the architectural blocks leave between the dentils—a row of projecting toothlike rectangular members below the cornice—two small distinctive marble disks side by side like a pair of spectacles. This is the "signature" of Domitian's architect Rabirius, and it proves that a restoration of the temple was planned during his reign (A.D. 81–96). Trajan had a hand in a later reconstruction. There are Cupids in the interior frieze, which prove that the temple was dedicated to Venus, Caesar's ancestor. To have gods for ancestors lent distinction to a Roman clan, though Caesar knew as well as any skeptic what it really meant. He knew his pedigree back to an ever-so-great grandfather, and God knew who *his* ancestor was. In the *gens Iulia* the line was traced back to Iulus the son of Aeneas, who was the son of Anchises and Venus.

The portico, like that behind Pompey's theater, was an art museum. (In its present state it is of the fourth Christian century.) Ancient authors mention a golden statue of Cleopatra (one of the dictator's few sentimental gestures?), a golden breastplate set with British pearls, and a bronze equestrian statue of Caesar on his famous horse which had human front feet!

The ground to the south of the Forum rises over fifty feet to the slopes of the Capitoline Hall. This difference in level was filled with three setback stories of luxury shops in massive rectangular blocks of *peperino*. The Street of the Silversmiths, the *Clivus Argentarius*, ran above and behind the shops at the Forum level. This whole complex survives.

In conclusion, nine more monuments and works of art rein-

FIG. 5.15   Rome, Forum of Caesar. (Fototeca)

force the theme of this chapter: the evidence of archaeology
about the importance of wealth and power in late Republican Rome. First, two bridges. The Pons Mulvius, which
carries the Via Flaminia—Rome's Great North Road—across
the Tiber, dates from 109, the censorship year of M. Aemilius
Scaurus, patrician, ex-consul, all-powerful in the Senate
through prestige and political manipulation. The bridge, in
tufa from Veii, has five arches, plus relieving arches, and is
the oldest Roman bridge in continuous use. The Pons Fabricius (Fig. 5.16), of 62, connects Rome's left bank with the
Tiber Island. Over its twin arches an inscription in very large
letters commemorates L. Fabricius, commissioner of streets
and bridges in that year; not much of a nabob, but if, as
seems likely, he was also tribune of the people in 62, he was
a powerful demagogue.

The round temple by the Tiber (Fig. 5.17) in the Forum
Boarium (cattle market) belongs in its first phase to the early
first century B.C. Though its footings are tufa, its superstruc-

FIG. 5.16   Pons Fabricius. (Author)

FIG. 5.17   Rome, Round temple by Tiber. (Felbermeyer)

ture is of expensive Pentelic marble. According to recent research its deity was Hercules Victor, patron of a rich and
powerful group of businessmen, the olive merchants.

The Casa dei Grifi (80–60 B.C.), on the Palatine under the
Flavian palace, is the most interesting Republican house in
Rome; from its rich wall decoration (some of it detached and
on display in the Palatine Antiquarium) it must have belonged to a man of wealth. Its décor includes fake incrustation (very early Pompeian Second Style: see chapter 8),
imitation marble and alabaster, vaults stuccoed in squares

and lozenges, and in lunettes, in white stucco, the griffins
from which the house is named, facing one another heraldically. Most interesting is the large bedroom (Fig. 5.18),
with fake treetrunk columns, panels in Pompeian red alternating with painted veined slabs in what is irreverently called
the fried-egg pattern, a frieze imitating green marble, and
a dado in a *trompe l'oeil* motif of red and white cubes, repeated in the center of the floor mosaic.

Nabobs of the late Republic built or acquired many seaside
villas. Cicero had one at Formiae (one of eight, of which
five others were on the sea). On the main road from Rome
to Naples, it was altogether too convenient, Cicero found,
for acquaintances wanting to stay overnight: "not a villa,"
he wrote to his friend Atticus, "but a public passageway."
Here, on December 7, 43 B.C., he was killed by Mark Antony's
gangsters. Some, without basis in fact, identify the villa with
the Villa Rubino, which has a Roman nymphaeum (artificial

FIG. 5.18   Rome, Palatine, Casa dei Grifi, bedroom.
(Palatine Antiquarium)

grotto with a play of water), and baths. Recently, interest has been shown in excavating working villas, owned but not always occupied by rich landowners. One of these is Posto, at Francolise near Capua, dating from the early first century B.C. It stand on a podium of squared blocks, and has a square courtyard with wells and an oil-separating vat, a timbered portico, and quarters for the owner or bailiff and the slaves.

The Boston Museum of Fine Arts possesses a fine realistic portrait head in terracotta (Fig. 5.19), from near Capua, of 60–50 B.C., which typifies the hard-faced men who made the Roman Empire. Perhaps it is a life mask. A 1967 critic called it the face of "an aged, careworn intellectual." It was earlier identified (without foundation) as L. Domitius Ahenobarbus, an enemy of Julius Caesar and ancestor of Nero.

One of the finest portrait bronzes of Roman antiquity is the bust of Cato the Younger (Fig. 5.20), from Volubilis in Morocco, perhaps Flavian, now in the Rabat museum. The fine-drawn aquiline profile is of a doctrinaire Stoic, anti-Caesarian, of whom Cicero said that he thought he was living in Plato's *Republic* and not amid the scum of Romulus. He committed suicide in 46 B.C. at Utica, in North Africa, rather than fall into Caesar's hands.

The Tomb of Caecilia Metella, at the third kilometer stone of the Via Appia, memorializes the nabob Metellus Creticus' daughter, married to Marcus Crassus (son of the triumvir), another nabob. She died about 40 B.C. Her tomb is a masonary drum derived from the tumuli of Caere and anticipating the mausolea of Augustus (Fig. 6.9) and Hadrian (Fig. 11.19).

Three men on horseback, Sulla, Pompey, and Caesar, subdued East and West for Rome and used part of the profits to change the face of Rome in forty years. They would have said that they did it out of what the Romans called *pietas,* a threefold loyalty to family, state, and gods. Each, to reflect credit on his family, which ruled the state, on the

FIG. 5.19   Boston, "Domitius Ahenobarbus."
(Courtesy Museum of Fine Arts; 01.8008)

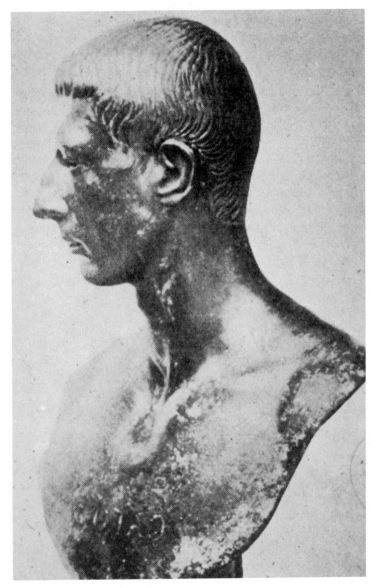

FIG. 5.20   Rabat, Museum, bronze bust of Cato the Younger.
(M. Janon)

gods his ancestors, and on the state his perquisite, erected great public buildings in the city to be his monument. Sulla's dramatic revamping of the old Forum, Pompey's theater and portico, and Caesar's new Forum made of a shabby civic center a metropolis almost worthy to vie with cities of the Greek East. Almost, but not quite, for the building material was still local stone, stuccoed tufa or the handsome lime-stone from Tivoli called travertine, which weathers to a fine gold and has ever since been Rome's characteristic building material. It was considered worthy in the Renaissance to build the fabric of St. Peter's. For its next transformation, this time into a city of marble, Rome had to wait for the rise to power of the greatest nabob of them all, Caesar's adopted son and successor, Octavian-Augustus.

6

Augustus: Buildings as Propaganda

In 1922, after the success of the Fascist march on Rome, Benito Mussolini felt acutely the need for an aura of respectability to surround his upstart régime. Another swashbuckling *condottiere,* 1965 years earlier, Caesar's heir Octavian, had felt the same need. Both resorted to the same method: an ambitious building program and a vigorous propaganda campaign designed to substitute for dubious antecedents a set of more or less spurious links with the heroes of the glorious past. About Fascist architecture the less said the better; the other point will be the subject of this chapter. In fourteen years (1924–38) Italian archaeologists changed the face of central Rome, and, in the process of glorifying *Il Duce,* added more to our knowledge of Augustan Rome than the previous fourteen centuries had provided.

Octavian's building activity, both before and after he took the title of Augustus, was prodigious. In his autobiography he boasts of restoring no less than eighty-two temples. He built many new ones besides.

Three temples, recently reexamined, deserve special mention. First, Apollo *in circo* [Flaminio], also called Apollo

Sosianus, directly across from the future site of the Theater of Marcellus. This was a complete restoration, at the hands of one C. Sosius. It had tufa footings, a marble-revetted podium, and Corinthian columns (three have been reerected; they have alternately broad and narrow flutes). The exterior frieze featured the triumphators' laurel, suspended between candelabra and bucrania (ox-skulls). In the cella were displayed, besides the cult statues, enough Greek statuary, classical and Hellenistic, to furnish a museum. A recent suggestion is that the sculpture came from the temple pediment, and represents Theseus fighting the Amazons, with Athena as the central figure. The interior frieze, miniature like that on the altar proper of the Ara Pacis (see below) had two themes: a procession, and Roman cavalry pursuing barbarians. Three fragments of the processional part survive, in the Conservatori Museum: the participants converged, as in the two major sections of the Ara Pacis. What is portrayed is probably the parade at the temple's inauguration, on Augustus's birthday, September 23, about 20 B.C. If it represents a triumph of Sosius, it underlines Octavian-Augustus's conciliatory spirit, for Sosius had fought against him in the naval battle of Actium. After Actium, Apollo meant much more to Octavian: he professed to owe his victory to the Apollo whose temple overlooked the scene. The largest fragment portrays a litter bearing a trophy and two bound prisoners; then three oxen arrayed for sacrifice, with their aproned attendants, naked to the waist, and a lictor. On the two fragments showing the part of the procession marching the other way, four bearers carry a litter containing scored round loaves of sacrificial bread and the head and ham of a pig; there are also a togate figure and another lictor. The building propagandizes Octavian-Augustus's magnanimity, piety, and artistic taste.

Even closer to the Emperor's heart must have been the temple of the Palatine Apollo, begun in 36, finished in 28.

In architectural detail (building stone and Corinthian capitals), it resembled Sosius's temple. Off its spacious portico opened the Palatine libraries, presided over by the polymath Varro, another pardoned former enemy. The Sibylline books (containing prophecies) were kept here, in a plinth of the cult statue. Its décor consisted of archaizing terracotta revetment plaques, portraying, among other subjects, Hercules contending with Apollo for the Delphic tripod (Fig. 6.1).

FIG. 6.1   Rome, Temple of Apollo Palatinus, Hercules-Apollo terracotta revetment. (Palatine Antiquarium; Istituto Centrale per il Catalogo e la Documentazione)

Hercules was a favorite with the Emperor, who saw in him a fellow burden-bearer and performer of labors: here, where Hercules loses, Octavian-Augustus subordinates one of his symbols, a mere heroized mortal, to another, a god.

In the temple of the Deified Julius (Fig. 6.2), dedicated in 29 in the Republican Forum, Octavian turned the prestige of his adoptive father to his own advantage. The comet whose appearance coincided with Caesar's murder was figured in the pediment, and the beaks of Antony's and Cleopatra's ships from Actium decorated the podium, which thus became yet another rostra, from which Augustus's stepson and successor Tiberius delivered the funeral oration over him in A.D. 14. The temple was flanked on one side by Augustus's arch (see below), and on the other by one commemorating Lucius and Gaius, his grandchildren and intended heirs. The temple portico was planted with the triumphators' laurels, which we last saw on the exterior frieze of the temple of Apollo Sosianus.

FIG. 6.2   Rome, Temple of Deified Julius. (Bini)

Augustus's entourage collaborated in his plans for building and renewing temples. His lieutenant and future son-in-law, Agrippa, built between 27 and 25 B.C. a Pantheon in the Campus Martius; its remains lie under the pronaos of the present, Hadrianic building, but face the other way. Its pediment probably contained an eagle perched on the civic crown of oak leaves awarded to Augustus in 25 for his having saved the lives of his fellow citizens. At the same time, Augustus received the right to decorate the door of his house with the laurel. Experts conjecture, from put-holes in the pediment of the present Pantheon, that Hadrian copied the eagle motif; it was copied again in the "ruptured duck" awarded to American veterans after World War II.

Tiberius in A.D. 6 restored the temple of Castor and Pollux in the Forum: the contemporary counterparts of the Heavenly Twins could have been Lucius and Gaius, or perhaps Tiberius's grandnephews, Nero and Drusus. Its interior frieze, like that of Apollo Sosianus, portrayed Romans and barbarians in conflict; its podium steps, like those of the temple of the Deified Julius, served as rostra. It is rare among Roman temples in being peripteral; *i.e.*, its columns go all the way round. Tiberius also, between A.D. 7 and 10, restored the temple of Concord at the west end of the Forum, dedicating it to Concordia Augusta, and made of it a museum.

Augustus embellished Rome, and his own glory, with his new Forum, a portico, his arch, his grandiose mausoleum, an Altar of Peace, and, in addition, parks and gardens, baths, a great library, markets, granaries, docks, and warehouses.

Ten years after another of Augustus's dynastic hopes, Marcellus, died in 23, Augustus dedicated a theater in his memory opposite the temple of Apollo Sosianus. There were theatrical masks in its keystones as there were in Augustus's house on the Palatine. It held 16,000, and in its architecture and building materials anticipated the Colosseum. Vases placed mouth-outward under the marble seats improved the acoustics. The top story was removed in the twelfth century and replaced with princely apartments. In the same year was built, with portico and cryptoporticus, the theater of Balbus, paid for by a general who had conquered Libyan tribes for Augustus. A rearrangement of the fragmentary Marble Plan of Rome places the theater under the Palazzo Mattei Paganica, in the Campus Martius. The Emperor took a great interest in the theater, as he should have: his whole life was staged. His dying words were said to have been, "Have I played well my part in life's farce?" Meanwhile Augustus himself lived in ostentatious simplicity in a modest house on the Palatine and encouraged the cult of antique austerity by restoring the hut of Romulus.

In the so-called House of Livia on the Palatine, one of the rooms is decorated with swags like those on the inner wall of the Ara Pacis. Augustus's own house, which adjoined, contained, besides the previously mentioned décor of masks, more swags—pine cones this time—also matched on the Ara Pacis, and a sanctuary of the hearth goddess Vesta. It is, of course, no accident that Augustus built his temple to his patron, Apollo, next to his own house.

One of the most remarkable houses of Augustus's time is the one under the Villa Farnesina, on the Trastevere side of the Tiber. The ancient villa, a vast rectangle with an ample exedra on the river side, was half-excavated in 1878–79, its stuccoes and frescoes removed to the Terme Museum and the area filled in. The house *may* have been built by Agrippa for the young Marcellus's marriage to Augustus's teen-age daughter, Julia: the decorative style fits this time. After Marcellus died in 23, Augustus married Julia to the middle-aged Agrippa. This may have been their second-hand honeymoon villa. The themes of its décor are Bacchic initiation, love, marriage, and genre scenes. In the stuccoes are sacred landscapes, initiation scenes, and a curious cautionary panel in which Phaethon asks his father Apollo for the loan of his

chariot, which he will drive recklessly to destruction. Julia
was as wild as Phaethon, but her father was not as lenient as
Apollo: she died in exile. The frescoes continue the Dionysiac
theme, but there are also intimate views of daily life: a
charming girl in lilac (Fig. 6.3) decants perfume; a bride
sits with her husband on their marriage bed; but a companion piece, perhaps more to Julia's taste, portrays profane love:
a prostitute making love in the presence of a male and a
female slave. A fresco of Aphrodite—with a flower—Cupid,

FIG. 6.3   Rome, villa under Farnesina, girl decanting perfume.
(Terme; Istituto Centrale per il Catalogo e la Documentazione)

and Persuasion continues the erotic theme. Julia, so often married, was notorious for extramarital affairs. "Yet why is it," someone asked, "that your children always look like your husband?" "I never take on passengers," she replied, "until I have the cargo safe in the hold." One whole bedroom, with striking black walls, portrays genre scenes of crime and punishment, featuring the judgments of the pharaoh Bocchoris, an Egyptian Solomon: these return to the cautionary tale motif of the Phaethon panel. In the riverside exedra are seascapes; and motifs of theatrical masks, perhaps suggesting that Julia inherited her father's passion for the theater.

Another famous wall painting of the 20s B.C., by one Studius, is the garden fresco discovered at the villa of Livia at Prima Porta, just north of Rome, on Rome's birthday, April 21, in 1863, and detached and removed to the Terme in 1951/2. It came from an underground dining room and gives a romantic, imaginative view into an orderly park—an earthly paradise—(Fig. 6.4), with trees, shrubbery, flowers, and birds. The earthly paradise is also, being Roman, a domesticated landscape: one of the birds is caged, and neat fences, of marble and cane, enclose the park. The trees in-

FIG. 6.4   Prima Porta, Villa of Livia, garden fresco.
(Terme; Istituto Centrale per il Catalogo e la Documentazione)

clude the oak (the civic crown was of oak leaves), the cypress, the palm (symbol of victory), the pine (whose cones figure elsewhere, as we have seen, in Augustan art). There are fruit trees also: quince, fig, pomegranate, cherry. The shrubs include laurel, another Augustan leitmotif. Livia's laurel was miraculously provided: a dove arrived carrying it in its beak; from its leaves the wreaths for triumphators were made. There are also myrtle, oleander, box, viburnum, ivy (associated with Bacchus and Hercules), and the acanthus, motif of the ubiquitous Augustan Corinthian capitals. The flowers shown are rose, poppy, iris, and chrysanthemum. Among the thirty species of birds are thrush, blackbird, nightingale, oriole, stilt, siskin, bunting, sparrow, flycatcher, wall-creeper, jay, partridge, dove (the laurel-bearer), and quail. No predators appear, for this is a landscape of Augustan peace, a magic time: in this garden, so real that precise identifications are possible, there are no seasons: flowers bloom and fruit ripens, all at the same time.

A terrace of the Prima Porta villa also housed the famous over-life-size statue of Augustus, now in the Vatican (Fig. 6.5: he was five feet seven; the statue is six feet nine). It epitomizes the Augustan program. Its ultimate model is classical Greek: Polyclitus' Doryphoros (Spear-bearer). The hairstyle and cock of the head imitate Alexander the Great; the Cupid at Augustus's feet alludes to his alleged descent from Venus, and perhaps also to his grandson Gaius. It acts as strut, implying a bronze original (marble needs propping; bronze does not), and is probably a copy made at Augustus's death in A.D. 14 of an original of 20–17 B.C. But the peak of propaganda is reached on the breastplate: at the top, celestial divinities—the protective sky-god, the Sun in his chariot, ushering in a new age. In the center, a Parthian gives back (a historical fact of 20 B.C.) to a uniformed Roman (Tiberius conceived as Mars) the standards captured from Crassus in

FIG. 6.5   Rome, Prima Porta Augustus. (Vatican)

53.* On the sides are personifications of Provinces pacified under Augustus, perhaps Dalmatia and Gaul; also Augustus's patron Apollo, with Diana. At the bottom is the fruitful earth, with two children, as on the Tellus panel of the Ara Pacis (see below).

At Augustus's death Rome was at last an Imperial metropolis: the city of brick had become a city of marble. Rome had gained grandeur, and lost freedom in the process. Toward the assessment of the gains and losses, the excavators' discoveries in Augustus's Forum, at his arch, in his mausoleum, and particularly in the difficult and ingenious recovery and reconstruction of his Altar of Peace have made the most important contributions.

Ever since 1911, Corrado Ricci had dreamed of excavating the site of Augustus's Forum (see Fig. 5.14), known to lie to the northeast of and at right angles to Caesar's, overlaid by modern construction. In 1924 Mussolini gave him his chance, and by 1932, when the Via dell' Impero was opened with Fascist pomp (see Fig. 5.13), the Fora of Caesar, Augustus, Nerva, and Trajan had all yielded up secrets to the archaeologist's spade.

Of Augustus's Forum, when Ricci began to dig, the most conspicuous part was the firewall at the back, separating it from the fire-trap slums of the Subura, ancient Rome's red-light district. The firewall is over 100 feet high, the exposed parts in travertine, the rest in *perperino* and *sperone*, the traditional Italic building stones of the period. This use of local materials, combined, as Ricci was to discover, with

* According to another interpretation, the uniformed figure is Romulus, the statue was originally set up in the temple of Athena in Pergamum, Asia Minor, and the pacified provinces are Galatia and Armenia. Still another view is that the implied deification would have been impossible in Augustus's lifetime, and the breastplate reliefs would have been impracticable in bronze; hence we have here a marble original, commissioned for Livia's villa; and it will have held a sprig of her famous laurel in its outstretched hand.

marble, is the symbol of the compromise, the amalgam of Italic and Greek materials, methods, and forms, which is the hallmark of the Augustan Age.

When the buildings cluttering the site had been cleared away, the plan (Fig. 6.6) was found to be based upon that of Caesar's Forum: a rectangular portico with a temple at the back. But the rectangle was enriched at the sides with curves, as at Palestrina earlier and in Bernini's portico in front of St. Peter's later. Each of the hemicycles had, let into the walls on two levels, niches two feet deep, big enough to hold statues of half life size, and above them Caryatids (copies of those which upheld the south porch of the Erechtheum in Athens), and, in shields, heads of Juppiter Ammon (who first greeted Alexander the Great as a god). Excavations in the south hemicycle as early as 1889 had turned up fragments of drapery in Carrara marble, and bits of inscriptions which, in combination with literary evidence, gave to the great Italian epigraphist Attilio Degrassi the clue to the subjects of the statues. The inscriptions, called *elogia*, recorded the *cursus honorum*, or public career, of a set of heroes, triumphing generals, or other prominent early Romans. The central figure in the south exedra was Romulus (also on the Altar of Peace). Three other examples are Aulus Postumius, who, with the help of Castor and Pollux (the household gods of the Julian clan), beat the Latins at the battle of Lake Regillus in 496, and built his divine helpers a temple in the Forum; Appius Claudius the Blind, who built the Appian Way (312 B.C.) and an aqueduct; and Sulla—nabobs and builders all. But there was space in the two levels of hemicycle niches, and in others hypothetically restored in the portico's rectilinear wall, for over fifty statues with *elogia*.* So Degrassi sought other stones similarly inscribed: some turned up in the most unlikely places.

One had been used as a marble roof tile of Hadrian's

---

* At least one scholar thinks the upper level contained trophies, not statues.

Fig. 6.6   Rome, Forum of Augustus, model by I. Gismondi. (Fototeca)

Pantheon; it was in the Vatican collection. Another was found in a vineyard near Rome's north gate, the Porta del Popolo. The former immortalized one Lucius Albinius, who took the Vestal Virgins in his wagon to Caere for safety when the Gauls were threatening Rome in 387 B.C. The latter was of Sulla's great rival Marius, the friend of the people. The dimensions, letter heights, and letter styles of both made their origin in Augustus's Forum extremely likely. A set of seven more had been known since the seventeenth century or earlier as coming from the site of the Forum of Arezzo, ancient Arretium, in Tuscany. The texts of some of these turned out to be copies of *elogia* from the Forum of Augustus. This justified the inference that, in this matter of a Hall of Fame, provincial cities imitated the metropolis. Thus those *elogia* from Arezzo for which no Roman prototype had been found might yet give a clue to what the Roman collection had once contained. This inference enriches the list by the names of Manius Valerius Maximus, conciliator of class struggles, and Rome's first dictator (494 B.C.); Lucius Aemilius Paullus, one of the greatest *triumphatores* of them all, who beat the Macedonians at Pydna in 168 B.C., and symbolized the union of Roman traditions with Hellenism, as Augustus aspired to do; Tiberius Sempronius Gracchus, father of the reforming Gracchi; and Sulla's lieutenant Lucius Licinius Lucullus, whose brother was responsible for the terraces and hemicycles at Palestrina.

The south hemicycle and portico, then, ingeniously connected Augustus's name with a set of nabobs, builders, successful generals, philhellenes, and men remarkable for piety to the gods or popularity with the masses. What of the north hemicycle? Here Ricci discovered the *elogium* of Rome's and Augustus's legendary ancestor, *pius Aeneas* himself, who was placed centrally, opposite Romulus, in the north exedra, and appears on the Altar of Peace; a set of the Kings of Alba Longa; Caesar's father; Marcus Claudius Marcellus, Augustus's much beloved heir, whose untimely death Vergil movingly mourns in the *Aeneid*, and whose ashes lay in Augustus's mausoleum; and Nero Claudius Drusus, Augustus's stepson, who also is figured, like Aeneas and Romulus, on the Altar of Peace. The Hall of Fame on this side of the portico was apparently intended to connect the legendary Kings of Alba and Rome with the Julio-Claudian dynasty. And the climax of it all was yet to come. At the end of the north portico Ricci excavated a square room with a pedestal at the back. On the pedestal he found a cutting for a colossal foot, seven times life size (Fig. 6.7). Forty feet up the back wall were the put-holes for the struts of a huge statue. Whose? The Forum's temple was dedicated to Mars, but the place for the god is in his temple. The most likely candi-

FIG. 6.7   Rome, Forum of Augustus, colossal footprint. (Fototeca)

date is the *Dux* himself, Augustus, father of his country, in whom Roman history came, in more senses than one, to a full stop.

Medieval limekilns tell, as usual, how the rich marbles that decorated both portico and temple were broken up and melted down into whitewash, but three marble Corinthian columns sixty feet high give some idea of the temple's grandeur. Its podium, lofty in the Italic fashion, was not solid marble, simply tufa revetted or veneered with thin marble slabs, an economical, and, some might say, dishonest way of making a city of marble of the desired Hellenic appearance. The statue base at the back of the temple (which was apsidal to match the hemicycles in the porticoes), nearly 30 feet wide, would hold at least three figures. A relief in Algiers probably copies the cult group: it portrays Venus, Mars, and Julius Caesar. Mars Ultor has on his breastplate griffins, symbols of vengeance; on his epaulets, horns of plenty; on his helmet, a sphinx (Augustus's signet); on his shield, the civic crown. Caesar, descendant of Venus, has a hole in his head where his comet was inserted in metal. The pediment is represented on the Claudian Altar of Piety in the Villa Medici: it shows, from left to right, the Palatine personified, Roma, Venus with Cupid, Mars in the center, Fortuna, Romulus, and the Tiber personified. The temple itself was vowed, the literary sources tell us, at the battle of Philippi (42 B.C.) to Mars Ultor, avenger of the murder of Julius Caesar, and Caesar's sword was piously preserved as a relic in it. The Forum did not neglect the arts. Like Caesar's, and like Pompey's portico, it was a museum. It did service also for literature: we are told that lectures were delivered in the hemicycles. It was more than a Hall of Fame for Augustus and his family. In the temple, the Senate deliberated over war and peace and received foreign potentates; here aristocratic youth assumed the toga of manhood; here triumphators deposited their insignia. Thus Augustus made it a center for the army, the administration, and the conduct of foreign policy. It was a great dynastic showpiece, deliberately distanced from the everyday concerns of the Roman people. Begun in 37 B.C., the Forum took thirty-five years to finish. By 2 B.C. other propaganda devices—especially the arch, the Altar of Peace, Vergil's epic, Livy's history, and Horace's lyric—had, as we shall see, given the desired respectability to Augustus, the Prince of Peace.

It was the victory of Actium (31 B.C.), over the combined fleets of Antony and Cleopatra, that enabled Octavian to pass as the Prince of Peace. In 1888–89, in the old Forum, between the Temples of the deified Julius and of Castor, were excavated the footings of an arch, originally with a single passageway, later enlarged to three. This arch was identified from literary sources as the one erected by Augustus to commemorate that victory, enlarged later when another occasion for propaganda arose. The arch itself is a routine affair, with several precedents, though one might ponder the propriety of thus gloating over Antony, a former colleague and a Roman citizen. (Gamberini, the excavator, even found, in the bottom of square stone receptacles beside the arch, laurel seeds, which suggest that the tree of victory— previously mentioned in connection with the temple of the Deified Julius—was prominent in the landscaping of the arch.) But, given the Roman propensity in general, and Augustus's in particular, for propagandizing in stone, the question naturally arose what opportunity for self-advertisement the arch offered. The answer was not given until Degrassi published another book in 1947.

For many years archaeologists had believed that on the walls of the nearby Regia had been engraved the *Fasti Consulares* (lists of Roman consuls from the founding of the Republic and probably of the kings as well), and the *Fasti Triumphales* (lists of triumphing generals from Romulus to

19 B.C. I have remarked in another book * how much one can learn of a people by what they make lists of: Greeks, of Olympic victors; Americans, of baseball averages; Romans, of statesmen and military heroes). But in 1935 Brown's first study of the Regia proved that the part of its wall where the *Fasti* would have begun was masked, in the rebuilding of 36 B.C., by another structure, and that the space available, carefully measured for the first time by Brown, did not fit the surviving *Fasti*, which were discovered in 1546 and are still preserved in the Conservatori Museum. Clearly the Regia was not the place where the *Fasti* were inscribed. Since two-thirds of the extant fragments were found between the Temple of the Deified Julius and the Temple of Castor, and since their dimensions suited those of the footings of the Arch of Augustus, the inference was clear. It was on the arch (Fig. 6.8) that the consular *Fasti* were carved, and this is now the universally accepted opinion. They were displayed on either side of the lateral passageway, where pedestrians could read them, the consular lists framed by pilasters with a pediment above (reconstructed in the museum by Michelangelo), the list of *triumphatores* on the corner pilasters of the enlarged arch. The result of this display was again, as in Augustus's Forum, to connect the upstart Octavian with a more respectable or heroic past. His name appears twice among the *triumphatores* (the slab that referred to Actium is unfortunately missing) in a list that began with Romulus and contained the names of the greatest heroes of Roman history; in the consular lists his name figured twenty-four times. This collocation and repetition could do him no harm.

In the consular lists the names of Mark Antony and his family have suffered *damnatio memoriae;* that is, they have been first inscribed and then chiseled out. In the list of *triumphatores,* on the contrary, Antony's name is allowed to

* *The Roman Mind at Work* (Van Nostrand, Princeton 1958, reprint, Krieger, Huntington, N.Y. 1980).

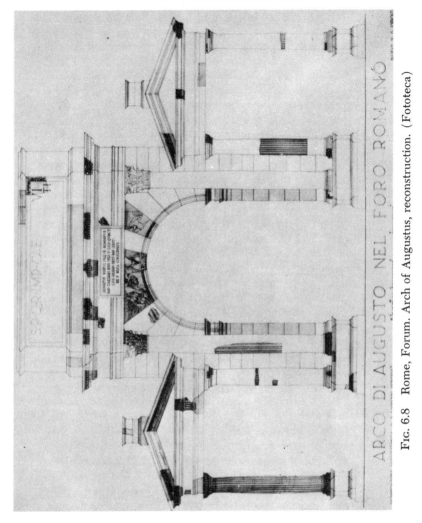

FIG. 6.8   Rome, Forum. Arch of Augustus, reconstruction.   (Fototeca)

stand. What is the legitimate inference from this? Clearly it is that the two lists were inscribed at different times, and that on the first occasion our *condottiere* felt a certain insecurity, which by the time of the second had disappeared. Literary sources date the second occasion in or shortly after 19 B.C., after the Roman standards disgracefully lost by Crassus at Carrhae had been recovered from the Parthians. In these eleven years or so the *condottiere* Octavian had become Augustus, the Reverend One, Expander of Empire, Father of his Country, Prince of Peace. Within those years Vergil's *Georgics* had cast an aura of beauty over Octavian's resettlement of veterans on the land; the *Aeneid* had connected this modern Aeneas, the pious one, the bearer of burdens, with his legendary ancestors; Horace's Roman Odes had praised Augustus's religious and moral reforms; and Livy's history had put into Augustan prose the lays of ancient Rome. Augustus could afford to be magnanimous to his enemies: he had seen to it that most of them were dead.

But it was not enough that the past be controlled and rewritten, and connected with the present on splendid monuments. Augustus must control the future, too; even after his death men must admire and worship him and his dynasty. To this end he began (literary sources tell us it was in 28 B.C.) in the Campus Martius a massive mausoleum (Fig. 6.9), which should be reminiscent in shape of the great Etruscan *tumuli* of centuries before, and in mass of such wonders of the world as the Mausoleum at Halicarnassus or the pyramids of Egypt. This monument, which through the centuries has been successively fortress, circus, park for fireworks displays, bull ring, and concert hall, was stripped to its gaunt core in 1935, as another part of the Fascists' Augustan plan to attach themselves to the memory of Augustus. The excavators, Giglioli and Colini, found within the circular ring of the mausoleum's vertical outer wall a series of concentric vaulted corridors in concrete, rising four stories or 143 feet,

FIG. 6.9   Rome, Mausoleum of Augustus. (Fototeca)

surrounding a central hollow cylinder where Augustus's ashes were to lie. A statue of the great deceased would have surmounted the cylinder, and the whole massive structure would have been heaped with earth and planted with cypresses. Before the door stood the bronze tablets bearing Augustus's autobiography—a calmly audacious fabrication of history, it has been justly called. In the corridor around the central cylinder were placed the marble containers for the urns of members of the dynasty. Some of the containers were found *in situ,* though their ashes—and, ironically, Augustus's as well—had long ago disappeared.

It was Augustus's fate to outlive his lieutenants, his relatives (see the family tree, Fig. 6.11), and all his favorite candidates for the succession. There lay, for example, the ashes of his stepson Drusus, his nephew, the young Marcellus, and his grandchildren, Lucius and Gaius; his lieutenant Agrippa; his sister Octavia, once given in a dynastic marriage to Mark Antony; his stepson Tiberius's one-time wife Vipsania Agrippina, divorced to give place to Augustus's daughter. Agrippina survived Augustus; who knows what

FIG. 6.10   Vienna, Kunsthistorisches Museum, Gemma Augustea.
(P. MacKendrick and H. Howe, *Classics in Translation*, 2, p. 370)

palace intrigue brought her ashes here? Her one-time husband's ashes rested here, too, and those of Germanicus, Tiberius's adopted son. (Tiberius and Germanicus also appear
on the Gemma Augustea, a large cameo in Vienna [Fig.
6.10], probably to be dated between A.D. 7 and 12. It assimi-
lates Augustus to Jupiter, portraying him in the company of
the goddess Roma, Italia, Cupid his ancestor(!), Victory,
Ocean, and either the civilized world or the Roman people
personified, which crowns him with laurel. Capricorn, his
zodiacal sign, is in a medallion over his head. Roman soldiers
raise a trophy, with Tiberius's zodiacal sign, Scorpio, on the
shield; it is uncannily like the famous World War II photograph of the flag-raising at Iwo Jima. The trophy will rise
over captured barbarians: a soldier savagely pulls a barbarian
woman by the hair.) Also in the mausoleum were the ashes
of the mad Emperor Caligula, of Claudius, Vespasian, Nerva,
and Septimius Severus's consort Julia Domna (for the Seve-

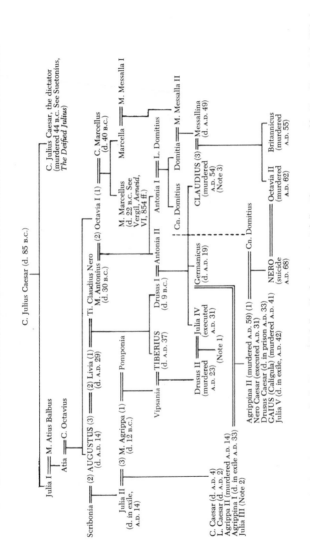

GENEALOGICAL TABLE OF THE JULIO-CLAUDIAN CAESARS

NOTICE that Julius Caesar left no descendants, but adopted his great-nephew Augustus. Connections were later traced by descent from his daughter Julia, his stepsons Tiberius and Drusus, or his sister Octavia. The names of emperors are in capitals. Numerals in parentheses show the order of marriages. Single lines indicate blood relationship; double lines, marriage; the dotted line, that the Cn. Domitius is the same person.

FIG. 6.11   Family tree of the Julio-Claudians.
(P. MacKendrick and H. Howe, *Classics in Translation*, 2, p. 370)

NOTE 1. A daughter of Drusus II and Julia IV married Rubellius Blandus; their son, Rubellius Plautus, was executed by Nero. NOTE 2. Julia III had a daughter who married Junius Silanus. NOTE 3. After the death of Messallina Claudius married his niece Agrippina II; there were no children.

ran dynasty, too, had need of respectability).

In stripping the mausoleum to its core, and building a deplorable neo-Fascist *piazza* on one side of it, an equally deplorable concrete shed for the reconstructed Altar of Peace on the other, the archaeologists of the thirties stripped Augustus, too, of his pretensions. Yet the decayed grandeur, the disappointed hopes, the inevitable passing of régimes, strike their own note of pathos and mortality:

> *"My name is Ozymandias, King of Kings:*
> *Look on my works, ye mighty, and despair."*

However unfortunate the building which protects it may be, the reconstructed Altar of Peace in the Field of Mars must be recognized as one of the great triumphs of Italian archaeology. Sculptured reliefs from this structure were first discovered, though not recognized as such, as long ago as 1568, in the underpinnings of what is now the Palazzo Fiano, on the Corso, Rome's *cardo*, which overlies the ancient Great North Road, the Via Flaminia. Other soundings were made in 1859 and 1903, and the reliefs were first recognized as belonging to the altar in 1879. But it was not until 1937–38 that G. Moretti carried through the incredibly ingenious and patient work that led to the almost complete recovery and reconstruction of the altar and the historic sculptured frieze surrounding it.

A colossal engineering problem arose because the Palazzo Fiano rested upon wooden piles driven into the water which in this part of Rome underlies most of the buildings. These piles, and reinforcements to them pinned down some of the marble blocks of the altar itself. To get the blocks out by ordinary methods, even if the water level had made it possible, would have caused the collapse of the building. Previous excavators had resorted to driving narrow, damp, dark tunnels, with incomplete results. Moretti resolved on more heroic measures; the solution is a credit to modern Italian engineering. The weightiest and worst-supported part of the palace lay directly over the altar; there were deep splits in the palace walls; only the extraordinary tenacity of the *pozzolana* mortar held them together. With infinite capacity for taking pains, the damaged parts of the walls were taken down and, by injection of liquid concrete, restored segment by segment, brick by brick. (The Italians call this process *cuci e scuci*, sew and unsew.) The subsoil was so uneven in profile and so soaking wet that a new masonry substructure was impossible. Moretti, in consultation with his engineers, determined to shift the weight of the palace wall onto a sort of enormous sawhorse or *cavalletto* (Fig. 6.12) of reinforced concrete. Holes were drilled sixty-five feet to a firm footing and filled with concrete; on this were built concrete piers to support the legs of the sawhorse. Between each pier and the corresponding leg was inserted a hydraulic jack (*martinetto*) adjustable to suit the various stresses exerted by the bearing walls. A grid of steel girders ran from pier to pier for reinforcement.

Once the corner of the building was supported by the concrete sawhorse, the problem was only half solved, for water covered the altar up to the top of the outside steps. Pumping was labor in vain; it would only have weakened the substructure of the palace and adjoining buildings. What were needed were dikes, to keep the water out while the area inside them was emptied. But a cement dike was impossible, because of the maze of water, gas, and sewer mains, heat, power, and light-conduits which, at all levels and in all directions, crisscrossed the subsoil of this busy part of modern Rome. A trench about 5 feet wide was dug, with a 230-foot perimeter. From a horizontal pipe laid in it, fifty-five three-inch pipes ran down vertically at equal intervals to a

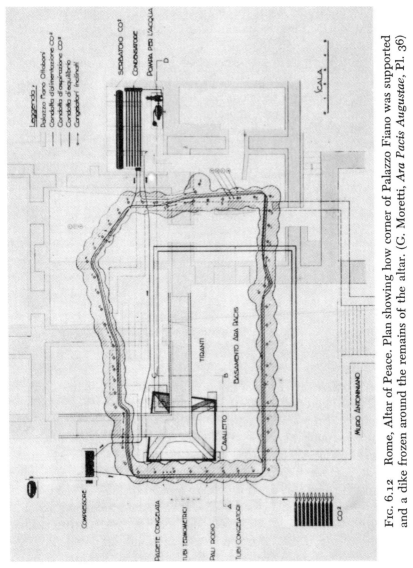

FIG. 6.12   Rome, Altar of Peace. Plan showing how corner of Palazzo Fiano was supported and a dike frozen around the remains of the altar. (G. Moretti, *Ara Pacis Augustae*, Pl. 36)

depth of 24 feet. Into these pipes was pumped carbon dioxide under a pressure of eighty atmospheres. Radiation from the refrigerant in the vertical pipes froze the surrounding muddy earth, and the impenetrable dike was a reality. The water inside covering the altar was then pumped out, and all the architectural blocks and fragments could be removed. Thus succeeded one of the most difficult and delicate excavations ever made. All was finished to meet a deadline, the bimillennary of Augustus's birth, September 23, 1938.

What Moretti now had to work with in his reconstruction was not only the slabs and fragments he had just extracted, but also the finds from previous excavations going back to 1568 (Fig. 6.13). Over the intervening years these had been scattered. Most of the 1568 finds had been sawn into three lengthwise (for the slabs were over two feet thick, too heavy for easy transport) and shipped to Florence to the Grand Duke of Tuscany, who then owned the Palazzo Fiano site in Rome. One slab was in the Vatican Museum, another in the Villa Medici (seat of the French Academy in Rome), still another in the Louvre. The finds from the 1859 dig had also been kept unrestored in the palace, and then transferred to Rome's Terme Museum. One slab was found in re-use face down as a cover for a tomb in Rome's Church of the Gesù.

These were all decorative elements. Under the Palazzo Fiano still remain the tufa footings and some of the travertine pavement (Fig. 6.14). These, though they were not removed, made it possible to visualize and reconstruct the plan. The altar itself, in the center of its enclosed platform, proved to be U-shaped, with the open end of the U facing west, toward the Campus Martius, and approached by a flight of steps. The whole was fenced off by a marble wall about thirty feet square and sixteen feet high with wide doorways on east and west. Since the pavement sloped, and there was provision for drainage, the inference was warranted that

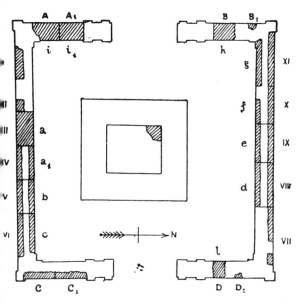

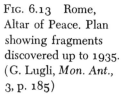

Fig. 6.13 Rome, Altar of Peace. Plan showing fragments discovered up to 1935. (G. Lugli, *Mon. Ant.*, 3, p. 185)

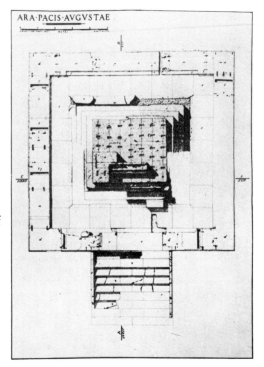

Fig. 6.14 Rome, Altar of Peace. Plan showing results of Moretti's excavation, still *in situ* under the Palazzo Fiano. (Moretti, *op. cit.*, Pl. 5)

the altar was originally open to the sky.* Each face of the enclosure wall bore two wide horizontal decorative bands separated by narrower bands, on the outer face, of meanders, on the inner, of palmettes. On the outer face the wide upper band bore a frieze with over 100 figures; the lower one motifs from nature: acanthus scrolls, bunches of grapes, the swans of Augustus's patron Apollo, and a lively population of small animals. The inner face carried, above, a motif of swags of fruit festooned between ox-skulls (*bucrania*); below, a series of long, narrow, recessed, vertical panels, giving the effect, in marble, of a wooden fence. Many of the slabs were found where they fell and were easily fitted into their proper place in the reconstruction (Fig. 6.15). Of the slabs in museums casts were taken. Thanks to careful observation of joins, repeats of floral motifs, the identity of historic figures, veins in the marble, and treatment of unexposed surfaces, these slabs, too, found their proper places. The job was done in the workrooms of the Terme Museum, with twenty-four large cases of fragments to work with, plus the full slabs and casts. The altar was finally rebuilt on the banks of the Tiber next to Augustus's mausoleum.

The result was worth the effort, for the Altar of Peace is universally acknowledged to be the greatest artistic masterpiece of the Augustan Age, blending Roman spirit with Greek forms, occupying in Roman art the same exalted position as the Parthenon frieze in Greek, and destined to inspire, as we shall see, many monuments with historic subjects in the following decades and centuries.

The figured upper panels on the enclosure's outer face are the most interesting part of the monument. On the north and

* In 1980, German archaeologists working in Rome unearthed, incised in the pavement of what was in antiquity a square adjoining the Ara Pacis, an enormous calendar-sundial, measuring 520 by 244 feet (Domitianic, but an Augustan version underlies it), inscribed with the names of the signs of the zodiac in Greek, and of the months in Latin. Its gnomon (pointer—a 100-foot obelisk) was so placed that its shadow fell across the Ara Pacis on Augustus's birthday.

Fig. 6.15   Rome, Altar of Peace, G. Gatti's reconstruction. (MPI)

Fig. 6.16   Rome, Altar of Peace, frieze with portrait of Augustus. (MPI)

south faces a procession moves westward. It is imagined as turning the corner of the enclosure and entering the doorway to sacrifice at the altar. The heads on the original north (now west) side were heavily restored in the Renaissance, but the fasces, the laurel crowns, the senatorial shoes and rings, the cult objects carried make it clear that the procession is of magistrates and priests. The original south (now east) side, which faced the city, must have been considered the most important half, and here, indeed, many historical figures of Augustus's family and court have been identified. It is noteworthy how the division of the friezes into dynastic and nondynastic halves parallels the arrangement of the Hall of Fame in Augustus's Forum.

The face in the upper right corner of the fragmentary left panel in Fig. 6.16, though cracked badly across the eye (for the whole weight of the Palazzo Fiano rested upon it for centuries), is recognizable from other portraits, from what remains of the profile, and from the treatment of the hair, as Augustus himself. The figures in the spiked caps to the far right are *flamines,* priests of Jupiter and Mars. The figure second to the left of the first *flamen,* all by himself in the background, is a spectator, the very type of the old Republican Roman. Lictors with the fasces precede the figure to the spectator's left of Augustus. This figure, then, must be the consul of the year, with the other consul on the other side of the Emperor.

But of which year? The consuls of the year 13 B.C., when the building of the altar was officially decreed, were Varus (who fell in the Teutoberg forest twenty-two years later) and Tiberius. Those of the year 9 B.C., when the altar was consecrated, were Drusus and Quinctius Crispinus. Now the slab pictured in Fig. 6.17 contains on its left edge, on either side of the veiled background figure with her finger on her lips (who is Augustus's sister Octavia) a family group. This has been identified almost certainly as Drusus (in uniform,

FIG. 6.17 Rome, Altar of Peace, frieze with family group of Julio-Claudians. (MPI)

FIG. 6.18 Rome, Altar of Peace, frieze probably portraying Agrippa, Julia, and Livia. (MPI)

with short tunic) and his wife, Antonia Minor, holding their
son, Germanicus, by the hand. Drusus can hardly be in two
places at once. Therefore the consuls on the earlier slab are
those of 13 B.C., and the whole procession is imagined as
that of the altar's *constitutio,* when the marble version was
not yet finished, not yet, perhaps, even begun. This hypothesis explains the treatment of the enclosure's inner face,
where the recessed panels represent a temporary wooden
fence. The swags in marble relief, of barley, grapes, olives,
figs, apples, pears, plums, cherries, pine cones, nuts, oak
leaves, ivy, laurel, and poppy—all the riches of a fertile Italy
at peace—were originally painted, like della Robbia terracottas, against a blue background. They must have been
intended to render the natural festoons swinging in the open
air against the blue sky. The *paterae,* or sacrificial bowls, in
two alternating patterns of gilded marble, which hang above
the swags, must be imagined as suspended from an upper
crossbar.

The persons in Fig. 6.18 are of the greatest historical
interest. The tall man with a fold of his toga over his head,
whose careworn face and pronounced Roman nose make a
recognizable portrait, can be identified from other likenesses
as Augustus's lieutenant Agrippa, acting as Pontifex Maximus. The child clinging to his toga is then one of his sons,
Gaius or Lucius. Gaius, the elder, born in 20 B.C., would
have been, in 13, of the age represented here; a modern
symbol of Aeneas's son Ascanius, or Romulus, the son of
Mars. The woman in the background with her hand on his
head would then be Gaius's mother, Julia, Augustus's daughter, whom he was later to banish for her immoral conduct.
The older woman in the foreground, the most carefully
wrought female figure in either frieze, would then be Julia's
stepmother, the redoubtable Empress Livia.

The family group to the right of Drusus in Fig. 6.17 is
also pregnant with history. The shapely woman with her

hand on the small boy's shoulder is identified as Antonia Major, Mark Antony's daughter by Octavia. The small boy grasping a fold of his uncle Drusus's cloak grew up to father the Emperor Nero. The girl to the spectator's right of the small boy is his sister Domitia; her father, Lucius Domitius Ahenobarbus, later commander of the Roman army in Germany, has his hand raised over her head. The elderly background figure with the kindly, lined face is perhaps Maecenas, Augustus's secretary of state for propaganda, the patron of Vergil and Horace.

The whole atmosphere of the procession is very Italian, quite intimate and informal, without central focus. Its members face in all directions and are so incorrigibly chatty that Octavia must command silence, finger to lips. Here, in these realistic groups, are the living likenesses of some of the men and women whose ashes later lay in Augustus's mausoleum, of some of the men and women who made a Golden Age. Here are the pages of history made flesh, and here are all the basic ideas of the Augustan program: the pretense of the revived Republic, in the consuls and lictors; the emphasis on religion, in the *flamines* and the veiled Pontifex; the dynastic hopes, in little Gaius; the subvention of literature, in Maecenas.

The east and west ends of the enclosure each contain, on either side of the doorways, a figured panel, four in all, of which two are well preserved. The one to the right of the main (west) entrance portrays a grave, bearded figure (Fig. 6.19), veiled, like Augustus, and offering sacrifices, with the aid of two acolytes, upon a rustic altar before a small temple containing tiny figures of the Penates as Castor and Pollux, whose connection with the *gens Iulia* we have already noted. The sow in the lower left corner is the famous one with the thirty piglets, whose discovery was to tell Aeneas where to found his city. (What purported to be the original sow and all the piglets, pickled in brine, was on display in a Latin town in Augustus's age.) From the sow the inference is that the bearded figure is Aeneas; he symbolized the past of Rome, and the ancestry of Augustus.

The panel to the left of the east entrance (Fig. 6.20) has as its central figure a full-breasted woman, whose face closely resembles the Livia of the south frieze. She has fruits in her lap, chubby naked babies in her arms, a miniature cow and a sheep at her feet, grain and poppies behind her. She is flanked by obviously allegorical figures of Air (riding a swan) and Water (riding a sea monster). Fresh water gushes from an amphora in the lower left corner; a salt-water harbor (indicated by waves, and perhaps the arch in the background) is at the lower right. Surely this is *Saturnia Tellus,* the fruitful earth of an Italy at peace, which Vergil sang of in the *Georgics,* rich in crops, flocks, and herds, but fruitful most of all in *men.* Of the two fragmentary panels, the west one is restored as a scene of Mars, the shepherd, the wolf, and the twins Romulus and Remus. (The Mars was acquired from a private owner in Vienna, whose Roman art dealer had told him it came from the Palazzo Fiano.) The east one, the least well preserved of all, probably represented the goddess Roma seated upon a trophy of arms, like Britannia on an English penny. Thus one pair of end panels is symbolical, while the other is mythological; the processional frieze deals with contemporary history. The whole makes a tripartite arrangement which is artistically very satisfying. At the same time, victorious Rome, fruitful Italy, the remote founder, and the first king, are all symbolically related here, as in other Augustan monuments, to the contemporary scene and the fortunes of the dynasty.

After the grandeur of the enclosure, the decoration of the altar itself seems modest and unpretentious, perhaps deliberately so. Winged sphinxes support rich volutes, the graceful S-curves that bound the altar table on either side. Beneath, there is a sacrificial scene, with the six Vestal Virgins neatly

FIG. 6.19 Rome, Altar of Peace. Aeneas sacrificing. (MPI)

FIG. 6.20 Rome, Altar of Peace. Tellus or Italia. (MPI)

arranged in order of size. In the sacrificial scene itself, the victims are a steer, a heifer, and a fleecy sheep. The attendants carry the sacrificial knives, platters, pitchers, and other paraphernalia. One twists the horns of the steer, another the tail of the heifer, to keep them moving. Altar and enclosure together provide our most complete visual record of a Roman state religious ceremony. And the whole complex, with its religiosity and historicity, is prolific of descendants: the Arch of Titus, the Cancelleria reliefs (to be discussed in Chapter 9), Trajan's Column (to be discussed in Chapter 10), his arch at Beneventum, the Arch of Constantine, the Column of Marcus Aurelius, the Arch of Septimius Severus (to be discussed in chapter 12). It is the prototype of them all, and the most masterly: tranquil, unpretentious, stately yet intimate, delighting in nature, perfectly balanced between country and city, perfectly symbolizing the Augustan Peace, when men would beat their swords into plowshares and study war no more. But within 100 years the altar began to be neglected. Perhaps, looking behind the façade, some old Republicans were moved to ask, "Where is the Altar of Liberty?"

A Forum, an arch, a tomb, a gem, an altar: taken together, as recent archaeology has revealed them to us, they epitomize the Augustan Age. In the Forum and the arch, the past recaptured, and pressed into the service of the régime. In the altar, the heroic and warlike past implicit in the orderly and peaceful present. In the tomb, posterity, the future generations, invited to marvel at the dynasty and what it has wrought. Behind all this, we can see that Augustus, the most ruthless power politician of them all, was simply continuing the careers of the great captains and dynasts of the past, like Caesar, Pompey, and Sulla. The refulgence of the monuments but reflects his monolithic control of the state, his cracking open of the seams of the old régime. In the history of art and architecture, Augustus's contribution is the applying of a standardized scheme of décor, as he applied a standardized scheme of administration, to the whole Empire. Henceforward Rome is the producer. She crystallized the styles and reexported them to the world which lay at her feet. Next we shall see how the Julio-Claudian Emperors, from Tiberius to Nero, exploited what Augustus had begun.

7

Hypocrite, Madman, Fool, and Knave

Roman historians branded the Julio-Claudian successors of Augustus—Tiberius (A.D. 14–37), Caligula (37–41), Claudius (41–54) and Nero (54–68)—as a hypocrite, a madman, a fool, and a knave. The hypocrite spent millions rehabilitating Asia Minor after an earthquake; the madman provided Ostia with a splendid aqueduct, the fool built for the same city a great artificial harbor; the knave rebuilt Rome—after burning it down first, his enemies said—with a new and intelligent city plan. But it would be easy to interpret the Julio-Claudian age as one of conspicuous consumption and conspicuous waste: there were many who fiddled before Rome ever burned. Thus both Tiberius and Caligula built on the Palatine grandiose palaces. Tiberius's early retirement to Capri meant that he never lived in the Domus Tiberiana. It lies in the northwest quadrant of the Palatine and has not been entirely excavated. But we know it had a peristyle, and the east cryptoporticus has been excavated: in its stuccoed vault are Cupids boxing. Graffiti naming the Egyptian divinities Isis, Serapis, and Apis may have some connection with the nearby Aula Isiaca, a Republican house under the Basilica of Domitian's palace, which contains frescoes with Egyptian themes. But Nero's Golden House, as we shall see, outdid them all. Tiberius's monstrous barracks of A.D. 21–23, measuring 1,430 by 1,235 feet, at the city wall, for the praetorian guard, introduces a sinister note. Claudius's Altar of Piety, modeled on Augustus's Altar of Peace, shows how derivative official art can be. Amid the complexity of this half-century, as archaeology reveals it to us, I have focused on limited examples from each reign: a stately pleasure dome of Tiberius by the sea at Sperlonga; a pair of extraordinary houseboats, probably Caligula's, from the Lake of Nemi; the curious subterranean basilica at the Porta Maggiore in Rome, which flourished briefly and mysteriously in the reign of Claudius; and Nero's fabulous Golden House.

In August 1957, road improvements near Sperlonga, on the coast about sixty-six miles southeast of Rome, offered G. Iacopi of the Terme Museum the opportunity for partially restoring, and closely examining, the ruins of a well-known villa there, commonly called the Villa of Tiberius. Making soundings near the villa in a wide, lofty cave fronting on the beach (Fig. 7.1), partly filled with sea water, Iacopi discovered that the natural cave had been made over into a *nymphaeum* or *vivarium:* a round artificial fish pool, with a large pedestal for statuary in the middle and artificial grottoes opening behind (Fig. 7.2). In the pool and the grottoes, buried under masses of fallen rock, Iacopi and his assistants found an enormous quantity—at last accounts over 5500 fragments—of statuary. The fallen rock gave a clue for dating at least one phase of the cave's existence and a possible confirmation of the popular name for the adjoining villa. For the historian Tacitus mentions that in A.D. 26, Tiberius, dining in a natural cave at his villa at Spelunca, was saved from being crushed under falling rock by the heroism of his

FIG. 7.1 Sperlonga, Cave of Tiberius. (G. Iacopi, *I ritrovamenti*, etc., Fig. 8)

FIG. 7.2 Sperlonga, Cave of Tiberius, reconstruction. (G. Iacopi, *op. cit.*, Fig. 18)

prefect of the praetorian guard, Sejanus, who protected him with his own body.° The cave of the near-accident at Sperlonga is probably the very one that Iacopi explored, though his discoveries suggest that there were additions after Tiberius's time.

The exploration was carried on under difficulties of several kinds. The Italian budget for archaeology is notoriously inadequate; the cave was subject to flooding from springs and lashing by winter storms; and it contained a dangerous quantity of ammunition and explosives stored there in World War II. The first difficulty was temporarily overcome by the generosity of the engineer in charge of the road building nearby; the second, by installing three pumps and building a dike; the third, by keeping an ordnance expert constantly on duty.

When the finds from the cave were first reported in the press, great excitement was caused by the announcement that among the finds were fragments of a Greek inscription giving the names of three sculptors (from Rhodes, where Tiberius spent the years 6 B.C. to A.D. 8 in retirement) mentioned by Pliny the Elder as having carved the Laocoön group now in the Vatican. The sculptors' names recur on Tiberius spent the years 6 B.C. to A.D. 2 in retirement) men- the Sperlonga fragments to a Laocoön group, but this has now proved vain. The current interpretation of the Sperlonga sculptures is based on a record kept by the road engineer of the findspots of the various fragments. They fall into

° After this near-tragedy Tiberius never again returned to Rome, but ruled from his villa on the Island of Capri, in the Bay of Naples, indulging, according to his enemies, in arcane perversions. The villa is perched atop a 1,000-foot cliff from which the Emperor allegedly had suspected conspirators thrown, "after prolonged and exquisite tortures" (Suetonius). The villa centers on a courtyard 100 feet square, with vaulted cisterns beneath. A huge exedra with a sea view was the audience chamber; to the north were sequestered private quarters, small (only four rooms) but richly decorated. The Emperor's mania for privacy produced Suetonius's gossip about unspeakable orgies. West of the villa is a massive structure with walls thirteen feet thick and dark vaulted rooms. It may have served as a signal tower for receiving news from Rome, as an astrological observatory, or as both: the suspicious monarch kept a court astrologer.

four major groups: (1) A Polyphemus group, from the right branch of the cave (Fig. 7.2), visible from the dining area in the center of the rectangular pool; (2) a Scylla group, from the center of the circular pool; (3) a pair of heroes, from the left side of the division between the pools; and (4) Odysseus and Diomedes quarreling over the Palladium (statue of Athena) from Troy, from the right-hand side.

(1) The Polyphemus, two-and-a-quarter times life size, has been strikingly restored (Fig. 7.3), on the evidence of a relief in Catania and a head in Boston, from an original of 180–159 B.C. The giant sprawls in his cave in a drunken stupor; companions of Odysseus are on the point of boring out his single eye with a sharpened stake; Odysseus intently supervises: his head bears a striking resemblance to that of the Laocoön by the same sculptors.

(2) The Scylla group is reconstructed from sections of a ship, six dogs' heads (one biting into a sailor's shoulder), five victims, two fishtails, and gobbets of flesh. It is held together by a representation of the hull of Odysseus' ship, with an anguished steersman who may be Odysseus himself. Scylla, with her girdle of yapping curs and her mermaid bottom half, was portrayed on the far side of the ship: a fragment shows her gigantic hand seizing a seaman by the hair. It is to this group that the inscription of the three Rhodian sculptors is attached.

(3) This is a pair of figures related to the celebrated Pasquino torso at the northwest corner of the Palazzo Braschi in Rome, to whose base in the fifteenth century lampoons (pasquinades) used to be affixed. The Pasquino belonged to a group representing either Menelaus with the body of Patroclus or Ajax with that of Achilles. Since the general theme of the Sperlonga sculptures seems to be an *Odyssey* in stone, the figures here are conjectured to be Odysseus with the limp body of Achilles.

(4) Odysseus and Diomedes are shown quarreling over

FIG. 7.3 Sperlonga, Cave of Tiberius, Polyphemus group, reconstruction. (Felbermeyer)

the Palladium (Fig. 7.4, the primitive statue of Pallas Athena on which Troy's safety depended). Pious Romans believed that Aeneas brought it to Rome. The Sperlonga version, from a Hellenistic original of about 150 B.C., is in the style of an earlier century.

The Sperlonga villa lasted down into the late Empire. An inscription, in letters that might be Severan, describes how a certain Faustinus adorned the grottoes with sculpture for the pleasure of his Imperial masters. Unless the inscription is a late copy, this Faustinus cannot be, as Iacopi thought, the friend of the poet Martial, who flourished under Domitian. NAVIS ARGO, an inscription in mosaic on the rock-cut prow of a ship at the entrance, is puzzling: is it the generic name for a ship, was Odysseus' ship so named, or was the mosaicist confused?

These four groups by no means exhausted the fancy or the purse of Tiberius and his successors: there is also Ganymede borne to heaven by an eagle (carved so as to be seen to best effect from below, and therefore possibly belonging to a pedimental treatment of the cave façade). There are heads of gods and heroes, satyrs and fauns, a charming Cupid trying on a satyr's mask, a delightful head of a baby with ringlets over its ears—all either in the fanciful, complex, sometimes tortured style of Hellenistic Pergamum and Rhodes or in Imperial copies thereof. The bizarre taste of the place has a counterpart in the Blue Grotto on Capri, which also held sculpture groups. Whether the taste is Tiberius's or that of later Emperors, it symptomatically reflects the gap between the ostentatious rich and the church-mouse poor that was one day to contribute to the Empire's fall.

The same fantastic extravagance marks our next finds. Seventeen miles southeast of Rome, cupped in green volcanic hills, lies the beautiful deep blue Lake of Nemi, the mirror of Diana. Here divers, as long ago as 1446, reported, lying

FIG. 7.4   Sperlonga, Cave of Tiberius. Head of statuette
of Athena. (Iacopi, *op. cit.*, Fig. 11)

FIG. 7.5
Lake Nemi,
Borghi finds
(1895) from
ships. (G.
Ucelli. *Le navi
di Nemi*, p.
19)

on the bottom in from sixteen to sixty-nine feet of water, two ships, presumably ancient Roman. A descent was made in a diving bell in 1535. Another attempt in 1827 used a large raft with hoists and grappling irons, and an art dealer tried again in 1895. All three efforts were chiefly successful in damaging the hulls, tearing away great chunks without being able to raise the ships to the surface. The 1895 attempt did, however, produce a mass of tantalizing fragments (Fig. 7.5): beams; lead water pipe; ball bearings; a number of objects in bronze, including animal heads holding rings in their teeth, a Medusa, and a large flat hand; terracotta revetment plaques, a quantity of rails and spikes, and a large piece of decking in mosaic. This treasure trove, displayed in the Terme Museum, naturally whetted appetites, not least Mussolini's. He determined to get at the ships by lowering the level of the lake, a colossal task undertaken eagerly by civil and naval engineers enthusiastic about classical civilization. The job was made easier, but no less expensive, because there existed an ancient antificial outlet, a tunnel a mile long, dating from the reign of Claudius, which could be used to carry off the overflow. The pumps were started on October 20, 1928, in the presence of the *Duce*. After various vicissitudes over a space of four years, the lake level was lowered seventy-two feet. By November 1932 the first ship was installed in a hangar on the shore, and the second (Fig. 7.6) lay exposed in the mud.

The ships proved to be enormous by ancient standards, of very shallow draft, very broad in the beam (one was sixty-six feet wide, the other seventy-eight) and respectively 234 and 239 feet long (Fig. 7.7). They were larger than some of the early Atlantic liners. Their 1100-ton burden gave them ten times the tonnage of Columbus's largest ship.

The task of freeing the ships of mud and debris, recording the finds level by level, reinforcing the hulls with iron, shoring them up, raising and transporting them to the special museum built for them on the lake shore proved in its way to be as great a challenge to Italian patience and ingenuity as the job of excavating the slabs and fragments of the Altar of Peace from under the Palazzo Fiano. There was always the danger of the ships' settling in the mud in a convex curve, springing the beams. The excavating tools used were made entirely of wood; iron would have damaged the ancient timbers. As each section of the hull emerged from the water which had covered it for so many centuries, it was covered with wet canvas to keep it from deteriorating.

The hulls proved to be full of flat tiles set in mortar. These overlaid the oak decking, and over these again was a pavement in polychrome marble and mosaic. Fluted marble columns were found in the second ship, suggesting a rich and heavy superstructure (Fig. 7.8). A round pine timber from the first ship, thirty-seven feet long and sixteen inches in diameter, with a bronze cap ornamented with a lion holding a ring in its teeth, proved to be a sweep rudder, one of a pair. It showed that these enormously heavy vessals (the decking material alone must have weighed 600 or 700 metric tons) were actually intended to be practicable, and to move about in the waters of the lake.

Clay tubes, flanged like sewer pipe to fit into each other, were arranged in pairs to make an air space between one level of deck and another. This suggests radiant or hypocaust heating, as in a Roman bath: these floating palaces, or temples, or whatever they were—perhaps both—had bathing facilities. Wooden shutters warrant the inference that the ships were provided with private cabins. A length of lead water pipe stamped with the name of Caligula has been used to date the ships to that reign (and indeed in some ways they accord well with Caligula's reputation for madness), but of course there is nothing to prevent lead pipe of Caligula's short reign (A.D. 37–41) from being used in Claudius's. Many scholars, on the evidence of the art objects

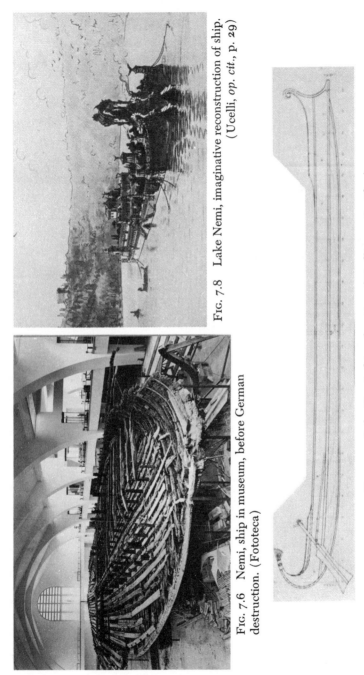

FIG. 7.8 Lake Nemi, imaginative reconstruction of ship. (Ucelli, *op. cit.*, p. 29)

FIG. 7.6 Nemi, ship in museum, before German destruction. (Fototeca)

FIG. 7.7 Lake Nemi, ship, elevation. (Ucelli, *op. cit.*, Pl. 4)

found, would date the ships in the latter reign, though D. E. Strong, inexplicably, called them Neronian.

Boards in the bottom of the hold were removable to facilitate cleaning out the bilge. This was done with an endless belt of buckets, some of which were found and are on display, restored, in the museum. Over the ribs of the hull was pine planking, then a thin coating of plaster, then a layer of wool treated with tar or pitch, finally lead sheathing clinched with large-headed copper nails.

The second ship had outriggers supporting a platform for the oarsmen, and a bronze taffrail decorated with herms—miniature busts tapering into square shafts. A number of mechanical devices of great technical interest was found: pump pistons; pulleys; wooden platforms (use unknown), one mounted on ball bearings, another on roller bearings; a double-action bronze stem valve (perhaps for use in pumping out the bilge), which had been welded at a high temperature (1,800° Fahrenheit); anchors, one with the knot tied by a Roman sailor still intact, another with a moveable stock, anticipating by over 1,800 years a similar model patented by the British Admiralty in 1851. Its use is to cant the anchor, giving it a better bite in the mud.

In 1944 the retreating Germans wantonly burned the ships in their museum. Their gear, stored in a safe place, survived. From careful drawings made at the time the ships were raised, models were made to one-fifth scale. They are now on display in the restored museum.

The ships did not contain within themselves clear evidence about what they were used for. Whether they had some religious purpose in connection with the nearby Temple of Diana, or were used as pleasure-craft, or both, they reflect, like the cave at Sperlonga, the mad extravagance that increasingly characterized the Roman Empire on its road to absolutism.

Rome's Porta Maggiore accommodates two highways, three superimposed aqueducts, and a baker's tomb. The latter, outside the walls as required by law, belongs here topographically but not chronologically: it dates from about 30 B.C. The baker, M. Vergilius Eurysaces, enjoyed under Octavian a government contract to supply bread; his tomb, handsomely revetted in travertine, shows he was proud of his trade. The aristocracy could boast with public buildings; the bourgeoisie had to make do with tombs like this. The cylinders (Fig. 7.9)—some upright, some horizontal, separated by an inscription in which his name figures prominently —are containers for flour. The frieze above unashamedly records the details of baking: weighing, milling, sifting, kneading, cutting, baking, weighing, distributing; the work is done by slaves in tunics, supervised by overseers in togas; toga-clad also are the magistrates to whom the loaves are finally consigned. We shall see the same pride in bourgeois pursuits in the house of Caecilius Jucundus and the shop of Verecundus, in Pompeii.

In 1917, on Rome's birthday, April 21, a landslip beside the Rome-Naples railway line outside the Porta Maggiore (see map, Fig. 12.16, 8) revealed, forty-two feet beneath the tracks, a hitherto unsuspected and most remarkable underground, vaulted, stucco-ornamented room, the "basilica." It provides a third major example of archaeology's contribution to our knowledge of the Julio-Claudian age. To protect the basilica against damage from seepage and vibration from trains—240 a day pass directly above—it was enclosed in 1951–52, at a cost of over $500,000, in a great box of waterproof reinforced concrete. Its footings were anchored nearly twenty-four feet beneath the level of the basilica pavement.

One entered the chamber in antiquity—it was always underground—down a long vaulted ramp which made a right-

FIG. 7.9   Tomb of Eurysaces. (Fototeca)

angle turn and emerged in a little square vestibule, whose skylight provided the basilica's only natural light. Beyond the vestibule was a vaulted nave (Fig. 7.10) ending in an apse, and two side aisles. The profiles of the piers upholding the vaults, and of the arches connecting the nave with the side aisles, are irregular; and the piers are set at eccentric angles (Fig. 7.11). This suggests a curious method of construction. A trench must have been dug through the surface tufa corresponding to the desired perimeter of the building. Then six square pits were dug, one for each pier, and the outline of the arches and doorways formed in the virgin soil. Then mortar was poured in. When it had set, the entrance corridor was dug and the interior of the basilica emptied of earth through the skylight in the vestibule. Then vault, piers, and walls were stuccoed. In the late Republic and after, Roman artisans showed great skill in ornamental stuccowork, a far cry from the wattle-and-daub in the primitive huts which is the remote ancestor of the refined work in the basilica. It is a symbol of how far on the road to sophistication Rome had traveled from her humble beginnings.

In the basilica the stuccowork is divided by moldings into squares, rectangles, and lozenges, filled with figures in low relief of great delicacy and elegance. Some are simple scenes of daily life, and many others are part of the standard repertory of Roman art, but the key motifs will bear, as we shall see, a single, serious interpretation. Not all scholars are in agreement on this point: one thinks the place is simply a summer retreat, another that its purpose was funerary. The apse, the focal point of the whole structure, was reserved for a special scene of central importance.

The central panel of the central vault shows a naked human figure, a pitcher in his hand, carried off by a winged creature. (The interior of the figure is eaten out; this is due not to vandalism but to the depredations of a parasitic insect

FIG. 7.10   Rome, subterranean basilica at Porta Maggiore, general view. (Fototeca)

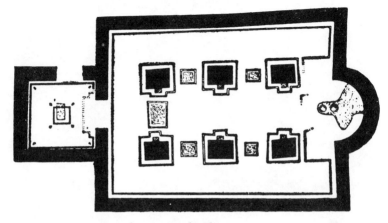

FIG. 7.11   Rome, subterranean basilica at Porta Maggiore, plan.
(*Legacy of Rome,* p. 407)

related to the termite.) In the four surrounding panels are
four other motifs. A hero wearing a lion's skin shoots with a
bow a monster guarding a maiden chained to a rock. A
beautiful, seated, half-naked woman cradles a statuette in
her left arm; a bearded middle-aged man stands before her.
A young man in a short tunic, carrying a leafy branch or a
shepherd's crook, leads off a woman by the hand. A veiled
female figure takes from a tree guarded by a serpent a
fleecy object to give to a man kneeling on a table nearby.
How are these scenes to be interpreted? Do they share a
common motif? According to the French Professor Jérome
Carcopino, they do.

The central subject is Ganymede borne heavenward to be
Jupiter's cupbearer. The hero with the lion's skin is Hercules
rescuing Hesione. The woman with the statuette is Helen
with the Palladium, the ancient image on which Troy's safety
depended; the wise Ulysses stands before her. Or it might
be Iphigenia, in faraway Tauris, about to bear past the
Thracian King Thoas the statuette of Artemis which will

release her brother Orestes from torment by the Furies. In the next panel, if the young man is carrying a branch, he is Orpheus bringing Eurydice back from Hades; if he is carrying a shepherd's crook, he is Paris kidnaping Helen. The veiled female is of course Medea getting the Golden Fleece for Jason. The common theme is deliverance. Ganymede, liberated from earthly ties, is borne on wings to the bliss of Heaven. Hercules can free Hesione because, according to some versions of the myth, he has been initiated into the mysteries. The statue, whether of Athena or of Artemis, guarantees the safety of the city or person who possesses it. Helen, in some accounts, can read the future and assuage men's pain; or, if the theme is Orpheus and Eurydice, we may recall that in an early version of the myth the ending was happy. Jason and Medea are freed from fear of the dragon through rites of magic initiation.

Does the great scene in the apse (Fig. 7.12) harmonize with the interpretation? In it, on the right, a graceful veiled woman, holding the lyre of a poetess, descends a cliff into the sea. She is pushed by a baby winged figure standing behind her. Beneath, waist deep in the water, a figure with a cloak outspread stands ready to receive her and escort her to the opposite shore. There, on another cliff, stands an imposing naked male figure, in his left hand a bow, his right outstretched in blessing. Behind him sits a young man thoughtfully supporting his head on his hand. Below in the sea yet another figure holds an oar and blows a horn in greeting. Any Roman intellectual would recognize the scene: it is Sappho, encouraged by Cupid, received by Tritons, blessed by Apollo, making the lover's leap to join her beloved Phaon for eternity. This is not suicide, but liberation from earthly love into an eternity of perfect harmony of the senses with the sublime and the supernatural. The scene is consistent with the others, and provides a further clue to the interpretation of the whole. For Pliny the Elder, in his

FIG. 7.12   Rome, subterranean basilica at Porta Maggiore, apse.
(Fototeca)

encyclopaedic *Natural History*, says that the myth of Sappho
and Phaon was made much of by a sect called neo-Pytha-
goreans, inspired by the number mysticism, and the belief
in immortality, of their founder, Pythagoras of Samos, who
flourished in the late sixth century B.C. These beliefs were
refined in the Hellenistic Age and taken up by heterodox
Roman intellectuals, like the splendidly named scholar P.
Nigidius Figulus, senator and clairvoyant, who at Octavian's
birth prophesied his world rule, but died in exile in 45 B.C.

This elegant underground chamber, so restrained and
literary in décor, so small in size (it measures less than
thirty by thirty-six feet) is just the place for a chapel for

such an élite and aristocratic sect of ancient Freemasons. The hypothesis is borne out by the discovery beneath the floor of the bones of a puppy and a suckling pig, the preferred *pièces de résistance* for a neo-Pythagorean cult meal, perhaps the meal that inaugurated the chapel.

And still other motifs in the stucco decoration strengthen the hypothesis, by stressing redemption, salvation, and initiation: a winged victory; a soul arriving in the Isles of the Blest; a woman with a flower, symbolizing Hope; a scene of Demeter, the earth goddess, and Triptolemus, the hero of agriculture, of whom much was made in the Eleusinian mysteries. Other reliefs show the reverse of the coin: the punishment of the uninitiate. The satyr Marsyas is flayed alive for presuming to challenge Apollo to a competition in music. The Danaids, for the crime of murdering their husbands, perform forever the useless labor of drawing water in perforated jars. There are other sinners: Medea with her slain sons; Pasiphaë, the monstrously adulterous Cretan queen; Phaedra, trying her wiles on her sinless stepson, Hippolytus, over-chaste votary of the maiden-goddess Artemis; King Pentheus murdered for scoffing at the Dionysiac mysteries; his mother, Agave, carries his severed head aloft in Bacchic frenzy. To these has not been given the true neo-Pythagorean vision of the truth; they are portrayed here to symbolize their doom to a private Hell of their own making.

Two long panels on either side of the spring of the central vault reinforce the general intellectual tone. In one, schoolboys recite their lessons before a seated schoolmaster with a ferule in his hand. In the other, the Muse of Tragedy attends the coming-of-age ceremony of a Roman adolescent. (Some interpret this scene as a marriage; if so, the sect will have allegorized it in some way.) We know that the sect was open to both sexes; reliefs in the wall panels of the basilica show men and women making offerings.

The stuccoes of the vault were in excellent condition when

found. (They have since suffered from dampness, now being corrected by air conditioning.) Also, they show no traces of addition or repairs, but the wall panels were desecrated in antiquity by vandals—the consoles for offerings ripped off, the lamps and chapel gear carried away. It looks as though the chapel had had a short life, and the cult a violent end. Will history provide a date? Tacitus mentions in his *Annals* a rich Roman, Titus Statilius Taurus, known to have owned property near the basilica, who fell foul of Claudius, was accused of practicing *magicas superstitiones,* and escaped his sentence by committing suicide in A.D. 53. The style of the stuccoes fits this date, the décor of the basilica fits the cult, its state when found fits Tacitus's story. We may suppose that everything within reach was looted, the chamber filled in, and probably never seen again until the spring day 1864 years later when the landslide by the railway revealed its existence.

In 1907 the German archaeologist F. Weege, following in the footsteps of Renaissance explorers of 1488, made his way through a hole in the wall of the Baths of Trajan, near the Colosseum (see map, Fig. 12.16, 9), to find himself in a labyrinth of underground vaulted corridors and rooms partly filled with rubble, which had once been part of an Imperial palace, the Golden House of Nero. Setting lighted candles at every turning to guide his way back, he explored as many as he could of the eighty-eight rooms of this small part of the palace complex, sometimes crawling with lighted candle over rubble that filled a room nearly to the vault, while spiders, centipedes, and other, nameless creatures scuttled away from him into the darkness.

The rooms had been filled with rubble by Trajan, with a twofold purpose: to make a firm substructure for his baths, and to continue the work of the Flavians in damning the memory of the conspicuous consumption and conspicuous waste of the hated Nero. Thirteen hundred and eighty-four years later, when the underground rooms were rediscovered, among the visitors was Raphael, who decorated a loggia in the Vatican Palace in the style of the fantastic paintings on Nero's walls. Since the buried rooms were grottoes, the paintings were "grotesques"—as often, the word has survived, while its history has been forgotten. Other visitors were Caravaggio, Velasquez, Michelangelo, and Raphael's teacher, Perugino. The names of many a famous artist are scrawled right across the face of the ornaments of the vaults. An Italian poem, written not long after the discovery of America, speaks of artists' underground picnics in the Golden House. The picnickers crawled on their bellies to enjoy their subterranean meal of bread, ham, apples, and wine.

The result of Weege's more scientific investigation was the working out of a new plan. The western half of the complex (Fig. 7.13) proved to be conventional, with the rooms grouped about a peristyle with garden and fountain. East of Room 5 on the plan, recent excavation has disclosed a nymphaeum with a mosaic of Polyphemus. Rooms 37 and 43 have alcoves: it is easy to imagine them as the Imperial bedchambers of Nero and his beautiful red-haired wife Poppaea. In Nero's bedchamber were hung the 1,808 gold crowns he won in athletic competitions in Greece, if competitions they can be called, when all the prizes were awarded to Nero in advance, and armed guards drove off all would-be rivals.

The eastern wing (Fig. 7.14) is more unorthodox in plan, and more interesting. The main approach opened into Room 60, the Hall of the Gilded Vault, so called from the ornate painted stucco ceiling, divided into round and rectangular fields in gilt, green, red, and blue, depicting mythological and erotic scenes, very different in tone from the restraint of

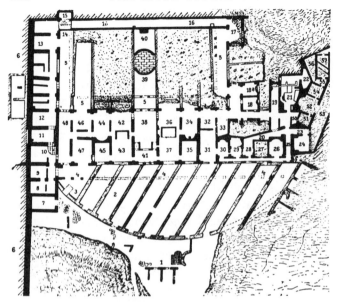

FIG. 7.13   Rome, Golden House, west wing.
(G. Lugli, *Roma antica*, p. 358)

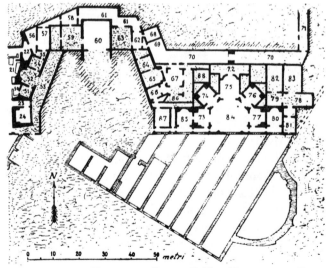

FIG. 7.14   Rome, Golden House, east wing.
(G. Lugli, *op. cit.*, p. 359)

the subterranean basilica. Hippolytus, off to the hunt, receives a letter containing incestuous proposals from his stepmother Phaedra. Satyrs rape nymphs, Venus languishes in the arms of Mars, Cupid rides in a chariot drawn by panthers. And yet we are told that the painting in this pleasure dome was done by the solemn dean of Roman artists, Fabullus himself, the John Singer Sargent of his day, who always painted in full dress, wearing his toga.

Room 70 is a vaulted corridor 227 feet long, with sixteen windows opening to the north in the impost of the vault, which is painted sky-blue as a *trompe l'oeil*. Seabeasts, candelabra, and arabesques, sphinxes with shrubs growing out of their backs, griffins, centaurs, acanthus leaves, Cupids, gorgons' heads, lions' heads with rings in their mouths, dolphins holding horns of plenty, winged horses, eagles, Tritons, and swags of flowers make up the riotous décor. In recesses in the walls, impressionistically painted landscapes and seascapes attempt the illusion of the out-of-doors. Halfway down the corridor the vault is lowered. Here it supported a ramp which led to the gardens above.

Room 84 is octagonal, lighted by a hole in the roof, anticipating, as we shall see, Hadrian's Pantheon. (A predecessor is a similar but smaller [eight-meter diameter] octagonal room with cupola, under the podium of Hadrian's temple of Venus and Rome, dated by its masonry to the late Republican or early Augustan period.) Perhaps this was the state dining room, described by ancient sources as hung on an axis and revolving like the world. Two German scholars have conjectured that the floor was on wheels and was moved by water power. Its ivory ceilings slid back and dropped flowers and perfumes on Nero's guests.

The most controversial room of all is the apsidal number 80, decorated with scenes from the Trojan War: Hector and Andromache, Paris and Helen, and Thetis bringing Achilles his shield. Nero was fascinated by the Trojan War: it was an

epic of his own composition on the fall of Troy which he re-
cited as Rome was burning. The recital took place at his
seaside villa at Antium, modern Anzio. It was filled with
such famous sculptures as the Apollo Belvedere in the Vatican, the Borghese gladiator in the Louvre, and the Maiden
of Anzio in the Terme. It had an onyx dado, and landscape
frescoes. What was in the Roman apse? Equivocal Renaissance reports place the finding of the Vatican Laocoön
somewhere in this area, the apse is of a size to fit the statue,
and the subject is appropriate to a room full of Trojan motifs.
The statue's baroque quality would have appealed strongly
to Nero's taste. This is the circumstantial evidence for Room
80 as the findspot of one of the most notorious statues of
antiquity. That this survey of the Julio-Claudian age should
approach its end, as it began, with mention of the Laocoön,
suggests how conventional was the repertory of Roman taste.

But a description of the rooms of the Golden House is
not quite the whole story. In 1954 the Dutch archaeologist
C. C. Van Essen published the results of careful probing in
the whole section of Rome for half a mile around the Colosseum, where he found traces of Nero's palace in a number of
places on the perimeter. For the Golden House was much
more than the complex of rooms just described. It was a
gigantic system (Fig. 7.15) of parks, with lawns, groves,
pastures, and a zoo. Over its central pool later rose the great
bulk of the Colosseum. Within these grounds, twice the extent of Vatican City, was a great Versailles in the midst of
the teeming metropolis. The eighty-odd rooms we have been
describing made up but one of several palaces in the
grounds. And an American, Miss E. B. Van Deman, working
from some very unlikely looking architectural blocks piled
beside the Temple of Antoninus and Faustina in the old
Forum, was able in 1925 to restore on paper (Fig. 7.16) the
monumental approach, over 350 feet wide, to the palace

FIG. 7.15   Rome, Golden House, reconstruction drawing of whole area.
(Fototeca)

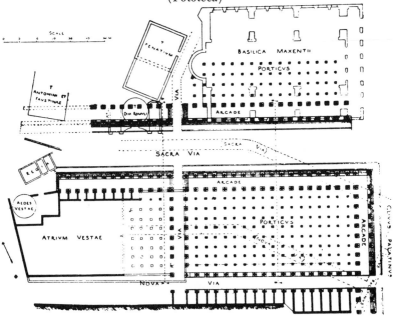

FIG. 7.16   Rome, the Neronian Sacra Via.
(E. B. Van Deman, *Mem. Am. Ac. Rome,* 5 [1925])

grounds from the old Forum and Palatine. It was a mile long, with arcades of luxury shops, and eight rows of pillars. Its plan is concealed today under mounds of dumped earth between the Hall of the Vestals and the Arch of Titus. Beside it rose a colossal statue of Nero, 120 feet tall, now marked by a pattern in the pavement. When Hadrian desired to remove the statue to make room for his Temple of Venus and Rome, it took twenty-four elephants to do the job. But decades before, his predecessors the Flavians had done what they could, with the Baths of Titus and the Flavian Amphitheater (the proper name of the Colosseum) to erase the memory of Nero's monstrous extravagance and turn his palace grounds to public use.

The four archaeological examples from the Julio-Claudian age discussed in this chapter were chosen for their intrinsic interest, not to illustrate a thesis. But they do prove a point all the same. Tiberius's *al fresco* dining room, with its monstrous and tortured statuary (even though some of it be later in date); Caligula's houseboats, with their incredibly heavy profusion of work in colored marble, mosaic, and bronze; Nero's Golden House, with its labyrinth of gaudy and overdecorated rooms of state, all testify to a decadent extravagance beyond Hollywood's wildest aspirations. By comparison, the cool, quiet taste of the subterranean basilica is an oasis and a relief, but even this is a commentary on Claudius's intolerance. And it has about it an air of holier-than-thou Brahminism, the furthest possible contrast with the warmth, the close contact with common people, which marked the Christianity that was to be preached in Rome not long after the basilica sect was outlawed. One cannot but marvel at the staying power of the organism that could survive this prodigality, this cleavage between class and mass, for over three centuries. But as we focus our attention upon the excesses of court and of metropolis, we ought not to forget that in the municipal towns of Italy and the Empire life went on, more modestly, quietly, and decently. Archaeology gives us precious proof of this in a pair of buried cities of the Flavian Age, Pompeii and Herculaneum.

8

The Victims of Vesuvius

One day in 1711 a peasant digging a well on his property in Resina, on the bay five miles southeast of Naples, came upon a level of white and polychrome architectural marbles, obviously ancient. This chance find led to the discovery of what proved to be the buried town of Herculaneum, destroyed in the eruption of Vesuvius on August 24, A.D. 79. Workmen digging in 1748 by the Sarno canal, nine miles farther along the bay, found bronzes and marbles on a site which an inscription, discovered fifteen years later, identified as Herculaneum's more famous sister city, Pompeii. Thus began a saga of excavation which has told the modern world more about ancient life than any other dig in the long history of archaeology, and this in two towns which have left almost no record in literature. In a few hours of a summer afternoon the eruption stopped the life of two flourishing little cities dead in its tracks: dinner on the tables, the wine shops crowded, sacrifices at the moment of being offered, funerals in progress, prisoners in the stocks, watchdogs on their chains. The townsfolk had not even time to gather their possessions. Ironically, going back for their little hoards of gold and silver spelled death for many of them, under the hail of pumice stone and ashes which asphyxiated (Fig. 8.1) or engulfed them. A particularly affecting cluster of victims, with their children and possessions, is preserved near the Nocera Gate. Several, struck down while trying to climb a stair in the House of Fabius Rufus (Insula Occidentalis, in the southwest corner of the city), were wearing gold rings and bracelets, and carrying a chest loaded with silver coins. At Herculaneum, on the afternoon of the eruption, rain turned the volcanic ash to mud, which solidified, burying the town thirty to forty feet deep. Electric drills and mechanical shovels are needed to dig there, so progress has been slow. Even Pompeii, under its shallower layer of pumice pebbles and light ash, is still only about three-fifths excavated.

For a century and a half after their rediscovery the two sites were treated almost entirely as a quarry for works of art, as a plaything for the various dynasties that misruled Naples, and as a romantic stop on the Grand Tour. The discovery of ancient artifacts here revolutionized the taste of Europe: Ludwig of Bavaria built a replica of a Pompeian house at Aschaffenburg; Winckelmann, the great Romantic art historian, conceived here many of his notions of the wonders of Greek art; and Casanova's brother copied some of the paintings, and did a brisk business in forgeries. Nelson's mistress, Lady Hamilton, was a frequent visitor: her husband was British ambassador to Naples. Goethe was impressed by Pompeii's smallness; Napoleon's marshal Murat supervised the dig; and Garibaldi made Alexandre Dumas his Director of Antiquities here. A generation of Victorians sobbed over *The Last Days of Pompeii*, and the young Queen herself visited the site in 1838.

But it was not till the era of scientific archaeology—which came to Pompeii and Herculaneum with Fiorelli in 1860— that the buried cities began to add their never-ceasing stores to the sum of our knowledge of ancient town planning,

Fig. 8.1   Pompeii, victims of Vesuvius, from House of Cryptoporticus.
(V. Spinazzola, *Pompeii: . . . Via dell'Abbondanza,* 1, p. 443)

public life, private life in town and country houses, trade
and tradesmen, religion, and art.

One of the results of scientific excavation at Pompeii was
to reveal at last the town plan (Fig. 8.2), after decades
spent in sporadic digging for treasure trove, in cutting paintings out of walls, filling in the excavated houses, and moving on without system to a new area. The plan as now
revealed (Fig. 8.3) shows the least regular streets in the
southwest quadrant of the town around the Forum; this,
therefore, should be the oldest part; and in fact architectural
terracottas found here, in the so-called *Foro Triangolare,* are

FIG. 8.2 Pompeii, air view.
(University of Wisconsin Classics Dept. collection)

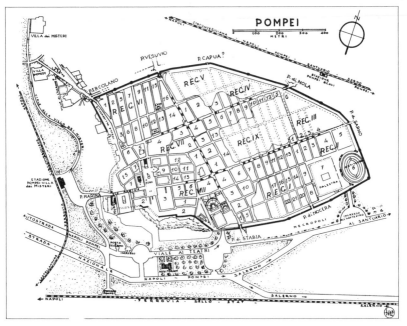

FIG. 8.3 Pompeii, plan. (MPI)

dated in the sixth century B.C. This forum contains the remains of a Doric temple, dedicated either to Hercules or to Minerva, dated in its earliest phase from the sixth century B.C. The triangular colonnade is from Pompeii's Samnite period, about 150 B.C. In front of the temple is an enclosed altar, perhaps venerated as the tomb of the founder. Elsewhere the pattern of a rectangular grid is clear, making possible the division of the city for purposes of archaeological reference into nine regions. Each region is subdivided into numbered blocks, or *insulae;* each *insula* into numbered houses. The whole 160 acres, big enough for a population of from fifteen to twenty thousand, is surrounded by a wall in which archaeologists, on the basis of building materials and techniques, have detected four phases. The earliest, with a facing of squared limestone, dates from the fifth century B.C.; the latest, marked by the addition of high towers, from the time of Sulla, who settled some of his veterans here in a colony grandiosely named the *Colonia Veneria Cornelia Pompeianorum.* Masons' marks from the third phase (280–180 B.C.) are in Oscan letters, the alphabet of ancient Italy's major language, next after Latin and Greek. Inscriptions (street signs, for example, or directives for soldiers being mustered to man the walls) show that Oscan persisted as Pompeii's third language, along with Latin and Greek (for the area around Naples had originally been settled by Greeks, and they kept their culture), down almost to the time of the eruption. The wall shows the marks of the stone catapult balls of the Sullan siege; some of the balls were found preserved as souvenirs in houses, used as garden decorations, or as plugs for impluvia drains. After the Sullan phase the wall was allowed to fall into disrepair, mute evidence of the security of the Augustan peace.

Whatever curtailment of liberty seemed a price worth paying for security in Rome, Pompeii at least enjoyed an active political life. The evidence is a vast series of election "posters," painted in red and black on house and shop walls. In these, individuals and groups (for example, the fullers or laundrymen, the fruit vendors, the fishermen, dyers, bakers, goldsmiths, muleteers, and a private club of gay blades who call themselves the *seribibi*, late drinkers) urge their fellow citizens to vote for candidates for aedile, the highest municipal office. For one block of supporters the candidate's gratitude must have been extremely limited: the notice read: "The sneak-thieves support Vatia for the aedileship." In the house of C. Julius Polybius (IX. 13.1–3) the householder himself urges his own election. The bases for the invitations to vote for a candidate like "Vote for *X*: he won't squander public funds," will have a strong appeal for the modern reader.

There was no interference with due process, to judge by the basilica in the Forum, where Pompeii's legal business was transacted: it is Pompeii's largest and most important public building. Tiles found in it stamped in Oscan come from a level which shows that the building dates at least from 120 B.C. Across the Forum from the basilica is the *comitium*, for town meetings and elections: at the south end of the Forum are three buildings, identified as the meeting place of the town council, with municipal offices on either side.

Pompeii was well-supplied, too, with public amenities. The streets were paved, and supplied at the main intersections with stepping stones, which did not interfere with the passage of high-axled wagons, though some stepping stones were removed in 1815 to allow the Queen of Naples's coach to pass. (Until the 1950s visitors with a taste for ostentation could be carried through Pompeii in a sedan chair.) Lead water pipes found everywhere show that all but the very humblest houses were supplied with running water. There were no less than three sets of public baths, of which the largest was under construction when the catastrophe came. The baths had radiant heating and elegant stuccoed vaults. There were separate sets of rooms for men and for women, and an enormous number of lamps found in one establishment shows that it was in use also in the evening hours. The Stabian Baths had a waterwheel operated by slaves on a treadmill principle: it brought water up in endless buckets from a deep well in the northwest corner.

That the intellectual as well as the physical needs of the population were catered to is deduced from the existence of a library, formerly called the Sanctuary of the Public Lares, on the northeast side of the forum. Its plan resembles that of the library at Timgad (*NASS*, 232), and that of Celsus at Ephesus (*GSS*[2], 468). It has natural light, niches for books, protection against damp, and exedrae for statues; for example, of Minerva, goddess of wisdom. The scrolls kept here would help to explain the literary content of graffiti and frescoes. There are also two stone theaters: one open to the sky, with a capacity of 5,000; one roofed, a *théatre intime*, for about 800. Both antedate the earliest stone theater in Rome. But the Pompeians did not push the intellectual life to extremes. Reservoirs under the orchestra probably supplied water ballets, though it has also been suggested that they were used to freshen the air or to supply water organs. The portico behind the large theater was remodeled in Nero's reign to make a barracks for gladiators, complete with armory and lock-up, where three of them were found asphyxiated in the stocks. The amphitheater has seats for 12,000. Legends scrawled on its walls, and on house walls all over town, testify to the gladiators' popularity with their fans: gladiatorial records are registered (twenty-four fights, twenty-four victories; the losers most often are murdered and forgotten), and one champion is recorded as SVSPIRIVM PVELLARVM, the one the girls sigh for. Eighty-two advertisements for fights have been catalogued, many of them on the walls of tombs! Though some fights were commercial ventures, many were given by the town magistrates to enhance their popularity.

But Pompeii's greatest contribution is to our knowledge, almost indecently intimate, of the private life of its inhabitants. This information comes primarily from the town houses (for example, Fig. 8.4, a cutaway model of the House of the Tragic Poet [VI. 8.3]), which shows vestible, atrium, tablinum, peristyle, and wall decoration: Bulwer-Lytton in *The Last Days of Pompeii* chose this as the house of Glaucus) and the suburban and rustic villas. The best guidebooks go into some detail on seventy-eight of these in Pompeii, and thirty-one in Herculaneum; hundreds more go unrecorded. In the face of this *embarras de richesse*, rigorous selection is necessary, and a description of a few houses and villas must suffice. To represent town houses I choose the "House of the Moralist" (*Regio* III, *Insula* iv, House 2–3), on the Via dell' Abbondanza, a shopping street of above-average houses. (The aristocratic quarter was in *Regio* VI.) Excavations on this street were carried out by Vittorio Spinazzola between 1910 and 1923 according to a method new in Pompeii, which

FIG. 8.4 Pompeii, House of Tragic Poet, cutaway model, from EUR. (Fototeca)

made the dead street come alive with extraordinary vividness. Spinazzola's meticulousness preserved and reconstructed the traces of upper stories, with windows, balconies, and loggias; of gardens, with the discovered roots of their trees and plants replaced by modern ones of the same species. The colorful painted signs and notices on the house and shop fronts, instead of being detached as in the past and transferred to the museum in Naples, were left *in situ,* protected by glass and awnings; the house interiors, with their furniture and wall paintings, were kept intact. All this Spinazzola published in 1953 in a colossal book of 1,110 folio pages, with over 1,000 figures and ninety-six large plates. His account is the more important because the House of the Moralist, having been kept inviolate by volcanic ashes for so many centuries, was badly damaged by Allied bombs in 1943. The Houses of the Vettii, of the Faun, and of Sallust suffered; also walls, gates, the Antiquarium, and much else. (There were Germans quartered in the hotels near the excavation entrance.) The plan (Figs. 8.5 and 8.6) of the House of the Moralist shows two dwellings thrown into one. The smaller, on the left, has typical features: its vestibule leading to an *atrium** off which open a summer and a winter dining room and a light well planted with flowers and shrubs. The winter dining room is frescoed in glossy black; it has a vaulted, coffered ceiling, and a high window closed by a shutter planned to slide into the wall. The usual peristyle, or rectangular portico behind the *atrium,* is missing, its function supplied by the loggias on the upper floor and the large sunken garden behind the larger house. The garden was planned as a little grove sacred to Diana. Her statue was found in the middle of the garden, with a little bronze incense burner in the shape of a ram still in place on its pedestal, and large trees planted around it. The pleasant summer dining room fills the garden's southwest corner. In it the marble-topped

---

* A central hall, the central part of whose roof sloped inward to a central opening for rainwater, which fell into a square pool below.

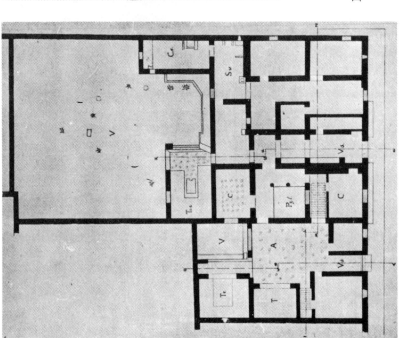

Fig. 8.6 Pompeii, House of the Moralist, reconstruction.
(Spinazzola, *op. cit.*, 2, p. 756)

Fig. 8.5 Pompeii, House of the Moralist.
(Spinazzola, *op. cit.*, 2, p. 728)

FIG. 8.7   Pompeii, House of the Moralist, triclinium.
(Spinazzola, *op. cit.*, 2, p. 752)

table was found set for a meal or sacrifice (Fig. 8.7). In the
corner was a brazier and a pitcher for hot water. Three
couplets painted on the wall prescribed etiquette for the
diners, and give the house its name: "Don't put your dirty
feet on our couch covers; if you bicker at table you'll have
to go home; be modest and don't make eyes at another man's
wife." There was a dumbwaiter to serve the pleasant loggias
on the upper floor overlooking the garden. The pointed jars,
amphoras, in the basement, suggest that the Moralist was a
wine merchant. A stamp found there gives his name: Gaius
Arrius Crescens. Election notices painted on the house front
show that he and his family were up to their ears in local
politics.

A sumptuous suburban dwelling is the sixty-room Villa of the Mysteries outside Pompeii's Herculaneum gate, the noblest and grandest known of its kind. It was built on a seaward-facing slope, with a terrace and subterranean vaults. A careful analysis by its excavator, Amedeo Maiuri, of its building materials and décor shows six phases, of which the earliest, in squared blocks of local limestone, includes the rectangular block of rooms numbered 2–8 and 11–21 in the plan (Fig. 8.8), and is dated 200–150 B.C. At this stage the villa was surrounded on three sides by a pleasant open portico, and the curved exedra or belvedere (see the plan) did not yet exist. The next stage, marked by the use of handsome light gray tufa instead of limestone, includes the peristyle and small *atrium (atriolum* in the plan), and the modest bathing rooms (42–44) beyond. It dates from the time of Sulla. The next two periods are dated from the prevalent styles of wall painting, to be discussed in the section on art below. They take the villa's building history through the reign of Augustus. In the Julio-Claudian period—the date is again made precise by the style of painting—the villa became useful as well as ornamental: the rustic quarters 52–60 were added, and an upper floor overlooking the vestibule. The latter is more elegant than the rustic quarters, less so than the noble eastern rooms. The inference is that in this period the owner used the villa only occasionally, leaving the management of its business end to a resident factor who lived on the upper floor (see the reconstruction, Fig. 8.9), where he could keep his eye on the bailiff and the slave farm hands. The portico (P1–4) was now provided with a windowed wall between its columns, and the sunrooms (9–10) were created, with their splendid view, open to the southern sunshine, ideal for a winter siesta.

When the volcano finally struck, the villa was undergoing extensive remodeling, having apparently not yet recovered from an earlier catastrophe for which there is other evidence,

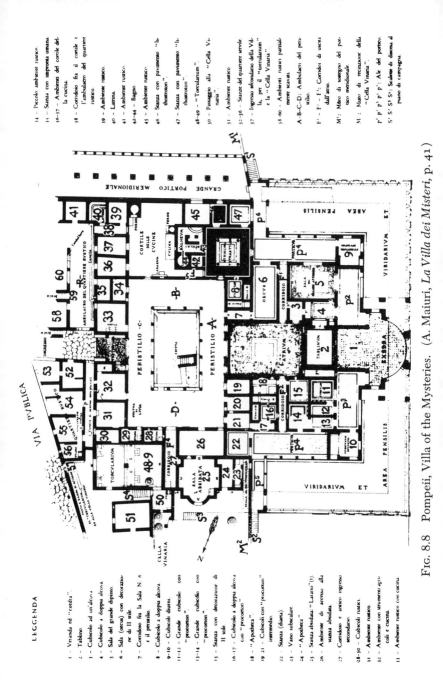

FIG. 8.8 Pompeii, Villa of the Mysteries. (A. Maiuri, *La Villa dei Misteri*, p. 41)

LEGGENDA

1 - Veranda ed "exedra".
2 - Tablino.
3 - Cubicolo ad un'alcova.
4 - Cubicolo a doppia alcova.
5 - Sala del grande dipinto.
6 - Sala (oecus) con decorazione di II stile.
7 - Corridoio fra la Sala N. 6 e il peristilio.
8 - Cubicolo a doppia alcova.
9-10 - Cubicoli diurni.
11-12 - Grande cubicolo con "procoiton".
13-14 - Grande cubicolo con "procoiton".
15 - Stanza con decorazione di II stile.
16-17 - Cubicolo a doppia alcova con "procoiton".
18 - "Apotheca".
19-21 - Cubicoli con "procoiton" intermedio.
22 - Stanza (diaeta).
23 - Vano subscalare.
24 - "Apotheca".
25 - Stanza absidata: "Larario"(?).
26 - Ambiente di accesso alla stanza absidata.
27 - Corridoio e antico ingresso secondario.
28-30 - Cubicoli rustici.
31 - Ambiente rustico.
32 - Ambiente con strumenti agricoli e cucina.
33 - Ambiente rustico con cucina.

34 - Piccolo ambiente rustico.
35 - Stanza con imposta umana.
36-17 - Ambienti del cortile del-la cucina.
18 - Corridoio fra il cortile e l'ambulacro del quartiere rustico.
39 - Ambiente rustico.
40 - Latrina.
41 - Ambiente rustico.
42-44 - Bagno.
45 - Ambiente rustico.
46 - Stanza con pavimento "lithostroton".
47 - Stanza con pavimento "lithostroton".
48-49 - "Torcularium".
50 - Passaggio alla "Cella Vinaria".
51 - Ambiente rustico.
52-56 - Stanze del quartiere servile.
57 - Ingresso secondario della Villa, per il "torcularium" e la "Cella Vinaria".
58-60 - Ambienti rustici parzialmente scavati.
A-B-C-D: Ambulacri del peristilio.
F¹ - F² - F³: Corridoio di uscita dall'atrio.
M¹: Muro di sostegno del portico meridionale.
M¹: Muro di recinzione della "Cella Vinaria".
P¹ P² P³ P⁴ P⁵ P⁶: Are del portico.
S¹ S² S³ S⁴: Scalette di discesa al piano di campagna.

both archaeological and literary: an earthquake in A.D. 62. The master's quarters were found empty of their contents, as though after the earthquake he had moved out altogether, and sold his elegant furniture at auction. A stamp reveals the name of the new owner: Lucius Istacidius Zosimus. Istacidius is a noble Samnite (Oscan) name; Zosimus is Greek. The inference is that the new owner was a freedman of the former master, who bought up the property and turned the entire establishment into a farmhouse. Evidence of the tasteless change from elegance to stark practicality was found everywhere: piles of mortar, columns and architraves taken down and stored, rooms closed off, an ugly new wall run straight across one of the most tasteful rooms in the master's quarters (6), a heap of onions piled on a mosaic floor in an alcoved master bedroom, farm tools in the graceful southwest sunroom (9). The apsidal room (25) was apparently destined to become a shrine to the Emperor. In it the statue of Augustus's consort, the Empress Livia, in painted marble with the head inserted in a second-hand torso (which was found [Fig. 8.10] propped against the peristyle wall) was apparently to be set up.

On the rustic side of the villa, business was going on as usual. The winepress (Fig. 8.11) was ready for use in the coming vintage; rough wine was ready in large amphoras protected by woven straw like a modern *fiascone* of Chianti or Vesuvio. Farm tools (picks, hoe, shovel, hammer, and pruning hooks) were found hanging in a room (32) beside the vestibule. The porter was on duty. He was found dead in his dark little room (35), on his finger a cheap iron ring set with an engraved carnelian, by his side the five bronze coins which may have been his life savings. He must have heard the dying screams of the adolescent girl whose skeleton was found in the vestibule nearby. Three women were crushed in the rustic quarters (55) when the roof fell in. The excavators found their disordered skeletons, their gold

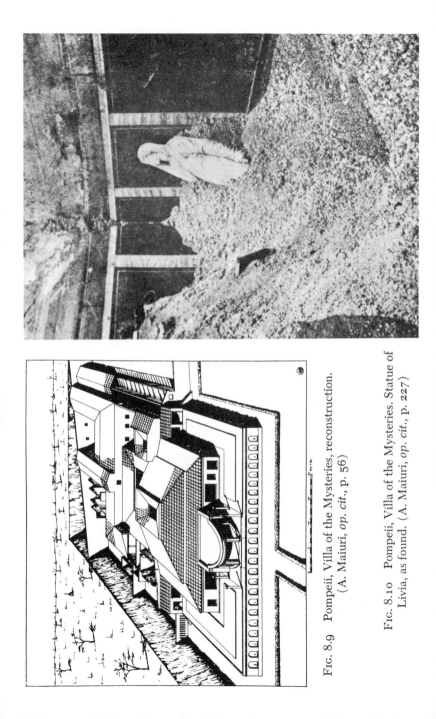

FIG. 8.9 Pompeii, Villa of the Mysteries, reconstruction.
(A. Maiuri, *op. cit.,* p. 56)

FIG. 8.10 Pompeii, Villa of the Mysteries. Statue of
Livia, as found. (A. Maiuri, *op. cit.,* p. 227)

Fig. 8.11   Pompeii, Villa of the Mysteries. Wine-press, reconstructed.
(Maiuri, *op. cit.*, p. 101)

rings and bracelets, a necklace of gold and glass paste beads, and, lying nearby, ten silver coins. In the cryptoporticus were found the bodies of four men, with wine or water jugs by their side. They had hoped the sturdy vaults would hold, and they did, but the mephitic fumes proved deadly. (Altogether, it is calculated that Vesuvius claimed 2,000 victims in Pompeii.) The nine wretched cadavers in the Villa of the Mysteries were the last inhabitants of a mansion which in its day had been one of the most elegant in all Italy.

Though space does not permit a detailed account of the fascinating things Herculaneum has to tell us, the subject of suburban villas cannot be left without mentioning a famous one there, still not fully explored, where in 1752 were found, in a narrow room with cupboards, a vast number of what were at first taken for charred billets of wood. Later, traces of writing were found on them: they turned out to be papyri, a whole library of 1,800 rolls. A machine invented to unroll them ruined more scrolls than it unwound, but finally, by 1806, ninety-six were deciphered. They proved to be works of an Epicurean philosopher named Philodemus, to whose patron Lucius Calpurnius Piso (father of Caesar's wife Calpurnia) and his descendants the villa may have belonged. It had a gracious peristyle, gardens, fishponds, and a belvedere overlooking the sea at the end of a long graveled walk. In the garden was found a whole gallery of sculpture in bronze and marble, now included among the most famous pieces in the National Museum in Naples. Here a cultured Roman patrician could combine in the ideal Epicurean way the calm contemplation of the beauties of nature and of art with the philosophic study of the atomic structure of the universe. The villa deliberately evokes the Garden of Epicurus. In the 1960s a classical art historian persuaded the oil millionaire J. Paul Getty to commission a replica of the Villa of the Papyri to house his sculpture collection in Malibu Beach, California (Fig. 8.12).

FIG. 8.12   Malibu Beach, Museum, Courtyard.
(J. Paul Getty Museum)

At Torre Annunziata (perhaps ancient Oplontis), three miles west of Pompeii, lies a seaside villa, half practical, half elegant, which may have belonged to Nero's redheaded wife, Poppaea. The east half contained the farm hands' quarters: farm tools were found in one of the rooms. The elegant western half includes a sumptuously painted suite of private baths and a lavishly decorated reception room (*oecus*). In the calidarium of the baths is a Third Style fresco of Hercules in the garden of the Hesperides, with a poet playing the lyre. At the time of the eruption, the villa was undergoing redecoration after the earthquake of 62, but five rooms of splendid earlier Second Style survive. One of these, to the right of the entrance atrium, displays comic masks. The oecus features a sanctuary of Apollo, with the Delphic tripod and a gate opening into an orchard; a two-story peristyle is shown in perspective, with a peacock (Fig. 8.13) perched on the oval window opening into it. The villa had no less than twelve gardens, planted with trees, shrubs, flowers, and herbs: chestnuts, citrus trees (started in pots), olive, apple, poplar or plane, cypress; boxwood hedge, ivy,

FIG. 8.13   Torre Annunziata, peacock fresco.
(Carlton Cleeve, Ltd., London)

oleander, myrtle, daisies, chrysanthemums, and roses. Sculpture adorned the gardens: a baby boy with a goose, a nude Venus unlacing her sandal, and a pair each of centaurs and "centauresses," which served as fountains; one of the centauresses plays the lyre.

A more rustic villa, between Pompeii and Boscoreale to the north, shows what the establishment of a capital farmer of the first century A.D. was like. The owner's quarters were modest. Business came first: most of the ground floor is taken up with stable, wine and oil presses, threshing floor, and slaves' quarters. Slaves were a problem: one rustic villa has quarters for thirty and stocks for fourteen. The Boscoreale wine store had a 23,000-gallon capacity, and enough stone jars were found to hold 1,300 gallons of olive oil. The proprietor of another Boscoreale villa, however, was not without his fondness for aesthetic ostentation. In a wine vat here was found in 1895 a treasure of 108 embossed silver vessels and 1,000 gold coins. The coins, representing a sum far larger than was needed for current expenses, were probably intended for a real-estate investment. The treasure was bought by the banker Count Edward de Rothschild, much to Italian disgust, and presented to the Louvre. One pair of cups represents a series of skeletons—one garlanded, another with a heavy bag of money, a third with a roll of papyrus, a fourth with a lyre—the whole bears the legend, the tragic irony of which the proprietor of the villa was to discover: "Seize hold on life; tomorrow is uncertain." Another treasure in silver, of 118 pieces, all now securely in the Naples museum,* was discovered in 1930 in a nail-studded chest in the strong room under a town house (I.x.4) called the "House of the Menander," after a fresco of the dramatist on the walls. The silver service included casseroles, platters, twenty-eight plates, trays, ladles, spoons, pastry molds, pepper shakers, pitchers, wine cups, two of them embossed with the Labors of Hercules, others with Cupids chariot racing, and other rural, hunting, and mythological scenes (the loves of Mars and Venus and the birth of Dionysus).

* Security is relative. The earthquake of November 23, 1980 allegedly destroyed 1,000 objects in the Naples Museum. It slightly damaged 100 buildings in Pompeii, including the Stabian Baths, the House of the Vettii, a brothel, and several houses on the Via dell'Abbondanza.

But it is not only the nabobs, their villas, and their treasures which Pompeii reveals to us. Ancient tradesmen, their
lives, work, and tastes, about which literature tells us almost
nothing, become more real for us here than anywhere else
in the ancient world except Ostia. In the market facing the
Forum the excavators found fruit in glass containers, and
the skeletons of fish and sheep. There are inns for muleteers
and carters by the city gates, and innumerable wine shops—
the bar open to the street, its top pierced to hold cool amphoras of wine or covered bronze vessels for hot drinks
(Fig. 8.14). Wine prices are scratched on walls, together
with other *graffiti* of more or less extreme indecency, referring usually to the oldest of the professions. One says, "I am
yours—for two *asses*" (the *as* was a small copper coin worth,
at the time this *graffito* was scribbled, about two and a half
cents). Another, in large letters over a bench at the Porta
Marina, advises loungers to READ THIS SIGN FIRST, and offers
the charms of a Greek prostitute named Attiké at sixteen
asses. Euxinus' wineshop (I.11.10), at the sign of the phoenix
and peacocks, has a vineyard, a monstrous wine jar (capacity
375 liters), and rooms and two latrines behind. It was a doss
house or bordello; a graffito states, in effect, that gentlemen
prefer blondes. The House of Fabius Rufus (Ins. Occ.) contains some literary graffiti. (Others are tags from the love poets,
and from Vergil, including the first line of the *Aeneid* in a
childish hand, low down on the wall. Did Pompeian schoolboys read the poem all the way through? There are no quo-
tations from books ten through twelve. But the majority are
monotonously obscene, featuring oral sex and a prostitute
who boasts of having had 1,300 men. Besides graffiti, Pompeii has a good deal of mediocre erotic art, most of it kept
prudishly under lock and key but visible upon payment of
a tip to a guard: it features erections, large phalloi, the positions of the act of love, especially anal; perversions involving
animals, strip teases, and steatopygy. This sort of thing should

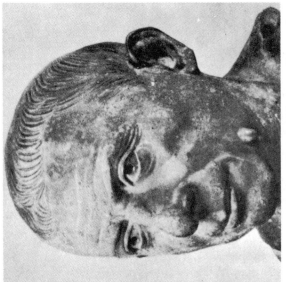

FIG. 8.14 Pompeii, *thermopolium* or bar. (MPI)

FIG. 8.15 Naples, National Museum. Bronze bust of Caecilius Jucundus, from Pompeii. (B. Maiuri, *Il Museo Nazionale di Napoli*, p. 71)

FIG. 8.16 Pompeii, House of D. Octavius Quartio, garden, reconstruction. (Spinazzola, *op. cit.*, 1, p. 418)

not be overemphasized: it is a part also of the ordinary life
of any modern Mediterranean (or American) city. The
prevalence of graffiti prompted the more sober-sided Pompeians to write more than once on the walls (of the large
theater, amphitheater, and basilica) the couplet, one of the
most famous of the hundreds found at Pompeii:

> *"I wonder, wall, that you do not go smash,*
> *Who have to bear the weight of all this trash!"*

Other *graffiti* complain of unrequited love: "I'd like to bash
Venus' ribs in" (from the basilica), or "Here Vibius lay alone
and longed for his beloved" (perhaps from an inn). Snatches
from the love poets, Ovid and (strangely) the tortured, neu-
rotic Propertius, are frequent, along with tags of Vergil re-
membered from schooldays. *Graffiti* keep a running account
of daily purchases of cheese, bread, oil, and wine; or the
number of eggs laid daily by the chickens. A reward is offered
for the recovery of a stolen bronze pitcher. Income property
is advertised for rent, or gentlemen's upstairs flats (*cenacula
equestria*). A metalworker, doing a brisk business in chamber
pots, has scratched on his wall a memo of the days on which
fairs are held in nearby towns. He made surveyors' instruments as well: our only example of a surveyor's plane table
(*groma*) comes from his shop. In a bronze-bound chest in
the house of a rich freedman banker, Lucius Caecilius Iucundus, were found his complete (and involved) accounts, on
153 wax tablets, part of a total of over 11,000 which Pompeii
has yielded. He profited from small 1 percent to 2 percent
commissions on public auctions; for example, of a mule, boxwood, slaves, linen, a fullery, pasture land: the median
transaction was for 3,059 sesterces ($103.50, uninflated). He
never stood for municipal office, perhaps to avoid conflict of
interest, for he was a municipal employee. His clients were
middle class, vintners, shopkeepers, and the like. His bronze
bust, with its shrewd, ugly, kindly face, warts and all
(Fig. 8.15), was also found in the house. It reveals the very

type of the *nouveaux riches,* not in the least ashamed of being "in trade," who came to be the ruling class in the last days of Pompeii.

In 1959, excavation for the Naples-Salerno autostrada brought to light, about 500 meters south of Pompeii, a stately mansion (portico with garden, pool, statues, frescoes, and mosaics) whose five dining rooms, together with finds of maritime gear (oar, anchor, and strakes), made it likely to be a club for shipowners. In one of the dining rooms was found a wicker hamper containing some sixty wooden tablets recording financial transactions, many involving one C. Sulpicius Cinnamus of Puteoli. The writing is not on wax, but on lacquer, and perfectly preserved, because the hamper had become encased in mud, which prevented its being carbonized. The transactions (one bilingual) include bonds posted for appearance in court, rentals, loans (some marked "paid") on security of perishable commodities, probate, auctions (of slaves and of purple cloth, to pay bad debts), records of interest, receipt for a ship's cargo (wine, vinegar, and Sicilian saffron). They date from A.D. 35 to 61.

The wealth of tradesmen can be judged by the quality of the decoration of their houses. The most lavish decoration is in the House of the Vettii (I.15.1), freedmen brothers, clients of Caecilius Iucundus. Their names are known from bronze seals found in the house; their ironbound strongbox was also found. In their garden they displayed bronze and marble statues (six of them carried off by thieves in 1978 but recently recovered in West Germany). The most famous frescoes are miniature, showing Cupids doing what bourgeois humans do: target practice, chariot racing (but their steeds are antelopes), plying the trade of florists, *parfumeurs,* goldsmiths, fullers, bakers, and vintners. The major paintings would illustrate a mythological handbook. Bacchic themes predominate, but other motifs include Hero and Leander, Jupiter and Leda, Pan puzzled by a hermaphrodite, Daedalus and Pasiphae, the punishment of Ixion, Achilles disguised as a maiden, a drunken Hercules about to rape Auge, priestess of Athena at Tegea; and scenes from the Theban cycle, including the baby Hercules (son by Jupiter of the Theban princess Alcmene) precociously strangling a snake.

Many houses were workshops, for the ancient world's slave economy did not foster the factory system. Thus in the house of the jeweler Pinarius Cerialis (III,IV,4), also handsomely frescoed, his showcase was found, containing 114 fine engraved cornelians, agates, and amethysts—some of the work unfinished—and the tiny, delicate tools of his trade. In the House of the Surgeon (VI.1,9–10), surgical instruments were found, including probes, catheters, gynecological forceps, pliers for pulling teeth, and little spoons, perhaps for extracting wax from the ears. These provide our best evidence for ancient surgical techniques.

Stephanus's *fullonica* (laundry: I.vi.7) was found with the imprint of the fallen front door left clearly in the ashes. The padlock was on the outside, from which the inference is that this establishment served as laundry only; if it had been a dwelling, the lock would have been on the inside. A skeleton behind the door had with him a bag of 107 gold and silver coins. Since two-thirds of them had been minted years before, under the Republic, one assumes that this was not merely the day's take, but a hoard—all the shop's moveable capital. Built in at the back were the small vats where the dirty clothes were trodden, to get out the dirt and grease, and the larger ones for rinsing. The upper floor and courtyard were used for drying: in the courtyard wall were found the small putholes for the canes over which the wet clothes were hung. Near the entrance was the clothes press, in which a pressing board was worked down upon the folded clothes by means of a pair of large wooden screws.

Across the street from the laundry a painted shop front shows the operations of a felter's establishment, where wool was matted together with a fixative, under repeated manipulation and pressure, until it acquired a consistent texture, like a piece of cloth. Felt was in demand for caps, cloaks, slippers, and blankets (the latter for both man and horse). The shop sign shows workmen at tables holding the carding comb and knives of their trade. In the middle of the picture other men, naked to the waist, are at work at shallow troughs impregnating the wool with the coagulant (Pliny the Elder says it was vinegar), which is being heated by a stove beneath the troughs. To the right, the proprietor—his name was Verecundus—proudly holds up a red-striped finished sample. To the left, Mercury, the patron of tradesmen, is painted emerging from a Tuscan temple with a money bag in his hand ("Hurrah for profit," says a Pompeian mosaic). Below is the proprietor's wife at a table, in spirited conversation with a female customer who is trying on slippers. No literary discussion, primary or secondary, can match the vivid concreteness of this archaeological record.

The house (II.v.1–4) of Decimus Octavius Quartio (or Marcus Loreius Tiburtinus—authorities differ about the occupant's name) may have belonged to a potter, to judge by a small kiln, with the potter's stool and samples of his wares, found in a workroom. This is interesting enough, but more interesting still is this tradesman's taste, as revealed by his house and garden. Hardly a corner of the house is left unfrescoed, and the paintings include two ambitious cycles: nine episodes from the saga of Hercules; and fourteen from the *Iliad*. (The House of the Cryptoporticus [I.vi.2–4] presents twenty-five *Iliad* episodes from an original 86, badly damaged when the last owner, an obvious Babbitt, turned the cryptoporticus into a wine cellar and made over the dining room for public use.) The potter was, in addition, a connoisseur of gardens; his is the most charming that Pompeii can boast. His *impluvium*—for catching rainwater in the atrium—is double-walled, for flower boxes; behind the *atrium* is a formal flower bed, with walks around it on three sides; the chief feature of the sunken back garden (Fig. 8.16), nearly twice the area of the house itself, is a pair of long, narrow fish pools, planned perpendicular to each other to form a T and trellised (Fig. 8.17) so that vines could grow over them. The walls of the pools were painted blue to deepen the color of the water. At one end of the crossbar of the T is the pleasantest *al fresco* dining alcove imaginable. Statuettes embellish the alcove and the sides of the pool. There is a little shrine in the alcove; another, with a fountain, where the two pools meet; still another, with a fountain in front of it, two-thirds of the way along the upright of the T. Putholes in the garden wall show that there were shed roofs there to protect exotic plants and flowers. The plum trees, oaks, shrubs, arbors, and plants with which the garden was filled in orderly rows, with walks between, have been re-planted, after identifying them from their roots found in the ashes. Forty-four amphoras were found buried to their necks in a row along one side of the garden. Perhaps they served as flower pots; it is equally possible that they were a wine store, for this potter's house has no wine cellar. In a corner and under the arbors along the walks there were wooden seats and little marble tables, for rustic picnics in the pleached shade. The difference of levels, the fountains, shrines, statues, arbors, trees, and the painted colors, red, gray, green, yellow, and blue, all judiciously restored, make this age-old garden extraordinarily vivacious. Here archaeology has once more given the lie to the hackneyed stereotype of the lifelessness and colorlessness of classical antiquity and has proved that in landscape gardening, at any rate, there is something to be said for the *bourgeois* taste of Pompeian tradesmen.

A market garden is a feature of the House of the Ship Europa (I.15.3) near the amphitheater. There are grapevines, fruit and nut trees, plants in pots, and areas for bed-

FIG. 8.17   Pompeii, House of D. Octavius Quartio, garden, with trellis and pool.
(Spinazzola, *op. cit.*, 1, p. 396)

ding out young plants. The American excavators found 416 root holes, for, among others, onions, cabbage, vines, beans, chickpeas, and olive. The plants and trees were watered from cisterns. Twenty-eight perforated vases held exotics: cherry, peach, apricot, pistachio, and lemon (which Romans did not eat, but used as a mouthwash or against moths). At the back of the garden were kennels, pigsties, byres, and hencoops.

Some had a taste for music, too, to judge by some frescoes in the small but gracious House of Fabia (I.vi.15). One portrays the mistress of the house with sheet music in her hand. Another shows what appears to be a music lesson, our only example of the lyre being played four hands. Indeed archaeology, by revealing these middlebrows to us in three dimensions, their shops and artifacts, inns and bars, street signs and *graffiti*, loves licit and illicit, tools and equipment, their tastes and pleasures, has given us, especially in Pompeii, a truer picture of the average, ordinary ancient Italian man than Latin literature provides. For Latin literature, with some exceptions like Plautus's plays, tends to be written by highbrows for highbrows. (Yet paradoxically, the best literary picture of an ancient Babbitt, Petronius's Trimalchio, *was* drawn by a highbrow for highbrows.)

Pompeii has enriched, too, our knowledge of the ancient Italian's relation to his gods. The archaeological documents for Pompeian religion include the temples, innumerable household shrines, wayside altars, frescoes, inscriptions, and *graffiti*. Of the ten temples, three, ruined in the earthquake, had not been repaired at the time of the final debacle, seventeen years later. One had reverted to the use of a private association, and two were dedicated to the Imperial cult, to which generally only lip service was paid: for example, the cynical *graffito* from Agrippa Postumus's villa in nearby Boscotrecase: "Augustus Caesar's mother was only a woman."

Of the rest, only the temple of the Egyptian Isis shows real signs of the prosperity that comes from devout support. Fragments of painting from the Black Room of this villa, reconstructed on paper, proved to contain Egyptian religious motifs: a crocodile god, a jackal, the sacred bull Apis, and Ammon (equated with Roman Jupiter). But the truth is that the real god of Pompeii—as of most other cities ancient and modern—was the God of Gain. The state religion, cold and formal, offered little comfort: the warmth and promise came from Oriental religions, of which the worship of Isis was one and Christianity another. There is no firm evidence of Christianity's having penetrated Pompeii by A.D. 79, unless the ominous *graffito* "SODOMA, GOMORA" be taken as a sign. But Pompeii, close to the Italian end of the trade route from Alexandria, is permeated with things Egyptian, and there is much evidence of enthusiasm for the cult of Isis. The earliest building stones of the temple (VII.vii) belong to the end of the second century B.C., and were thrown down in the earthquake of A.D. 62. (A lararium in the House of Caecilius Iucundus bears two reliefs [Fig. 8.18] in a primitive style, portraying two results of the earthquake. In the first, the temple of Jupiter in the forum, flanked by a pair of equestrian statues [of the Dioscuri], tilts at a crazy angle, as does the monumental arch to the left of it, whose actual core still stands. On its right is an altar, beside it a bull for sacrifice, with a priest, and sacrificial instruments. The other scene Caecilius could have witnessed from his house: the Vesuvius gate leans precariously; to the left, the water-distribution tower, still under repair in 79, to the right a cart drawn by a mule team; beyond, a rustic altar beside a tree. One of the reliefs having been stolen, the other is kept under lock and key.) The temple of Isis, however, was not left derelict after the earthquake: it was immediately reconstructed from the ground up in the name of a six-year-old boy, who was rewarded for his piety by honorary member-

FIG. 8.18 Pompeii, House of Caecilius Jucundus, stucco reliefs of earthquake damage. (Author)

ship in the town council. The cult, with its promise of personal immortality, received rich gifts from its votaries. Its marble lustral basin, for holy water; statues and statuettes, including of course the goddess herself, with her rattle that kept off evil spirits; the striking bronze bust of an actor-donor; lamps; sacrificial knives; the ornamental marble curb of a well; candelabra; and rich frescoes, some with likenesses of white-robed, shaven-headed priests, which decorated the precinct and the walls; all are now among the treasures of the National Museum in Naples.

Family cults flourished in Pompeii more than the official religion, to judge by the fact that nearly every house and workshop has its private shrine, usually housing busts of ancestors (for in their ancestor worship the Romans were downright Japanese), and adorned with a picture of a snake, representing the family's Genius, or guardian spirit. Sometimes, as in the House of the Cryptoporticus, there is a handsomely decorated private shrine to one of the Olympian deities, in this case Diana. The trades had their patron saints: Mercury (god also of thieves) for commerce; Minerva, who invented weaving, for the clothmakers; the hearth goddess Vesta for the bakers. The front of the felter's shop described above is emblazoned with a magnificent Venus in a chariot drawn by four elephants. Sex, too, had its enthusiastic worshipers: a dyer's vat (IX.vii.2) bears a relief of an enormous winged phallus, set in a temple whose *acroteria* are also phalluses, of smaller size. (Representations of the male member were thought to ward off the evil eye.) But perhaps the perfect symbol of the religion of this tradesmen's town is a fresco in the House of the Cryptoporticus, in which the family of Aeneas (the symbol of Rome) is shown guided to its destiny by Mercury, the god of trade.

Is all this great art? A fair answer to the question should come from an analysis of what is usually regarded as the masterpiece of Pompeian painting, the painting in Room 5 of the Villa of the Mysteries.

This analysis must be prefaced by a word about the four more or less successive styles into which archaeologists have succeeded in dividing the vast corpus of Pompeian painting.

The First (or "incrustation") Style, found in buildings (*e.g.*, at Palestrina) dated by their fabric and technique from 150 to 80 B.C., uses colored stucco to imitate marble dadoes, rusticated blocks, and revetments. An excellent example is the House of Sallust (VI.2.4). The sumptuous House of the Faun (VI.12.2), which may have belonged to Sulla's nephew, contained, besides the famous bronze statue from which it is named, mosaics contemporary with the First Style, of which the most famous depicts Alexander winning the battle of Issus. Statue and mosaic are now in the Naples Museum.

The Second (or "architectural") Style (80–*ca.* 15 B.C.) imitates architectural forms, uses perspective, and throws the field to be painted open to mythical or religious subjects. A famous example of the Second Style is the bedroom from the villa of Fannius Synistor at Boscoreale, north of Pompeii, now in New York's Metropolitan Museum. Paintings from its oecus are divided among New York, Naples, and Brussels: one of them probably portrays the philosopher Menedemus with his pupil Antigonus Gonatas; there are personifications of Macedonia and Persia; there are Dionysus and Ariadne, the Three Graces, a woman playing the lyre, a man enthroned, with a seated woman, and a woman with a shield.

The Third (or "Egyptianizing") Style (*ca.* 15 B.C.–A.D. 62) flattens out painted architectural detail into framed panels like hanging tapestries, worked out with fine detail in a miniaturist's technique. A selection of Third Style paintings follows: (1) The House of Ceres (I.19.3), with an idyllic sacred landscape. (2) The House of the Floral Bedchambers (I.9.5), with scenes, in a room which may have been a chapel, in which Bacchus appears with Isis and

Osiris; a garden fresco like that from Livia's Prima Porta villa, with identifiable fauna (doves, magpies, blackbirds, jays, and swallows) and flora (anemone, myrtle, ivy, laurel, palm, and oleander; crabapple, citron, cherry, and pear). An Apis (sacred bull), and vessels for Nile water add to the Egyptian motifs. The dining-room paintings portray the fall of Icarus, and Actaeon set upon by his own dogs. (3) The House of Jason (IX.5.18–21) has scenes which have been interpreted as representing impiety punished (Jason's wicked uncle, Pelias; Marsyas, Apollo's challenger in music; Phaedra, Medea; but there are also scenes which do not fit: Achilles' human and semi-equine tutors, Phoenix and Chiron; Hercules and Deianeira), so that probably the main intent is decorative: if there is a guiding thread, it is the lost epic cycle. (4) The Villa San Marco at Stabiae (Castellammare di Stabia, on the Bay of Naples south of Pompeii), perhaps belonged to Claudius's freedman Narcissus. It has fifty rooms, a veritable picture gallery: gods, goddesses, Seasons, nymphs (Daphne, Europa), muses (Melpomene), a disobedient son (Phaethon), a monster (Medusa), and scenes from tragedy (Oedipus, and Iphigenia in Tauris, with the statue of Artemis). A new site museum houses some of the paintings. (5) To this period belongs the Boscoreale silver treasure, 103 pieces, including a full service for eating and drinking: ten four-piece place settings. On some of the cups are skeletons, many labeled with famous names and bearing wise saws about death and pleasure. Some pieces have political implications: Augustus receiving the province of Africa; Tiberius (in whose reign the set is dated) at sacrifice, and in a triumphal chariot. (6) Also Third Style is the "Villa Imperiale" near Pompeii's Marine Gate. Grandiose but probably not imperial, it was revealed by bombing in 1943. It has in the dining room Theseus victorious, Ariadne abandoned, Daedalus and Icarus, Sappho and Alcaeus, Mars and Venus, but also women in genre scenes: the eve of marriage; singing to a lyre accompaniment; listening to a reading. The bedroom, with a picture window for the sea view, has Atalanta, Meleager, and the Calydonian Boar.

The Fourth, or "ornamental" Style is usually dated A.D. 62–79, but it does not form an orderly sequence with the Third: there are overlaps and throwbacks. An example is the House of the Dioscuri (VI.9.6–7). On its Fourth-Style walls seven different hands have been distinguished. The subjects treated include Perseus and Andromeda, Theseus victorious, Ariadne abandoned, Achilles among the women, Iphigenia in Tauris, Hercules enslaved to women's work by Omphale; Meleager, Endymion the Moon's beloved, Phaedra and Hippolytus, Dirce punished, Pan and a hermaphrodite, and a puzzling scene in which a seated woman (witch? Penelope?) in a conical hat gives a drink (magic potion?) to a traveler (Odysseus?).

Examples of the last three styles occur in the Villa of the Mysteries, but the great sequence from which the Villa takes its name is of the Second Style.

In this sequence, against a background of glossy Pompeian red, are painted in tempera, almost life-size, a series of twenty-nine figures subdivided into ten groups. At the left of the door in the northwest corner (as one enters from Room 4) a boy reads what is apparently a ritual from a papyrus roll; a woman, perhaps his mother, points to the words with a stylus. Next is a scene of ritual washing of a myrtle branch; one of the servers, in deep décolleté, and with pointed ears, carries the papyrus ritual roll at her waist in a fold of her *stola*. In the next group a fat, blonde-bearded, naked old Silenus plays a lyre, a faun plays his pipe, and his consort gives suck to a goat. Then comes the figure of a woman in motion so violent that her drapery swirls about her as she raises a hand in horror at one of the scenes that follows. But between her and the scene that repels her are three other groups. First, another trio, of a Silenus and two fauns. The Silenus is giving one of the fauns a drink out of a silver bowl; the other faun frightens the drinker with a Silenus mask held so as to be reflected in the surface of the wine. Second, the central scene, in the center of the east wall, portrays a naked god, identified as Bacchus by the thyrsus (the staff tipped with a pine cone) which lies athwart his body, and by the vine leaves in his hair, leans back in the lap of a figure who must be his bride, Ariadne. Third, a kneeling woman unveils an erect purple-draped object, surely the Mystery of Mysteries, a phallus. Beyond her is the scene of horror (Fig. 8.19): a half-naked female figure, perhaps Nemesis, or her Etruscan equivalent, Vanth, with huge black wings, raises a whip to scourge a woman, surely the candidate for initiation, who cowers, her back bare, her face buried, in the lap of a seated woman who strokes the victim's disheveled hair to comfort her. Beyond her a naked Bacchante whirls in an orgiastic dance, clicking castanets high in the air above her head. In the last two scenes a woman in bridal yellow, on an elegant ivory stool, does her hair while a Cupid holds a mirror. Another Cupid, with his bow, looks on. And finally, a matron, with her mantle draped over her head like a priestess, sits, leaning on a cushion of purple and gold, on a chair with a footstool, and watches gravely.

This fresco, which clearly portrays a Dionysiac ritual, and connects it with marriage and fertility, has undeniable power. It packs into a confined space—it is less than sixty feet long, on three sides of a room measuring only 16 by 23 feet—movement, rest, fear, horror, magic, abandon, and orgy. It illustrates better than anything else from Pompeii how the Augustan age assimilated Hellenistic Greek art into an Italian idiom. Yet somehow the final impression, here and in lesser examples of Pompeian painting, is that the artist is working from a memory of great paintings seen in collections or museums, from a repertory, or from sketch books of

FIG. 8.19   Pompeii, Villa of the Mysteries, fresco: woman being scourged. (MPI)

famous works of art. His work is well above the inn-sign or wallpaper level, he is competent and sophisticated: no hack, but no genius either. And so, with all respect for the natural enthusiasm of the excavator, the question with which this section began must be answered in the negative. This is not great art, but it is the next thing to it, and no modern *bourgeoisie* since the sixteenth-century Dutch has had the taste to fill its houses with such able work. But we must conclude that the great value of Pompeian art is in documentation, of the practical taste of ordinary people.

Maximilian, later to be Emperor of Mexico, when he visited Pompeii in 1851, found it terrible—its rooms like painted corpses. Since then, modern archaeological methods (scientific, not miraculous) have brought the corpses to life. What archaeology has presented to us here, as at its best it always does, is not things but people, at work and play, in house and workshop, worshiping and blaspheming, and after their fashion patronizing the arts. So vividly does archaeology reveal them that we are moved to say with Francis Bacon, "*These* are the ancient times, when the world is ancient, and not those which we account ancient, by a computation backwards from ourselves."

As the rain of ashes was covering Pompeii, and the river of mud engulfing Herculaneum, life in Rome, that Eternal City, went on. It was the age of the Flavians. Vespasian, the bourgeois founder of the dynasty, died just a month before Pompeii was buried. He and his sons, the good Titus and the wicked Domitian, enriched Rome with splendid art and architecture.

9

Flavian Rome

Two *fora,* an amphitheater, an arch, a sculptured relief, a palace, a stadium: these may stand as typical of archaeology's contributions to our knowledge of the Flavian age. As in the Julio-Claudian dynasty, the buildings and the sculpture epitomize the atmosphere of the time, the last three decades of the first century A.D. After the excesses of Nero and the bloodbath of A.D. 69—a year of civil war which saw three Emperors in succession, Galba, Otho, and Vitellius, raised to the purple and then murdered—the Roman people wanted "normalcy." Under Vespasian and Titus they got it; under Domitian the pendulum swung again—and so did the headsman's ax.

Flavian architecture and art sum up, too, the personalities of the Emperors. The bluff, no-nonsense Vespasian, the Emperor of reconstruction, symbolized, in his majestic Forum of Peace, what one of his staff called the "immense majesty" of the peace he had brought to a war-torn world, and the dynasty gave credit, in the frieze of the *Forum Transitorium,* to the artisan class which was its ardent supporter. Vespasian, true to his bourgeois origins, built for the people, over the pool of Nero's Golden House, the great amphitheater which

posterity was to call the Colosseum. Reversing a Neronian
impiety, he restored the Temple of Claudius on the Caelian
Hill. The temple itself is not preserved, but the buttress
walls and porticoes of its vast terrace on three sides still
remain, with handsome Claudian-style rustication; that is,
with the margin of the block finished smooth, the rest left
quarry-rough (Fig. 9.1). The Marble Plan shows the temple

FIG. 9.1   Rome, Temple of Claudius, west terrace wall. (Fototeca)

set at the back of a formal garden (see model, Fig. 9.2, 13).
Domitian summed up the great moment of Titus's short life
when he immortalized his capture of Jerusalem on his arch
at the top of the old Forum. Domitian, would-be *triumpha-
tor*, would-be rival of his great predecessors, nevertheless
erected at the west end of the Forum Romanum a temple to
his deified father and brother. He gave it fluted Corinthian
columns 50 feet high, and a frieze portraying sacrificial instruments, one block of which is now in view in the Tabularium
arcade, and he exalted, in the reliefs found in 1939 under the
Cancelleria Palace in Rome, the military prowess of the dynasty which in his view culminated in himself. He took over
Vespasian's *Forum Transitorium*, to thrust himself into a
class with Augustus and his own father; reared on the Palatine a palace to outdo the Golden House; and, with philhellenism genuine or affected, built in the Campus Martius
a stadium for footraces in the Greek fashion.

Since very little of Vespasian's Forum of Peace remains
above ground, recourse for information about it must be had
in the first instance to literature. Pliny the Elder, who was
on Vespasian's staff, described it as one of the most beautiful
squares in the world, embellished as it was with loot from
Nero's Golden House, and trophies of war, including the
famous seven-branched gold candlestick from the temple in
Jerusalem, carved in relief on the Arch of Titus.

A fragment of the previously mentioned Marble Plan of
Rome (Fig. 5.12), the Forma Urbis, inscribed with the.let-
ters CIS (Fig. 9.3), is easily restored to something like
[Forum Pa]CIS, Forum of Peace. It shows a colonnaded
portico approached by steps. An open space is incised with
a series of three long indented strips, apparently representing formal garden plots. The fragment also shows one right
angle of a structure which should be an altar.

Faced with the thousand pieces of the Marble Plan,

MUSEO
DELLA
CIVILTÀ
ROMANA

PLASTICO DI ROMA

1 STADIO DI DOMIZIANO
2 CIRCO FLAMINIO
3 CIRCO MASSIMO
4 ODEON DI DOMIZIANO
5 TEATRO DI BALBO
6 TEATRO DI MARCELLO
7 TEATRO DI POMPEO
8 DOMUS AUGUSTANA
9 PALAZZO DI TIBERIO
10 FORO DI TRAIANO
11 FORO DELLA PACE
12 TEMPIO DI SERAPIDE
13 TEMPIO DEL DIVO CLAUDIO
14 TEMPIO DI COSTANTINO
15 TERME DI CARACALLA
16 ANFITEATRO FLAVIO
17 TERME DI TITO
18 TERME DI TRAIANO
19 TERME DI DIOCLEZIANO

FIG. 9.2   Rome, model. In center, Palatine, with Domitianic buildings.
(Felbermeyer)

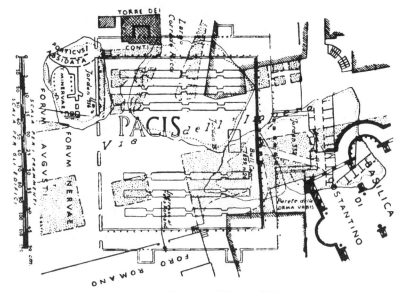

FIG. 9.3   Rome, Forum of Peace, Colini and Gatti reconstruction
from *Forma Urbis*. (G. Lugli, *Roma antica*, Pl. 6)

archaeologists play the fascinating game of making joins, as
in a jigsaw puzzle. In 1899 Lanciani announced the discovery
of a new fragment which joined with the piece showing the
Forum Pacis. It filled out the rectangular shape of the altar,
added two more rows of garden plots, and supplied another
side to the portico, at right angles to the other. This side
had two rows of columns, four of which were represented as
of larger dimensions than the others, and as standing on
plinths or square bases. These two fragments made possible
restoration, on paper, of a considerable part of the Forum's
plan. Given the Roman architectural principle of axial symmetry (which means that what appears on one side of the
axis of a Roman plan will have a twin on the other), Lanciani could be sure that the altar belonged in the middle of
one side of the portico-surrounded space, toward the back.
He could restore two more column bases; and, knowing that

there must have been three rows of garden plots on either side of the altar, and that the scale of the Marble Plan was 1:200, he could arrive at the original length of one inner side of the portico: about 325 feet. But there paper hypothesis had to rest, awaiting excavation.

The opportunity did not arise until 1934, in connection with systematizing and beautifying with lawns the borders of Mussolini's grandiose new Via dell' Impero, cut, as we saw (pages 167 and 188), through slums from the Colosseum to the Piazza Venezia. The two projecting columns of the *Forum Transitorium* ("Forum of Nerva"), southeast of the Forum of Augustus, were cleared, under the direction of A. M. Colini, of medieval and modern detritus down to their plinths (Figs. 9.4 and 9.5); the podium of the Temple of Minerva, at the end of this Forum, uncovered (most of its stones had been used in 1606 to build the Acqua Paola on the Janiculum); and the *peperino* wall behind the projecting columns isolated. Close in back of this wall, on the Forum of Peace side, Colini found large columns in African marble, which, he inferred, marked the missing northwest side of that Forum. Its general location had been known since 1818, but only now was there a *precise* point in modern Rome's subsoil from which, with the help of the Marble Plan, the true dimensions of Vespasian's portico could be measured. Also, another fragment of the Marble Plan, not joining the two previously mentioned, showed the very stretch of wall and the columns which Colini had been excavating, as well as the plan of Minerva's temple, the podium of which he had uncovered.

Now that the plan of Vespasian's Forum could be precisely fitted into the plan of modern Rome, it became clear that some fragments of large, fluted white marble columns, found in the southeastern part of this area as long ago as 1875, belonged to the part of the portico where the larger columns shown on the Marble Plan would fall. Colini now

FIG. 9.4 Rome, *Forum Transitorium*, Colonnacce before excavation.

FIG. 9.5 Rome, *Forum Transitorium*, Colonnacce after excavation.

(M. Scherer, *Marvels of Ancient Rome*, Pls. 162 and 165)

made another join on the Marble Plan, adding to Lanciani's fragment another piece, previously known but not connected, which showed the Temple of Peace at the back of the portico. It was an apsidal building, wider than it was deep, with a pedestal for the cult statue indicated in the apse. If it survived today it would come within a few feet of touching the north corner of the Basilica of Maxentius. The south side of the rectangular hall to the right of it coincides with the actual wall of the church of Sts. Cosmas and Damian, which was the findspot—in 1562—of the fragments of the Marble Plan itself. This square hall was one of the libraries of Vespasian's Forum. Since the principle of axial symmetry nearly always operates, and since the Romans usually built their libraries in pairs (one Latin, one Greek), Colini quite reasonably restored on paper another rectangular hall to the left of the apsidal temple. A section of the polychrome marble pavement, excavated by Colini east of the church wall, was less than an inch thick, too thin to be exposed to the weather. Colini inferred that it must have been part of the flooring of the library in which the Marble Plan was displayed.

An ingenious combination—"joins" recognized on the Marble Plan, actual excavation, and inference—had now made the Forum's general outline clear, but Colini was not yet done. Overlying the Forum's outer (northeast) perimeter wall, as he had plotted it, rose the medieval Torre dei Conti, built by the brother of Pope Innocent III. Reexamining the ancient remains, in squared travertine, ordinary tufa, and *peperino,* beneath this tower, Colini was able to establish that they formed part of Vespasian's Forum, a great ornamental rectangular niche on its northeast side, with two columns of African marble in front of it. Symmetry would dictate another matching niche farther to the southeast in the same wall, and a pair on the opposite side to correspond. Pink granite columns found in the excavations belonged to the portico; marble gutters proved that it had a pitched roof.

Finally, in 1938, the plan was complete enough for a model of the Forum to be made (Fig. 9.6) for Mussolini's Mostra Augustea della Romanità, now called the Museo della Civiltà Romana, a great exhibition of models and photographs of Roman architecture and engineering, casts of inscriptions, and replicas of artifacts.

But Vespasian's Forum, famous as it was, and valuable as its restored plan is to illustrate archaeological inference at work, is overshadowed by his mightiest monument, which has survived to become the very symbol of pagan Rome to modern times: the Flavian Amphitheater or Colosseum. More perhaps than any other classical monument, its stones are steeped in blood and memories: in the blood of gladiators and wild beasts, and perhaps of Christian martyrs, in memories of medieval battles, Renaissance plundering of stone (much of the travertine in St. Peter's came from it), and

FIG. 9.6   Rome, Imperial Fora, model.
(F. Castagnoli, *Roma antica*, Pl. 4)

Victorian moonlight visits. Having resisted earthquakes, fire, and demolition, it is now menaced by the vibrations of modern traffic. Work on strengthening its walls against this new threat has been going on since 1956.

For sheer mass the Colosseum deserves its name. It is a third of a mile around, and the Italian engineer G. Cozzo has calculated that 100,000 cubic meters of travertine went into its outside wall, over four times as much into the whole structure. The achievement here, however, is not mere massiveness but precise engineering, careful calculations of stresses and strains, avoidance of crowding at entrances and exits, perfect visibility, and ingenuity in the arrangements for getting the wild beasts into the arena. (Perhaps this is the place to recall that the architectural detail of the building owes much to the Sanctuary of Fortune at Praeneste, and to the Tabularium in the Forum; also that it was upon the Colosseum that Charles Follen McKim based his design for the Harvard Stadium.) The site chosen (Fig. 12.16, 9–10), the bed of the pool of Nero's Golden House. was good propaganda and good engineering. It was good for public relations to turn a detested Emperor's pleasure grounds into a place for public enjoyment. (Neither Vespasian nor the Roman mob would have thought of the slaughter of men and beasts as anything but enjoyable; their attitude at best was that of Hemingway to a bullfight.) From the engineering point of view, it saved much excavation to pump out the pool and use it for the substructure of the arena, and in the low, soft ground, footings could go deep: eight feet of concrete under the *cavea*. Besides, the huge mass of debris from the demolished Golden House could be cannily reused in the new fabric. The first step was to erect a skeleton of travertine piers, a double row, built of squared blocks held together not with mortar but with metal clamps. The holes where these clamps were wrenched out, 300 metric tons of them, in the metal-starved Middle Ages, are visible today throughout the fabric. Differences in construction suggest that the huge project was divided into four quadrants, each assigned to a different contractor. Most of the work is honest, so that, for example, one cannot get the proverbial penknife blade into the joints between the blocks of the piers, but in the northwest quadrant the work is shoddy. This is precisely the section that has given the most trouble under the strain of the traffic vibrations of modern times.

Inside the second concentric ellipse of piers begins a set of radial walls which supported the seats. The slope of the seats was precisely calculated for perfect visibility. The vaults of the lower levels were left open until the upper-level piers were finished. This made possible the use of derricks to lift heavy blocks to the upper levels. The third-story piers have one course of blocks projecting, to provide a step to support the scaffolding required for building the wall on the fourth level. This wall is built of smaller blocks than those used on the lower levels, to facilitate lifting, and it is full of second-hand materials: column drums, for example, which may have come from the Golden House. The outer face of the fourth-level wall is equipped with 240 consoles, projecting brackets jutting out from the wall to support masts. Corresponding to each in the cornice above is a hole for the mast. The mast, Cozzo argues persuasively, was fitted with rope and pulley. The rope descended obliquely and was fastened to another below which ran elliptically at a convenient height above the podium of the arena. Awnings, fixed to these ropes, could be rolled up or down in strips as the sun's position dictated. Awnings being made of canvas, this duty was assigned to detachments of sailors—the logical Roman administrative mind at work.

When the skeleton was finished, the space between the piers in the radial walls was filled in: on the ground level with tufa, on the second level with lighter materials, brick and cement. Only then were the vaults completed. The stairs were ingeniously planned to give access from the ground direct to each level separately. This both emphasized distinctions (VIPs in the lowest tier, women at the top; compare the separate second-balcony stairs in modern theaters) and facilitated entrance and exit. Each outside entrance—there were originally eighty—bears a Roman numeral. This corresponded to a number on the admission ticket, and divided the 45,000 or 50,000 spectators into manageable groups.

The arena proper was surrounded by a wall, high enough to protect the spectators from the beasts (VIPs not being regarded as expendable), but not so high as to block the view of the arena from the seats behind. Slots in the top of this wall are the postholes for a dismountable fence, which supplied additional protection. Literary sources say it was of gilt metal surmounted by elephants' tusks. In front of the fence ran a catwalk where archers were stationed to shoot beasts which got out of hand.

The arena was originally floored with wooden planking, removable for the mock naval battles which were staged here in the early years of the amphitheater's existence. Since this had been the site of Nero's artificial pool, flooding must have been comparatively easy. But though slaves fought and killed each other in these naval battles, they were less sanguinary, and therefore less popular, than gladiatorial contests or beast fights, and changing back and forth from murder on water to murder on land was a nuisance, so the naval battles were transferred elsewhere. The area below the arena floor was then filled in with complicated substructures, which finally revealed their secret to Cozzo in 1928.

The area under the catwalk in each quadrant contains eight cell-like rooms, each big enough to hold a man, and approached by a short corridor. Opening out of each corridor, forward and to the left of a man sitting in the cell, are three adjoining shafts, a small square one, a large rectangular one, and another square one of medium size. How are these to be explained? Cozzo reasoned that a beast was released from his cage near the center of the substructure, into the corridor (1) shown in Fig. 9.7, with a portcullis (a) at the end of it. The portcullis was raised, and the beast charged into the transverse corridor (2). This was too narrow for him to turn back; he was therefore forced to go forward into the open elevator cage (3). The attendant in the cell then released a counterweight, whose rope ran in one shaft while the weight itself rose and fell in another, one shaft on either side of the elevator proper. The elevator door then closed; the elevator rose, activated by the counter‧weight, to position (4) in Fig. 9.7. The beast emerged into the narrow upper-level corridor (5–6), raced up the ramp (7), and emerged, slavering for fresh meat, through the trapdoor (8) into the arena.

This is not the only ingenious device in the Colosseum. The substructure piers along the arena's long axis are cut obliquely. Why? Cozzo reasoned that on them rested, at an angle below the horizontal, hinged sections of the arena flooring, on which stage sets could be placed; the whole section of flooring could then be raised by counterweights to the arena level, to provide appropriate backdrops or scenery for the fights. Against such backdrops, scenes from myth or

FIG. 9.7
Rome, Colosseum, beast elevator, elevation. (Cozzo, *Ingegneria Romana*, Fig. 175)

history were acted out, the protagonists tortured to death before delighted spectators. We hear of 11,000 beasts, and 5,000
pairs of gladiators, fighting to the death in one session in the
arena. In 1937, demolition of houses east of the Colosseum
revealed the ground plan (Domitianic) of part of the gladiators' barracks, with armory, infirmary, baths, and, for training bouts, a miniature amphitheater, with seats for rabid
fans (Fig. 9.8). New joins on the Marble Plan have revealed
another nearby, called the Ludus Dacicus, and therefore
probably Trajanic, celebrating his victory over the Dacians.
To celebrate the millennium of Rome, in A.D. 248, elephants,
elk, tigers, lions, leopards, hyenas, hippopotamuses, a rhinoceros, zebras, giraffes, wild asses, and wild horses (captured in Africa; see Fig. 13.5) were slaughtered in the
Colosseum. This market of flesh did not cease till the sixth
Christian century. As late as the reign of Odoacer (476–
493), senators' names were still being inscribed on reserved
seats.

Fig. 9.8   Rome, Colosseum, model, showing colossal statue of Nero
(left center), Arch of Constantine (bottom left), and gladiators'
barracks (right center). (P. Bigot, *Rome Antique*, fac. p. 44)

Vespasian did not live to see the Colosseum completed. It was dedicated, still unfinished, under Titus in A.D. 80. The chief surviving monument of Titus's reign is his arch, commemorating his conquest of the Jews in A.D. 70, but, since the inscription upon it refers to him as deified, it is clear that the arch was not finished until after his death. Built of valuable Pentelic marble, it would never have been preserved if it had not been incorporated, in the Middle Ages, into a fortress of the powerful family of the Frangipani. The last vestiges of the Frangipani tower were not removed from the arch until 1821. It was then reinforced and its missing portions restored in travertine. In 1980 it, along with Trajan's Column (chapter 10) and the arches of Septimius Severus and of Constantine (chapter 12) were covered with scaffolding and green wire mesh to protect them against pollution. The arch of Titus is chiefly famous for the use in it of Rome's first Composite (Ionic plus Corinthian) capitals, and for the relief on its inner jamb showing (Fig. 9.9) Titus's army carrying in triumph the spoils of Jerusalem, including the table of the shewbread, the seven-branched candlestick, and the silver trumpets. In the relief opposite, Titus stands in a four-horse chariot, with the goddess Roma leading the horses, and Victory crowning him with a laurel wreath. The frieze under the cornice, not unrelated to the small inner altar frieze of the Altar of Peace, portrays a procession of priests, sacrificial animals, and troops carrying on their shoulders small platforms bearing representations of cities and places conquered by Roman arms, including a personification of the River Jordan. The motif in the highest part of the inner vault, showing Titus—who was a burly man—carried off to heaven by an eagle, is as conventional as the Ganymede in the vault of the underground basilica at the Porta Maggiore. In the years since Augustus, Roman official art had become conventional without ceasing to be historical.

The arch appears, with other Domitianic buildings, on a

FIG. 9.9 Rome, Arch of Titus, showing relief with spoils of Temple at Jerusalem. (Fototeca)

relief (Fig. 9.10) from the tomb of the Haterii, found in
1848 near Centocelle, on the Via Labicana three miles southeast of the Porta Maggiore, and now in the Vatican. The
arch on the relief bears little resemblance to the actual
monument; the Colosseum, on the other hand, is shown with
the original statues in its arcades: eagles above; Hercules,
Apollo, and Aesculapius below. The other monuments shown,
no longer extant, are (1) the Arcus ad Isis in the Campus
Martius near the Pantheon (perhaps the cats which prowl
there have Egyptian blood); in the attic of the arch is a
prisoner, probably of the Jewish War, chained to a palm
tree: the motif recurs on the Trajanic reliefs at Adamklisi
(*Dacian Stones Speak*, Fig. 4.22); (2) the arch shown in
side view once stood at the east end of the Circus Maximus;
the statue is of Magna Mater, but not the one on the Palatine; (3) the hexastyle temple shows a cult statue of Jupiter,
either Capitolinus or Tonans, both temples restored by Domitian. The tomb must have been commissioned by a contractor who worked on these buildings: the inference is
warranted by the crane (Fig. 9.11) on another relief from
the tomb: its ropes and pulleys lifted building blocks; it was
worked by slaves in a treadmill. The reliefs of the tomb itself
tell as much as those of Eurysaces' tomb about the pretensions and beliefs of the haute bourgeoisie. At the top, the
deceased, a woman, reclines on a banqueting couch; she
appears again in the tomb's pediment. The children, one of
them wearing the lion's skin of Hercules, who play at the
foot of the couch recur in medallions below. An old woman
throws incense on an altar bearing Bacchic symbols in relief.
To the right is a miniature temple featuring a statue of Venus,
with masks of ancestors above. The tomb proper is shown,
with paneled and figured bronze doors, flanked by plaques
of Cupids, symbolizing the Seasons; they recur, riding sea
monsters or playing with garlands, in the central panels of
the side wall, and again in the lower register. Bacchus' grape-

FIG. 9.10　Rome, Vatican, Tomb of Haterii, Domitianic buildings.
(Vatican Museum)

FIG. 9.11　Vatican, Tomb of the Haterii, crane and tomb proper.
(Alinari/Editorial Photocolor Archives)

vines twine about the columns, surmounted by eagles, which also appear on the ridgepole. The side wall had pilasters embellished with fruit, flowers, and grain ears. The lower reliefs portray Virtues. In the lowest register we see Hercules with basket and shovel: he is resting from his labor of cleaning the Augean stables. In the center of the lowest register is the half-open door of the tomb, with a veiled woman (the deceased?) in the opening; to the right, a fountain house. The relief's lower left quadrant shows a puzzling structure, perhaps the ustrinum, for cremation; above it, a canopied altar with Cupids wielding thunderbolts.

To the good Titus succeeded the wicked, psychopathic, tyrannical Domitian, the greatest builder-emperor since Augustus, and one under whom the Empire took a long stride on the road to absolutism. His building activity rivaled that of Augustus, and one of his favorite areas was the Campus Martius. Recent excavation under the Palazzo Farnese has revealed a complex of buildings which may be the stables for the various factions of chariot horses, one phase of which is Domitianic. One evidence of Domitian's self-aggrandizement turned up unexpectedly in 1937, under the Palazzo della Cancelleria in the Campus Martius (Fig. 12.16, 11), seat of the papal chancellery, and an enclave of Vatican City. Curiously, the palace already had an intimate connection with the Flavians: many of the stones in its fabric were robbed in the late fifteenth and early sixteenth century from the Colosseum. In connection with extensive repairs to the building, deep excavations beneath it revealed the tomb of the consul Aulus Hirtius, a lieutenant of Julius Caesar's who died in office, and in battle against Mark Antony, in 43 B.C. Leaning face inward against this tomb were five slabs which proved to be part of a marble historical relief. A sixth slab was found later nearby, still within papal jurisdiction; a seventh, found under the sidewalk, technically outside the

Pope's control, was first claimed by the Roman civil authorities. But a trade was made for the slab of the Altar of Peace then in Vatican hands, and all the slabs are now reunited in a courtyard of the Vatican Museum.

The seven slabs combine into two sections of some sixteen figures each, almost complete (Fig. 9.12a, b). The more fragmentary of the two contains near its right end an instantly identifiable figure, with the characteristic beaked profile of Vespasian (Fig. 9.13). He is saluting, whether in greeting (*adventus*) or farewell (*profectio*) is controversial, a young man, surely one of his sons. Comparison with known portraits of Titus and Domitian leads to the conclusion that it is the latter who is represented here. The salutation is taking place in the presence of lictors, Vestals (identified from their characteristic headdress), *apparitores*, or escorts (at either end), a helmeted female figure (the goddess Roma or, according to some, the war goddess Bellona, or the personification of martial courage), and two male figures, one bearded (the Genius of the Senate), and one beardless, with a cornucopia (the Genius of the Roman People). The other section is at once more complete, more difficult to interpret, and more interesting. Several of the conventional figures recur: the lictors, Roma, the two *Genii*. There are also six soldiers (in the uniform and with the arms of the praetorian guard); the wing of a Victory; a helmeted female wearing the *aegis*, the characteristic breastplate of Minerva; the helmeted, bearded male figure beside her must be another divinity, Mars. The remaining figure, the first on the second slab from the left (see Fig. 9.14), is rendered in profile, and is clearly intended as a portrait, but close examination, by Dr. F. Magi, when he was Director of the Vatican Museums, shows that it was reworked in antiquity.

Here archaeological ingenuity again goes to work. The two sections of the total relief obviously (from the similar technique and the recurrence of conventional figures in

FIG. 9.12 (*top and bottom*)   Vatican City. Cancelleria reliefs:
procession of Domitian; greeting by Vespasian
(Musei Vaticani)

both) belong together. The presence of Vespasian places
both sections in the Flavian age. Of the three Flavians, only
Domitian was sufficiently hated to have had *damnatio
memoriae* practiced upon him, to alter his portrait into another's. And the most conspicuous alteration of the head
consists in hacking off a fringe of curls on the forehead; such
a fringe was Domitian's characteristic hairstyle. It remains
to inquire whose the new profile is. In the context, it must
be an emperor. The most likely candidate is Domitian's successor, Nerva, the first of the "five good Emperors." The new
profile, with its irregular nose, lined forehead, and sunken
cheeks, suits the known iconography of that tired old man.
Left with the question why, then, the portrait of Domitian
on the other section of the relief was left undamaged, Magi
argued that the Senate, on second thought, had considered
the alteration into Nerva not enough: the relief was dis-

FIG. 9.13　Vatican City. Cancelleria reliefs. Detail of head of
Vespasian. (Musei Vaticani)

mantled altogether, and its slabs carefully stacked against
Hirtius's tomb for the future use of one of the stonecutters
whose yards are known to have been numerous in the area.

Two questions remain: the occasion for carving the relief
in the first place, and the building that housed it. The occasion for greeting Vespasian must be the most memorable
one of his reign: his triumphant return from Jerusalem in
A.D. 70. The occasion for greeting Domitian must be an
equally memorable one, almost certainly his setting out on
a campaign, or his return from a military victory (because
of the prominence of the winged figure and the Mars on the

FIG. 9.14　Vatican City. Cancelleria reliefs. Detail showing
how head of Domitian was transformed into that of Nerva.
(Musei Vaticani)

relief). Domitian's military successes were not many; the likeliest is his campaign of A.D. 83 against a German tribe, the Chatti. If carving the monument would take a year, as competent sculptors report, the earliest possible date for the finished relief would be A.D. 84; on grounds of style, Jocelyn Toynbee and Erika Simon would date it eight or nine years later. To celebrate the same victory, Domitian built the Temple of Fortuna Redux (Good Luck and Safe Return), and this temple, Magi thinks, is a reasonable place to suppose the reliefs to have been displayed. (Heinz Kähler, however, would assign them to the Domitianic predecessor of Hadrian's Pantheon.) In them the whole Roman state is portrayed as asking of the founder of the Flavian dynasty and of his son the peace and prosperity which the Julio-Claudians had failed to give. Like the fresco of the Villa of the Mysteries at Pompeii, the relief is not great art but a great document, a measure of the distance Roman sculpture had traveled in the scant century since the Altar of Peace. It is a courtier's exaltation of a monarch; a solemn, highly rhetorical affirmation of imperial sovereignty and pride in Rome's dominion. And perhaps there is a moral in it, too: it summarizes the history of the dynasty, from the triumphant reception of the first Flavian to the explosion of hate which damned the memory, by altering the face, of the last. And these slabs, the expression of a despot's pride, end leaning against the simple tomb of a lieutenant of Julius Caesar, who died fighting, he would have said, to save for his fatherland its free institutions.

In A.D. 86 Domitian set about continuing the work begun by Vespasian on the narrow Forum between the Forum of Peace and that of Augustus, which we have had occasion to mention earlier. (The final dedication was not to occur until Nerva's reign.) In effect this Forum was an ingenious device to monumentalize the street which led from the old Republican Forum to the unsavory Subura district and workers' quarter to the north. Caesar's Forum was Venus' precinct (the temple embellished by Domitian with a frieze of Cupids); Augustus's belonged to Mars. A convention had been established, a canonical way of doing things: hence, Vespasian dedicated his larger Forum to Peace, the *Forum Transitorium* to Minerva, with a small temple of Janus at the south end. Domitian, his devotion to Minerva already established by his having given her prominence on the Cancelleria relief, now remodeled Vespasian's temple to her, raising it on a high podium. The podium alone remains, with its relieving arch marking where the Cloaca Maxima or great sewer passed below. But the original monumentalizing of the street by Vespasian had involved building a colonnade, of a type common in the frescoes of the Pompeian Third and Fourth Styles. Along its architrave, which was richly decorated on its under side, ran a continuous frieze, the technique of which resembles that of the Cancelleria relief on a small scale, for the art of the Flavian reigns is recognizably related. The dentils in the cornice show between them, as we saw (p. 169), the characteristic "spectacles signature" of the architect Rabirius, who may have worked for Vespasian as well as for Domitian.

The surviving section of the frieze portrays Minerva among the nine Muses, and the punishment of Arachne, who for presuming to rival Minerva's skill at weaving was turned into a spider. The sculptor took the occasion to carve artisans (the figure of a fuller survives) and household scenes, of spinning, weaving, and dyeing, all under Minerva's special patronage. One sees the wool basket, the upright loom, the scales for weighing the day's stint, and the proud display of a finished roll of cloth. In the attic above the surviving section of the frieze stands the goddess in relief, wearing the characteristic cloak of a Roman general!

Recent excavation has added little to earlier knowledge

of this Forum, but it is of absorbing interest for what it adds to our portrait of the Flavians. Domitian takes over his father's plan, and pushingly insinuates himself, as it were, between his father and the Empire's founder, both of whom he envied and tried to emulate. But it was beyond even his effrontery to associate himself with the Minerva who was patroness of artisans; nothing could be more incongruous than his connecting his elegant dilettantism with the homely arts of the household. The frieze is probably a part of Vespasian's plan: its theme suits his plain personality, and the references to handicrafts suit its location on a street leading to a worker's quarter. The support of the workers (and of their wives, whose influence was all the more important to win because it was indirect) was worth having, and meanwhile Minerva's connection with the Muses (the creative arts and literature) could be turned by Domitian to his purpose: he desired to be known as a patron of the arts.

The showiest surviving result of Domitian's patronage of the art of architecture is his palace on the Palatine, planned by the famous Rabirius and finished perhaps in A.D. 92. Here is a return, after the comparative austerity of his father's and brother's reigns, to the baroque extravagance of Nero. The palace reflects Domitian's personality and is indebted to earlier, and seminal of later Roman architecture. In the basilica (plan, Fig. 9.15,*F*) the Emperor was judge; in the throne room (*E*), autocrat; in the lararium (*G*), pontifex maximus. The throne room, with its colossal niches for statues, was built for an Emperor with delusions of divinity. The dining room (*H*) had a dais to elevate the god-Emperor above his guests, but the peristyle (*D*), originally faced with marbles polished like mirrors (to reflect possible assassins), was planned by a terrified mortal who feared stabs in the back. (Blocks from the peristyle cornice show, as in the *Forum Transitorium,* Rabirius's

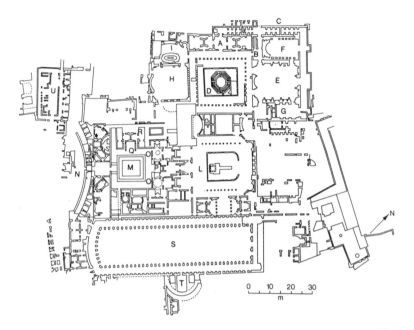

FIG. 9.15   Rome, Palatine, Palace of Domitian, plan. (Fototeca)

FIG. 9.16   Rome, Palatine, Palace of Domitian, reconstruction.
(F. Castagnoli, *Roma antica*, Pl. 44.1)

"spectacles signature.") The restless inward and outward curves of the rooms at *A* in the west block (the public part) of the palace, and at *O* in the eastern private quarters, were made possible by the flexibility of poured concrete, which, as we saw in chapter 5, makes it possible to enclose space in any shape (see reconstruction, Fig. 9.16). This fluidity appealed to Hadrian, the most gifted amateur architect among the emperors, and he imitated it, as we shall see, in his Villa near Tivoli.

The *impluvium* (pool for rain water) in the peristyle (*M*) of the private quarters contained a fountain, and is curiously treated with cut-out segments of circles, with cuttings in its top face for setting statues. This combination of plays of water and works of art is in the taste of the Sperlonga villa of Tiberius: ancient sources find a parallel between that monarch's suspicious, tyrannical nature and Domitian's. The small temple in the upper peristyle (*L*), connected with the "mainland" by a curious seven-arched bridge, was built, to judge by its materials and technique, two centuries later than Domitian. But his is the "stadium" (*S*). Its portico makes it unlikely that it was ever a track for running races in the Greek style; he was to build such a stadium full-scale in the Campus Martius in A.D. 93. The Palatine stadium, in spite of its apsidal imperial spectator's box (the model for Bramante's Vatican Belvedere), was probably a garden for shady strolling. Perhaps Hadrian had this plan in mind when he built the "Painted Porch" or "Poecile" of his villa, to which we shall return. It is hard to realize that all this splendor lies only 100 yards from the site of "Romulus's" straw hut. The difference measures the distance Roman culture had traveled in 800 years.

One used to be able to sit under the umbrella pines of a summer evening and hear symphony concerts played in Domitian's stadium garden. On such occasions it seemed less of a pity that the Palatine is incompletely excavated.

Here, on this hill of dreams, as Miss Scherer calls it, one could imagine Domitian's palace rich with many-colored marbles, bright with paintings and gold. One could wander in the dappled light among oleander and lemon trees, golden broom and scarlet poppies, and admire how the mellow brick glowed rose-colored in the afternoon sunlight. One could appreciate the mood of the Romantics for whom, a century and a half ago, all Rome had this dreamlike quality. One can argue that their attitude may not have been scientific, but it produced the classical revival in architecture. Here is the old dilemma, but its horns are properly labeled not art and science, but sentiment and intelligence. If we want truly to understand ancient Rome, the choice is clear. Sentiment is not a Roman quality; intelligence is. The atmosphere of Domitian's reign was not dream but nightmare. The natural beauty of the Palatine is attractive but adventitious; the essence of the place is of another kind, starker, grander, more disciplined, than a nineteenth-century water color, and behind it looms always the shadow of violence.

Domitian also had a summer palace in the Alban Hills, perhaps on the very site of Alba Longa. The papal residence at Castel Gandolfo occupies the site today. In Republican times Cicero's enemy Clodius, and Pompey had villas here. The palace complex is on three terraces, five hundred meters long, but narrow. At the top were servants' quarters, a slave cemetery, and cisterns. The middle level contained the palace proper, long and narrow, with the rooms grouped around three courtyards in a row. An avenue with nymphaea led westward to a small theater, where Domitian could indulge his taste for things Greek: stuccoes in a corridor under the cavea portrayed Bacchus, the Muses, and Medea. The main feature of the lowest terrace was a cryptoportico with skylights and caissoned vaults, forming a monumental entrance to the palace. There were also stalls for animals due to be slaughtered in the nearby circus, in plan like the hippodrome on the Palatine. The whole complex was surrounded by a wall, reflecting the Emperor's persecution mania and fear of violence.

Not violence but intelligence, and the affectation of Hellenism, lies behind Domitian's stadium (for Greek games) and odeum, or music hall (for literary and musical competitions) in the Campus Martius (Fig. 12.16,12). The shape of the stadium has been preserved almost intact in the loveliest of Rome's squares, the Piazza Navona (Fig. 9.17). As a part of Mussolini's ambitious new city plan in 1936, a great new street called the Corso del Rinascimento was constructed, running north and south through the Campus Martius. It provided an opportunity for definitive examination of the stadium's remains, which had been preserved in the cellars of shops and the crypts of churches. This Colini undertook; he emerged from his molelike labors with a plan (Fig. 9.18) and a model (Fig. 9.19) of the stadium, a prime example of what archaeology can do with bits and pieces. Nowadays remains of the hemicycle are visible under an insurance building outside the north end of the *piazza,* and one travertine pier is to be seen under the arcade of the Corsia Agonale, in the middle of the stadium's east side. Beneath this area are traces of the footings, of cement poured in caissons, thicker and stronger the farther east they go, to support the increasing weight of the rising tiers of seats above. Brick stamps found here date the building to A.D. 93 or a little after, with evidence of major repairs under Hadrian (another Greek lover) and Caracalla (another violent despot).

Colini found that Domitian's architect, to compensate for providing here only one *ambulacrum* or vaulted corridor for sauntering, where the Colosseum had two, widened his

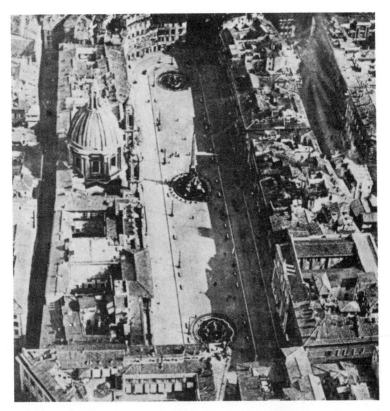

Fig. 9.17   Rome, Piazza Navona, air view.
(A. M. Colini, *Stadium Domitiani*, frontispiece)

corridor at regular intervals between the stairs to provide
halls where spectators—the stadium had seats for 30,000—
might congregate between footraces. The stadium was built
in a repeated sequence: stair, entrance, hall, entrance, stair,
which gives classical orderliness and efficiency to the plan
(perhaps Rabirius's). This was the last great public building
in Rome to use conventional classical décor. In the center
of the west side was the Imperial box: the crypt of the
church of Sant' Agnese marks its substructure. Here the
good saint allegedly suffered martyrdom, condemned by the

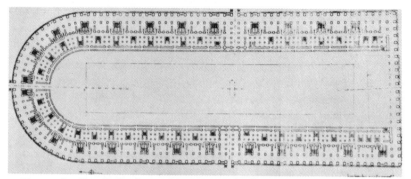

FIG. 9.18   Rome, Stadium of Domitian. (Colini, *op. cit.*, Suppl. Pl. B)

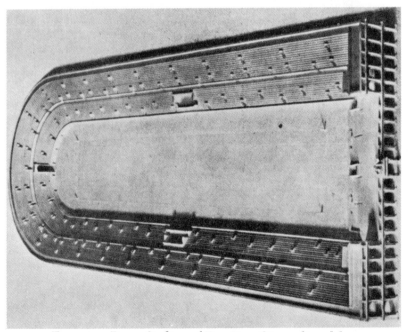

FIG. 9.19   Rome, Stadium of Domitian, Gismondi model.
(Colini, *op. cit.*, Pl. 16)

Emperor Diocletian to the brothels in the stadium arcades. The whole building profited by the experience of the Colosseum's builders, as they in turn had profited from the experience of the builders of the Theater of Marcellus. Thus its exterior was adorned with engaged columns, Doric on the first level, Corinthian on the second. But the total effect was deliberately different, graceful where the Colosseum was massive, dedicated to Greek footraces instead of Roman blood-sports. The only thing of its kind outside the Greek world, the stadium was a deliberate flouting of Roman tradition. This was in Domitian's manner. The Roman people rejected it, in theirs. To them, Greek footraces represented foreign degeneracy, nudism, and immorality. No sooner was the tyrant murdered (in a courtier's plot sparked by his wife) than they went back to their simple pleasures of watching the murder of gladiators and wild beasts. Domitian's odeum, traces of which were found south of the stadium in 1936–37, did not suffer the same fate, for it could be used for pantomime (Fig. 13.1) and other degraded forms of dramatic art.

Here then, is a part, a small part, of what archaeology can tell us of the prodigious Flavian activity in architecture and in art. It will be noticed that, not for the first or the last time in Roman history, the greatest tyrant is also the greatest builder. (He is also Rome's last great emperor who did not come from the provinces.) Absolutism was the price Rome paid for its grandeur. But, in the century after Domitian's murder, absolutism marked time. Nerva's successor, the Spaniard Trajan, is the second of the "five good Emperors," under whom the metropolis and its port prospered, and the provinces lived content.

10

Trajan: Port, Forum, Market, Baths, and Column

Archaeologically speaking, the most important sites in Italy to illustrate Roman events and the Roman way of life in the happy reign (A.D. 98–117) of Trajan—called *Optimus Princeps*, "best of princes"—are the port of Ostia, which he endowed with a new harbor, and his Forum, the last and grandest of the Imperial Fora.

Our present knowledge of Ostia, extending far beyond the early *castrum* discussed in chapter 4, is due in large part to the devoted skill of Guido Calza. Under some pressure from Mussolini, who wanted the dig finished for an exposition scheduled for 1942 (but never inaugurated), he supervised the removal in four years of over 600,000 cubic yards of earth, recovering some seventy of the 170 acres enclosed within Ostia's Sullan wall. What he uncovered he rejuvenated but did not falsify: his method was much the same as Spinazzola's in Pompeii. This was his principle, more honored in the breach than the observance: "Better to brace than repair, better repair than restore, better restore than embellish; never add or subtract." His aim was not to suppress inconvenient ugliness, but to remove impediments to study and understanding. He restored mosaics, making a clear distinction between the old *tesserae* and the new, re-erected columns, put balconies back in place, and rebuilt wooden ceilings to protect houses from the weather. He detached wall paintings, reinforced them with cement and wire mesh, and replaced them—covered with glass and protected against mold by the insertion of lead plates into the wall below the painting, to retard the spread, by capillary action, of dampness. He sealed the tops of walls, freed flights of stairs from rubble, opened out windows which had been bricked up in late antiquity. He planted trees, and set a privet hedge to mark the line of the city wall. He restored the ancient drainage system. The result of all this careful work was to present to the modern world a picture of Roman life under the Empire only a shade less vivid than Pompeii. And the picture is not of a provincial town, but of the very vestibule of Rome itself, in fact a Rome in miniature, for Ostia gives an excellent notion of what life in the metropolis was like at the height of the Empire. And thanks to the careful work on the brick stamps by Professor Herbert Bloch of Harvard, most of the buildings excavated can be dated with a very fair degree of precision, so that Ostia's development can be accurately traced from end to end.

We know from an inscription that Trajan's artificial harbor, whose completion marked the beginning of Ostia's peak of prosperity, was begun in A.D. 104. Ostia proper was at the very mouth of the Tiber, but silting, which today has put the beach of modern Ostia (Ostia Lido) three miles beyond the seawall of the ancient town, early made the city docks impracticable for any but the smallest vessels. So Trajan built his harbor beside (indeed over the necropolis of) Claudius's, two and a half miles northwest of the town. The traffic in grain and luxury goods to feed and pander to the more or less refined tastes of the largest and richest city in the world made Ostia vastly prosperous. The evidence is building activity, dated by brick stamps, impressed on building tiles, and bearing the names of consuls, tile manufacturers, or both. There was a slight time lag, while prosperity built up. Only 12 percent of the datable buildings in Ostia belonging to Trajan's reign; 43 percent were built or restored under Hadrian. Then activity tapers off again: 17 percent of the buildings are of Antonine date (A.D. 138–192), while only 12 percent belong to the age of the Severi (A.D. 193–235). Thereafter Ostia, whose fortunes rose with Rome's, declines with her also.

The most illuminating way to describe what archaeology has to tell us about Ostia is to follow the plan used for Pompeii, treating in order the town and its population, municipal life and public amenities, housing arrangements, trade and industry, and the evidence for Ostia's religious life. Art in Ostia is, naturally, less well preserved than at Pompeii, but what survives sometimes rises above the level of pure documentation: in sculpture, striking portrait heads of Themistocles, Hippocrates, anonymous Roman men and women, Trajan, and perhaps the philosopher Plotinus (A.D. 205–270; Fig. 10.1); Cupid and Psyche coyly embracing; Mithras slaying the bull; in painting, nothing to compare with Pompeii; in mosaic, a crowded hunting scene from the Baths of the Seven Sages, and sea monsters from the Baths of Neptune; trademarks from the Piazzale delle Corporazioni; and some elegant *opus sectile* (tiles of colored marble cut in geometric shapes) from the House of Cupid and Psyche and from a Christian building where the Decumanus meets the sea. The recovery of the decorative design of this last building is a triumph, after six years of patient struggle with this gigantic jigsaw puzzle. (An ancient graffito shows the ancestors of the modern craftsmen working with opus sectile on a table.) The walls of the main hall were divided into three registers: the two most striking portray, the one a haloed Christ in a medallion, and the other lions (which look like large puppies) and tigers. A

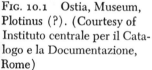

FIG. 10.1   Ostia, Museum, Plotinus (?). (Courtesy of Instituto centrale per il Catalogo e la Documentazione, Rome)

rectangular exedra at the end, was done in imitation opus reticulatum. The building was the seat of a guild; the walls are dated 385–388.

The plan of Ostia (Figs. 10.2 and 10.3) is regular but not regimented. It has unity in variety; it combines utility, a monumental quality, and the scenic. Its backbone is the major east-west street, the *decumanus*, nearly a mile long, and once colonnaded, which runs from the Porta Romana straight to the Forum. Beyond the line of the west *castrum* wall it forks sharply to the left, ending at the Porta Marina, which once fronted directly on the sea. The main north-south street, the *cardo*, began at the Porta Laurentina on the south—Ostia's triplicity of gates is an Etruscan heritage —and ran, shaded and porticoed, northwestward to the dazzling whiteness of the colonnaded, marble-enriched Forum. Then it split in two on either side of Hadrian's Capitolium and passed north between balconied houses to the river. Sixteen percent of Ostia's total area, exactly the same pro-

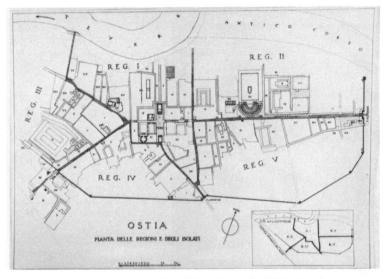

FIG. 10.2   Ostia, plan. (G. Calza, *Scavi di Ostia*, 1)

FIG. 10.3   Ostia, air view. (H. Kähler, *Rom und seine Welt*, Pl. 199)

portion as a modern city such as Madison, Wisconsin, was devoted to streets. Twelve percent of Ostia was taken up by baths, 15 percent by warehouses (for Ostia was first and foremost a commercial town), and 57 percent by houses, most of which are middle-class apartment blocks. Knowing the total housing area available, and calculating twenty-six square meters of space for each person, and an average apartment height of three stories, Meiggs reckons the maximum population at fifty to sixty thousand.

The evidence for Ostia's municipal life comes mostly from inscriptions, over six thousand of them, many unpublished. They show that Ostia, like most Italian towns, imitated Rome: since Rome had a pair of chief municipal officers, the consuls, Ostia had a pair also, the *duoviri*. One of them, C. Cartilius Poplicola, whose marble-faced tomb stands just outside the Porta Marina, was elected to this office eight times. There was a town council of 110 members, which met in a marble-floored council house facing the Forum. Legal activity went on across the street in the basilica, also paved with marble and provided with a pleasant portico facing the Forum. It had a charming frieze of Cupids carrying garlands. Both buildings are of Domitianic or Trajanic date; the prevalence of marble in them can be explained by the ease with which the stone could be brought by ships in ballast. There was a municipal plutocracy, whose names occur and recur on honorific decrees (praising them for benefactions), and on tombs near the Porta Romana and Porta Marina. The names are those of businessmen and freedmen, not of the old Roman aristocratic families. And as the years wore on, men seldom held office more than once, for it grew to be an expensive honor. If taxes assessed by the Imperial treasury were not collected in full, town officers had to make up the deficit out of their own pockets.

Public amenities included a theater, baths, and a fire department. The theater, built in Augustus's reign (about 12 B.C.), and often restored and enlarged, is surprisingly small: it seats only four thousand, and is used nowadays for outdoor performances of Greek and Roman plays. Cisterns under the center rear seats served the water ballets fashionable in late antiquity. Behind the stage building is a portico where theater patrons could saunter, with a temple in its midst built by Domitian. In a combination of business with pleasure typical of Ostia, seventy offices face the four sides of the portico. These offices, to be discussed in more detail below, were maintained by local branches of firms from all over the Empire.

Ostia was well equipped with public baths, five of which are especially interesting and are described here. (1) The Baths of the Swimmer (V.x,3), named from a mosaic, have late Domitianic brick stamps and contained frescoes, a palaestra, and much North African pottery. (2) The Baths of Neptune, Hadrianic and Antonine, near the theater (*Regio II, Insula* iv), have a large entrance hall paved with a spirited mosaic showing Neptune driving four sea horses, surrounded by Tritons, Nereids, dolphins ridden by Cupids, fabulous sea monsters of every kind, and two young men swimming. Excavation under the mosaic revealed nothing earlier than Claudius, except for a single unstratified Proto-Villanovan pot handle. Other Proto-Villanovan ware was found when a sewer was being dug in Ostia Antica village, a quarter-mile east of the entrance to the site. (3) The Baths of the Seven Sages (*Reg.* III,x) are named from a painting in the dressing room which depicts the seven wise men of Greece, each labeled with an off-color couplet describing in some detail the intimate connection between constipation and the intellectual life. (4) The Terme del Invidioso (V.v,2) were Julio-Claudian, rebuilt between A.D. 100 and 150. Their walls were painted with yellow cups on a red ground; pottery found under a mosaic floor goes back to the third century

B.C. The most interesting of all are (5) the Forum Baths (*Reg.* I,xii), built in the reign of Antoninus Pius. A 1956 study by an American heating engineer, E. D. Thatcher, underlines how well the Romans understood the principles of radiant heating (of floors, walls, bathing pools, and even vaults), and of orienting the bathing rooms to catch the maximum amount of sunlight, and to provide a windbreak Thus, although the large windows were not glazed, the rooms were usable on most days of the year, even in winter, with the additional provision, proved by put-holes, of a rigging of canvas for the coldest days. If the windows had been glazed, bathers could not have acquired a tan, whose therapeutic and fashionable implications were the same for an Ostian as for us. Thatcher calculates that an unglazed room in the Forum Baths was usable 98 percent of the time: hence glazing was not worthwhile. The Romans knew, as the Forum Baths show, that the flow of heat is always from a hotter body to a colder one, and that air temperature alone is no criterion of comfort. In fact one may be comfortable in a much lower air temperature than that found in most American houses and public buildings, provided one does not lose more heat than one is generating at the time. The floor and wall surfaces of the Forum Baths radiated enough warmth to keep bathers comfortable in relatively cool air with unglazed windows. The courtyard of the baths was paved with white mosaic to reflect light and heat. A room which commanded a maximum of sunlight had radiant heat in the floor only, not in the walls. The various rooms of the baths were heated to different temperatures; Romans achieved with differently heated areas what we achieve with thermostats. The whole complex of the Forum Baths, Thatcher concludes, shows a sophistication in the use of radiant heating well beyond what modern engineers have achieved.

Though brick construction made Ostia more nearly fire-

proof than a modern city of frame dwellings, the grain for
the dole stored in the city's numerous warehouses was too
valuable a commodity to risk. A cohort of firemen detached
from the main corps in Rome was therefore kept at the ready
in barracks behind the Baths of Neptune (*Reg.* II,v). The
barracks, built under Hadrian, surround an arcaded courtyard with rooms opening off, where excavation under a
mosaic found nothing older than Claudius. A latrine with a
shrine in it thriftily combines cleanliness with godliness. At
the end of the courtyard opposite the entrance is a platform
which still bears the bases of statues of emperors worshiped
by the firemen as a part of the Imperial cult.

As at Pompeii, so at Ostia, the houses are the most interesting part of the city, not least because Ostian houses differ
completely in plan from those of Pompeii. The Imperial
Palace, some 200 meters west of the main excavated area,
dates from the reign of Antoninus Pius: it had baths, courts,
a peristyle, apartments on a large scale, a Mithraeum, and a
carpetlike mosaic, now in the Vatican. But the great majority
of Ostian residential structures are apartment houses—tall,
many-windowed brick blocks, with or without shops on the
ground floor. They were designed to be rented out in flats,
with separate access to the upper stories from the street.
Some have balconies, opening both on the street and on
garden courtyards. There, many families shared the pergolas,
fountains, trees, shrubs, pools, and statue-studded lawns, as
they shared also the large common latrines. The paintings
from three houses have been published in color: those of
the Painted Vaults (III,v,1), of the Yellow Walls (III,ix,12
and 21), and of the Muses (III, ix,22). In one house or another, four phases, Hadrianic to post-Severan, have been
distinguished. The House of the Painted Vaults runs the
gamut of tastes, from an elegant octagonal ceiling with
Pegasus, a peacock, and Cupids and pygmies fishing to an
erotic daub as crude as anything in Pompeii. The House of

the Yellow Walls has scenes of Hercules fighting against the river god Acheloüs, and a Maenad with a Silenus. The House of the Muses is named from panels representing these divinities, with their patron, Apollo. These houses were for the rich. The Casa dei Dipinti (*Reg.* I.iv.4; see Fig. 10.4) is a middle-class block, built in Hadrian's reign. The ground-floor flats have mosaic floors and paintings of mythological scenes, figures of poets and dancers, landscapes, and fantastic motifs. At the end of the garden is yet another of Ostia's combinations of the useful with the ornamental: a number of large *dolia,* terracotta jars sunk in the ground for storing oil or grain. Despite the panegyrics of the excavators, there is a certain deadly sameness about these flats where the lower middle class lived their lives of quiet desperation, as they do in the unfashionable quarters of Rome today.

The occupants of Ostia's flats were largely minor civil servants or tradesmen. There are eight hundred shops, including four fullers' establishments, like those at Pompeii, where workmen cleaned garments by soaking them in vats full of urine and jumping up and down on them: the vats have side rails to facilitate this process.

The livelihood of these people came from Ostia's two artificial harbors (Fig. 10.5). The earlier, begun under Claudius in A.D. 42, is now the site of Rome's main airport, whose engineers have preserved the traces (Fig. 10.6) of the two curving moles which enclosed a basin over 650,000 square yards in area. Ostia's famous four-story lighthouse, repeatedly portrayed in relief and mosaic, stood two-thirds of the way along the left mole—on the cement-filled hull of a monstrous ship, 104 meters long, which had brought from Egypt the obelisk now in Rome's Piazza S. Pietro. The harbor opening was 200 meters wide; by its left edge were found seven wrecks, a veritable marine graveyard. They are now housed in a small museum in front of the Fiumicino airport building. Ancient sources say there was an artificial

FIG. 10.4   Ostia, Casa dei Dipinti. Gismondi's reconstruction.

FIG. 10.6 Ostia, harbors of Claudius (traces of the mole show in a different tone in the air photograph), and of Trajan (the hexagon). (Italian Ministry of Aeronautics)

FIG. 10.5 Ostia, harbors. (Calza, *op. cit.*)

FIG. 10.7 Ostia, harbor of Trajan, model. (Mostra Augustea della Romanità, *Catalogo*, Fig. 104)

island between the arms of the moles, with a lighthouse
on it, which became the symbol of Ostia: A canal, now the
Fiumicino branch of the Tiber, connected the harbor with
the main stream. The south bank of the canal, opposite the
harbor, was used as a dumping ground for marble, rough-
cut from the quarry, awaiting shipment upstream or carriage
to Ostia. Over one hundred blocks, mostly polychrome, have
been catalogued, from all over the Empire: violet-veined
pavonazzetto (peacock-stone) from Phrygia, green *cipollino*
from Euboea, *rosso antico* from Attica, *giallo antico* from
Numidia, red-and-yellow-veined *portasanta* from Chios, red
porphyry from Egypt, green porphyry from the Pelopon-
nese; also onyx from Galatia, and alabaster from Egypt,
Syria, or local sources.

Grandiose as it was, the harbor was ill-protected from pre-
vailing winds: a storm in A.D. 62 wrecked two hundred ships
anchored or berthed in it. Trajan therefore built a smaller
but more efficient basin (Fig. 10.7): hexagonal in shape, 378
meters on a side, and with numbered berths where ships
might tie up to discharge their cargoes directly into warehouses on all six sides. A complicated entrance with a right-
angled turn protected it completely from the hazards which
had plagued Claudius's harbor; it also was connected with
the Claudian canal. Around it were baths, a temple, a small
theater, and an Imperial palace. Nowadays it is a safari park,
where visitors may combine the pleasures of ruins with ward-
ing off the attentions of mandrils and giraffes.

The ships which unloaded at the quays of Claudius's or
Trajan's harbor came from all over the Mediterranean. Their
agents had their in-town offices in the portico behind the
Augustan theater, called by the Italians the *Piazzale delle
Corporazioni*. Each office had an emblem in mosaic before
its door, indicating the commodity it imported or the service
it rendered. These mosaics, plus inscriptions, document the
greatest variety of goods and services, giving a clear idea

how busy the port of Rome was in the high Empire. The commodities included furs, wood, grain, beans, melons, oil, fish, wine, drugs, mirrors, flowers, ivory, gold, and silk. Among the service personnel were the caulkers, cordwainers, grain measurers, maintenance men for the docks, warehouses, and embankments; shipwrights, bargemen, carpenters, masons, muleteers, carters, stevedores, and divers for sunken cargoes. The home offices, often recorded in the mosaics, include ports famous or forgotten in North Africa, Sardinia, Gaul, and Spain. Ostia proper, as well as the ports, was full of warehouses where these multifarious goods were stored. Their plan, multistoried around a courtyard, was to influence the luxurious *palazzi* of the Renaissance. (When McKim, Mead, and White built the Boston Public Library, for example, their ultimate model was an Ostia warehouse.) The headquarters (*scholae*) of the various guilds grew, in the second and third centuries, to be very luxurious, with airy courtyards and temples in imported marble, which testify to the power and prosperity of these ancient labor unions. Perhaps, then as now, the labor leaders were more prosperous than the rank and file, for in Ostia as in Pompeii, the multitude of small shops, fishmongers, fullers, and millers, and the omnipresent *thermopolia,* or bars, are humble enough, often with dark, cramped living quarters behind or on a mezzanine.

Ostia's world-wide trade made her a melting pot, and her temples emphasize the fact. Besides the temples of the Imperial cults and the official religion, like the Temple of Rome and Augustus, Hadrian's lofty Capitolium, and the half-scale Pantheon, all in the Forum, there are the four unpretentious tufa and stucco temples (built between 80 and 23 B.C. and reconstructed under Trajan) which share a platform in a large porticoed precinct west of the theater (II.viii,2). They were probably dedicated to Ceres, Fortuna, Venus, and Spes. The temple of Hercules (I.xv,5), just pre-Sullan, is built of tufa and travertine and stands in a triangular pre-

cinct, in which was found a relief interpreted to show that
the cult statue was found in the sea and was believed to have
oracular powers. Representing foreign cults is, near the Porta
Laurentina (*Reg.* IV,i), the temple of the Phrygian Great
Mother, where her emasculated priests once clashed their
cymbals. Near the Porta Marina (*Reg.* III,xvii) is the temple
of the Egyptian Serapis, conveniently located for sailors just
in from the Levant. Widening the airport road uncovered a
synagogue, built in the first century A.D., and beautified in
the second. It has the menorah (seven-branched candlestick), shofar (ram's horn, blown on Rosh Hashannah, the
new year, and Yom Kippur, the day of atonement), an aedicula to house the Torah (books of the Law), a bema (pulpit)
to read it from, mosaics, and a Greek inscription mentioning
the Ark of the Covenant. Jews took Roman names, thus concealing their numbers. Everywhere there were shrines of the
Persian Mithras: eighteen of them have been found, ranging
in date from A.D. 160 to 250. They always occupy a retired,
obscure corner of a pre-existent building; they are apparently intended to symbolize the cave where Mithras was
born to his life of struggle with the powers of darkness for
the immortal souls of men. They are usually oblong with
shallow benches along the sides, with an altar or cult statue
at the end. The favorite cult statue is of Mithras slaying the
bull; being washed in the blood of a freshly slaughtered bull
brought redemption into immortality to Mithras' votaries.
One Ostian Mithraeum, that of Felicissimus (*Reg.* V,ix; see
Fig. 10.8), has a mosaic pavement representing the seven
stages of initiation, somewhat like the degrees of freema-
sonry. Each has its appropriate symbol: the Crow, the
Bridegroom, the Soldier, the Lion, the Persian (with a scimi-
tar), the Sun-runner, and the Father, or Worshipful Master.
The cult was for men only: it appealed to merchants, freedmen, and soldiers.

In the fourth century in Ostia some of these were won

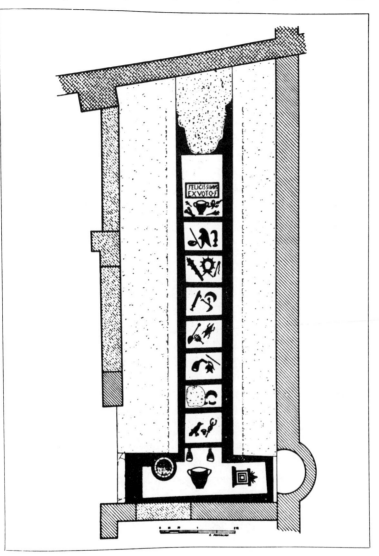

FIG. 10.8   Ostia, Mithraeum of Felicissimus.
(G. Becatti, *Scavi di Ostia*, 2, p. 107)

away by another Oriental religion, Christianity. A house
(*Reg.* IV,iii) with a mosaic of the communion chalice, set
with the Christian symbol of the fish (the initial letters of
the word for "fish" in Greek stand for "Jesus Christ, Son of
God, Savior") may have been the residence of the bishop.
A remodeled bath (*Reg.* III,i) made over into a humble
Christian basilica, may be the place where Augustine worshiped in A.D. 387, as recorded in his *Confessions*. Part of
the tombstone of his mother, Monica, who died in Ostia,
was found in the 1950s in the neighboring modern village of
Ostia Antica. The altar of the Mithraeum next to the basilica
was found smashed by Christian wrath into a thousand
pieces.

When Saint Augustine worshiped in Ostia, the city was
already in full decline. The Emperor Constantine had re-
voked its municipal status, and assigned it to the village
called Portus, which had grown up around Trajan's harbor.
The cemetery of Portus, on Isola Sacra, the island between
the Fiumicino and the principal mouth of the Tiber, contains a few Christian burials. It is chiefly noteworthy for the
class distinctions it reveals between the wealthy in their fine
vaulted brick tombs, embellished with paintings and mosaics
(very like those found in the cemetery under St. Peter's),
and the poor, whose ashes rest in the miserable amphoras
stuck in the low-lying ground. Terracotta reliefs from tomb
façades show the same bourgeois pride in one's trade which
we saw in the tomb of the baker Eurysaces: they portray the
activities of, among others, a toolmaker, doctor, miller, water
seller, and midwife. By the end of the fourth century, burials
in this cemetery ceased, mute and pathetic evidence of the
decline of Portus itself. Ostia proper agonized on to its end.
The flat slabs of inscriptions are re-used as shop counters, or
to mend pavements. Architectural marbles are sawed up into
latrine seats. Statues are reduced to lime or used, whole or
decapitated, to repair breaches in the city wall. The water

pipes break and are not repaired, fallen house walls are left lying, rubble piles up forty feet deep. Sacked by the barbarian, decimated by malaria, Ostia by the fifth century was desolate, and the road to Rome overgrown with trees. Only a Christian chapel by the theater, marking the spot where a Christian was martyred, was left to mark the spot.

Besides embellishing the Forum at Ostia with its basilica and council house, Trajan, through his architect, the Syrian Apollodorus of Damascus, adorned Rome with the last, largest, and finest of the Imperial Fora (Figs. 5.14 and 9.6). We know from an inscribed record, the *Fasti Ostienses*, found in re-use to repair a floor in an ancient private house in Ostia, that it was dedicated in January, 112; the Column on May 18, 113. Its general plan has been known since the French excavations of 1812. Its inspiration is the porticoes of Caesar's Forum and the apses and the Hall of Fame of Augustus's Forum. In conception it is axially symmetric and tripartite: the Forum proper, the basilica, and the famous Column behind, flanked by a pair of libraries. Hadrian in 121 added the Temple of the Deified Trajan, now destroyed, which closed the vista to the west.

The Forum proper lay at right angles to the Forum of Augustus, its façade bowed slightly out, like the *Forum Transitorium*. Its entrance was through a triumphal arch, added in A.D. 117, after Trajan's death. From it may have come the panels now in the passageway of the Arch of Constantine, by the same hand as the reliefs on the column, showing Trajan victorious over the Dacians in battle, and his triumphant return to Rome. In the middle of the great porticoed square, over 620 feet wide, with apses on either side, was placed a great equestrian statue of Trajan. It was still there in 357, when Constantius II remarked that never horse had such a stable. The Forum's vast space was not wasted: it was used for promulgating laws and distributing the dole;

schools were held in the exedrae.

At the back of the open square which forms the Forum proper lay the basilica, its two short sides curved, like the sides of the Forum, into apses. It was deliberately designed with military connotations, to be reminiscent of the head-quarters building of a Roman camp. Besides the usual legal and commercial functions of a basilica, it was used for manu-mitting slaves. The basilica presents its long side to the Forum as Italian basilicas regularly did, but was much grander than the basilicas of Alba, Cosa, or even the Basilica Julia in the old Forum. The basilica had two double rows of columns, in gray granite and polychrome marble: the yellow *giallo antico*, from Numidia; the striated green *cipollino*, "onion-stone"; the purple-streaked *pavonazzetto*, "peacock-stone"—Italian masons have over 500 different names for marble. The architraves were marble, crystalline white from Mt. Pentelicus in Attica. The walls were veneered with mar-ble from Carrara. There was a frieze 32 meters long, with more scenes from the Dacian wars, some of which may have been incorporated into the Arch of Constantine; in the colon-nade were Dacians, where the Forum of Augustus had Caryatids. The roof was plated with gilt bronze. It was this magnificence which the Christians sought to imitate in their great early basilica churches in Rome, where the high altar stood in the place of the judges' tribunal: Old St. Peter's, Santa Sabina, St. John Lateran, St.-Paul's-Without-the-Walls, San Lorenzo. Trajan's goodness as *optimus princeps* was legendary to early Christians; Trajan's basilica supplied a noble model for early Christian churches; Pope Sixtus V did Trajan a grave injustice when he replaced his statue at the top of the Column with one of St. Peter.

Behind the basilica a pair of small libraries, one Greek and one Latin, faced the tiny square in the midst of which rose Trajan's 100-foot column. Its shaft, of Parian marble, was wound about with 155 scenes on the twenty-three spirals of the great scroll, whose bands grow wider the higher they go, so that they were "readable" to a great height, especially from the library balconies. Unrolled, the scroll would be 650 feet long. It described in 2,500 figures the events of Trajan's two campaigns, of A.D. 101–102 and 105–106, against the Dacians. The intent was not celebratory nor encomiastic, but documentary, combining Hellenistic technique with Roman historicism. The Dacians were the ancestors of the modern Romanians. It is because of Trajan's conquests, imposing Roman culture, that Romanians speak a Romance language, derived from Latin, today. (A more extended treatment and illustration of the column will be found in my *Dacian Stones Speak*, pp. 71–94, Figs. 4.3–20.)

To what that great scroll has to tell us about the Roman attitude—and the sculptor's—toward the art of war we shall return. For the moment another matter is of interest: the inscription on the column base. It states that the column marks the height of earth that was removed to make room for it. For centuries it was inferred that Trajan's engineers had cut away a whole saddle connecting the Esquiline with the Capitoline Hill. But in 1907 Boni published the results of excavations around the base of the column, which revealed a street, a wall, and houses, dated by their pottery—Arretine and earlier—to the late Republic. Hence there probably never was a saddle of hill here: the footings of the column were trenched through the pavement of Boni's street. What then does the inscription mean? Boni fixed his eye on the terraced slope of the Quirinal to the north of the Forum, and concluded—rightly, as later excavation proved—that what Trajan was referring to was the cutting down and terracing of this slope for some purpose to be connected with the Forum. What that purpose was did not transpire until 1928, when Corrado Ricci cleared the area of medieval and later accretions and discovered the six levels of Trajan's Market (Fig. 10.9).

FIG. 10.9   Rome, Trajan's Market. (Fototeca)

The terrace treatment clearly goes back for inspiration to the Sanctuary of Fortune at Praeneste. Brick stamps show that the Market was built before the Forum: the shape in which the hill was dug out left space for the Forum apse. Form follows function: the hemicycle shows the classical virtues of symmetry, regularity, and creative exploitation of tradition, but the shape is practical, too: it allows space for nearly twice as many rooms (150) as would have been possible with a rectilinear front. The shop fronts are good looking as well as utilitarian. The ground floor rooms are handsomely framed in travertine; the second level windows are arched, and framed with pilasters, much as at Praeneste, but without the axial symmetry. Instead, Trajan's architect presented a deliberately irregular skyline, curving streets, changing vistas, elaborate internal communications, clearly defined volumes, and "rhythmic shadow" (MacDonald). The pediments are alternately curved and triangular; the triangular pediments are sometimes deliberately broken, never coming to an apex—a trick of style imitated with success by eighteenth-century English furniture designers like Chippendale. But this is an old thing in a new way, for here the material is not stone but brick, the beautifully proportioned rose-red Roman kind, used unashamedly without a polite overcoating of stucco or marble, like the rose-red arcades of Renaissance Bologna.

Some of the rooms have drains in the floor for carrying off spilled liquid; the inference is that these were wine or oil shops; those without such provision would be for dry commodities, such as grain. There are 150 of these shops altogether, all more or less identical. The whole complex has the air not of private enterprise but of a government project, and it seems a reasonable guess that here we have the headquarters of the *annona*, the government dole of wine, oil, and grain—cargoes of the ships that docked in Trajan's port of Ostia.

Access to the second level is by stairs at either end of the hemicycle, not in the middle. The split approach is borrowed from the exedra of Terrace VII at Praeneste. (It was brick stamps in these stairs that enabled Bloch to date this complex in the first decade of the second century A.D.) The second-floor shops open onto a semicircular vaulted corridor with windows facing the Forum. The complex includes annular, barrel, and ramping vaults: one involves six different curves. On the third level, variety within unity, plus ease of access for wagons, is achieved by a semicircular street onto which the third-level shops open. A straight stretch of paving running north and south, called the Via Biberatica—Pepper or Spice Street—and concealed by the façade, contains shops

with balconies, as at Ostia. Stairs ascend from this level to a
great rectangular cross-vaulted basilical hall, with shops
opening off it at two levels. A Republican ancestor is the
market hall at Ferentino, on the Via Latina 75 miles southeast of Rome. Modern architectural historians rhapsodize,
and justifiably, over the Trajanic hall's spaciousness, simplicity, clarity, and unencumbered noble space. (There is
just one column in the whole complex.) Though the hall's
plan and elevation may owe something to Near Eastern
bazaars, it is admirably suited to the Italian climate and life-
style. Some archaeologists think this was the place where the
dole was distributed; others see in it ancient Rome's whole-
sale grain, oil, and wine market, like the Pit in Chicago
where bidding fixes the day's commodity prices. The inter-
connecting suites of rooms on the fifth and sixth levels, with
their niches for shelves or cabinets, are clearly not shops, but
offices for administrative personnel. One large centrally located room, with a view over the whole complex, would be
a good place for the office of the superintendent of the entire
affair, the *praefectus annonae*. The size of this complex, and
the care expended upon its plan reflect the growing secu-
larizing and urbanizing of Roman Imperial culture.

Trajan's Baths (Fig. 10.10), whose large southern exedra
sinks its footings into the Domus Aurea, were begun after
104 and inaugurated in 109. The architect was again Apollodorus of Damascus. He built a colossus, with overall dimensions of 1072 by 1023 feet; the building proper measured 617
by 689 feet. Unlike the Market, the baths (partly restored in
1976) were axially symmetrical and had marble revetments.
They are the ancestor of the colossal baths of Caracalla, Diocletian, and Constantine. An entrance at the north led into a
porticoed open swimming pool, beyond which was a vast
cross-vaulted central hall, flanked by palaestras and exedras.
South of the central hall was the small tepidarium; south of
this, the larger caldarium; both were double-apsed. An al-

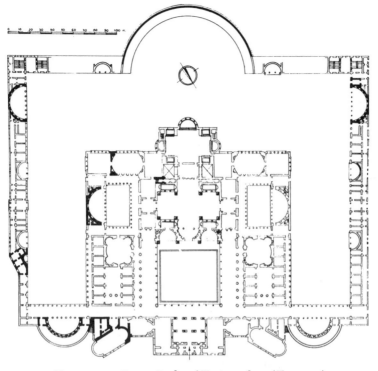

FIG. 10.10   Rome, Baths of Trajan, plan. (Fototeca)

most circular hall in the southeast corner of the main building has on its wall a modern marble plan of the baths. An
exedra in the southwest corner of the whole complex has
been partially restored; it was probably a library.

Trajan's Market did not let his people forget his generosity. Trajan's Column did not let them forget his prowess
in war. Though casts have often been made of the reliefs on
the column—the earliest to the order of Francis I of France,
in 1541—the best photographs were not taken until 1942,
when a scaffolding erected around the column to protect it
from air attack made close-ups possible. In 1980 scaffolding
went up again, this time as support for wire mesh against

pollution, a more insidious enemy. The *optimus princeps* appears no less than 60 times, larger than life. He dominates the sea voyages (handling the tiller personally), the marches, the river crossings, the councils of war, the reviews, the encounters in the open field, the sieges, the sacrifices, the building operations, the reception of ambassadors, and the submission of enemy chiefs.

Because of the fascinating detail of the reliefs (all reproduced in sketches in Coarelli's admirable *Guida archaeologica di Roma*, pp. 118–27), Trajan's Column tells us as much about the Roman army and navy as Pompeii and Ostia do about civilian life. Nor is this all: we learn a great deal, too, about provincial and native customs and culture. Most important, the unknown sculptor has impressed his personality and his feelings upon what he carved. There is an occasional touch of rough humor—a slave falling off a mule, a Dacian ducked in the Danube—and a scene or two in which Trajan, deprecating the humility of submissive native chiefs, seems to be following Vergil's advice to spare the meek. But the dominant note is Vergil's, too: the horror of war. Some of the detail is worth recording.

The army and navy first. The transports, with oars in two banks and auxiliary sail, have ramming beaks which are adorned with an enormous eye, for luck, or with a sea monster. The soldiers are jacks-of-all-trades: we see them woodcutting and reaping, but most often at the interminable work of building palisaded camps, with tents of skins—a new camp every night when they were on the march. They built their permanent camps of squared stones: the sculptor shows the soldiers carrying them in slings on their shoulders, or in baskets. The walls had towers, with balconies, from which flaming torches gave signals by night. Catapults were mounted on the battlements; other catapults are horse or mule drawn, or mounted on improvised wooden bases like stacked rail-

road ties. We see the standards of the legions—the famed
Eagles—and the standard-bearers, wearing animal heads for
helmets, like Hercules. On the march, the men carry their
gear in bundles on the ends of their pikes, like tramps with
their worldly goods done up in bandannas.

We see something of provincial towns and their citizens.
The army embarked from an Adriatic port, Ancona or Brindisi, and sailed across to Illyricum. Here the cities ape Rome,
with arches, columned temples, theaters, and amphitheaters.
The citizens turn out in a body, leading their children by the
hand, to greet their Emperor with upraised right arms, as in
a Fascist salute, and to offer sacrifice. The Danube is crossed
on a great bridge, the work of Apollodorus, with masonry
piers and wooden superstructure. Then one is in wild country, with exotic flora and fauna, including an especially
bloodthirsty wild boar. The natives live in straw huts, and
wear trousers: this last, to a Roman, sure proof of barbarism.
In battle they use short hooked swords and carry sinister
dragon-head standards. Their cavalry, horses and all, are
protected from head to foot with scaly armor.

It is exciting, but it is terrible: it is said to have inspired
Dante's *Purgatorio*. Dacian women burn Romans alive or,
according to another interpretation, Moesian Quisling women
are torturing Dacians and Sarmatians; Romans impale the
severed heads of Dacians before the walls of their camp
(Fig. 10.11), or present them, dripping with gore, to the
Emperor. A Dacian is assassinated with a sword thrust as he
pleads for mercy. Bodies are trampled underfoot in battle,
prisoners are dragged along by the hair. The Dacian king
commits suicide rather than fall into Roman hands; his subjects burn their capital to the ground to deny it to the
Romans; the chiefs commit mass suicide. The story of the
first campaigns is separated from the second by a Victory
writing on a shield; immediately thereafter the deadly, mo-

FIG. 10.11   Rome, Trajan's Column, detail.
(P. Romanelli, *La colonna traiana,* Fig. 60)

notonous round begins again. The pathos of some of the
scenes heightens the horror, as when two comrades tenderly
carry from the field the limp body of a mortally wounded
Dacian youth, or a whole tribe, babies in their mothers' arms
and children on their fathers' shoulders, comes to make the
act of submission. At the end is shown the looting—Dacian
treasure loaded on the backs of mules. These scenes, with
their implied criticism of warfare, are the closest the Romans
ever came to pacifism, but Roman achievement is glorified
by heroizing the defeated. There is general agreement that
the layout of the reliefs is based on a master plan, perhaps
drawn up by Apollodorus of Damascus. Then individual

scenes were divided among five sculptors, of very varying degrees of competence.

The province won with so much blood, sweat, and tears by Trajan was consolidated by his successor Hadrian (who had fought in the campaigns) and taught the arts of peace. Hadrian, that restless traveler, spent little of his reign in Rome, but he adorned the city with some of its grandest buildings, for which he himself probably drew the plans. He also built near suburban Tivoli a villa greater than Versailles.

11

An Emperor-Architect: Hadrian

About Trajan's successor Hadrian (A.D. 117–138) archaeology and literature, interlocking, tell us so much that we can write his biography from his buildings, with an occasional assist from written sources. The buildings of his reign are numerous and brilliantly designed. We shall take as examples three from Rome and five from the unique complex of his Villa near Tivoli: the Temple of Venus and Rome, the Pantheon, and his mausoleum; the *Teatro Marittimo*, the *Piazza d'Oro*, the "Stadium," the Small Baths, and the Canopus. All can be dated with more precision than usual, because in Hadrian's time the practice became general of stamping bricks with the names of the consuls of the year they were made. Professor Bloch's accurate study of, and sound inference from, over 4,600 stamps, most of them from Hadrian's reign, have put all students of Roman archaeology deeply in his debt.

An attempt to understand Hadrian through his buildings rests upon the hypothesis that he was himself his own architect, inspired by the ferment of building activity in Rome in Domitian's and Trajan's reigns, when he was growing up. The hypothesis is perhaps justified by an inference from an anecdote recorded by Dio Cassius, a Roman senator and consul from Bithynia in northwest Asia Minor, who wrote in Greek a history of Rome from the beginning to A.D. 229. Dio's story is that once when Trajan was in conference with his architect, Apollodorus of Damascus, Hadrian interrupted; Apollodorus, angered, said, "Oh, go and design your pumpkins!" We infer that Apollodorus' reference to "pumpkins" was intended to pour scorn on certain of Hadrian's designs for vaults, involving pumpkinlike concave segments with re-entrant groins between, such as are still to be seen in Hadrian's Villa, in the vestibule of the Piazza d'Oro, and in the Serapeum at the end of the Canopus (Fig. 11.1). The same anecdote records that Apollodorus so piqued Hadrian, later, by his criticisms of the design of the Emperor's Temple of Venus and Rome, that Hadrian had him first exiled

FIG. 11.1   Tivoli, Hadrian's Villa. Serapeum at Canopus: the "pumpkin" vaults are in the half-dome. (Piranesi)

and then put to death. This is how Hadrian is established as an architect, and a vindictive one at that.

Hadrian's most baroque flights of architectural fancy are to be seen at his villa near Tivoli, where the various complexes of buildings are scattered over an area 1000 yards one way by 500 yards the other. The buildings, which far outdid Nero's Golden House in extent and grandeur, include palaces, large and small, for manic and for depressive moods (plan [Fig. 11.2] A,G,R,S,T,U,V,W), guest-quarters (B), a pavilion (C), dining rooms (D,E,K), baths (F,O,P), a library (the apsed building to the right of G), porticoes (H,J), pools (between H and J, and northwest of X), slave quarters (J,N), a stadium (L), many cryptoporticoes (for example, M), firemen's barracks (between A and M), a palaestra or wrestling ground (Q), and a vaulted temple of Serapis (X). Excavation, and the carrying off of statues, with which Roman museums are crammed, began as early

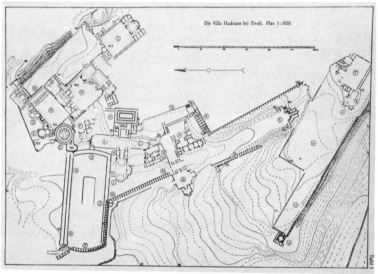

FIG. 11.2   Tivoli, Hadrian's Villa.
(H. Kähler, *Hadrian und seine Villa bei Tivoli*, Pl. 1)

as 1535 and continues to the present. It has been followed by reconstruction (Fig. 11.3; it includes some of the Praetorium [Fig. 11.2 (R)] after bombing in World War II) and general tidying up: the Italian authorities report the clearing away of 13,200 pounds of briers!

The setting of Hadrian's villa near Tivoli takes full advantage of landscape: the view embraces mountains in one direction, distant Rome and the sea in the other. There is the color of pines, olives, ripe grain, pasture, and vineyard, the sound of cicadas by day and nightingales at twilight. And when the villa was new, everywhere was the sound of water and the color of marble. For this enormous Folly, this Roman Versailles, the immensity of all this space devoted to the whims of one man, untrammeled by any limitations of technique or money, is the perfected product of 200 years of Roman experience in elegant country living. Its builder occupied it but little. Eleven of the twenty-one restless years of his

Fig. 11.3   Tivoli, Hadrian's Villa, model. The round building (left center) is the Teatro Marittimo; the Piazza d'Oro is at the upper left; the Canopus, with colonnade, pool, and Serapeum, is near the center of the upper right quadrant. (MPI)

reign were spent in foreign travel. He named parts of his villa for famous buildings and places he had seen in the Greek East: the Academy and the Painted Porch (*Stoa Poecile*) in Athens, the Canopus near Alexandria. He even created a mile of cryptoporticoes which he called a "Hell" (*Inferi*, the Lower Regions): in his tortured life he had been there, too, as we shall see. There are many more crypto-porticoes than used to be thought. Many are service tunnels —to keep the slaves out of their finicky master's sight—but the access road was partially sunken, for aesthetic effect and to reduce noise; the great trapezoidal crypt by the Inferi has stalls for 131 animals; and one waterproofed gallery with ten

FIG. 11.4   Tivoli, Hadrian's Villa, Teatro Marittimo, air view.
(H. Kähler, *Rom und seine Welt*, Pl. 188)

branches opening off one side and eleven off the other, which used to be thought of as prison cells for slaves, or as wine-cellars, has been plausibly explained as designed to store snow for cooling drinks! But the buildings are idiosyncratic, not imitative, except in the creative Roman way. Hadrian, the Spaniard, was quick to learn. He always spoke Latin with an accent (his Greek was better), but his architecture was pure Graeco-Roman, using the architectural vocabulary of the past to create a new architectural language of his own.

His earliest architectural essay at the villa, to judge from the brick stamps, is the so-called *Teatro Marittimo* (the round complex at *G;* see also Fig. 11.4). Its earliest bricks date from the first year of his reign. (Of course the bricks need not have been used in the year they were made, and indeed will often have been put aside for several years to season.) Some bricks in the fabric of the *Teatro Marittimo* are dated A.D. 123, an *annus mirabilis* in Roman brick pro-duction, to meet the vast requirements of Hadrian's many projects, some ready to build, some still on the drawing board. These bricks point to later restorations of the original plan, but the point here is that the fundamental design, very characteristic of Hadrian, must have been laid down early. Much light on this complex, and on the villa as a whole, has been cast by the sensitive, perceptive work of the German Heinz Kähler, who, undaunted by the burning of all his carefully drawn plans in World War II, redid and published them in 1950, illuminating as never before our picture of Hadrian as man and architect.

The entrance to the *Teatro Marittimo* was through a portico to the north (at the bottom of the air photograph) which approached a door in a high circular brick wall, insur-ing complete privacy from the rest of the villa. Inside the wall was a circular portico, concentric with the portico a moat. The *Teatro Marittimo* is now restored (through the philanthropy of an Italian tire manufacturer, impressed by the likeness of its plan to his product), and the moat is filled with water. When it was dry, its floor showed a pair of grooves in an arc, one on either side of the main axis. The grooves were made by the rollers of a drawbridge worked from a small room on the edge of the inner circle. On the site of one of the drawbridges there is now a permanent foot-bridge, visible in the air photograph. On the circular island, the columned arc between the drawbridges is a vestibule where the Emperor might receive his friends. Beyond it is a diamond-shaped peristyle, originally with a marine thiasos (a revel of sea divinities) in its architrave, and a fountain in the middle: its sides are segments of circles which if projected would be tangent to the outer wall of the moat. Beyond the peristyle is an apsidal room; the apse has the same arc as the vestibule. This would be a pleasant place for intimate dinner parties. The rooms on either side might be bedrooms. A broad window opens from the dining room onto the moat, with a view directly on an alcove let into the circular wall on the axis of the far side. From the alcove the view leads through eleven differently shaped and differently lighted spaces back to the entrance portico and a far-distant fountain to the north.

It remains to describe the rooms east and west of the peristyle. The central apsidal room of the three on the west (to the right of the peristyle in the air photograph) is a deep bath with a window over the moat. Steps lead up to the low sill: Hadrian could choose between tub and moat for bathing. To the south is the dressing room, to the north the steam bath and furnace room. East of the peristyle is a circular room whose interior cross-walls form a double *T*, creating two alcoves for reading. Each would be appropriate to its season: the eastern for winter mornings and summer afternoons, the western for summer mornings and winter afternoons. The two adjoining rooms would be just right for a small library, of some 1,500 rolls, half Greek and half Latin; the main library lay conveniently to the southwest (right center in the air photograph). It is tempting to see in this

suite of rooms the study where the Emperor wrote his re-
signed, sentimental, mannered little poem to his soul (or is
it to the soul of his beloved Antinous?):

> *"Little soul, gentle and drifting,*
> *Guest and companion of my body,*
> *Now you will dwell below in pallid places,*
> *Stark and bare;*
> *There you will abandon your play of yore."*

The remaining odd corners would house latrines, little con-
servatories, cupboards, and pantries.

This earliest Hadrianic building perfectly expresses one
aspect of the man: his genius, his moodiness, his striving for
form, his restlessness. With its wall, its moat, and its drawbridge, it is all designed for privacy and quiet. From any
room one gets a view of variously lighted sections of space:
chiaroscuro to match moods grave and gay. In the midst of
axial symmetry, unrest is everywhere: in the curved forms,
in the abrupt switches from light to dark, from roofed to
open spaces, from horizontal architraves to the vertical play
of the central fountain. The unrest is central: the midpoint
is water and inaccessible. Tension and split are expressed in
the divided bridge approach. All is indirection, schizophrenia,
avoidance of forthrightness. As an architectural exercise, it
is uniquely abstract, a proposition of Euclid in brick and
marble, at one moment seeming to involve nothing but circles, at another, nothing but squares. It is probably no accident that its total diameter is almost exactly the same as the
Pantheon's. It would have suited the complexity of Hadrian's
mind to design a grandiose habitation for all the gods to the
self-same dimensions as this splendid toy, the habitation of
a restless, schizophrenic man whom his subjects worshipped
as a god. The gods had made Hadrian in their own image;
seconded by flattering courtiers, he was returning the compliment.

Excavation has shown that the "Stadium" (Fig. 11.2,*L*) is

FIG. 11.5   Hadrian's Villa, "Stadium," model. (DAI)

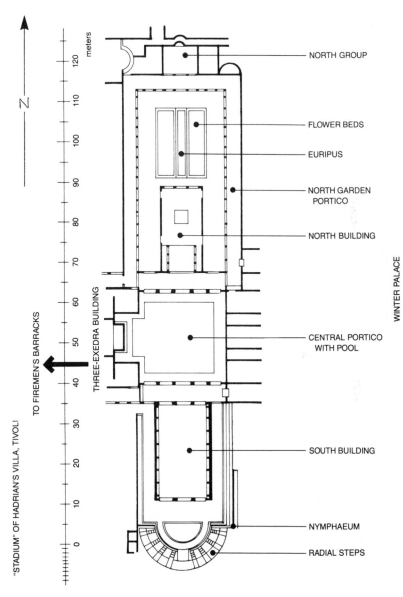

Fig. 11.6   Hadrian's Villa, "Stadium," plan. (DAI)

more complicated than had been thought. The model (Fig. 11.5) shows that the plan centered on a portico faced by buildings on all four sides. The south building (model, center) was too wide to roof with a vault: it must have been timber-trussed. The spacious peristyle opened southward onto a nymphaeum, where water flowed down eight little radial flights of three steps each, as in the Piazza d'Oro. The northern building had a three-nave vestibule, a flat roof, an opus sectile floor, and, running east and west on its north side, a long narrow pool ("Euripus": best seen in the plan, Fig. 11.6; there is one like it in the garden of the House of D. Octavius Quartio in Pompeii [Figs. 8.16 and 17]). This was flanked by flowerbeds. West of a central pool, flanked by statues, was a three-exedra building; the complex on the east of the pool was intended to supply rest and refreshment for a small number of guests. The lofty central hall on the west was barrel-vaulted; there were smaller vaulted halls on either side; above and behind, a hip-roofed building, with brick-stamps of A.D. 123, ceiling frescoes, and a miniature bath room in the southwest corner; behind this again, the "Firemen's Barracks" (Fig. 11.2,H) with brick stamps of 126: a swimming pool with a cryptoporticus below.

Between 118 and 121 was built the bath complex (Fig. 11.2 F) just south of the Teatro Marittimo. Its most interesting feature is the so-called Heliocaminus, circular in plan, with seats in tiers, and a coffered half-dome. It was a steam room, or laconicum: a predecessor can be seen in the baths of a villa of Domitian near Sabaudia, 42 road-miles southeast of Rome. A contemporary parallel is in the Large Baths here (plan, P); there is one from the next reign in the Forum Baths at Ostia. One of the villa's many cryptoporticoes ran beneath the heliocaminus.

The next building in Hadrian's architectural biography is his Temple of Venus and Rome (Fig. 12.16,13), built facing the Colosseum to rival the most splendid buildings of Athens and the Greek East. Its length matched that of the Olympieion in Athens (135 by 354 feet), restored by Hadrian. The Emperor's well-known Philhellenism is symbolized by a statue found in the Athenian Metroön, and now in the Agora Museum, whose cuirass carries, in relief, both Athena and the Capitoline Wolf. Literary sources give the foundation date of the temple of Venus and Rome as Rome's birthday, April 21, A.D. 121; the brick stamps, of 123, 134, and the fourth century, tell the story of long years of building and late restoration. The essence of the plan is two cellae back to back, one for Venus and one for the goddess Roma, perhaps made apsidal by Maxentius in 307 (Figs. 11.7 and 11.8), though reputable scholars still believe the apses are Hadrianic. They may be interpreted as a colossal architectural pun. Venus is a goddess of love, Love is AMOR, and AMOR is ROMA spelled backward. The symbolism does not stop here. Hadrian is Caesar: his is the heritage, if not the blood, of the Julian line, and the temple is a reminder of the greatness of Rome, firmly established by Augustus, and smiled upon by Augustus's ancestress, Venus. The design was the butt of the criticisms that cost Apollodorus his life. He had said that the temple should have been set on a high podium, which could have housed various paraphernalia useful in the Colosseum opposite, and that the cellae had been designed too low for the statues in them: "If the goddesses wish to get up and go out, they will be unable to do so." The first half of Apollodorus's criticism is unjustified: Hadrian was designing a Greek temple, not an Italic one. About the second half we cannot judge for certain, for brick stamps allegedly show the apses to belong to the fourth century reconstruction, but the proportions, are Hadrianic (Fig. 11.9). The temple was set in the midst of a forest of sixty-six columns of gray granite. When it was reexcavated in 1932, some of the columns were reerected; the positions of others were ingeniously marked by clumps of shrubbery trimmed to the proper shape. The

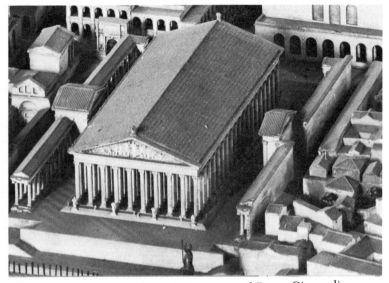

FIG. 11.7   Rome, Temple of Venus and Rome, Gismondi
model. (F. Castagnoli, *Roma antica*, Pl. 27.2)

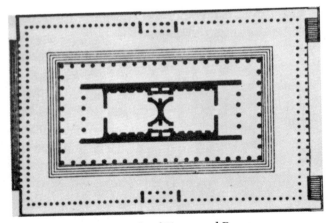

FIG. 11.8   Rome, Temple of Venus and Rome.
(Castagnoli, *op. cit.*, p. 85, Fig. 2)

FIG. 11.9
Rome, Temple of Venus and Rome,
apse (note size of scale figure).
(Author)

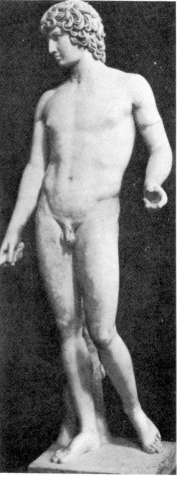

FIG. 11.10   Antinous. (Author)

excavators found under the pavement an octagonal room interesting in itself, and significant for its place in Roman architecture. The level at which it was found is lower than that of Nero's Golden House. (Hadrian's temple was built in the grounds of what had once been the Golden House; the reader will recall the twenty-four elephants needed to move the colossal statue of Nero and make room for the temple.) The octagonal shape appears in the dining room of the Golden House itself, in Domitian's palace on the Palatine, and in a room in the Small Baths at Hadrian's villa (O on the plan, Fig. 11.2). The cupola of Nero's octagonal dining room, together with its lighting through a hole in the roof, reappears on a grand scale in the Pantheon. This is what we mean by saying that Hadrian adapted to his own new architectural language the vocabulary of pre-Neronian, Neronian, and Domitianic buildings. Here once again modern archaeology illuminates the development of Roman architecture by demonstrating and dating the classical use of new things in old ways, and old things in new.

Shortly after the consecration of the Temple of Venus and Rome, Hadrian set out on the first of his great tours of his Empire. He visited the western provinces, making arrangements, among other things, for the building of the great wall bearing his name that runs from Tyne to Solway in the north of England. He visited the provinces of Africa, Cyrene and Crete. Finally, in A.D. 123, he reached Bithynia, and there met Antinous (Fig. 11.10), the sulky, langorous, addolescent boy who, for the remaining seven years of his short life, and even more after his tragic death by drowning—perhaps suicide—in the suburb of Alexandria called Canopus, was to dominate Hadrian's existence and inspire his whole creative activity. It is not surprising that the Emperor, childless and unhappily married, should find deep satisfaction in the company of this boy. The psychological aspects of the affair, and the possible effect of Hadrian's infatuation upon his archi-

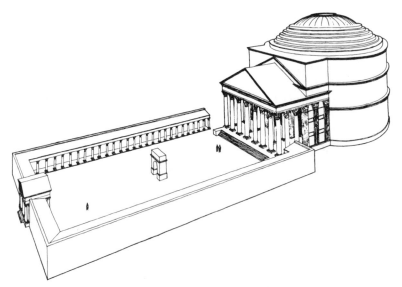

Fig. 11.11   Rome, Pantheon, reconstruction drawing.
(MacDonald, *ARE*, Fig. 8, p. 96 [Yale U. Press])

tecture have been treated with delicacy and understanding
by Marguerite Yourcenar and Eleanor Clark.

The first Hadrianic building that could have been designed after the meeting with Antinous is the Pantheon (Figs.
11.11; 12.16,14), "the oldest important roofed building in the
world that still stands intact." The reconstruction drawing
(Fig. 11.11) shows the purpose served by the portico: to de-
lay until the last possible moment the full visible impact of the
immense rotunda. One has to be within about 200 feet of the
façade before one sees the dome. The portico underlines the
urban setting; the conventional pediment pays tribute to the
Roman state religion; the rotunda symbolizes "the immense
majesty of the Roman Peace" (Pliny the Elder). On the
evidence of the brick stamps, its framework was complete by
A.D. 125, and the whole building perhaps finished by 128.
Until 1892 the building passed as the work of Augustus's

lieutenant Agrippa, because the inscription that runs across
the architrave of the rectangular porch in front of the drum,
"Marcus Agrippa built this when he was consul for the third
time" (27 B.C.), was taken at its face value. But in 1892 the
entire fabric was found to be full of stamped bricks of Hadrianic date, and the building therefore Hadrianic throughout (with Severan restorations, also recorded in an inscription). The Agrippa inscription partly follows the Roman
practice of repeating the original dedication in a restored
structure, and partly reflects the Emperor's mock modesty.
His involuted nature found satisfaction in seldom inscribing
his own name on the buildings he designed. His contempo-
raries knew well enough who the architect was. And the
elaborate mystification served also to point up his identifying
himself with Augustus, which we saw first in the Temple of
Venus and Rome. Whether Hadrian thought of himself as a
new Augustus or not, certainly Augustan domed buildings at
the seaside resort of Baiae, on the Bay of Naples, influenced
his architecture. Hadrian played the game out in the way
he handled the transition between the circular and the rectangular parts of his plan (Fig. 11.12). On either side of the
entrance to the drum, behind the porch, he designed rectangular projections with huge half-vaulted apses cut out of
the front: one of these apses would have contained a statue
of Agrippa, the other of Augustus. And Romans passing between them (through the great bronze entrance doors that
still survive) would marvel at how self-effacing was their
Emperor-architect.

The interior (Fig. 11.13) carries forward that liberation
of religious architecture from the Greek tyranny of the rectangular box, which can only come about through the use of
poured concrete, and which we saw first in the Sanctuary of
Fortune at Praeneste. Here Hadrian plays with geometrical
abstractions, as in the Teatro Marittimo. The game is to describe a sphere in a cylinder: if the curve of the dome were

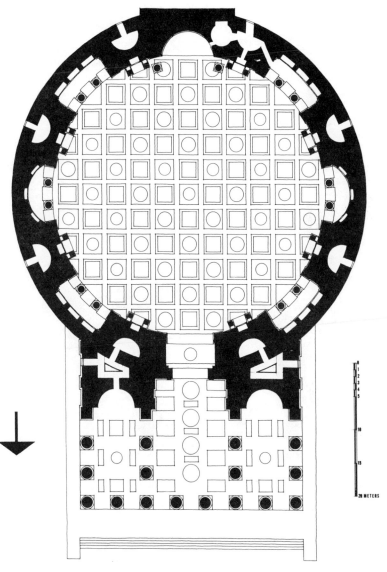

FIG. 11.12   Rome, Pantheon, plan.
(MacDonald, *ARE*, Fig. 9 [Yale U. Press])

Fig. 11.13   Rome, Pantheon, interior, 19th-century reconstruction,
drawing by fellows of French Academy in Rome.

projected beyond the point where it meets the vertical walls of the drum, the bottom of the curve would be just tangent with the floor. The very pavement, with its alternation of squares and circles, plays up the geometrical *jeu d'esprit*. (Under the porch lies the simple rectangular plan of Agrippa's temple.) Furthermore, both the plan and the interior view show that the walls of the drum are not solid, and that they continue the architect's vast toying with geometrical concepts. The walls are lightened with niches (for statues; one, of Venus, wore Cleopatra's pearls in her ears). The niches are alternately rectangular and curved; the result is that the hemispherical cupola is supported not on a solid wall but on eight huge piers. In order to reduce the bearing weight of the superstructure upon the niches, elaborate brick relieving arches were built into the concrete fabric above the apertures. They were concealed by polychrome marble revetment, and run as barrel vaults right through the walls. The cupola itself is designed with 140 sunken stepped coffers, to lighten it, to exaggerate the perspective, and to play yet again with the alternation of curve and straight line. The concrete of the cupola, which is thinner toward the top, is made with pumice, the lightest material available. The vast rotunda (its volume is 70,000 cubic meters) both magnifies imperial might and diminishes individual humanity: Hadrian used it as an audience hall. It seems to consist entirely of space, light, and color. The polychrome marble décor includes *giallo antico*, red porphyry, green-black and blue-veined marble, and there was much gilding. As the day waxes and wanes and the light from the cupola shifts across the patterned floor, "Hadrian's sun-show spins on with the rotation of the earth" (MacDonald). Symbolizing as it does the Imperial concern for all lands and peoples, it is as much an embodiment of its age as the Parthenon, Santa Sophia, or Chartres.

The Pantheon is lighted solely through the great hole,

thirty feet across, at the top of the cupola. (The building is
so large that the inconvenience from rain is negligible.) The
best possible idea of the perfection of this great building
is to be gained by looking down into the interior from high
above, from the edge of the hole in the roof. This dizzy
height, at which one may glory or despair according to the
measure of one's acrophobia, is reached by a stair behind the
left apse in the porch. The stair gives access to the cornice at
the top of the drum; one then walks half-way round the
cornice, which is wide but unrailed, to the back of the drum,
where a flight of steps, only half-railed, leads up over the
lead plates (the original gilt bronze was sent to Constantinople in the seventh century), to the aperture, from which
those with a head for heights can gauge the aesthetic satisfaction of realizing that the interior is exactly as high as it is
wide. The total effect, massive, daring, playing with space,
yet not entirely successful technically, reflects the man.

One wonders what Hadrian's tortured and cynical spirit
would make of the vicissitudes his building has suffered.
What preserved it was its being given by the Emperor Phocas in 609/10 to Pope Boniface VIII; it became the church
of Santa Maria ad Martyres. A Barberini pope in the seventeenth century used the bronze of the porch roof to make the
canopy over the high altar of St. Peter's, and guns for the
papal fortress, Castel Sant'Angelo (which had once been
Hadrian's mausoleum); of this vandalism the wags of 1625
made the famous epigram, "*Quod non fecerunt barbari fecerunt Barberini*," which might be paraphrased, "The Barberini
rush in where barbarians fear to tread." At the same time
Bernini added a pair of ridiculous bell towers—called "the
ass's ears"—which were not taken down until the nineteenth
century. Perhaps Hadrian would be better pleased to know
that men like himself were buried in his building (a great
creative artist—Raphael—and two Italian kings), and that
his Pantheon has been the most imitated of all ancient build-

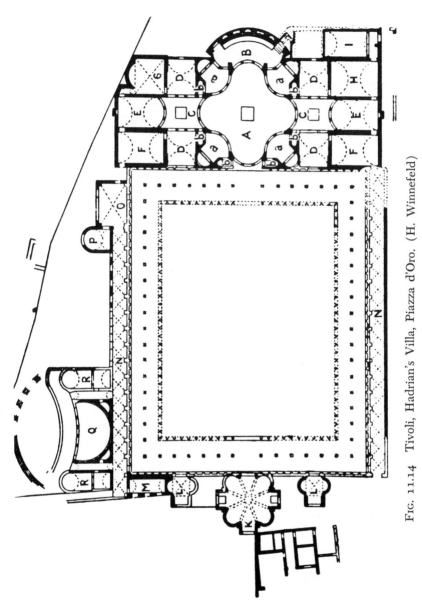

FIG. 11.14   Tivoli, Hadrian's Villa, Piazza d'Oro. (H. Winnefeld)

ings—by great architects from Palladio through Thomas Jefferson to Frank Lloyd Wright.

While the Pantheon was being built, an activity unexampled in the history of Roman architecture was going on at the villa. To the fruitful years after 125 belongs the uniquely inspired plan (Fig. 11.14) of the most important palace in the villa complex, called the *Piazza d'Oro,* the Golden Square. Its "pumpkin" vestibule (*K* in the plan) has already been mentioned. In many of its features, including the hole in the roof, the eight supporting piers, and the alternation of curved and rectilinear niches, it is a quarter-scale Pantheon. But there is greater frankness in the display of the structure, both internally, in the groined vault, and externally, where the octagonal plan is left clearly visible, instead of being concealed by the skin of the drum, as in the Pantheon. Except perhaps for the cross-vaulted passages *N,N,* the portico is conventional; excavation in the summer of 1958 revealed footings for formal flower beds, as in the portico of Pompey's theater, and in Vespasian's Forum of Peace.

The part of the complex which shows Hadrian's full genius is the palace block, south of the portico (plan *A-I*). Here the vastness, sweep, and richness of the *Piazza d'Oro* comes to its climax in a design which has been called lyrical, feminine, and even Mozartian. Here, if anywhere, can be detected the influence of Antinous. The frieze motif, for example, is Cupids (hunting, and riding sea monsters), but since this theme is borrowed from the *Teatro Marittimo,* which, at least in its earliest phase, antedates Antinous, too much should not be made of it. (But Hadrian's fondness for the chase is reflected in the eight medallions from an unidentified building which adorn the Arch of Constantine. Hadrian there, shown making a dedication to Apollo, has been metamorphosed into Constantine and given a halo [Fig. 11.15]. But Antinous is present in all the medallions; in the one illustrated he has been apotheosized into Apollo himself. The beasts involved are

FIG. 11.15   Rome, Arch of Constantine, Hadrianic medallion.
(Fototeca)

bear, boar, and lion, dedicated respectively to Silvanus,
Artemis, and Hercules.) The focus of the Piazza d'Oro is
the four-leaf-clover room at *A*, with a fountain in the middle.
Its walls sweep in and out, with a sinuous, wavelike move-

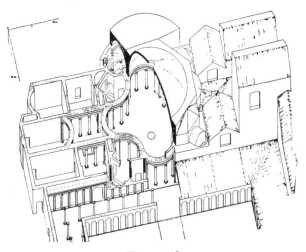

FIG. 11.16
Tivoli, Hadrian's Villa, Piazza d'Oro, reconstruction.
(H. Kähler, *Hadrian*, Pl. 16)

ment, as though the room were alive and breathing. The outswinging arcs open into light-wells (*C,C; B* is a curved nymphaeum, with statue niches alternately curved and rectilinear, from beneath which the water flowed down steps into a reflecting pool; the fourth side is the entrance). The inswinging arcs open into bell-shaped rooms (*a,a,a,a*). These serve to counter the thrust of the centrally pierced cupola (see the reconstruction, Fig. 11.16), which may have successfully solved the problem of transition from octagonal ground plan to circular dome. The cupola was supported (none too well, for it has fallen and left no trace) on eight delicate piers, in what we now see to be Hadrian's standard but ever-varied manner. The six tiny apsidal rooms (*b*) are latrines; their water supply came from fountains at the back of the bell-shaped diagonal rooms, yet another example of the Roman combination of the useful with the ornamental.

Off the central clover-leaf open on each side five rectangu-

lar rooms (*I* is a late addition), all but one barrel-vaulted;
the exception (*G*) had a cross-vault. Each set opens onto a
light well. At the back of the central room (*E*) in each set
is a statue niche. The view from the back of these rooms
runs, as in the *Teatro Marittimo,* through variegated light
and shade. *E* was diagonally lit from the light-well; the light-
well itself, a variant on the conventional atrium, had probably a square *compluvium,* or open skylight; the central
room was lit by the round cupola-aperture, and so on. The
whole design, with its indirect lighting, plays of water, and
works of art, is light and gay, reflecting the Emperor's brief
years of pleasure with his *innamorato;* what the Empress
Sabina thought is not recorded. But here again is the tension
that comes from an inaccessible midpoint. And whose statues
were in the niches? Whatever may have been the case in
Antinous's lifetime, after his death Hadrian deified him,
identifying him with Apollo, Dionysus, Hermes, Silvanus,
Osiris, and other gods, and surrounded himself with remind-
ers of him in marble. Of the statues of Antinous in Roman
museums, a number variously estimated at from sixteen to
thirty comes from the villa.

At the villa, the Small Baths (Fig. 11.2,o), dated 121–126,
"seem to have as their principal object the discarding of the
obvious" (Ward Perkins). Rooms are dovetailed as in a jigsaw puzzle (Figs. 11.17 and 11.18); they are square, rectangular, cruciform, circular, elliptical, polygonal; there are
barrel- groined-, lunette-, quadrispherical, and cross-vaults,
domes and semidomes, stabilized by the interpenetration and
reciprocal thrusts of the rooms themselves, with an assist
from the monolithic quality of Roman concrete. Some floors
were of opus sectile. The large windows facing west were
probably unglazed, as at Ostia. The circular sunroom (plan,
K) has a cupola with an oculus, like a miniature Pantheon.
The octagonal atrium or vestibule (*J*) has alternately concave and convex walls, which rise imperceptibly into a dome.

The east court, a palaestra or garden, may have had a balcony for spectators. The highly baroque curving north wall, built to match the "Stadium" adjoining, has three high pedimented niches flanked by columns supported by heavy travertine corbels. The tepidarium (T) resembles in shape, perhaps intentionally, the Poikile (Fig. 11.2,J). To variety of shape and lighting was added variety of color: polychrome marble; red, blue and green in the mosaics, vault painting in red, cream, and yellow. It is, in sum, a highly innovative building, but functionally quite workable.

Hadrian's happiness was short-lived. In A.D. 128 he set out again on his travels, accompanied by Antinous. They wintered at Athens, which Hadrian enriched with monuments, passed over into Asia Minor, and down through Syria into Egypt. Here, in 130, Antinous died, probably a suicide, to please his master or to avoid his passion. Hadrian's grief was more baroque than any of his buildings. From this point his life becomes one long death wish. The most massive symbol of this is his mausoleum, whose great concrete drum, approached by Hadrian's bridge, the *Pons Aelius* (nowadays the Ponte Sant' Angelo), still dominates the right bank of the Tiber near St. Peter's. The latest Hadrianic bricks in it are dated A.D. 134; it must have become an important part of the Emperor's plans when he returned to Rome, mourning Antinous, in 132 or 133. Its plan goes back to Etruscan *tumuli*, via the Mausoleum of Augustus—creative imitation again. The square block on which the drum rests has almost exactly the dimensions of the Augustan monument's diameter. A spiral ramp leads up to the tomb chamber in the very center of the drum. Carlo Fontana (1634–1714) made of the cover of Hadrian's sarcophagus a baptismal font for St. Peter's. The mausoleum's top was spread with earth and planted with cypresses, the trees of death (Fig. 11.19), and the whole surmounted by a colossal group in bronze, perhaps of Hadrian in a four-horse chariot, now replaced by the

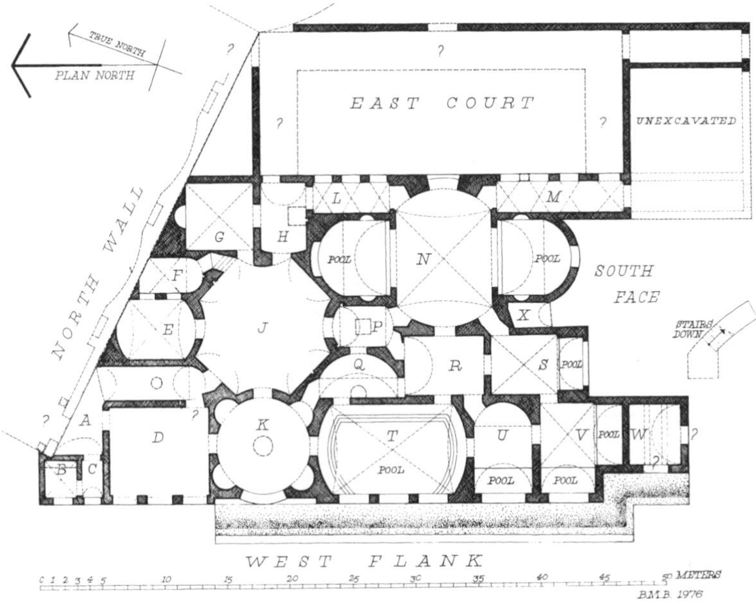
TRUE NORTH
PLAN NORTH
EAST COURT
UNEXCAVATED
NORTH WALL
SOUTH FACE
STAIRS DOWN
L
M
G
H
N
POOL
POOL
F
E
J
P
X
Q
R
S
POOL
O
A
D
K
T
POOL
U
V
POOL
W
B
C
POOL
POOL
WEST FLANK
0 1 2 3 4 5 10 15 20 25 30 35 40 45 50 METERS
B.M.B. 1976

FIG. 11.17 Tivoli. Hadrian's Villa, Small Baths, plan. (MacDonald & Boyle, JSAH 39.1 [1980] ©1980, Society of Architectural Historians)

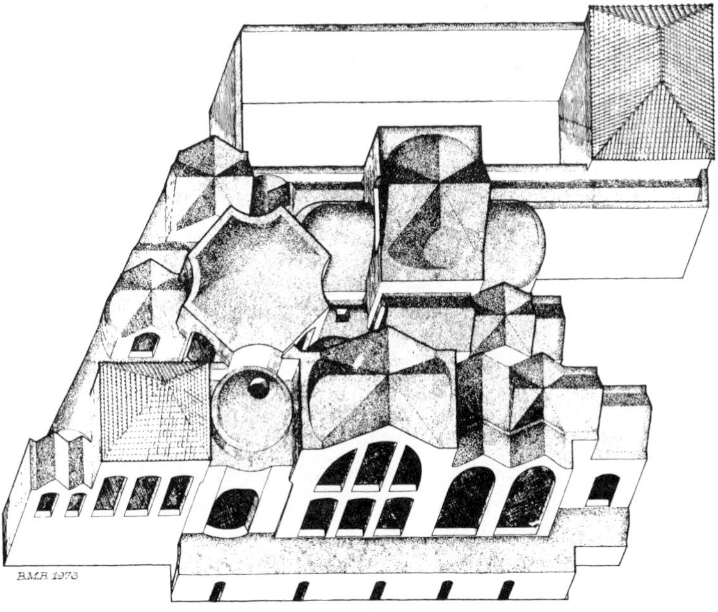
B.M.B. 1973

FIG. 11.18 Tivoli. Hadrian's Villa, Small Baths, axonometric reconstruction. (MacDonald & Boyle, JSAH 39.1 [1980])

Fig. 11.19
Rome, Hadrian's Mausoleum, reconstruction.
(S. R. Pierce, *Journ. Rom. Stud.* 15 [1925])

archangel Michael, who gives the mausoleum its present
name, Castel Sant' Angelo. It is possible that one of the
bronze horses which grace the basilica of San Marco in
Venice came from Hadrian's quadriga. When the death he
longed for agonizingly came, from dropsy, in A.D. 138, Hadrian's ashes were laid beside those of the wife he had never
loved, in the core of the monument which symbolized his
despair at the death of the only creature to whom this
strange man had ever given his affection. The great pile has
been successively fortress, prison (immuring, among others,
the great Renaissance scientist Giordano Bruno), and, since
1934, military museum.

But before his death Hadrian dedicated one more section
of the villa to mourning his loss. This is the Canopus (Figs.
11.1 and 11.20), named for the suburb of Alexandria where
Antinous met his untimely and unhappy end. The original
plan may have antedated Antinous's death—the latest stamps

Fig. 11.20   Tivoli, Hadrian's Villa, Canopus, view. (Fototeca)

reported by Bloch are dated A.D. 126—but after the disaster Hadrian, deliberately turning the knife in the wound, must have made this complex a memorial of the place where it happened. For the approach is along a pool (excavated and restored 1954–1957) intended to be reminiscent of the canal which gave access to the Canopus at Alexandria. The latest finds make it possible to restore the pool with its south end fitted with dining couches. The north end is apsidal, edged with a curious colonnade whose architrave is flat over one pair of columns and arched over the next pair. Along the sides were found perfect (and entirely unimaginative) copies of the Caryatids, the maidens who upheld the south porch of the Erechtheum; these would be memories of past happiness in Athens. Flanking the maidens were Sileni. Other marbles, adorning the apsidal north end of the colonnade, included, in order, an Amazon, a Hermes, a river god representing the Tiber, another representing the Nile, an Ares, and another Amazon. Casts of these have been set up in their places beside the Canopus; the originals are in the site museum adjoining. All this uninspired archaism is depressing; in the aging, heartbroken Hadrian taste and inspiration alike are dead.

The colonnade led to the terminal half-dome (another "pumpkin," it will be recalled) and secondary structures, the whole long known as the Serapeum (there was such a temple in the Alexandrian Canopus). It is complex in plan, at once *nymphaeum* and temple, with its hemicycle deepened at the back into a long narrow apsidal gallery in which some commentators have seen a deep sexual significance. Here Hadrian has turned, to catalyze his flagging inspiration, to older civilizations, dead or dying like himself. Once again, for the last time, and feebly, he has made of what they have to offer something uniquely his own. In the Canopus, as in the Teatro Marittimo and the Piazza d'Oro, there is no single satisfactory viewpoint: the result is an effect of motion, in curved space, in varied light and shade, involved with water, the whole a polyphonic counterpart to Hadrian's own restlessness.

The buildings we have studied present a partial portrait of the man. Hadrian the hunter, the soldier, the statesman comes out clearly in reliefs, coins, and inscriptions we have not room to treat. But the buildings reflect the dilettante Hadrian, uneasy, moody, whimsical, formal, distant, unapproachable, tense, self-conscious, cold. They show many facets of his character: in the Teatro Marttimo, his love of privacy, and his restlessness; in the Temple of Venus and Rome, the neat, abstract quality of his mind, his sense of humor, his self-conscious pairing of himself with Augustus; in the Pantheon, abstraction and Augustus again, plus an awareness of his own grandeur; in the Piazzo d'Oro, complication, involution, febrile gaiety. In the mausoleum, the obsession with his own grandeur and with the memory of Augustus recur, and something new has been added: death wish and posturing with grief. These last two attitudes are to be read again in the fabric of the Canopus, together with a failure of creativity which marks the beginning of the end.

Hadrian is not the only Emperor whose personality may be read in the artifacts of his reign, but he is unique in being himself his own architect, and so innovative that his work marks a turning point in the history of Roman architecture. This in turn creates a problem. How much in his work is genuine self-expression, how much mere playing with form? But the very putting of the question gives insight into Hadrian's character. The key is schizophrenia: unrest and self-consciousness where there might have been the easy confidence born of unchallenged Empire; loneliness in the midst of a crowded court; genius that failed; a love that killed. These are the contradictions that have caused Hadrian to be saluted—a dubious compliment—as "the first modern man." His architecture, as Professor Brown says, embodies the scope, power, and purpose of the Roman Empire, in its use of ductile materials, patron's support, accumulated experience, and unflagging inventiveness. And in it, perhaps more eloquently and poignantly than in any other Roman work, the mute stones speak.

12

Antonines through Constantine
(A.D. 138–337)

With Hadrian an era ends. Juvenal, who wrote during his reign, is the last secular classical Latin poet of importance. Hadrian's successor, Antoninus Pius (A.D. 138–161) was modest and plain living where Hadrian had been flamboyant and extravagant. The autobiography (written in Greek) of *his* successor, Marcus Aurelius (161–180), is throughout a tacit criticism of Hadrian: his boy-love, his architecture, his dilettantism. Marcus Aurelius's son and successor, Commodus (180–192), was a monstrous megalomaniac beside whose excesses those of Caligula, Nero, or Domitian pale into insignificance. The next dynasty, the Severi (193–235), founded a military absolutism that degenerated into anarchy (235–284). Under Diocletian (284–305) absolutism is intensified and grows more rigid. Under Constantine (306–337) the Empire's creative center shifts to Constantinople (old Byzantium made new, in the Greek east), a new religion triumphs, and the story of Christian archaeology begins. True, the two centuries from Hadrian through Constantine are represented by some of Rome's most impressive surviving monuments: the Temple of Antoninus and Faustina, the

Columns of Antoninus Pius and Marcus Aurelius, the Arches of Septimius Severus and of Constantine, the Baths of Caracalla and Diocletian, Aurelian's Wall, and the Basilica of Maxentius. And in the 200 years after Hadrian, Roman skill in military and civil engineering, as exemplified in baths and aqueducts, roads and walls, continues unabated.

Indeed the years from the Antonine through the Constantinian dynasties, too often neglected by literary classicists, are so fruitful in monuments of architecture and art that rigorous selection will be necessary in discussing them. Even so, we shall be dealing with a plethora of archaeological evidence, including a sumptuous villa, two temples, four arches, two columns, two sets of baths, and a trio of public buildings—for show, imperial pomp, and amusement—besides the works of engineering mentioned above. And the thread that runs through it all is the evidence of increasing absolutism as the Roman Empire careers toward its fall.

A suburban villa whose construction forms a bridge between Hadrian's and Piazza Armerina (see chapter 13) is Sette Bassi, at the sixth milestone of the Via Latina, southeast of Rome. Archaeologists have distinguished three phases here (A.D. 140–160). The earliest was a conventional, compact residential block (Fig. 12.1), involving a covered atrium, peristyle, and smaller courts, all at the back of an extensive garden peristyle. The west wing (to the right in the model) belongs to Phase II: it was built on a man-made terrace, and had a nymphaeum-exedra, and a façade of nonfunctional arches. It was bombed in World War II, and the great windowed wall of its façade fell in 1951. In Phase III was added a huge (1,000-foot) buttressed cryptoporticus, with round towers at either end: it enclosed the peristyle garden, some baths, and two large, high reception halls. The brickwork, as in Trajan's market, is left unveneered, some of it in *opus vittatum*—a technique involving bands of tufa in-

FIG. 12.1 Sette Bassi villa, model. (DAI)

serted between courses of brick. The plan is tighter than that of Hadrian's Villa. A lineal descendant is the villa of Maxentius, about a mile and a half out on the Via Appia (Fig. 12.18).

Piety was a hallmark of the first two Antonine Emperors, who were singled out by Gibbon as presiding, like Nerva, Trajan, and Hadrian before them over "the period in the history of the world during which the condition of the human race was most happy and prosperous." Antoninus Pius built in the old Forum for the worship of his deified wife Faustina (died 141) the familiar temple (Fig. 12.2), whose broken pediment (of 1602) reminds us that the temple survives because it was incorporated into the church of S. Lorenzo in Miranda. Its walls are of peperino tufa, once marble-revetted; its frieze, of Greek island marble, bears griffins heraldically facing, and vegetable motifs. The stairs (modern restoration), incorporating an altar, lead up to six unfluted cipollino columns 55 feet high, with white marble Corinthian capitals. Graffiti on the shafts present crude sketches, by idlers, of statues once visible from the temple porch; e.g., Hercules and the Nemean lion. Fragments have been found of the sculpture that once adorned the temple: Faustina enthroned, Antoninus himself, heroized (i.e., semi-nude). An inscription records that on his death in 161 he too was deified and worshiped here. There are also bits of an altar with representations in relief of Neptune, Juno, Vulcan, Minerva, Venus, and Mercury—and traces of the narrow precinct in which the temple stood.

Antoninus was called Pius because of his veneration for Hadrian, his adoptive father. The three-dimensional evidence of this is the Hadrianeum of 145, the 49-foot Corinthian columns of one side of which line the Piazza di Pietra, and are incorporated in Rome's Bourse. A barrel vault supported the steps; the cella was barrel-vaulted and coffered; the pedestals of the pilasters on the cella's inner wall bore

FIG. 12.2   Rome, Forum, Temple of Antoninus and Faustina.
(Fototeca)

personifications of the provinces of the Empire, some of
which are still on the temple, others in the Conservatori
(Fig. 12.3), in Naples, in the Vatican, and in private collections. On the plaster casts in the Terme have been recognized Bithynia (home of Hadrian's favorite Antinous),
Armenia, and Moesia. The seven originals in the Conservatori courtyard include (according to the most trustworthy
identifications, based on attributes and coins) Mauretania,
Achaea, Moesia or Thrace, Dacia (?), Gallia, Hispania or
Germania, and Libya. Those in Naples probably represent

379

FIG. 12.3   Rome, Conservatori, province panels from Hadrianeum. (Fototeca)

Scythia, Phrygia, and Parthia. Interspersed with the personification panels are trophies: armor, captured standards (including the Dacian dragon, as on Trajan's Column), shields,
lances, a battle-ax. Though the trophies are military, they
imply that hostilities are over, and all the provinces are
peaceful. Peace was Hadrian's policy. Under Trajan, the
Roman Empire reached its greatest extent; Hadrian saw
himself as a consolidator, his mission to put the provinces in
order. A propagandist under Pius, the Asiatic Greek rhetori-
cian Aelius Aristides, expressed a rosy view of what the
Roman peace meant under that Emperor: the world as a
Common Market, enjoying citizenship generously shared by
the Romans; one long holiday, the world a weaponless garden, competition in beautifying cities the only rivalry; Rome
as confirming the civilization founded by Athens; the Romans succeed in combining world rule with democracy.

The next Antonine monument in date is the base of the
column of Antoninus Pius, erected in the Campus Martius
after his death in 161, and now in the apse of the Cortile
della Pigna in the Vatican (Fig. 12.4), whither it was moved
in 1789 after its discovery in 1703. The column shaft has
disappeared: it was a plain 48-foot monolith of red Egyptian
granite. Quarried as early as 105/6, it was originally intended
for the temple to the deified Trajan in his Forum. The base
bears an inscription and three reliefs: an apotheosis and two
decursiones (mounted funeral cortèges), one for each new
Emperor (for Marcus Aurelius [reigned 161–180] had his
adoptive brother, L. Verus, as his colleague until the latter
died in 160). In the apotheosis panel Antoninus and Faustina,
conceived as Jupiter and Juno, flanked by eagles, are being
borne off to heaven by a naked winged figure personifying
either the Golden Age or Aion, a Mithraic symbol for Eternity. He holds a snake-girdled globe emblazoned with the
moon, stars, and three signs of the Zodiac: Pisces, Aries,
Taurus, under the first of which Antoninus died. Witnesses

Fig. 12.4   Vatican, Column of Antoninus Pius, base. (Fototeca)

of the apotheosis are the goddess Roma and a personification of the Campus Martius, holding an obelisk. Roma is a
helmeted Minerva type, splendidly accoutered, with an
arrow-filled quiver, a Gorgon on one shield, the wolf and
twins on the other. The *decursiones* are virtually identical:
they portray, rather dumpily, seventeen horsemen riding
counterclockwise round ten infantrymen. Six of the seventeen wear senatorial shoes: they are priests of the Imperial
cult. The figure third from the bottom right in each relief
represents Marcus and Lucius respectively. The infantrymen are the Emperor's praetorian bodyguard; two of them
are standard bearers. The emphasis is on piety. It used to be
held that the apotheosis was "court art" and the *decursiones*
"plebeian," but a more sensible view now prevails: all three

reliefs are official art, which by now embraces both the traditional and the innovative.

From an arch, now destroyed, of Marcus eleven panels survive—three in the Conservatori, eight on the Arch of Constantine, where the grave, bearded face of the philosopher-Emperor has been made over into a smooth-shaven likeness of Constantine, much as Domitian became Nerva on the Cancelleria reliefs. The Conservatori panels, dated A.D. 176, are unaltered, and symbolize qualities which Marcus wished his people to identify with himself: Clemency, Victory, Piety. In the Clemency relief two bearded barbarian chiefs kneel in supplication before the mounted Emperor, who holds out a forgiving hand. On the Victory panel Marcus, with a winged Victory over his head, rides in a four-horse chariot past a temple—perhaps of Fortuna Redux—and is about to turn through a triumphal arch. The chariot bears likenesses in relief of Neptune, Juno, and Minerva above, and two more Victories below. The spokes are Hercules's clubs; the hub-cap, a lion's head. In front of the chariot stands a lictor looking up adoringly; his fasces appear in low relief on a pilaster of the arch behind him. A stubble-bearded trumpeter, blasting away, completes the scene. The Piety panel shows the Emperor sacrificing, in the presence of the Genius of the Senate, the Flamen Dialis (priest of Jupiter), and Marcus's chief of staff, Ti. Claudius Pompeianus. At the altar stand a camillus (acolyte), and a flute player; the sacrificial priest, half-naked, with his ax; and the victim, a fine bull; behind him an attendant shoulders a situla for the entrails. In the background is the Capitoline temple and a portico adjoining, topped by reliefs of gladiators fighting wild beasts. The pedimental details are clear: flanking Jupiter are Minerva and Juno; below them, the moon and sun; across the bottom, Vulcan, Hercules, Jupiter's eagle, and Juventus (Hebe), the cupbearer of the gods. The Arch of Constantine panels (posthumous) can be more briefly described, since they contain many motifs derived from Trajan's Column. On the north side, an *adventus*, Marcus arriving in Rome on foot, escorted by Mars and Venus. Victory, holding a garland, files over his head; the background is again the temple of Fortuna Redux and the triumphal arch, also decorated with a garland. In the other north panels we see the Emperor (1) leaving Rome with war elephants, and saluted by Via Flaminia personified as a half-naked woman kneeling on a wheel; (2) distributing largesse; and (3) questioning a German prisoner. On the south side he was portrayed—again metamorphosed into Constantine—addressing his troops, among whom are standard bearers in animal-skin caps and others in a variety of helmets and cuirasses. The other south side panels show various war episodes and a sacrifice.

From 166 dates the most famous equestrian statue from antiquity: the gilt bronze of the Emperor in uniform greeting his troops (Fig. 12.5), which Michelangelo brought in 1538 from the church of St. John Lateran to his Capitoline piazza. In 1980, it was removed, pitted with pollutants, for restoration. A copy will replace it.

To the Antonine or Hadrianic period belongs the first phase of a five-story apartment block, which, like the ones at Ostia, is carved into the south foot of the Capitoline Hill. The ground floor has shops with mezzanine sleeping quarters, as in Trajan's market; such shops can be seen still in the older parts of Trastevere. One shop with a vat served a fuller. The rooms grow smaller and smaller as one ascends; they are poorly decorated and would have been crowded—the block would hold 380—dark and dirty, a veritable rabbit warren for the poor: genteel starvation in a third-floor back, such as Martial and Juvenal complain of. The block lasted into the fourth century; a regionary catalogue of that date records 46,612 *insulae,* but only 1,797 old-fashioned Pompeian-type *domus.*

FIG. 12.5   Rome, Capitoline Hill: equestrian statue of Marcus
Aurelius, now dismantled. (Fototeca)

The most important monument of Marcus's reign is his column in the Piazza Colonna, superficially resembling Trajan's: 100 Roman feet tall, it records in a continuous spiral, in 116 scenes, the events of two campaigns of the 170s in Marcus's German Wars, separated by a Victory inscribing a shield. The column shares its key motifs with Trajan's: the Emperor addressing troops (Fig. 12.6, bottom spiral), receiving embassies, performing sacrifice, leading attacks. But the emphasis is different: the Emperor is more isolated, aloof, absolute; the horrors of war are more crudely stressed. The message is beat, club, drag, burn, kill: villages are destroyed (Fig. 12.6, upper spiral), prisoners taken; barbarians flee, are exiled; Quisling barbarians behead loyal ones at Roman behest. Tribesmen are assassinated in a pit, speared by Romans from above; their women dragged by the hair, transported, butchered. The violence and anguish on the column reflect the fragility of an age in which a philosopher is forced to make war. Roman art here expresses ideas which its Hellenistic antecedents were not created to express: this is its creative originality, veiled and constrained until, as now, it burst the serene but fixed equlibrium of classical humanism. The most famous scene, the Miracle of the Rain, personifies a downpour which gave the Romans victory over the Quadi, who lived in what is now Moravia. The storm allegedly came in answer to Christian prayers, and indeed the atmosphere created is more mediaeval than classical: the rain god, winged, shaggy, lowering (Fig. 12.6, middle spiral, far right), would not be out of place adorning a portal of Chartres cathedral. And the soldiers escorting the baggage train, holding their shields over their heads as protection against the deluge—primitively portrayed—well illustrate what art historians mean by plebeian as opposed to "aulic" or official art.

The Antonine dynasty ended with the assassination of

FIG. 12.6   Rome, Column of M. Aurelius, three spirals. Miracle of the Rain, extreme right, central panel (Fototeca)

Marcus's unworthy son Commodus (192), described by Renan as a "stupid butcher's boy." Its successors, the African Severans (193–238), added to the Palatine buildings, restored the age-old shrine of Vesta in the Republican Forum, repaired the aqueducts, and built monumental arches, baths, and roads. The additions to the Palatine appear clearly in the model (Fig. 12.7): they include the baths—raised on a two-storied, blind-arched terrace (like Palestrina's) at the south corner of the hill, above the curve of the Circus Maximus—and the curious false façade below the baths to the right, called the Septizodium. It is a three-storied columned screen, like the architectural backdrop of a Roman theater, intended to impress Severus's fellow Africans as they entered Rome from the south by the Via Appia. A similar one, in Cincari, Tunisia, portrayed, in niches, the seven planets: Saturn, Jupiter, Mars, Sun, Venus, Mercury, Moon, and the name Septizodium suggests a similar interpretation of the Roman one. It was dismantled under Sixtus V (1585–90), and some of its stones used in his chapel in S. Maria Maggiore. From the "Paedagogium" (schoolroom), probably Severan, just under and to the left of the exedra in the model (Fig. 12.7), comes a graffito: the so-called Mocking Crucifix, now in the Palatine Antiquarium. It portrays a crucified man with the head of an ass, to the left another man, and a legend scrawled in Greek, "*Alexamenos is worshiping his god.*" The likeliest interpretation is that this is pagan mockery of Christian worship. The building standing in its own precinct, to the upper left of the aqueduct in the model, is a temple of the Sun, erected by the adolescent fanatic Elagabalus (reigned 218–225), and made by him into a religious museum, enshrining an aniconic (nonrepresentational) Cybele, the actual hearth of Vesta, the Palladium (the primitive statue of Minerva allegedly brought by Aeneas from Troy), and the *ancilia,* the quivering spears of Mars, presagers of war. The temple underlies the church and monastery of S. Se-

Fig. 12.7 Rome, Palatine, model with Septizodium. (Felbermeyer)

bastiano on the Palatine's northeast corner, and has never been properly excavated.

Septimius Severus's wife, the bluestocking Julia Domna, a deeply religious woman, restored the round shrine of Vesta after a fire in 191. Ironically, the shrine was subject to fires precisely because the sacred flame was kept burning in it. It reproduces the shape of a primitive hut. Julia Domna also restored the Atrium Vestae adjoining, where the six Vestals lived. Two stories rose round a rectangular fountained court bordered by statues of the redoubtable virgins, some of which are preserved in the Terme; their subjects, according to inscriptions, were in office between 201 and 380. One inscription has suffered *damnatio memoriae:* its subject turned Christian. At the building's east end were six cellae for the Lares whom the Vestals served; the virgins' living quarters were on an upper floor on the Palatine side. The ground floor rooms housed a grain mill and kitchen. An apsidal hall at the southeast corner was the Vestals' dining room.

In 196 Severus restored the Aqua Marcia, originally built between 144 and 140 B.C. This, then, is an appropriate place to discuss the system of aqueducts as an outstanding feat of Roman engineering. The eleventh and last of the ancient aqueducts was built by the Emperor Alexander Severus in A.D. 226; the earliest, the Aqua Appia, dates back to the same builder and the same year—312 B.C.—as the Queen of Highways, the Via Appia. The network (Fig. 12.8) supplied Rome with over 250,000,000 gallons of water every twenty-four hours. When New York was thrice the size of Severan Rome, its aqueducts supplied only 425,000,000 gallons daily.

We owe our knowledge of Rome's aqueducts to three people, one ancient and two modern: Sextus Julius Frontinus, water commissioner under Trajan, whose book on aqueducts survives; Dr. Thomas Ashby, former director of the British School at Rome; and Miss Esther B. Van Deman of

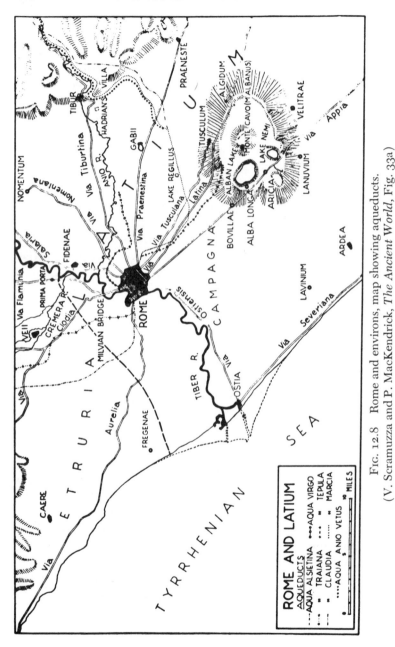

FIG. 12.8 Rome and environs, map showing aqueducts.
(V. Scramuzza and P. MacKendrick, *The Ancient World*, Fig. 33a)

the American Academy. For over thirty years, before modernity removed the traces, this devoted pair tramped the rough country between Tivoli and Rome, plotting the courses of the major aqueducts. Their definitive work is well-nigh as monumental as the aqueducts themselves. Together they explored the mazy course of the aqueduct channels, above ground and below, along crumbling cliffs and the edge of deep gorges, over walls, through briers, across turnip fields, in the cellars of farmhouses and wineshops. They climbed and waded; Ashby explored downshafts "with the aid of several companions and a climber's rope," and when they were through, the courses and the building history especially of Rome's four major aqueducts, the Anio Vetus (272–269 B.C.), the Marcia (144 B.C.), the Claudia (A.D. 47), and the Anio Novus (A.D. 52)—all repeatedly repaired—were better known than they had been since Frontinus's day, and fellow archaeologists were in a position to draw from their detailed pioneer work important conclusions about Roman hydraulic engineering and about Roman culture.

Following Frontinus's indications, Ashby and Miss Van Deman found the sources of the four great aqueducts at over 1,000 feet above sea level, in springs or lakes in the upper reaches of the Anio valley, near Subiaco, Mandela, and Vicovaro. The airline distance of the sources from Rome varies from twenty-four to twenty-seven miles, but to follow the contours the aqueducts took a circuitous course, so that their actual length is from forty-three to sixty-two miles. Though the modern reader associates Roman aqueducts with the magnificent lines of arches (Fig. 12.9) stretching across a once-empty Campagna near Rome, the fact is that well under a third of a Roman aqueduct's course was normally carried on arches: the rest was tunnel or sidehill channel. The reason for this was in part economy, in part strategic considerations: an aqueduct below ground is harder for an enemy to find and cut. When the Goths finally did cut the

FIG. 12.9   Aqueducts near Capannelle, reconstruction (painting).
(Deutsches Museum, Munich)

aqueducts in the sixth century A.D., the seven hills of Rome
became, and remained for centuries, unfit for civilized
habitation.

The four aqueducts, Ashby and Miss Van Deman found,
followed the course of the Anio fairly closely from their
source to just below Tivoli, where, having lost half their
altitude, they turned south along the shoulder of the hills to
Gallicano. In this stretch, at Ponte Lupo, the Aqua Marcia
crosses a gorge on a bridge that would test the mettle of the
most seasoned archaeologist, for it epitomizes Roman con-
structional history in stone and concrete for almost nine
centuries. After Gallicano the intrepid pair traced the aqueducts' course westward, where, by a system of tunnels, in
verted siphons (the Romans knew that water would rise to

its own level), and side-hill channels they cross the broken gorges of the Campagna to a point south of Capannelle race-track, six miles from Rome, whence they proceed on the famous arches to the Porta Maggiore. From reservoirs in the city the water was distributed in lead pipes (one, of Hadrianic date, has walls three inches thick, and weighs eighty-eight pounds per running foot), with a strict priority, first to public basins and fountains (the Aqua Julia alone supplied 1,200 of these), next to baths (extensions of the Marcia supplied those of both Caracalla and Diocletian), then to private houses. Surplus was used for flushing the sewers. Attempts were made to control the priorities by running the pipes for private use only from the highest levels of the reservoirs, but Frontinus complains bitterly of illegal tapping.

In the Gallicano-Capannelle stretch special archaeological ingenuity is required, first to find the channels, and then to decide which belongs to which aqueduct. Where the channels have entirely disappeared, through the disintegrating action of floods, earthquake, tree roots, or plowing, the course can be defined by plotting the occurrence of heaps of calcium carbonate on the ground. This is the aqueduct deposit. Roman water is extremely hard, and the heaps mark where once there were downshafts (*putei*) for inspection and cleaning the channels, which without such maintenance would soon have become completely blocked with deposit. Frontinus says the downshafts occurred regularly every 240 feet, and Dr. Ashby found many at just this interval.

For distinguishing one aqueduct from another there are many criteria. The first is construction materials. The earliest aqueducts are built of cut stone, the latest of brick. Miss Van Deman was famous for her precise dating of building materials; she was the only archaeologist in Rome who could date a brick by the *taste* of the mortar. A second criterion is quality of workmanship. The Claudia, for example, is notoriously jerry-built: where abutments are found which

should be solid, but are instead one block thick, filled in
with earth behind, that channel belongs to the Aqua Claudia.
A third criterion is mineral deposits. Thus the Marcia was
famous for its purity; the crystalline lime deposits were
quarried in the Middle Ages, polished, and used to decorate
altars. The Anio Novus, on the other hand, is distinguished
by a singularly foul deposit. A fourth criterion is directness
of course: the older the aqueduct, the more sinuously it runs;
a channel found meandering by itself along the contours is
likely to be that of the Anio Vetus.

The total impression the aqueducts give is one of efficiency, organization, and heedlessness of expense, under the
Republic as well as under the Empire. They were built with
the spoils of wars or the tribute of provinces. The Marcia,
built with the proceeds of the loot of Carthage and Corinth,
cost 180,000,000 sesterces, or $9,000,000 uninflated. The
Tepula, of 125 B.C., was perhaps built with the profits from
the organization of the new province of Asia. From Agrippa's
time onward, and especially in Frontinus's administration,
the aqueduct service employed a large bureaucracy; overseers, reservoir-superintendents, inspectors, stonemasons,
plasterers (the stone-built channels were lined with two or
three coats of hydraulic cement), and unskilled laborers.
Maintenance was a constant problem. Arches needed propping, filling in, or brick facing; piers needed to be buttressed
or brick-encased. There was no attempt to produce high pressure: lead pipes would not have stood it, and for public use
it was not necessary. There was no attempt to make the
aqueducts financially self-supporting: their original building
was one of the benefactions expected of successful com-
manders. Since these nabobs expected a *quid pro quo* in the
gift of power, the aqueducts are a symbol, under the Republic, of irresponsible oligarchy, and under the Empire, of increasingly irresponsible autocracy, though "good" Emperors,
like Augustus, Claudius, Trajan, and Hadrian, had a hand in

them. In Augustus's reign were built the Julia, the Virgo, and the Alsietina. Trajan built a northern line from Lago di Bracciano to Rome's Trastevere quarter on the right bank of the Tiber: part of its course runs under the courtyard of the American Academy. Hadrian executed major repairs, datable by the omnipresent brick stamps. But even good Emperors knew no way of financing such public works except by bleeding the taxpayer. In municipalities, private capital was absorbed in such public enterprise, with no return in income or local employment commensurate with the capital involved. So one major conclusion from Ashby's and Miss Van Deman's work is that the Romans were better engineers than they were economists. Let the last word on aqueducts be Pliny the Elder's: "If one takes careful account of the abundant supply of water for public purposes, for baths, pools, channels, houses, gardens, suburban villas; the length of the aqueducts' courses—arches reared, mountains tunnelled, valleys crossed on the level—he will confess that there has never been a greater marvel in the whole world."

In 203 Septimius Severus built at the west end of the old Forum the monumental three-passage arch which bears his name. The layout of the ornamentation, in the summer of 1981 invisible under scaffolding, was the same on each face: in the attic, an inscription—in which the name of Septimius's son Geta, who was murdered by his brother Caracalla, has been erased—then pairs of panels with scenes of battle, siege, surrender, and imperial oratory; in the spandrels (the space between the curve of an arch and its enclosing rectangle), victories, seasons, and river gods; in the keystones, Mars and Hercules; above the minor arches, narrow friezes of triumphs, with personifications of conquered provinces and of Rome; in the plinths, soldiers with Parthian prisoners. The most instructive parts of the arch are the panels above the minor arches. They portray (1) on the Forum side, left,

Severus's departure for Zeugma or Carrhae, a battle, an
allocutio, and the lifting of the siege of Nisibis; (2) Forum,
right: siege of Edessa, surrender of the Osrhoeni and their
king, Abgar, and council of war. The scenes, all in the Tigris
Valley, are all dominated by Severus; (3) street side, left
(Fig. 12.10): successful attack on the rich and well-built
city of Seleucia-on-the-Tigris, which gives up without a
struggle, its leaders, tiny, swarming figures, kowtowing to
Severus and his sons (upper right). In the lower register we
see the nearby walled city of Ctesiphon: its king, with his
cavalry bodyguard, abandons it, but at the lower left a squad
of infantry makes a desperate foray from an open gate. The
lower right corner, badly weathered, seems to show Roman
soldiers attacking a fortified and defended suburban house;
(4) street side, right: Ctesiphon, attacked with siege-engines,
falls; the Emperor makes a speech. These panels, while they
owe something to the spiral reliefs on the columns of Trajan
and Marcus Aurelius, also reflect the conventions of paintings carried in triumphs, as in Republican days. A comparison with the Ara Pacis reliefs will show the difference
between classical and postclassical art, but the glorification
of the Emperor, begun under Augustus, is here carried to
unprecedented heights.

In 204 the money changers (*argentarii*) and cattle merchants of the Forum Boarium dedicated to the Severans the
Arch of the Argentarii in the Velabrum, partly preserved
beside the early mediaeval church of S. Giorgio in Velabro.
Of central interest are the interior panels, which originally
showed, on the left, Caracalla, the heir apparent, sacrificing,
with his father-in-law Plautianus and his wife Plautilla, or
his brother Geta, all of whom Caracalla murdered. The identification is conjectural because the panel has suffered *damnatio memoriae:* the figure or figures to Caracalla's right have
been chiseled away (Fig. 12.11). The same discourtesy has
been practiced on the figure of Geta or Plautilla, originally

FIG. 12.10   Rome. Arch of Septimius Severus, attack on Seleucia. (DAI)

shown sacrificing with Severus and Julia Domna on the right interior panel. The members of the Imperial family are presented as superior, quasi-divine figures.

His throne secured by family murders, Caracalla proceeded to carry out a grandiose project: his Baths. The Baths of Caracalla (Fig. 12.16,16), known to thousands of visitors as the summer setting for Rome's outdoor opera, were built on a vast platform, twenty feet high, with an area of 270,000 square feet, greater than that of London's Houses of Parliament. Excavations in 1938, when the Baths were being prepared for their metamorphosis into an outdoor opera house, revealed in the substructure vaulted service corridors, wide enough for vehicles, widening out at intersections into regu-

FIG. 12.11   Rome, Arch of Argentarii, Caracalla sacrificing, with *damnatio memoriae*. (Bini)

lar underground public squares, with provisions for rotary traffic. Access to the lower reaches was by stairs let into the central piers of the main building. The principal entrance to the Baths was to the north (over the edge of the platform at the top center of the air photograph, Fig. 12.12). It was flanked by numerous small rooms which in the difficult postwar years housed teeming families of Italy's homeless. (Their unique opportunity of a summer evening to admire the sleek prosperity of the operagoers recreated the gulf that yawned between haves and have nots in Imperial Rome, and contributed not a little to Italy's unrest.)

The main bath building was set in the northern half of the great open space provided by the platform, and was surrounded with gardens. Facing these on the perimeter was a variety of halls, for lectures, reading, and exercise. Those on the east and west were contained in curved projections (exedras). A part of the western exedra appears in the lower left corner of the air photograph. Beneath it, in a subterranean vault, was discovered in 1911 what was at that time the largest Mithraeum (shrine of the Persian god Mithras) in Rome.* To the south (lower right on the photograph), was a stadium whose seats were built against the reservoir which supplied the Baths: this was fed by a branch from one of the great aqueducts, the Aqua Marcia.

The main block of the Baths is distinguished for its axial symmetry. The most prominent room was the circular *caldarium*, or hot bath (just to the right of center in the photograph). It is between its main piers that the opera stage is set. Behind it the vast rectangular open space (82 by 170 feet) is most logically interpreted as a grand concourse whence the patrons of the baths (as many as 1,600 in peak hours) could move unimpeded to the bathing rooms of their choice. This central room was groin-vaulted in coffered con-

* In 1958 Dutch archaeologists excavated a larger one under the church of S. Prisca on the Aventine Hill.

crete, in three great bays supported by eight piers (Fig. 12.13). The rooms around the central rectangle, with their enormously thick walls, were ingeniously arranged as buttresses to resist the thrust of the colossal vaults.

The large open spaces at the east and west ends of the main block were exercise grounds. The exedras adjacent to their inner sides were decorated in the early fourth century with the splendidly satiric mosaics of athletes now in the Vatican Museum. With their broken noses, low foreheads, and cauliflower ears, they are the very type of overspecialized brutal brawn which intellectuals in all ages have delighted to ridicule.

The large rectangular area at the rear center was the cold swimming pool, or *frigidarium;* perhaps the rooms on either side were dressing rooms. Below the pavement of the baths the excavators discovered tons of *L-* or *T*-shaped iron bolted together in the form of a St. Andrew's cross. The possible inference is that some part of the Baths was roofed with iron girders, designed to support bronze plates ingeniously contrived to reflect sunlight onto the bathers below. (The evidence for the bronze plates and the sunroom is not archaeological but literary, and, chiefly because the literary source had little or no idea what he was talking about, has raised apparently insoluble controversy.)

There must always have been crowds, motley, colorful crowds, speaking many tongues, in the heyday of the Baths. There is easily room for 1,600 patrons at a time. We may imagine them bathing, sauntering, making assignations; conversing idly or upon philosophical subjects; thronging the lecture rooms, the library, the picture gallery; running, jumping, racing, playing ball, or watching spectator sports in the stadium at the back.

From Caracalla's reign came the original of the Antonine Itinerary (text to a road map), which, however, in its present

FIG. 12.12   Rome, Baths of Caracalla, air view. (Castagnoli, *Roma antica,*

FIG. 12.13   Rome, Baths of Caracalla, great hall, nineteenth-century reconstruction. (American Academy in Rome)

form is Diocletianic (284–306). It lists seventeen main routes, including the Appia, Clodia, Aurelia, Praenestina, Labicana, Latina, Salaria, Valeria, and Flaminia. Mention of the Antonine Itinerary affords an opportunity to discuss the major feat of engineering represented by Roman roads. These (see map, Fig. 4.1), echoing to the measured tread of marching legions, had made a large contribution to unifying Italy by the time that great consular highway, the Via Aemilia, opened up the Po Valley from Ariminum to Placentia in 187 B.C.,* but their work of carrying commerce and ideas was unceasing. Of course there were roads in Italy before the Romans: the name and route of the Via Salaria, from the salt pans at the Tiber's mouth up the valley into the Apennines, suggest that it must have been in use since prehistoric times. The Tiber itself, above Rome, has never been much used as a waterway. An adventurous pair of American archaeologists traveled from Orte to Rome (48 miles if done by rail) in a rubber raft in 1950. It took them five days. They reported no river traffic, no riverbank towns, the stream serving more as a barrier than a link. The Via Latina, named not for a Roman consul but for a people potent in central Italy until the Romans broke their league in 338 B.C., must count as a pre-Roman road, and its winding course along the foothills must antedate the draining of the Pomptine marshes and the laying down of the straight course across them from Rome to Terracina and thence to Capua of the *regina viarum,* the queen of roads—the Via Appia. It bears the name of a Roman censor of 312 B.C. This is the first of the great highways, and it deserves its fame for its bold conquest of natural obstacles and its arrow-straight course across the marshes. But its gravel surface was not replaced by stone pavement

* Some dates, and routes of roads not on the map, Fig. 1.4: Via Valeria, 307; Clodia (Rome-Saturnia), 287–285; Flaminia, 220; Cassia (Rome-Arretium), 154; Postumia (Genua-Aquileia), 148. Public works bring popularity: every milestone would remind the traveling voter of the road-builder's generosity.

until 293 B.C., and then only as far as the suburb of Bovillae. Its course, like that of many another Roman road, was not always so arrow-straight. In the hills behind Terracina it followed the contours; it was not until Trajan's time that another bold stroke of engineering cut through the high, rocky Pesco Montano to let the road pass by the more direct coastal route. (Some authorities hold that the Romans preferred straight roads because the front axles of their vehicles were rigid.) Trajan's engineers showed their pride in their work by incising monumental Roman numerals, still visible, to mark the depth of the cut every ten feet from the top down, until the road level was triumphantly reached at [CXX].

Along the Appia, and the other consular roads radiating from Rome, traces of the ancient stone paving are occasionally preserved. The paving blocks are usually *selce* (flint), polygonal in shape, and closely fitted without mortar. While most Roman roads prove on archaeological examination to consist of paving blocks laid in a trench and packed with earth and *selce* chips, it will be worthwhile to record the ideal method of laying a pavement—strictly speaking a mosaic pavement—as recommended by the architect Vitruvius, a contemporary of Augustus. The method illustrates the Roman engineer's infinite capacity for taking pains.

After the field engineer (1 in the reconstruction, Fig. 12.14), assisted by the stake man (2), had aligned the road with his *groma,* he ran levels with the *chorobates* (3) with the roadman's help (4). A plow (5) was used to loosen earth and mark road margins; then workmen dug marginal trenches (6) to the depth desired for the solid foundations. Laborers (7) shoveled loose earth and carried it away in baskets. The next step was to consolidate the roadbed with a tamper (8). Now the roadbed was ready for its foundation, the *pavimentum* (9), lime mortar or sand laid to form a level base. Next came the *statumen,* or first course (10), fist-size stones, cemented together with mortar or clay, the thickness varying from ten inches to two feet. Over this was laid the *rudus* or second course (11), nine to twelve inches of lime concrete, grouted with broken stone and pottery fragments. Next the *nucleus,* or third course (12), concrete made of gravel or coarse sand mixed with hot lime, placed in layers, and compacted with a roller. Its thickness was one foot at the sides and eighteen inches at the crown of the road. Finally, the *summum dorsum* or top course (13), polygonal blocks of *selce* six inches or more thick, carefully fitted and set in the nucleus while the concrete was still soft. Sometimes, when archaeologists have taken up a stretch of Roman road, they have found the selce blocks rutted on the under side: the economical contractors, happily untroubled by high-priced labor, had repaired their road by turning the worn blocks upside down. Standard curbs (14a and b) were two feet

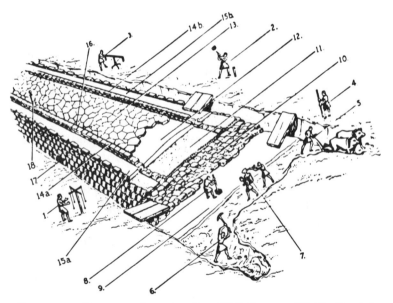

FIG. 12.14   Roman road construction. (U.S. Bureau of Public Roads)

wide and eighteen inches high; paved footpaths (15a and b) often ran outside them. Conduits (16) under the curb, with arched outlets (17) opening beside the right of way, took care of draining surface water. Milestones (18) marked the distance from Rome and the name of the Emperor responsible for repairs. From the names of successive Emperors on milestones of the same road, archaeologists have calculated that the average life of a highway was thirty to forty years.

Two points should be emphasized: first, this represents an ideal method of construction, not often exemplified in practice; second, to a modern engineer a road like this would seem insufficiently elastic, a five-foot wall in the flat, too rigid for the stresses and strains to which it was subjected. Hence perhaps the frequent need for repairs, but Roman traffic was lighter than ours, and the very fact that we can write about the roads at all is a tribute to their durability. Upon roads like these, under the Empire, traveled the imperial posting service, with relays of messengers, and posthouses where horses and carriages could be changed. Under exceptional conditions the Emperor Tiberius, using this service, once traveled 180 miles in a day, a rate of speed not equaled on European roads until the nineteenth century. Thus the competence of the Roman road builders made possible both the coldbloodedness of the Roman conquest and the security of the Roman peace.

One of the latest pieces of Roman engineering, to a knowledge of which archaeology has recently contributed, is Aurelian's Wall. It has been meticulously studied by a pupil of Ashby's, the late I. A. Richmond, formerly Professor of the Archaeology of the Roman Empire at Oxford. Two-thirds of it is still standing (Fig. 12.15), to the disgust of those interested in the unimpeded flow of Rome's traffic, to the delight of those in love with Rome's past. It was twelve miles long, twelve feet thick, sixty feet high; it had 381 towers, each with a latrine, and eighteen portcullised gates, nine of which

FIG. 12.15   Rome, Aurelian's Wall, from south, near Porta Appia.
(H. Kähler, *Rom und seine Welt*, Pl. 252)

survive (Fig. 12.16). Though the Renaissance humanist
Poggio Braccionini had examined the wall as early as 1431,
and the Frenchman Nicholas Audebert had studied it scientifically in 1574, Richmond was still able to make important
contributions. He emphasized, for example, that one-sixth
of the wall incorporated buildings: tombs, houses, park walls,
aqueducts, cisterns, porticoes, an amphitheater,* a fortress.
The inference is that the wall had to be built with speed and

* The Amphitheatrum Castrense, incorporated into the wall just south of
the church of S. Croce in Gerusalemme, was part of a late Severan Imperial
villa complex which included also baths and a circus. The amphitheater, measuring 286 by 246 feet, was brick-faced; its arches, filled in when it was
made part of the wall, were framed by Corinthian half-columns. Only two
of the original three stories survive. S. Croce, once an Imperial audience
hall, was made over into a church by Helena, mother of Constantine. Hers,
too, are the baths, a twelve-chambered reservoir of which is visible in the
Via Eleniana, 270 yards northeast of S. Croce. A quarter-mile southeast of
the Porta Maggiore, Aurelian's Wall crosses at right angles the Circus
Varianus, built to indulge Elagabalus's passion for chariot racing. Its north
wall was preserved by being used in 1585 to support the Acqua Felice.
Measuring 1,836 by 406 feet, it was not much smaller than the Circus Maximus (1,950 by 487).

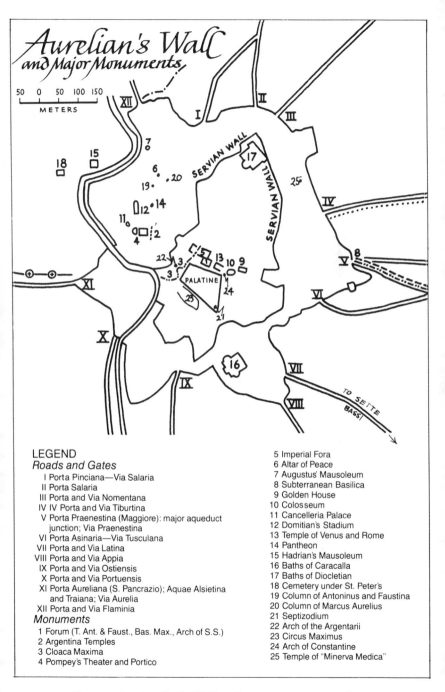

LEGEND
Roads and Gates

I Porta Pinciana—Via Salaria
II Porta Salaria
III Porta and Via Nomentana
IV IV Porta and Via Tiburtina
V Porta Praenestina (Maggiore): major aqueduct junction; Via Praenestina
VI Porta Asinaria—Via Tusculana
VII Porta and Via Latina
VIII Porta and Via Appia
IX Porta and Via Ostiensis
X Porta and Via Portuensis
XI Porta Aureliana (S. Pancrazio); Aquae Alsietina and Traiana; Via Aurelia
XII Porta and Via Flaminia

Monuments

1 Forum (T. Ant. & Faust., Bas. Max., Arch of S.S.)
2 Argentina Temples
3 Cloaca Maxima
4 Pompey's Theater and Portico
5 Imperial Fora
6 Altar of Peace
7 Augustus' Mausoleum
8 Subterranean Basilica
9 Golden House
10 Colosseum
11 Cancelleria Palace
12 Domitian's Stadium
13 Temple of Venus and Rome
14 Pantheon
15 Hadrian's Mausoleum
16 Baths of Caracalla
17 Baths of Diocletian
18 Cemetery under St. Peter's
19 Column of Antoninus and Faustina
20 Column of Marcus Aurelius
21 Septizodium
22 Arch of the Argentarii
23 Circus Maximus
24 Arch of Constantine
25 Temple of "Minerva Medica"

FIG. 12.16   Aurelian's Wall and major monuments, plan

economy, in the face of the threat of barbarians in north Italy and a depleted treasury. Strategic reasons, of course, dictated the protection of the aqueducts. The use of tomb-stones as latrine covers shows, says Richmond, that the wall builders "had their religious scruples under excellent con-trol." It was a sense of urgency and not solicitude for works of art that prompted them, when they built a garden wall at Porta San Lorenzo into the circuit, to leave the statues in their niches and pack them round with clay.

Richmond also found that in the phase of the wall identi-fied as Aurelian's by building materials and brick stamps, the workmanship differed sharply from one curtain to another. The inference from this was that various stretches were assigned to various gangs of workmen—mostly civilian, since the legions were needed in the North and for Aurelian's cam-paign against the Parthians in the East. These workmen belonged to the various city guilds, or *collegia,* some experi-enced in construction, some not, but all pressed into service in the emergency.

Richmond distinguished the bottom twenty-four feet of the wall as the original phase. It was built of brick-faced concrete—that its bricks were often second-hand is inferred from the many Hadrianic stamps—surmounted by a gallery with loopholes outside and an open, bayed arcade inside, with a crenelated wall-walk above. Access to the wall was by the towers only; Richmond inferred that the planner aimed to keep excited and irresponsible civilians from inter-fering with defense, and the wall detail from pilfering or philandering in the adjoining houses and gardens. In this phase the wall was plain, efficient, functional, simple, and uniform, built to a standard size and pattern. Its many gates show that there was no very formidable danger: the intent was to provide a barrier to shut chance bodies of undesir-ables out of the city, as on far-flung frontiers structures like Hadrian's Wall shut them out of the Empire.

In its second phase (under Maxentius, 306–312) another thirty-six feet of wall was fitted on to the base provided by Aurelian's. In some places the addition was only six feet thick, the other half of the original width being left as a passage for the circulation of materials and messages. A wall sixty feet high reduced the required number of defenders, since it had nothing to fear from an enemy equipped with scaling ladders. In this phase machines did the work of men: if there were two *ballistae* to a tower, the expensive and impressive total of pieces of artillery would have been 762. Heightening the wall meant heightening the tower, sometimes to five stories. A start was made toward monumentalizing the gateways, but it petered out. The effect, however, can be admired in the Porta Asinaria near the Lateran, which was restored in 1957–58. For the workmanship of this phase is identical with and therefore of the same date as the Basilica and Circus of Maxentius. When he was defeated by Constantine at the battle of the Milvian Bridge, and the capital moved to Constantinople, neither the money nor the motive for monumentality any longer existed.

The next major alteration is dated by inscriptions to A.D. 401–3, the reign of Honorius. It was prompted by the threat that the city might be sacked by Alaric the Visigoth. It involved second-hand stone facing for the curtains of the wall, and square bases for the towers. The photograph (Fig. 12.15) shows this Honorian phase at the Porta Appia. The upper stories of the round towers belong to Maxentius's addition, while halfway up the face of the curtain between the rectangular towers to the left of the grate can be seen the patching required to add Maxentius's brickwork to the battlements of Aurelian's original wall. (To distinguish the building phases of the Porta Appia, Richmond had to crawl into the base of a tower through a very small hole, while a small uninvited audience bet on his chances of sticking.) The new battlements were built in a way that shows that in this phase Rome could no longer afford artillery: archers replaced *ballistae*. By now the Empire is Christian, and crosses begin to appear on the keystones of the gate arches, as prophylaxis against the devil. Later, in what Richmond describes as "an age of vanishing standards of faith and hygiene," an indulgence of 100 days was granted for kissing one of these crosses. They were no help: the wall was assaulted by earthquakes (A.D. 442), and by Goths (A.D. 536 and 546), and repeatedly repaired. Belisarius in 547 restored it all, with the help of palisades, in twenty days, and equipped it with spring guns, the force of whose projectiles could impale five men, and with mantraps or deadfalls, harrowlike devices which could be pushed over on assailants. But the repairs are botched work, appropriate to what Rome had become: no longer an imperial capital but a minor metropolis of an outlying Byzantine province. All the same, the wall was never really breached till the advent of heavy artillery, when Garibaldi's men attacked the Porta San Pancrazio in 1849.

The half-century of military anarchy ended with the accession of Diocletian in 284. The symbol of his reign is the huge bath complex of 298–306 (Figs. 12.16,17 and 12.17), embracing the modern Piazza Esedra, Michelangelo's church of S. Maria degli Angeli, and the Terme Museum. Rome's Termini railway station, nearby, takes its name from these Terme, the largest of Rome's Imperial baths. They measured 1,235 by 1,202 feet; the central block 812 by 585. In the air photograph, the curve of the piazza probably represents the cavea of a theater incorporated in the bath complex; the domed building beyond the fountain was the tepidarium; its concave approach, the caldarium. The high windows of the Renaissance church lit the great central hall. The domed building near the left edge of the photograph, now a plane-

Fig. 12.17   Baths of Diocletian, present state, from the air.
(Fototeca)

tarium, was the southwest corner of the main block. Behind
and to the right of the church were the *natatio* (swimming
pool), an atrium, and the dressing room. Other parts of the
vast complex are visible in the wine cellars of the Grand
Hotel; the extreme southeast and southwest corners appear
as a bulge in a building in the Via Viminale, and as the
American church, S. Bernardo. The Baths' capacity was
3,000, nearly double that of Caracalla's. The libraries of Trajan's Forum were transferred here, to rooms off either side of
the Piazza Esedra curve. Ward Perkins well characterizes
these baths as simple, light, neat, efficient, and mature—an
architecture to be experienced, not described.

Diocletian also restored the Curia Hostilia in the north-west corner of the old Forum, preserved to our day through having been incorporated in the church of Sant' Adriano. Its bronze doors are copies; the originals were taken in 1660 to the Church of St. John Laterian. Its proportions were canonical: height one-half the sum of length and width. Within, it was impressive with coffered ceiling, an opus sectile floor, and a wealth of polychrome marble revetment: a veneer as false as the pretense of legislative autonomy in the rubber-stamp Senate. Two doors west of the Curia, under the church of San Martino, and in one of the shops in the front portico of the Forum of Caesar, was set up (393/4) the Secretarium Senatus, a law court for trying senators.

In the main Forum, just east of the temple of Antoninus and Faustina, is the so-called Temple of Romulus, a small round domed building flanked by apsidal halls: it still has its original bronze doors. The Romulus in question was the son of Diocletian's colleague Maxentius: the boy died in 309 and was deified. But the building is more likely to have been dedicated to the Penates, which ancient written sources locate near here. Romulus's mausoleum lies a mile and a half out on the Via Appia, a round, domed building, 114 feet across (the Pantheon is 140), in an archaizing rectangular precinct, measuring 338 by 412 feet, with engaged columns, 48 cross-vaulted bays, piers connected by arches. Adjoining was a suburban residence, which comprises baths, nymphaea, a cryptoporticus, a basilical hall 48 feet high, and the Circus of Maxentius, which held 10,000. Its starting gates and the imperial box are visible in the air photograph (Fig. 12.18); its spina (dividing wall down the center) was off axis, to allow for a number of chariots abreast at the start. There was an obelisk on the spina; it was installed in the central fountain of the Piazza Navona in 1651. The masonry is *opus vittatum;* hollow jars were let into the vaulting to lighten the weight.

Back in the Roman Forum, the basilica begun by Maxentius about 306, and finished by Constantine in 313 (Fig. 12.19), looms just east of the temple "of Romulus." It stands on a vast podium, measuring 325 by 211 feet; the nave alone was 260 feet long by 81 wide. The massive surviving coffered vaults belong merely to a side aisle: a single "chapel" will hold a symphony orchestra. An apse at the west end held a colossal statue of Constantine staring with majestic aloofness: its head, hand, and foot, seven times life size, are displayed in the Conservatori courtyard. Such massiveness belongs to the absolutist Empire, not to the Republic: it is therefore perhaps symbolic that one now enters the Basilica not from the old Forum but from the Via dei Fori Imperiali behind the building.

Constantine's arch (A.D. 312–315; Professor Richardson prefers 325/6), which rises between the Colosseum and the Temple of Venus and Rome, consists very largely of reliefs from earlier reigns in re-use, a procedure which enraged the late Bernard Berenson, who totally misunderstood it. It bespeaks not decadence but a desire on the part of the Senate, who dedicated the arch to Constantine, to preach a sermon in stone: be like only the good Emperors. Inscriptions on the arch refer to Constantine as liberator and avenger, working by divine inspiration (*instinctu divinitatis*), not of the Christian God but of the pagan Apollo. The scheme of the reliefs, in July 1981 invisible under scaffolding, is the same on each face of the arch: at the top, Dacian prisoners (Trajanic); between them, the panels already described from the arch of Marcus Aurelius; below, hunt medallions (Hadrianic); in the spandrels, Victories and rivers; on the plinths, Victories with prisoners. Here the ends of the arch also bear reliefs, thus providing a continuity somewhat like that of the scenes on the spirals of Trajan's and Marcus Aurelius's Columns. Each end bears three reliefs: a square panel with scenes from Trajan's Dacian Wars; medallions of the sun and moon: and

FIG. 12.18   Rome, Circus of Maxentius. (Fototeca)

Fig. 12.19 Rome, Basilica of Maxentius. (Fototeca)

long rectangular panels. The last two categories are Constantinian. The total narrative on the rectangular panels begins on the west end, with Constantine's departure from Milan, to march on Rome and unseat Maxentius. On the south face we see him victorious at Verona, and in the key battle of the Milvian Bridge, on the north edge of Rome, where he beat Maxentius, saw the cross and crown in the sky, and heard heavenly voices cry, "In this sign thou shalt conquer." (No hint of this appears on the relief.) On the east, Constantine enters Rome in triumph. On the north face, Constantine makes a speech (Fig. 12.20) in the old Forum. Behind the attentive listeners on the left are the Basilica Julia and the Arch of Tiberius; behind the figures on the right is the Arch of Septimius Severus. On the other north panel, Constantine distributes largesse. Here the barrier between official and plebeian art is broken. The Emperor sits, frontal and immobile; the figures surrounding him are graded in size according to rank: VIPs, bureaucratic accountants, VIP beneficiaries, and then an anonymous crush of tiny plebeian petitioners. The whole effect is of a parade of virtues: Constantine appears as defender, conquering warrior, ceremonialist, orator, and generous prince.

The four-way arch "of Janus" in the Velabrum near that of the Argentarii is also probably Constantinian, perhaps celebrating his triumph. Roma, Juno, Minerva, and Ceres appear in the keystones. The arch is unfinished: its niches perhaps were made for statues never put in place. The Cloaca Maxima runs beneath it: Janus had associations with water. And its passageway would shelter tradesmen and customers of the Forum Boarium in bad weather.

A fourth-century curiosity is the so-called Temple of Minerva Medica—actually a nymphaeum—in the Via G. Giolitti between the Porta Maggiore and the railway. It is a ten-sided building in brick and concrete (Fig. 12.21), 80 feet across, with ten large windows, semicircular exedras, and a cupola

FIG. 12.20   Arch of Constantine: allocutio. (Bini)

with ribbed vaults, which were built up concurrently with the concrete. It stood in the gardens of Constantine's erstwhile colleague Licinius, serving at first as a summerhouse or "folly." Later, heat ducts and a heated pool were added.

We end this survey with the setting up in 357 of a second obelisk, 106 feet high (now in the Piazza S. Giovanni in Laterano) on the spina of the Circus Maximus (Fig. 12.7) between the Palatine and Aventine Hills. The history of the Circus Maximus goes back a very long way, to the reign of the Etruscan Tarquin I (616–578 B.C.); the racetrack was in use until A.D. 550. During this long period the Circus was repeatedly restored, enlarged, and embellished, until under Nero it reputedly held 250,000. It was 1,950 feet long and 487 wide; on the spina, besides the obelisks, were seven eggs and seven dolphins, used in counting the laps, also various aediculae and small sanctuaries (Fig. 13.3). The four circus factions, the Whites, Reds, Greens, and Blues, actually the vestiges of plebeian political organization, came to take on the character of political parties, and feelings ran high. Em-

FIG. 12.21   Rome, so-called Temple of Minerva Medica. (Fototeca)

perors took sides with the Blues or Greens. "They frequented their stables," says Gibbon in the famous fortieth chapter of the *Decline and Fall*, "applauded their favourites, chastised their antagonists, and deserved the esteem of the populace by the natural or affected imitation of their manners." There was murder done: in Constantinople under Justinian the Greens massacred 3,000 Blues. Gibbon vividly describes the excesses: long hair, concealed weapons, brigandage, arson, violation of churches and of noble matrons, miscarriage of justice, whippings, hangings. In the notorious Nika riots 30,000 perished. "This wanton discord . . . invaded the peace of families, divided friends and brothers, and tempted the female sex . . . to espouse the inclinations of their lovers, or to contradict the wishes of their husbands. Every law, either human or divine, was trampled under foot, and as long as the party was successful, its deluded followers appeared careless of private distress or public calamity."

Our survey has now reached the brink of Rome's decline and fall, the latest point in ancient history to which it will take us. In the 1,300 years since the Palatine huts we have, with archaeology's help, traced Rome's rise to grandeur and her agonizing decline. Spiritually, Rome never fell. The Papacy in a sense is the ghost of the Roman Empire sitting crowned upon its grave: the symbol is the Popes' palace-fortress installed in Hadrian's mausoleum, or St. Peter's basilica overlying what is in part a pagan cemetery. It will be appropriate in the final chapter to confront Caesar with Christ, by describing a late Imperial hunting lodge in Sicily, and a tomb beneath the high altar of St. Peter's, which by the fourth century A.D. was believed to be the last resting place of the apostle who was a fisher of men.

13

Caesar and Christ

In the official Italian archaeological journal *Notizie degli Scavi* for 1951 were reported recent excavations of a grandiose villa near Piazza Armerina, in central Sicily, which had already received some notoriety in the press, for depicting "Bikini girls" in very brief bathing suits (Fig. 13.1). Of this villa traces had always existed above ground, and as early as 1754 the discovery had been reported there of a "temple" (probably the basilica numbered 30 in the plan, Fig. 13.2), with a mosaic floor. In 1881 the trilobate complex (46) was excavated, and in 1929 the great Sicilian archaeologist Paolo Orsi, the expert on prehistoric remains on the island, dug there. Major funds—500,000 lire—made possible large-scale excavation between 1937 and 1943, as a part of *Il Duce's* plans for a major celebration of the bimillennary of Augustus's birth. After the war, government support to the tune of 5,000,000 lire (which inflation reduced in value to $8,000, only a tenth as much as the earlier grant) made it possible to finish excavating the villa and to take steps (*e.g.,* the erection of a peculiarly ugly roof) to preserve *in situ* the mosaics which are its chief glory. This is one of the few excavations on Italian soil whose chief avowed intent was to encourage tourism, and it has succeeded. Piazza Armerina is

FIG. 13.1 Piazza Armerina, Imperial Villa, "Bikini girls" mosaic.
(B. Pace, *I Mosaici di Piazza Armerina,* Pl. 15)

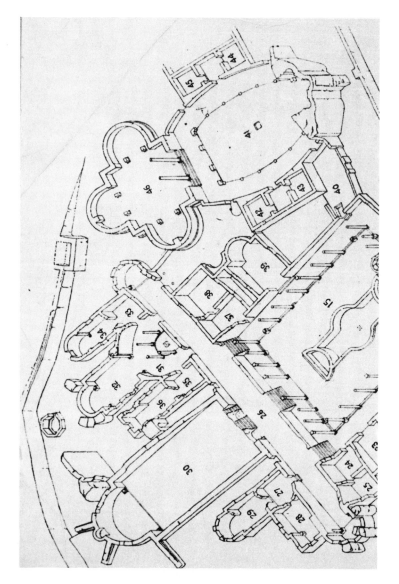

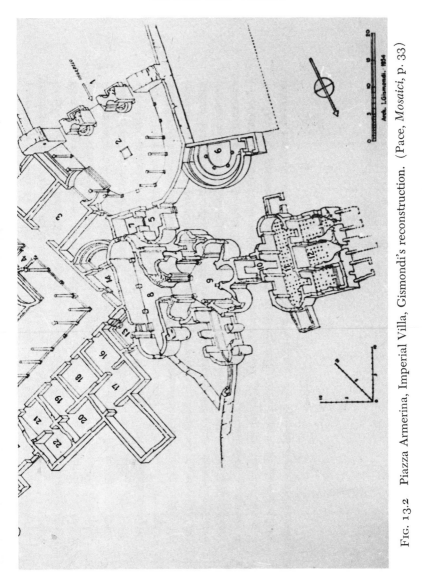

FIG. 13.2   Piazza Armerina, Imperial Villa, Gismondi's reconstruction.   (Pace, *Mosaici*, p. 33)

a boom town, boasting a new hotel, and its narrow streets are choked with sightseeing busses.

Both the mosaics and the villa's ambitious plan make it a sight worth seeing. There are forty-two polychrome pavements, involving the setting by the ancient workmen of 30,000,000 individual mosaic rectangles, or *tesserae*, over an area of more than 3,500 square yards, a complex unique in extent in the Roman world. The plan, too, is one of the most ambitious known to archaeology, rivaling that of Nero's Golden House, Hadrian's villa, or Diocletian's palace at Spalato on the Dalmatian coast. The villa lies three and a half miles southwest of Piazza Armerina, nearly 2,000 feet above sea level, on the west slope of Monte Mangone, in the midst of green orchards and pleasant groves of nut trees. Its altitude assured its being cool in summer; its setting under the lee of the hill protected it from winter winds. But the slope required terracing, and so the villa was laid out on four levels centering on three peristyles and a portico (plan 2,15,41,26). The parts are connected by irregular rooms (13,14,40). The technique of the masonry shows that the whole complex is of one build, characterized by asymmetrical symmetry, strange, twisted ground plans, a fondness for curves, and off-center axes, all of which shows a definite break with conventional classicism. The structure is light and elastic: the dome over the three-lobed state dining room (46), nowadays replaced by an unnecessarily ugly modern roof to protect the mosaics, was built of pumice concrete, lightened still further by setting in it lengths of clay pipe and amphoras, to reduce the weight of the superstructure on the bearing walls.

From a strange polygonal porticoed atrium (2) steps lead down to a porticoed horseshoe-shaped latrine (6) and to the baths (7–12), where spatial architecture runs riot, with single and double apses, a cloverleaf, and an octagonal *frigidarium* or room for taking a cold plunge (9). The middle terrace, east of the baths, centers on a huge trapezoidal peristyle (15), with a complex fountain, embellished by a fish mosaic, in the middle, and living rooms opening off to north and south. South of the peristyle a higher terrace is occupied by an odd elliptical court, shaped like a flattened egg, with a buttressed apse at the west end, the trilobate dining room at the east, and a triple set of conventional rectangular rooms, with mosaics of Cupids vintaging and fishing, to the north and south. The total effect is of an agreeable contrast between straight and curved walls. Returning to the rectangular peristyle, we find to the east of it a long double-apsed corridor, like the *narthex*, or long narrow portico, in front of an early Christian church. East of this is a suite of rooms centering on the vast- off-centered, apsed basilica—larger than Domitian's on the Palatine in Rome—which was the earliest part of the villa excavated. On either side of this is a series of rectangular and apsed rooms, the private quarters and nursery, to judge by the mosaics. An aqueduct limits the villa on the north and east. The servants' quarters are not yet excavated; they probably lay to the southwest, to the left of the monumental entrance (1). The whole is complicated, consistent, functional, organic, clearly the work of a master architect who will challenge comparison with the builder of the Sanctuary of Fortune at Praeneste or with Hadrian himself.

The mosaics must have been done over a number of years by huge gangs of craftsmen, probably imported from North Africa, since the technique resembles that of mosaics at Volubilis, Hippo, Carthage, and Lepcis. Mosaic-making is slow work; nowadays it takes a careful workman six days to lay a square meter of tesserae. To finish the job in the space of a few years would have required a swarm of as many as 500 artisans.

Apart from their vast extent and their subject matter—of which more in the sequel—the mosaics are of prime impor-

tance for the contribution they make to dating the villa.
About its date there is controversy. The late Biagio Pace
(who excavated here in the 1930s), relying on stylistic simi-
larities to late (fifth-century A.D.) mosaics in Ravenna and
Constantinople, dated the villa in about A.D. 410 and
ascribed its ownership to a rich Sicilian landed proprietor.
Some archaeologists, however, including Andrea Carandini,
the late Giuseppe Lugli, and Ranuccio Bianchi Bandinelli,
would date the mosaics between 320 and 360, because of the
presence under them of sherds of the African pottery called
terra sigillata *D*, which they date late. The mosaics would
then be Constantinian: Lugli argued that there would not
have been time to lay 3,500 square meters of tesserae before
Maximian's forced abdication in 306. Pace's pupil G. V. Gentili, who was in charge of the 1950 excavations, argues, following the Norwegian archaeologist H. P. L'Orange, for an
earlier date. Kähler and Ward Perkins follow Gentili's dating.
One piece of evidence not adduced by him is conclusive in
his favor. The double-apsed entrance (8) to the baths contains a spirited mosaic depicting the Circus Maximus in
Rome, full of life and movement, with the chariots of the
four stables, the Greens, Blues, Whites, and Reds, all represented. The Green—the Emperor's favorite—wins, not without a collision. Down the center of the oval track runs the
spina, or division wall, surmounted by various monuments,
including a single obelisk in the center (Fig. 13.3). Now it
is known that Augustus set up an obelisk in the Circus Maximus, and that in A.D. 357 Constantius II added another.
Therefore, any representation of the Circus with only one
obelisk must be earlier than 357. Pace's late date is therefore
excluded.

Is there any possibility of still more precise dating? Gentili
thinks there is. Beginning from the *a priori* proposition that
a complex architecturally and artistically as grand as this
must be beyond the means of any private citizen, however

FIG. 13.3 Piazza Armerina, Imperial Villa, Circus Maximus mosaic. (Dorothy MacKendrick photo)

FIG. 13.4 Piazza Armerina, Imperial Villa, small hunting scene, mosaic. (Pace, *Mosaici*, Fig. 30)

rich, he assumes that the villa must have been built to the order of an Emperor. Which one? To answer this question he looked among the mosaics for possible portraits, and he found them in several places. For example, in the vestibule (13) between the baths and the trapezoidal peristyle (15) there is an obvious portrait study of the mistress of the villa flanked by two children, presumably her son and daughter. The son has a squint. He is represented again, with the same squint, in the northeast apse of the *frigidarium* (9), in the room of the small hunting scene (23), and in the vestibule of Cupid and Pan (35). (The effect of the squint is achieved by setting one eye with a square tessera, the other with a triangular one.)

Now was the time to have recourse to the study, there to take down from the shelves the works of the Byzantine chronicler John Malalas. He records that Maxentius, the son of the Emperor Maximian Herculius (A.D. 286–305), Diocletian's colleague, was cross-eyed. Armed with this firm clue, Gentili examined the mosaics again, looking for proof or disproof that the villa belonged to Maximian. He found proof.*
Knowing that Maximian Herculius equated himself with Hercules, as his name shows, he looked for, and found, evidence in a colossal sculptured head of Hercules from the basilica apse, and in the mosaic, of preoccupation with that hero and his exploits. Over and over again, in the borders of robes, in foliage, and self-standing (in 4) he found representations of ivy, which was Hercules's symbol: the initial of its Latin name, *hedera*, is the initial of the hero's name. Furthermore, one of the most extensive and important mosaics in the villa, that in the state dining room (46), has as its subject the labors of Hercules. Gentili's case looks conclusively proven; it was buttressed when he took up the Circus mosaic (8), to back it with concrete and replace it, and

---

* But Settis, following Kähler, would attribute the villa to Maxentius, who inherited the title Herculius.

found under it a hypocaust containing coins of the late third century, presumably dropped by the workmen who laid the mosaic in the first place.

The subjects of the mosaics are in part more or less conventional mythological scenes. Odysseus hoodwinks the one-eyed Sicilian giant Polyphemus, making him drunk with a great bowl of wine (27); an obliging dolphin rescues the musician Arion from a watery grave (32), and Orpheus with his lyre charms a vast array of animals, including a goldfinch, a lizard, and a snail (39). Still more interesting are the mosaics which show Maximian's interests. He appears to have had three obsessions: hunting, the circus, and his children. The three scenes of the chase (23,26,33) have prompted L'Orange to suggest that the villa was built as a sumptuous hunting lodge, but the great basilica shows that it was adapted also to the uses of more formal protocol; the Imperial court must sometimes have met here.

The smaller hunting scene (23) is divided, in typical African fashion, into five bands (Fig. 13.4). At the top, two eager hounds, one gray, one red, are off in full cry after a fox. Next below, a young hunter identified by Gentili as Constantius Chlorus, Maximian's adopted son, accompanied by our old friend the squint-eyed Maxentius, sacrifices to Diana, the goddess of the hunt. The third band is devoted to fowling—with bird lime—and falconry, the fourth to the fox, gone to ground and besieged in his den by the dogs. In the fifth, on the left a stag is about to be caught in a net stretched across a forest path in the unsporting Roman way; on the right is a boar hunt with an unorthodox hunter just about to make the kill by dropping a large rock from above on the boar's head. In the center is a vivid huntsman's picnic. The hunters, wearing puttees, are sitting under a red awning. While they are waiting, one of them feeds the dog. A black boy blows on the fire, over which a succulent-looking trussed bird is roasting. Servants fetch bread from a wicker basket; another basket harbors two ample amphoras of wine.

This is an intimate *genre* scene. More impressive is the large hunting scene which crowds the whole 190-foot length of the double-apsed corridor (26). Here the aim portrayed is to catch exotic North African animals alive for the wild beast hunts in amphitheaters like the Colosseum. In the south apse is a female figure, probably symbolizing Africa, flanked by a tiger and an amiable small elephant with a reticulated hide. The figure in the opposite apse who has a bear on one side, a panther on the other may be Rome, the animals symbolizing her dominion over palm and pine. In this case Africa is the point of departure of the captured beasts, Rome their destination. Between the two apses the hunting scenes unfold amid fantastic architecture in a rolling wooded landscape sloping down to the sea in the center which is teeming with fish. On land, animals attack each other (a leopard draws blood from a stag's belly), and hunters in rich embroidered tunics hurl javelins, in the presence of the Emperor, at snarling lions and tigers at bay, and set traps baited with kid for panthers (the kid being spread-eagled in a way that looks curiously like a parody of the Crucifixion). The hunters act as bearers—their heads camouflaged with leafy twigs, like Birnam wood coming to Dunsinane—or drag a lassoed bison toward the red ship which will transport it to Italy. A horseman, having stolen a tiger cub, delays the mother's advance by dropping another cub in her path. A hippopotamus and a rhinoceros are among the game; smaller animals are hauled to the ships in crates on ox-carts; a live trussed boar is carried slung on a pole; a recalcitrant ostrich and an antelope are being pushed up a gangway (Fig. 13.5), while the gangway of another ship is groaning under the weight of an elephant with a checkerboard hide like the one flanking Africa in the apse. Just in front of this same apse a man is being used as bait to attract a fabulous winged griffin with the head of a bird of prey, whom a nearby hunter stands

Fig. 13.5   Piazza Armerina, Imperial Villa, large hunting scene, mosaic (detail). (MPI)

Fig. 13.6   Piazza Armerina, Imperial Villa, Labors of Hercules, mosaic (detail). (Pace, *Mosaici*, Pl. 7)

ready to capture. Settis sees here both pattern and symbol: the pattern is a recessed panel construction: land-fen-land-sea-EMBARCATION-sea-land-fen-land; the symbol, he alleges, is human victory over the passions, symbolized by wild beasts, by means of music (compare Arion), cleverness, or force. The crowded, vivid, barbarous artistry of this mosaic brings us to the very threshold of the Byzantine age; in Rome's past, only the Barberini mosaic at Palestrina can match it.

In Maximian's family even the children were brought up to take part in blood sports. Room 36, a child's room, perhaps Maxentius's—his squint-eyed portrait recurs in the anteroom (35)—portrays a child's hunt, in three bands, full of characteristic Roman insensibility to animal suffering. In the upper band, a boy has hit a spotted hare full in the breast with a hunting spear, while another has lassoed a duckling. The middle band portrays hunting mishaps: a small animal nips one fallen small boy in the leg; a cock attacks another with its beak and spurs. In the bottom register one boy clubs a peacock, a second defends himself with a shield against a buzzard, and a third has plunged his hunting spear into the heart of a goat.

The child's Circus (33), unlike the hunt, is rather fantastic than brutal. Around a spina with a single obelisk, as in room 8, run four miniature chariots drawn by pairs of birds in the appropriate stable colors: green wood-pigeons, blue plovers, red flamingoes, and white geese. As usual, Green wins, and is awarded the palm. Servants with amphoras sprinkle the track to lay the dust. It is all vivid, detailed, alive, more illuminating than a dozen pages in a handbook.

The masterpiece among the mosaics is clearly the labors of Hercules cycle in the *triclinium* (46). These were part of a standard repertory, available for copying from a book of cartoons (we have seen this sort of thing in Pompeii), but here the artist has stamped his own personality on the hackneyed scenes. In his hands they are at once learnedly allusive and bloodily violent. Thus the Augean stables, which Hercules cleaned by diverting a river to run through them, are simply suggested by a river and a pitchfork. Violence is often rather hinted at than insisted on, as in the slitlike eye of the dying Nemean lion, or the Picasso-like protruding eye of the terrified horse of Diomedes (Fig. 13.6). Sometimes the effect is gained by a topical touch, as when Geryon, the triple-headed giant, is given a suit of scaly armor, like the barbarians (cataphractarii) on Trajan's column. But the full baroque excess, as insistent as in the frieze from the Pergamene altar, or the Laocoön group, comes out in the scene in the east lobe where five huge giants, foreshortened with a technique which anticipates Michelangelo's on the ceiling of the Sistine Chapel, convulsively, despairingly, imploringly, yet full of impotent rage, turn their deep-sunk eyes to heaven as they strive to pull from their flesh Hercules's deadly arrows, steeped in the blood of the Centaur Nessus. Hercules fought the giants as Jove's helper; it is worth recalling that Diocletian called himself Jovius, and Maximian was Herculius. In the north lobe the apotheosis of Hercules is no doubt the mosaicist's enforced tribute to his Imperial master, but in the scenes of metamorphosis in the entranceways to the apses—Daphne into a laurel, Cyparissus into a cypress, Ambrosia into a vine—he is following his own paradoxical bent, accepting as it were the challenge of expressing so dynamic a. thing as the change from one form to another in the obdurate medium of mosaic. Ambrosia's metamorphosis was wrought by Dionysus, to save her from the lascivious clutches of the mythological King Lycurgus of Thrace. Kähler makes the point that since Alexander the triumph of Dionysus had been equated with the triumph of rulers, and supposes that each apse held a statue of the appropriate god or demigod.

The ten "Bikini girls" (38) come last, because these mosaics, which overlie another set, are obviously later than the rest. They owe their fame to the scantiness of their costumes, as brief as any to be seen on modern European beaches. Gentili thinks they are female athletes, being awarded prizes, but Pace may be nearer the truth in supposing that they are pantomime actresses, with tambourines and *maracas*, performing in a sort of aquacade, the blue *tesserae* in which they stand representing water. There is ancient evidence for this curiously decadent art form. Martial speaks of actresses dressed—or undressed—as Nereids swimming about in the Colosseum, and the Church fathers fulminate against such spectacles. When the orchestra of the most august of theaters, that of Dionysus in Athens, was remodeled in Roman times to hold water, we must suppose, since the space is too small for mock naval battles, that the place once sacred to the choruses of Aeschylus, Sophocles, and Euripides was thereafter used for the aquatic antics of just such actresses as the Piazza Armerina mosaics portray. Tastelessness and grandeur, conspicuous waste and a daring architectural plan: this paradoxical blend, so characteristic of the villa, explains both what is meant by decline and why it took the Empire so long to fall.

The villa at Piazza Armerina belongs to an age when Christians were persecuted: the motifs in the mosaics are almost aggressively pagan. But Maximian's son-in-law Constantine became in the end a convert to Christianity, and built, beginning about A.D. 322, in honor of St. Peter, a great basilica church on the Vatican Hill, replaced in the Renaissance by the present building. In 1939, at the death of Pope Pius XI, who had asked to be buried in the crypt of St. Peter's, excavations for his tomb created the occasion for transforming the crypt into a lower church. In lowering the floor level of the crypt for this purpose, the workmen came, only eight inches down, upon the pavement of Old St. Peter's, Constantine's church. This in turn rested upon mausolea with their tops sliced off, and their interiors rammed full of earth. At the direction of Pius XII, these mausolea were scientifically excavated.

What was revealed was a pagan Roman cemetery, in some places thirty feet below the floor of the present church. The mausolea were all in use and in good repair when Constantine began his church in A.D. 322: the earliest brick stamp found in the area dates from the reign of Vespasian, A.D. 69–79. The excavations were carried out under conditions comparable in difficulty only to the recovery of the Altar of Peace: the same constant battle with seepage, the same problem of underpinning one structure in order to read the message of another. Under these formidable difficulties, the cemetery was cleared, and archaeologists found the reason why Constantine moved a million cubic feet of earth and went so far as to violate sepulchers to build Old St. Peter's on just this site. Whatever modern walls it was necessary to build were carefully marked with Pius XII brick stamps, that future archaeologists might be in no doubt as to which masonry was modern and which ancient. The cemetery may now be visited by small groups with special permission, with well-informed commentary by a polyglot guide. The story he has to tell was not published until over ten years after the excavation began, in a massive two-volume *Report,* which stands fifteen and three-quarters inches high, contains 171 text figures and 119 plates, and weighs fourteen pounds. Fortunately its objectivity is as impressive as its bulk. The archaeological evidence is lucidly set forth, and no conclusions are drawn which exceed it.

We know from Tacitus that Nero, in his search for scapegoats on whom to shift the blame for Rome's great fire of A.D. 64, martyred Christians in an amphitheater on the Vatican Hill, and tradition has it that in this amphitheater St. Peter, too, suffered martyrdom. It was to test the validity of this tradition that Pius XII ordered the cemetery under St. Peter's excavated. What was found was a series of twenty-one mausolea and one open area (*P* in the plan, Fig. 13.7), all facing southward onto a Roman street. The mausolea are plain brick on the outside, highly baroque within, enriched with mosaics, wall paintings, and stucco work. There are both cremation and inhumation burials, but when the mausolea were filled in inhumation was beginning to predominate. Of the mausolea only *M* is entirely Christian in décor; others began as pagan, later admitting Christian burials, or adapt pagan motifs to Christian symbolism. *M* contains the earliest-known Christian mosaics, which Ward Perkins and Miss Toynbee call a microcosm of the dramatic history of Christianity's peaceful penetration of the pagan Roman Empire. They are dated by technique and motifs to the middle of the third century A.D. The subjects are Jonah and the whale, the Fisher of Men, the Good Shepherd, and, in the vault, Christ figured as the sun. The wall paintings of the cemetery are mostly pagan, the contractors' stock-in-trade, depicting in myth or in symbol the soul's victory over death. The great artistic interest of the mausolea is in the stucco work, held by some to be superior in quality to that of the subterranean basilica at the Porta Maggiore. Some of it is of unparalleled scale and complexity, excellently preserved (Fig. 13.8), and now protected from dampness by large, constantly burning electric heaters. Of stone sculpture in the round there is very little; it was probably removed by Constantine's workmen. But there are many marble sarcophagi with pagan and Christian motifs, testifying to the artistic revival enjoyed by the Roman world with the peace of the Church in A.D. 312. They show how the stonemasons carved them as blanks, filling in details like inscriptions and portrait busts to the customer's order. There is a pathetic one of a baby, who died, the inscription tells us, when he was six months old. There are reliefs of Biblical scenes: the children in the fiery furnace, Joseph and his brethren, the three Magi, and what may be the earliest Christian cross, dated about A.D. 340; (an alleged

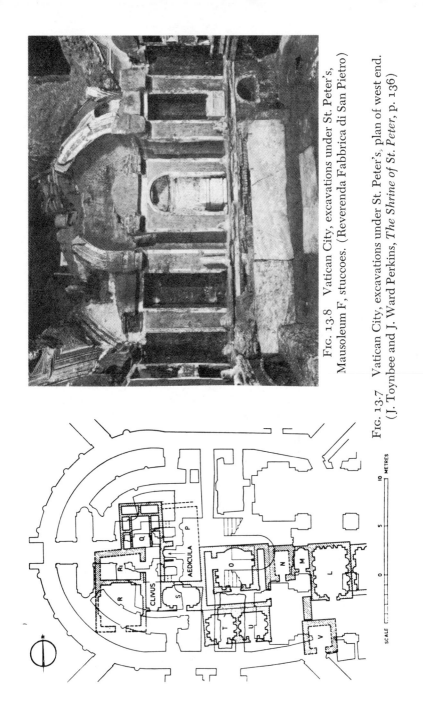

FIG. 13.8   Vatican City, excavations under St. Peter's, Mausoleum F, stuccoes. (Reverenda Fabbrica di San Pietro)

FIG. 13.7   Vatican City, excavations under St. Peter's, plan of west end. (J. Toynbee and J. Ward Perkins, *The Shrine of St. Peter*, p. 136)

cross at Herculaneum is more probably the scar of a ripped-away wall bracket).

The cemetery tells us something about the status and the religious convictions of its owners and occupants. Of the persons recorded in its inscriptions, over half have Greek names. They are freedmen or descendants of freedmen, many in the Imperial civil service. Some are tradesmen, some artisans. Only one was of Senatorial rank: his daughter's body was wrapped in purple and veiled in gold. The richness of the tombs bespeaks an attitude that is modern enough, or rather neither ancient nor modern, but a constant. Paradoxically, importance is attached to material things, to the race for riches and creature comforts, while at the same time there is a preoccupation with the after life, a return, after the skepticism of the earlier Empire, to a belief in a personal immortality in store for those who have led moral lives. The deceased are connected with the world they have left behind by tubes for libations, that wine and milk may be poured down on their bones. Heaven is variously conceived: as a place of blessed sleep, or, like the Etruscan heaven, a succession of banquets, wine, and gardens. Grief is swallowed up in victory; the dead have their patron heroes: Hermes, Hercules, Minerva, Apollo, Dionysus, the Egyptian Isis or Horus—and Christ.

But the pagan cemetery, interesting as it is for the light it casts on the middle class of the early fourth century of our era, is not the centrally important archaeological discovery under St. Peter's, nor does it supply the motive for Constantine's location of his church just here. That motive the excavators found in the open space they named "Campo P." Campo P is separated from mausoleum R by a sloping passage, called the Clivus; the drain under the passage contains tiles with stamps dated between the years 147–161, which fall within the reign of Antoninus Pius. A painted brick wall, since made famous as the Red Wall, separates the Clivus from Campo *P*. Into this wall are cut three superposed niches, two in the fabric of the wall itself, one beneath its foundations, which were actually raised on a sort of bridge at this point to protect the cavity. In front of the niches traces were found of a modest architectural façade, called the Aedicula, or little shrine.

In the cavity the excavators found human bones, which they have never identified further than to describe them as those of a person of advanced age and robust physique. The Aedicula penetrated above the pavement of Old St. Peter's and formed its architectural focus. The conclusion is inevitable that Constantine in A.D. 322 planned his basilica to rise just here (Fig. 12.16,18), at great trouble and expense, because he believed the lowest niche, under the Red Wall, to enshrine a relic of overarching importance—nothing less than the bones of St. Peter. (Opponents of this inference argue that Peter, as a convicted criminal, would not have been entitled to burial.) There is, however, no doubt whatever, on objective evidence, that the Aedicula was reverenced in the fourth Christian century as marking the burial place of the founder of the Roman church.

But this is not the end of the problem. The next question is, "How early can the burial, by objective archaeological evidence, be demonstrated to be?" The answer to this question must be sought, if anywhere, in the context of Campo *P*. This proved on excavation to be an area of poor graves, marked, like those of the necropolis of the Port of Ostia on Isola Sacra, simply by a surround and a pitched roof of tiles, without any of the pomp of costly marble sarcophagus or richly stuccoed mausoleum. It is to the class which would be buried in such pathetic graves as these that the earliest Roman Christians (of the age of Nero, A.D. 64) must have belonged. Since the *Report* was published, 24 more graves have been discovered in Campo *P*, and Professor Magi, whom we have already met in connection with the Cancelleria reliefs, has discovered, under the Vatican City parking lot, another cemetery, also of poor graves, of the first centuries A.D. Here, luckily, numerous brick stamps supply precise dates, and show that half the burials are of the reigns of Trajan and Hadrian. Inscriptions (99 more or less complete) record, among others, many Imperial slaves, and many of these have Greek cognomina. Longevity was not noteworthy, and none of the inscriptions is of a Christian. The graves in Campo *P* (Fig. 13.9) were found to lie at various levels: the deepest must be the earliest. The deepest is the one called by the excavators Gamma (see plan, γ, Fig. 13.9): it lies five and a half feet below the pavement of Campo *P*, and it partly underlies, and is therefore older than, the foundations of the Red Wall, which in turn is dated by the Clivus drain about the middle of the second century A.D. Grave Theta (θ) is higher, and therefore later, than Gamma. It is a poor grave, protected by tiles, one of which bears a stamp of Vespasian's reign (A.D. 69–79). It is unsafe method to date an archaeological find by a single brick stamp, which could be second-hand, used at any date later than its firing, even

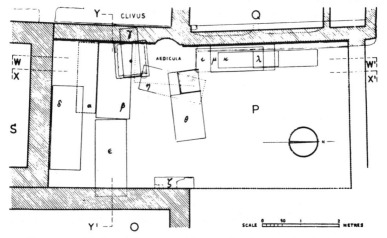

FIG. 13.9   Vatican City, excavations under St. Peter's, Campo P. (Toynbee and Ward Perkins, *op. cit.*, p. 141)

much later. But the stamp creates at least a presumption that Theta may be dated as early as A.D. 79, and, if so, Gamma must be earlier still. Since both these graves appear to have been dug in such a way as to respect the area just in front of the Aedicula, it follows that the bones in the lowest niche must be earlier than either grave.

This is the process by which it is possible (but not rigorously necessary, on the evidence) to date the bones before A.D. 79, perhaps in the reign of Nero; perhaps they are the bones of a victim of the persecution of A.D. 64; perhaps they are the bones of St. Peter. They were evidently disturbed in antiquity, for this is not a proper burial, but simply a collection of bones; the head, for example, is missing. The original burial must have lain athwart the line of the later Red Wall: when the builders of the Red Wall hit upon it, they may, knowing the legend of St. Peter's martyrdom in the amphitheater somewhere near this spot, have assumed that this was his grave, and so they arched up the Red Wall's foundations to avoid disturbing it. The next step was to build the Aedicula (Fig. 13.10), an act associated in literary sources with Pope Anacletus (traditional dates, A.D. 76–88). But since not even the most pious Catholics suppose the Aedicula to be this early, an emendation of the name into Anicetus (ca. 155–165) is defensible: it is paleographically plausible, and it suits the date of the Red Wall. The traces of the Aedicula as found were asymmetrical: its north supporting column had been moved to make room for a wall that was built sometime before Constantine to buttress the Red Wall, which had developed a bad crack from top to bottom. The excavators found the north face of this buttress wall covered with a palimpsest of *graffiti*, only one of which—in Greek—refers to St. Peter by name, though some others may do so in a cryptic way, and all testify that this spot was one of particular sanctity, much frequented by pilgrims. More recent examination has found Peter's name scratched on the Red Wall itself.

The shrine under St. Peter's is not the only spot in Rome

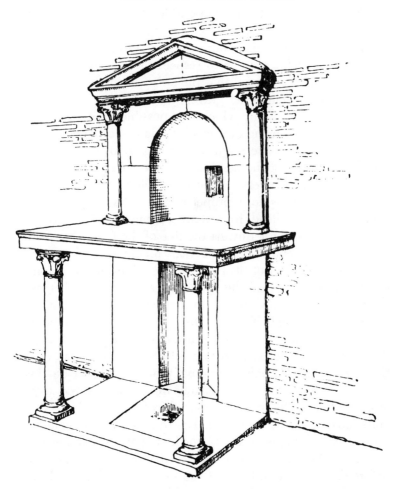

FIG. 13.10   Vatican City, excavations under St. Peter's. Aedicula, reconstruction by G. U. S. Corbett. (Toynbee and Ward Perkins, *op.
cit.*, p. 161)

associated with St. Peter. Another is under the Church of
San Sebastiano, two and a half miles out, just off the Appian
Way. Here excavation has found *graffiti* mentioning St.
Peter and St. Paul, a room for taking ceremonial meals, and

Christian tombs of the third century A.D.

Rome has 350 miles of these catacombs, narrow rockcut tunnels and tomb chambers with coffinlike recesses in tiers, sometimes with altar tops, sometimes with arched openings (arcisolia), for popes and martyrs. The catacombs of Sts. Callistus and Domitilla are near San Sebastiano; that of Priscilla is north of the city on the Via Salaria. A private one, discovered in 1955 at the Via Latina where the Via C. Baronio crosses, about three kilometers southeast of the Baths of Caracalla, is dated A.D. 315–350, and contains an unusual wealth of paintings on Biblical and pagan subjects, including Noah drunk, Jonah taking his ease under his vine, Daniel with a pair of tiny lions; the Last Supper; an anatomy lesson, with cadaver; the death of Cleopatra; and six labors of Hercules. In this catacomb Christians and pagans are buried companionably together. A century after Christianity was recognized as the state religion, the catacombs fell out of use except as centers of pilgrimage.

Some scholars believe, but without cogent archaeological evidence, that St. Peter's body, in whole or in part, was moved to San Sebastiano from the Vatican Hill, for safety during the persecutions under the Emperor Valerian in A.D. 258. This would explain the association of the San Sebastiano site with the apostle; the assumption that the bones were returned to the Aedicula after the danger was past would explain—though it is not the only possible explanation—the disturbed state in which the excavators found them.

In any case, in the years between the building of the Aedicula and the centering of Constantine's church upon it, there was continuity of pious commemoration of the spot. This is proved by the *graffiti* on the buttress wall, and by a series of burials, Alpha, Beta, Delta, Epsilon, and Mu (a, β, δ, ε, μ), all motivated by a desire to be buried as close as possible to the Aedicula, and all, to judge by their contents—remains of cloth in Beta, for example, showed gold threads—belonging to important people. Some scholars (not including the excavators) have supposed that these are the graves of early Popes.

This was the state of affairs in Campo *P* when the building of Constantine's basilica began. The Aedicula was made the focus of the whole building plan: it was left projecting above the pavement of the new church, and it was covered by a canopy upheld by twisted columns. (It is an extraordinary coincidence that Bernini, when he built the canopy over the altar of the Renaissance church, chose twisted columns to uphold it, though he could not possibly have known that Constantine's canopy also involved this detail.) Constantine's architect, in the classical tradition, paid the secular Roman basilica the compliment of creative imitation.

It was not until about A.D. 600 that the altar was placed directly over the shrine, and the presbytery raised to accommodate it. By that time, the tradition was firmly established that pious pilgrims should leave a votive coin in front of the Aedicula: here in the fill the excavators found 1,900 coins, Roman, papal, Italian, and from all over Europe, ranging in date from before A.D. 161 uninterruptedly down to the fourteenth century. Also about A.D. 600, at the same time as the placing of the altar directly over the shrine, the two upper niches in the Red Wall were combined into one, the Niche of the Pallia, where the vestments of newly consecrated archbishops were put to be sanctified by close contact with the bones of the first Bishop of Rome: a shaft in the floor of the niche led down to the grave.

The shrine and the Constantinian church survived the sacks of Rome both by the Goths in A.D. 410, and by the Vandals in A.D. 455; the Saracens in A.D. 846 were not so respectful. In their search for treasure they handled the Aedicula very roughly, and it is likely that it is from this sack, and not from the persecution of A.D. 258, that the disturbance of the bones should be dated. In any case, after the sack the life of the shrine went on as before, and in the Renaissance church as in its predecessor the shrine remained the focal point, one of the most venerated spots in Christendom.

With the shrine of St. Peter, venerable, still vital, going back to the two roots of Western civilization, pagan Rome (itself the transmitter of Greek culture) and Christianity, it is fitting that we should end our survey of what archaeology has to tell us about the culture to which ours owes so much. The two complexes, the grandiose pagan villa and the humble Christian shrine, which we have discussed in this chapter, are interrelated. The villa is one of the last manifestations of a culture that is played out, the shrine marks the beginning of a new culture that will produce its own grandiose monuments and in its turn be threatened by decline. In a sense, with the simplicity of St. Peter's shrine the historical cycle returns to the simplicity of primitive Rome. But it is not simply a matter of returning to beginnings and starting over again; the new culture stands upon the shoulders of the old. The Christian shrine has the look of a pagan tomb monument in the Isola Sacra necropolis; Constantine's church has the look of a pagan Roman basilica. The language of the Mass was Latin until 1963; the Pope is Pontifex Maximus. The striking thing is the continuity,* and this is the most important lesson that archaeology has to teach. Again beneath St. Peter's, as at so many other ancient sites, what the archaeologist digs up is not things but people. The remains in the niche under the Red Wall are not dry bones; they are live history. The breathing of life into that history is a major and largely unsung triumph of the modern science of archaeology, patiently at work over the last 100 years. To come to know a fragment of our past is to recognize a piece of ourselves. Perhaps, as archaeology interprets history, making the mute stones speak, we may come to know our past so well that we shall not be condemned to repeat it.

* A striking example of this was discovered in 1963 in Velia, in south Italy: a medical school, which flourished from Augustan times to the late Empire and trained both women and men. This was the ancestor of the Salerno medical school, which enjoyed such prestige in the Middle Ages.

Abbreviations

AJA: American Journal of Archaeology
AnalRomInstDan: Analecta Romana Instituti Danici
ANRW: Aufstieg und Niedergang der antiken Welt
ArchClass: Archeologia Classica
Archy: Archaeology
ArchLaz: Archeologia Laziale
BAR: British Archaeological Reports
BEFAR: Bibliothèque des Ecoles françaises d'Athènes et de Rome
BdA: Bolletino d'Arte
BullComm: Bulletino della Commissione archeologica comunale di Roma
CollEFR: Collection de l'Ecole française de Rome
CollLat: Collection Latomus
CronPomp: Cronache Pompeiane
DialArch: Dialoghi di Archeologia
EAAC: Enciclopedia di Arte Antica Classica
Helbig[4]: W. Helbig, Führer durch die öffentlichen Sammlungen klassischer Altertümer in Rom, 4th ed., by H. Speier et al. 4 vols. (Tübingen 1963–72)
HSCP: Harvard Studies in Classical Philology
JDAI: Jahrbuch des deutschen archäologischen Instituts
JRS: Journal of Roman Studies
JSAH: Journal of the Society of Architectural Historians
Lat: Latomus
MAAR: Memoirs of the American Academy in Rome
MEFR: Mélanges de l'Ecole française de Rome
MemLinc: Memorie dell'Accademia Nazionale dei Lincei
MemPontAcc: Memorie della Pontificia Accademia Romana di Archeologia
MonAnt: Monumenti Antichi

MonArtRom: Monumenta Artis Romanae
MonRom: Monumenti romani
MPI: Ministero della Pubblica Istruzione
NGM: National Geographic Magazine
NSc: Notizie degli Scavi di Antichità
PBSR: Papers of the British School at Rome
PdP: Parola del Passato
RE: A. Pauly, G. Wissowa, Real-Encyclopädie der classichen Alter-
     tumswissenschaft
RendNap: Rendiconti dell'Accademia di Archeologia . . . di Napoli
RendPontAcc: Rendiconti della Pontificia Accademia Romana di
     Archeologia
RM: Mitteilungen des deutschen archaologischen Instituts, Abteilung
     Rom
StudEtr: Studi Etruschi
StudMisc: Studi Miscellanei

Bibliography

General

Axel Boëthius, John B. Ward Perkins, *Etruscan and Roman Architecture* (Harmondsworth 1970).

R. Bianchi Bandinelli, *Rome the Center of Power, 500 B.C.–A.D. 200* (Paris 1969).

———, *The Late Empire: Roman Art A.D. 200–400* (*ib.* 1970).

O. J. Brendel, *Prolegomena to the Study of Roman Art* (New Haven 1979). Two essays, originally of 1953 and 1969.

F. Coarelli, *Guida archeologica di Roma* (Verona 1974).

L. Crema, "Architettura romana," *Enciclopedia Classica* III.x.3 (Turin 1957).

L. Curtius, A. Nawrath, E. Nash, *Das antike Rom* (Vienna 1957).

D. R. Dudley, *Urbs Roma* (London 1967). A sourcebook of literary texts.

EAAC, 7 vols. (Rome 1958–66) and Supplement (*ib.* 1970).

Enciclopedia universale dell'arte: "Romano antico". (Florence 1964); "Tardo antico," (*ib.* 1965). Good photos, authoritative text.

M. Hammond, *The City in the Ancient World* (Cambridge, Mass. 1972).

R. Helbig, *Führer durch die öffentlichen Sammlungen klassischer Altertümer in Rom*[4], ed. H. Speier (Tübingen 1963–72).

H. Kähler, *Rom und seine Welt*, 2 vols. (Munich 1958–60). Good photos, authoritative text.

A. G. McKay, *Houses, Villas, and Palaces in the Roman World* (London 1975).

Museo della Civiltà Romana, *Catalogo* (Rome 1958). The earlier edition, *Mostra Augustea della Romanità* (*ib.* 1938), has photographs and bibliography.

E. Nash, *Pictorial Dictionary of Ancient Rome*[2], 2 vols. (London 1968).

G. C. Picard, *L'art romain* (Paris 1962).

M. Scherer, *Marvels of Ancient Rome* (London and New York 1955).

R. E. Stilwell, ed., *Princeton Encyclopedia of Classical Sites* (Princeton 1976).

D. E. Strong, *Roman Art* (Harmondsworth 1976).

J. B. Ward Perkins, *Architettura romana* (Venice 1974).

CHAPTER 1: *Prehistoric Italy*

R. J. C. Atkinson, *Field Archaeology* (London 1946).

M. S. Balmuth, "The Nuraghi Towers of Sardinia," *Archy* 34.2 (1981) 35–43.

L. Barfield, *Northern Italy Before the Romans* (London and New York 1971).

G. Barker, R. Hodges, "Archaeology and Italian Society," *BAR International Series, Papers in Italian Archaeology* 2 (Oxford 1981).

P. Barocelli, "Terremare, Palatino, orientazione dei *castra* e delle città romane," *Bulletino Communale* 70 (1942), 131–44.

John Bradford, "The Apulia Expedition: An Interim Report," *Antiquity* 24 (1950) 84–95.

———, Ancient Landscapes (London 1957), 85–110.

"Civilta del ferro," *Documenti e studi di storia patria per le province di Romagna* 6 (1950).

F. von Duhn and F. Messerschmidt, *Italische Gräberkunde*, 2 vols. (Heidelberg 1924–1939).

P. G. Gierow, "The Iron Age in Latium," 2 vols. *Acta Instituti Sueciae* 24 (Rome 1964–66).

M. Guidi, *Sardinia* (London and New York 1963).

G. M. A. Hanfmann, rev. of Säflund (see below, chapter 1) *AJA* 45 (1941) 308–15.

C. F. C. Hawkes, *The Prehistoric Foundations of Europe* (London 1940).

L. A. Holland, "The Purpose of the Warrior Image in Capestrano," *AJA* 60 (1956) 243–47.

G. Kaschnitz-Weinberg, "Italien mit Sardinien, Sizilien, and Malta," in W. Otto and R. Herbig, *Handbuch der Archäologie*, 2 (Munich 1954), 311–97.

J. Kastelic, *Situla Art* (New York and London 1965).

W. F. Libby, "Radiocarbon Dating," *Science* 133 (Mar. 1961) 621–29.

G. Lilliu, "1000 Years of Prehistory: Sardinia, the *Nuraghe* of 'Barumini and its Village—a Recent Large-scale Excavation," *Illustrated London News* 232 (1958) 388–91.

H. L. Movius, Jr., "Age Determination by Radiocarbon Content," *Antiquity* 24 (1950) 99–101.

M. Pallottino, *Genti e culture dell'Italia preromana* (Rome 1981).

T. J. Peet, *The Stone and Bronze Ages in Italy* (Oxford 1909).

R. Pittioni, "Italien: urgeschichtliche Kulturen," *RE* Supplementband 9 (1962) cols. 105–372. Charts, maps, C^{14} dating.

I. Pohl, "San Giovenale: da villagio protovillanoviano a città 'Etrusca,'" *PdiP* Fasc. 191 (1980) 131–42.

Prima Italia: l'arte italica del primo millenio a.C. (Rome 1981). Catalogue of an exposition.

Popolazione e civiltà dell'Italia antica, vols. 4–7 (Rome 1975–78). Contributions by experts. Covers Proto-Villanovan, Villanovan, Etruscan, Etruscan language, race society, institutions, coinage, religion, art, synthesis.

D. Randall-MacIver, *Villanovans and Early Etruscans* (Oxford 1924).

D. Randall-MacIver, *The Iron Age in Italy* (Oxford 1927)
———, *Italy before the Romans* (Oxford 1928).

D. and F. Ridgway, eds. *Italy before the Romans* (London and San Francisco 1979). Articles by experts, on Veii, Este/Golasecca, Bronze to Iron Age, early Rome, the Etruscan city, North Italy, and Hallstatt/La Tène.

G. Säflund, "Le terremare," *Skrifter utgivna av Svenska Institutet i Rom* 7 (1939).

R. B. K. Stevenson, "The Neolithic Cultures of Southeast Italy," *Proceedings of the Prehistoric Society* 13 (1947) 85–100.

D. Trump, *Central and Southern Italy before the Romans* (London and New York 1966).

J. Whatmough, *The Foundations of Roman Italy* (London 1937).

R. E. M. Wheeler, *Archaeology from the Earth* (Oxford 1954, reprinted in Pelican Books, 1956).

CHAPTER 2: *The Etruscans*

N. Alfieri, "The Etruscans of the Po and the Discovery of Spina," *Italy's Life*, no. 24 (1957) 91–104.

——— and P. E. Arias, *Spina* (Florence 1958).

P. E. Arias, "Considerazioni sulla città etrusca a Pian di Misano (Marzabotto)," *Atti e Memorie della Deputazione di Storia Patria per le Provincie dell' Emilia e di Romagna* 4 (1953) 223–34.

S. Aurigemma, *Il R. Museo di Spina in Ferrara* (Ferrara 1936).

———, *Scavi di Spina* I, I.2 (Rome 1960–65).

L. Banti, *The Etruscan Cities and their Culture* (London 1973, from original of 1968).

R. Bianchi-Bandinelli, "Clusium . . . in età etrusca," *MonAnt* 30 (1925) 370–87.

R. Bloch, "Religion étrusque et romaine," *Histoire des religions de l'Encyclopédie de la Pléiade* (Paris 1970) 841–926.

———, "Volsinies etrusque: essai historique et topographique," *Mélanges d'archéologie et d'histoire de l'École française de Rome* 59 (1947) 9–39.

A Boëthius, *op. cit.*

J. Bradford, *Ancient Landscapes* 111–44.

O. J. Brendel, *Etruscan Art* (Harmondsworth 1978).

E. Brizio, "Relazione sugli scavi eseguiti a Marzabotto presso Bologna dal novembre 1888 a tutto maggio 1889," *Monumenti Antichi* 1 (1891) cols. 248–426.

V. Cacconi, V. Milani, *Profilo di una città etrusca: Populonia* (Pistoia 1981).

F. Canciani, F. von Hase, "La tomba Bernadini di Palestrina," *Latium Vetus* 2 (Rome 1979).

E. Colonna di Paolo, *Necropoli rupestri del Viterbese* (Novara 1978).

E. Colonna di Paolo, G. Colonna, *Castel d'Asso* 2 vols. (San Casciano 1970).

———, G. Colonna, *Norchia* 2 vols. (Florence 1978).

G. Colonna *et al.* "Scavi nel santuario etrusco di Pyrgi," *ArchClass* 16 (1964) 49–117.

———, "The Sanctuary at Pyrgi in Etruria," *Archy* 19 (1966) 10–23.

Corpus Inscriptionum Etruscarum, II.i,3 (Tarquinia) (Leipzig 1936).

C. D. Curtis, "The Bernardini Tomb," *MAAR* 3 (1919) 9–90.

———, "The Barberini Tomb," *ib.* 5 (1925) 9–51.

G. Dennis, *Cities and Cemeteries of Etruria*[3] 2 vols. (London 1878).

T. Dohrn, Helbig[4], no. 736 (1963). On Mars of Todi.

———, "Der Arringatore," *MonArtRom* 8 (Berlin 1968).

———, "Die ficoronische Ciste in der Villa Giulia," *ib.* 11 (1962).

Etruscan Culture, Land, and People (Malmö and New York 1962). A rich miscellany, centering on the King of Sweden's dig at S. Giovenale.

Etruschi e Cerveteri (Milan 1981). Exhibition catalogue, illustrating Lerici method.

M. Falkner, "Epigraphisches und archäologisches zur Stele von Lemnos," in W. Brandenstein, *Frühgeschichte und Sprachwissenschaft* (Vienna 1948) 91–109.

E. M. Forster, "Macolnia Shops," *Abinger Harvest* (London 1936).

H. Hencken, *Tarquinia and Etruscan Origins* (London and New York 1968).

J. Heurgon, *La vie quotidienne des Etrusques* (Paris 1961).

C. N. Lerici, "Periscope on the Etruscan Past," *NGM* 116.3 (Sept. 1959) 336–50.

———, "Periscopic Sighting and Photography to the Archaeologist's Aid," *Ill. London News* 232 (1958) 774–75.

G. A. Mansuelli," Sulle testimonianze piu antiche di Marzabotto," *Banti Studies* (Rome 1965) 241–47.

M. Moretti, *Nuovi monumenti della pittura etrusca* (Milan 1966). Descriptions and color photos of, e.g., Tomba della Nave and Tomba degli Olimpiadi; explanation of Lerici method.

M. Pallottino, *Etruscologia*³ (Milan, 1955), Engl. trans., Pelican books 1955.

———, *Etruscan Painting* (Geneva 1952).

———, "I frammenti di lamina di bronzo con iscrizone etrusca scoperti a Pyrgi," *StudEtr* 34 (1966) 75–209.

———, G. Proietti, *Il Museo Nazionale Etrusco di Villa Giulia* (Rome 1980).

L. Pareti, *La Tomba Regolini-Galassi* (Vatican City 1947).

E. Pulgram, *The Tongues of Italy* (Cambridge, Mass. 1958).

G. Ricci et al., "Caere: Scavi di R. Mengarelli," *MonAnt* 42 (1955) cols. 1–1186.

E. H. Richardson, *The Etruscans* (Chicago 1964).

———, *Etruscan Sculptures* (Mentor-UNESCO Art Book, New York 1966). Splendid color.

F. Roncalli, "Il 'Marte' di Todi," *MemPontAcc* series 3, 11.2 (1973) 11–121.

H. H. Scullard, *The Etruscan Cities and Rome* (London and New York 1967).

D. E. Strong, *The Early Etruscans* (London 1968).

M. Torelli, *Etruria* (Rome-Bari 1980). A guidebook.

J. B. Ward Perkins, "The Problem of Etruscan Origins," *Harvard Studies in Classical Philology* 64 (1959) 1–26.

G. E. W. Wolstenholme and C. M. O'Connor, eds., *Ciba Foundation Symposium on Medical Biology and Etruscan Origins* (London and Boston 1959). Important contributions by H. Hencken (29–47) and J. B. Ward Perkins (89–92), among others.

CHAPTER 3: *Early Rome and Latium*

A. Andren, "In Quest of Vulca," *RendPontAcc* 49 (1976/7) 63–84. Coins suggest cult statue of Jupiter Capitolinus.

A. Bedini, "Abitato preistorico in località Acquacetosa-Laurentina," *ArchLaz* 1 (1978) 21–8.

J. R. Brandt, "Ficana: rassegna preliminare delle campagne archeologiche 1975–7," *Itinerari ostensi* 2 (1977/8). See also *ArchLaz* 2 (1979) 29–36, and *StudEtr* 48 (1980) 529–30.

F. E. Brown, "The Regia," *Memoirs of the American Academy in Rome* 12 (1935), 67–88.

———, "New Soundings in the Regia," *Entretiens Hardt* 13 (1967) 47–63.

———, "La Protostoria della Regia," *RendPontAcc* 47 (1974/5) 15–36.

F. Castagnoli, *Lavinium*, 2 vols. (Rome 1972–75).

———, "Les sanctuaires du Latium archaique," *Comptes-rendus de l'Academie des Inscriptions* (1977) 46–76.

———, *EAAC* 6 (1965), s.v. "Roma."

G. Carettoni, "Excavations and Discoveries in the Forum Romanum and on the Palatine during the Last Fifty Years," *JRS* 50 (1960) 182–303.

Civiltà del Lazio primitivo (Rome 1976). Catalogue of an exhibition.

F. Coarelli, "Il sepolcro degli Scipioni," *DialArch* 6 (1972) 36–106. See also his *Guida archeologica di Roma*, 325–33.

———, "Il Comizio dalle origini alla fine della Repubblica," *PdP* 32 (1977) 166–238.

F. Coarelli, "Public Building in Rome Between the Second Punic War and Sulla," *PBSR* 45 (1977) 1–23.

———, ed., *Roma Medio-Repubblicana* (Rome 1973).

T. J. Cornell, "Aeneas and the Twins: The Development of the Roman Foundation Legend," *Proceedings of the Cambridge Philological Society* 201 (n.s. 21) (1975) 1–32.

L. Curtius, A. Newrath, and E. Nash, *Das antike Rom*[3] (Vienna 1957).

A. Degrassi, *Inscriptiones Latinae liberae rei publicae, I* (Florence 1957).

T. Frank, "Roman Buildings of the Republic: An Attempt to Date Them from their Materials," *Papers and Monographs of the Am. Acad. in Rome* 3 (1924).

P. G. Gierow, *op. cit.* in ch. 1.

E. Gjerstad, "Il comizio romano dell' età reppublicana," *Skrifter* 5 (1941) 97–158.

———, "Early Rome I," *ib.* 17 (1953).

———, "The Fortifications of Early Rome," *ib.* 18 (1954) 50–65.

———, "Legends and Facts of Early Roman History," *Scripta Minora*[2] (Lund 1960–61), pp. 3–68 of off-print. To be used with caution: unconventional dates.

P. G. Goidanich, "L'iscrizione arcaica del Foro Romano e il suo ambiente archeologico," *Memorie dell' Accademia d'Italia*, series 7, vol. 3 (1943) 317–501.

M. Grant, *The Roman Forum* (London and New York 1970).

R. Lanciani, *Ancient Rome in the Light of Recent Discoveries* (Boston 1888).

G. Lugli, *I monumenti antichi di Roma e suburbio* 3 (Rome 1938) 23–50.

———, *Roma antica: il centro monumentale* (Rome 1946).

———, *La tecnica edilizia romana* 2 vols. (Rome 1957).

G. Marchetti-Longhi, "L'area sacra del Largo Argentina," *MPI Guides* (Rome 1960).

A. H. McDonald, *Republican Rome* (London and New York, 1966).

A. Momigliano, "An Interim Report on the Origins of Rome," *JRS* 53 (1963) 95–121. Literary, linguistic, and religious evidence; rejects Gjerstad's late date.

R. M. Ogilvie, *A Commentary on Livy, Books 1–5* (Oxford 1965).

———, *Early Rome and the Etruscans* (London 1976).

Oxford Classical Dictionary[2] (Oxford 1970), art. "Tabula Pontificum."

R. E. A. Palmer, "The King and the Comitium," *Historia Einzelschriften* 11 (1969).

P. Pensabene, "Roma: Saggi di Scavo sul tempio della Magna Mater," *ArchLaz* 1 (1978) 67–71.

R. Peroni et al., "S Omobono: materiali dell' età di bronzo e degli inizi dell' età del ferro," *BullComm* 77 (1955–60) 3–143.

S.B. Platner and T. Ashby, *A Topographical Dictionary of Ancient Rome* (Oxford 1929).

J. Poucet, "Les Sabines aux origines de Rome," *ANRW* I.i (Berlin 1972). Disbelieves in joint Latin-Sabine culture.

S. M. Puglisi, "Gli abitatori primitivi del Palatino," *MonAnt* 41 (1951) cols. 1–98.

L. Quilici, "Collatia," *Forma Italiae* I.10 (Rome 1974).

———, *Roma primitiva e le origini della civiltà laziale* (Rome 1979). Excellent.

———, S. Quilici Gigli, "Antemnae," *Latium Vetus* 1 (Rome 1978).

———, "Crustumerium," *Latium Vetus* 3 (Rome 1980).

Ricerca su una comunità del Lazio protostorico: il sepolcreto dell'Osteria dell'Osa (Rome 1979). Exhibition catalogue.

L. Richardson, Jr., "Cosa and Rome: Comitium and Curia," *Archy* 10 (1957) 49–55.

I.S. Ryberg, *An Archaeological Record of Rome from the Seventh to the Second Centuries B.C.* (London 1940).

G. Säflund, "Le mure di Roma reppublicana," *Skrifter* 1 (1932).

V. Saladino, "Der Sakophag des . . . Scipio Barbatus," *Beiträge zur Archäologie* 1 (Würzburg 1970).

M. R. Scherer, *Marvels of Ancient Rome* (New York and London 1955).

I. G. Scott, "Early Roman Traditions in the Light of Archeology," *MAAR* 7 (1929) 7–116.

P. Somella, "Heroon di Enea a Lavinium: recenti scavi a Pratica di Mare," *RendPontAcc* 44 (1971/2) 47–64.

———, "Il culto di Minerva a Lavinium," *ib.* 46 (1973/4) 33–48.

C. M. Stibbe, "Satricum," *ArchLaz* 1 (1978) 56–59.

B. Tilly, "The Identification of Laurentum," *ArchClass* 28 (1976) 283–93.

P. Zaccagni, "Gabii: la citta antica e il territorio," *ArchLaz* 1 (1978) 42–6.

CHAPTER 4: *Roman Colonies in Italy*

G. Becatti, "Sviluppo urbanistico," in G. Calza, *Scavi di Ostia,* 1 (Rome 1953).

J. Bradford, *Ancient Landscapes,* 145–216.

F. E. Brown, "Cosa: The Making of a Roman City," *Jerome Lectures* 13 (Ann Arbor 1980).

———, "Cosa I: History and Topography," *MAAR* 20 (1951) 7–113.

V. J. Bruno, "A Town House at Cosa," *Archy* 23 (1970) 232–41.

———, "Underwater Discoveries at the Island of Diana (Giannutri) in the Arcipelago Toscano," *AJA* 77 (1973) 208.

T. V. Buttrey, "Cosa: the Coins," *MAAR* 34 (1980) 11–153 and plates. On hoard of 2,000 silver denarii.

F. Castagnoli, "I più antichi esempi conservati di divisioni agrarie romane," *Bulletino del Museo della Civiltà Romana* 18 (1953–1955). 1–9.

———, "La centuriazione de Cosa," *MAAR* 24 (1956) 147–165.

———, "Le ricerche sui resti della centuriazione," *Note e discussioni erudite a cura di Augusto Campana* 7 (Rome 1958).

F. Coarelli, *Etruscan Cities* (New York 1975) 148. On Giannutri. Good photos, but text, especially on Cosa, to be used with caution.

A. M. Colini, "Il tempio di Veiove," *BullComm* 12 (1942) 5–55.

J. Collins-Clinton, *A Late Antique Shrine of Liber Pater at Cosa* (Leiden 1979).

F. De Visscher and F. De Ruyt, "Les Fouilles d'Alba Fucens (Italie centrale) en 1949 et 1950," *L'Antiquité Classique* 20 (1951) 47–84 and later reports in successive volumes. See also report of 1955 campaign, *Notizie degli Scavi* (1957) 163–70.

S. L. Dyson, "Cosa: The Utilitarian Pottery," *MAAR* 33 (1976).

E. Greco, D. Theodorescu, "Poseidonia/Paestum I: La Curia," *CollEFR* 42 (1980).

G. Guiccardini Corsi Salviati, "La centuriazione romana e un' opera attuale di bonifica agraria," *Studi Etruschi* 20 (1948–1949) 291–96.

W. V. Harris, *Rome in Etruria and Umbria* (Oxford 1971), in ch. 5.

P. MacKendrick, "Asphodel, White Wine, and Enriched Thunderbolts," *Greece and Rome,* new series, 1 (1954) 1–11.

———, "Roman Colonization and the Frontier Hypothesis,"

in W. D. Wyman and C. B. Kroeber, eds., *The Frontier in Perspective* (Madison 1957) 3–19.

M. T. Marabini Moevs, "The Roman Thin-walled Pottery from Cosa," *MAAR* 32 (1973).

———, "Italo-Megarian Ware at Cosa," *ib.* 34 (1980).

J. Mertens, *Alba Fucens* 2 vols. (Rome 1969).

—— and S. J. de Laet, "Massa d'Alba (Aquila): Scavi di Alba Fucense," *Not. Scav.*, series 8, vol. 4 (1950) 248–88.

———, "L'urbanizzazione del centro di Alba Fucense," *MemLinc*, series 8, vol. 5 (1954) 171–94.

J-C. Richard, "Les origines de la plèbe romaine," *BEFAR* 232 (1978) 278–337. Historicity of Ancus Marcius's Ostia.

L. Richardson, Jr., "Excavations at Cosa in Etruria, 1948–1952," *Antiquity* 27 (1953) 102–3.

E. T. Salmon, *Samnium and the Samnites* (Cambridge 1967).

———, *The Making of Roman Italy* (London 1982). In *Ancient Peoples and Places* series; admirable.

Doris M. Taylor, "Cosa: Black-Glaze Pottery," *MAAR* 25 (1957) 68–193.

J. B. Ward Perkins, "Early Roman Towns in Italy," *Town Planning Review* 26 (1955) 127–54.

CHAPTER 5: *Nabobs as Builders: Sulla, Pompey, Caesar*

G. Carettoni, "Il fregio figurato della Basilica Aemilia," *Rivista dell'Istituto di Archeologia* 10 (1961) 5–78.

F. Coarelli, "Il complesso pompeiano del Campo Marzio e la sua decorazione sculturea," *RendPontAcc* 44 (1971/2) 99–122.

M. A. Cotton, "The Late Republican Villa at Posto, Francolise," *Suppl. Publ. BSR* (London 1979).

L. Crema, "Architettura romana nell'età della Repubblica," *ANRW* I.iv (Berlin 1973) 633–60, 46 plates. Favors Sullan date for Praeneste. Rare photos: nymphaeum of Villa "of Cicero," Pompeii (33); Tabularium plan (96).

A. Degrassi, "Quando fu costruito il santuario di Fortuna Primigenia di Palestrina?" *MemLinc* 14 (1969) 111–

27. About 110 B.C.

F. Fasolo and G. Gullini, *Il Santuario della Fortuna Primigenia a Palestrina* 2 vols. (Rome 1953).

G. Gatti, "Teatro e cripto di Balbo in Roma," *MEFR* 91 (1979) 237–313.

G. Bodei Giglioni, "Pecunia fanatica: l'incidenza economica dei tempii laziali," in F. Coarelli, ed., *Studi su Praeneste* (Perugia 1975) 3–76.

G. Gullini, "La datazione e l'inquadramento stilistico del santuario della Fortuna Primigenia a Palestrina," *ANRW* I.iv (Berlin 1973) 786–99. Dates complex shortly after 150 B.C. Good photos.

———, *Guida del Santuario della Fortuna Primigenia a Palestrina* (Rome 1956).

J. A. Hanson, *Roman Theater-Temples* (Princeton 1958).

H. Kähler, review of Fasolo and Gullini, *Gnomon* 30 (1958) 366–83.

———, "Das Fortunaheiligtum von Palestrina-Praeneste," *Annales Universitatis Saraviensis (Philosophie-Lettres)* 7 (1958) 189–240.

Phyllis W. Lehmann, "The Setting of Hellenistic Temples," *JSAH* 13.4 (1954) 15–20.

G. Lugli, *Roma antica* (Rome 1946) 177–79, 245–58 (Caesar's buildings).

———, *I monumenti antichi* 3 (Rome 1938) 70–83 (Pompey's theater).

A. M. and M. Moretti, "La Villa dei Volusii a Lucus Feroniae," *Tesori d'arte sul cammino delle autostrade* (Rome 1977).

A. H. McDonald, *op. cit.* in ch. 3.

Platner and Ashby, *op cit.* in ch. 3.

Giovanna Quattrocchi, *Il Museo Archeologico Prenestino* (Rome 1956).

A. Steinmeyer-Schareika, "Das Nilmosaik von Palestrina und eine ptolemäische Expedition nach Äthiopen," (Diss. Bonn 1978).

Eugénie Strong, "The Art of the Roman Republic," *Cambridge Ancient History* 9 (1932) 803–41.

E. B. Van Deman, "The Sullan Forum," *JRS* 12 (1922) 1–31.

C. C. Van Essen, *Sulla als Bouwheer* (Groningen 1940).

CHAPTER 6: *Augustus: Buildings as Propaganda*

B. Andreae, "Archäologische Funde und Grabungen im Bereich der Soprintendenzen von Rom 1949–1956/7," *Arch. Anzeiger* (1957) cols. 110–358.

E. Büchner, "Solarium Augusti und Ara Pacis," *RM* 83 (1976) 319–65.

———, "Horologium-Solarium Augusti: Vorbericht über die Ausgrabungen 1979–80," *ib.* 87 (1980) 355–73.

G. Carettoni, "Roma, Palatino: Scavo della zona a s.-o. della Casa di Livia, I: la casa repubblicana," *NSc* 21 (1967) 287–319.

———, "La zona augustea del Palatino alla luce di recenti scavi," *RendPontAcc* 39 (1966/7) 55–75.

L. Crema, *op. cit.* in ch. 5.

Curtius, Newrath, and Nash, *op. cit.* in ch. 3.

A. Degrassi, "Elogia," *Inscriptiones Italiae* 13.3 (Rome 1937).

———, "L'edifizio dei Fasti Capitolini," *RendPontAcc* 21 (1945/1946) 57–104.

———, "Fasti," *Inscriptiones Italiae* 13.1 (Rome 1947).

P. Fidenzoni, *Il teatro di Marcello* (Rome 1970).

C. Gasparri, "Aedes Concordiae Augustae," *MonRom* 8 (Rome 1970).

P. Gros, "Aurea Templa," *BEFAR* 231 (Rome 1978).

H. Ingholt, "The Prima Porta Statue of Augustus," *Archy* 22 (1969) 176–87, 304–18.

H. Kähler, "Die Augustus-Statue von Primaporta," *Mon-ArtRom* 1 (Köln 1959).

E. La Rocca, "La decorazione frontonale del tempio di Apollo Sosiano," *ArchLaz* 2 (1979) 75–6.

G. Lugli, *I monumenti antichi,* 3 (Rome 1938) 194–211 (mausoleum).

———, *Monumenti minori del Foro Romano* (Rome 1947) 77–84 (arch).

H. Mielsch, "Römische Stuckreliefs," *RM* Suppl. 21 (1974). Lists 132 items, including those of Farnesina.

G. Moretti, *Ara Pacis Augustae,* 2 vols. (Rome 1948).

H. Riemann, "Pacis Ara," *RE* 18 (1942) cols. 2082–107.

I. S. Ryberg, "The Procession of the Ara Pacis," *MAAR* 19 (1949) 79–101.

———, "Rites of the State Religion in Roman Art," *ib.* 22 (1955).

E. Simon, *Ara Pacis Augustae* (New York 1966).

D. E. Strong, J. B. Ward Perkins, "The Temple of Castor in the Roman Forum," *PBSR* n.s. 17 (1962) 1–30.

J. M. C. Toynbee, "The Ara Pacis Reconsidered and Historical Art in Roman Italy," *Proceedings of the British Academy* 39 (1953) 67–95.

E. A. Wadsworth, "Stucco Reliefs of the First and Second Centuries still Extant in Rome," *MAAR* 4 (1924).

P. Zanker, "Forum Augusti," *MonArtRom* 2 (Tübingen 1968).

———, "Forum Romanum," *ib.* 5 (*ib.* 1972).

CHAPTER 7: *Hypocrite, Madman, Fool, and Knave*

S. Aurigemma, *La Basilica sotterranea neopitagorica di Porta Maggiore in Roma* (Rome 1954).

G. Bandinelli, "Il monumento sotterraneo di Porta Maggiore in Roma," *MonAnt* 31 (1927) cols. 601–848.

M. Barosso, "Edifizio romano sotto il tempio di Venere e Roma," *Atti del 3° Convegno nazionale di storia di architettura romana* (1938, publ. 1940) 75–78.

M. E. Blake, *Roman Construction in Italy II: Tiberius to the Flavians* (Washington 1959).

A. Boëthius, *The Golden House of Nero: Some Aspects of Roman Architecture* (Ann Arbor 1960).

J. Carcopino, *La Basilique pythagoricienne de la porte majeure* (Paris 1926).

B. Conticello, B. Andreae, "Die Skulpturen von Sperlonga," *Antike Plastik* 14 (1974).

G. Cultrera, "Nemi—la prima fase dei lavori per il recupero delle navi romane," *NSc* (1932) 206–92.

G. Iacopi, *I ritrovamenti dell' antro cosidetto "di Tiberio" a Sperlonga* (Rome 1958).

A. Prückner, S. Storz, "Beobachtigungen im Oktagon der Domus Aurea," *RM* 81 (1974) 323–39.

P. Ciencio Rossetto, *Il Sepolcro del fornaio M. Virgilio Eurisace* (Rome 1973).

G. Säflund, "The Polyphemus and Scylla Groups at Sperlonga," *Stockholm Studies in Classical Archaeology* 9 (1972).

G. Ucelli, *Le navi di Nemi* (Rome 1940).

E. B. Van Deman, "The Sacra Via of Nero," *MAAR* 5 (1925) 115–26.

C. C. Van Essen, "La topographie de la Domus Aurea Neronis," *Mededeelingen der Kon. Nederland. Akad. van Wetenschappen,* afd. Letterkunde, nieuwe Reeks, Deel 17 (Amsterdam 1954) 371–98.

J. B. Ward Perkins, "Nero's Golden House," *Antiquity* 30 (1956) 209–19.

F. Weege, "Das Goldene Haus des Nero," *JDAI* 28 (1913) 127–244.

CHAPTER 8. *The Victims of Vesuvius*

B. Andreae, ed., *Neue Forschungen in Pompeii* (Recklinghausen 1975).

J. Andreau, "Les affaires de M. Jucundus," *CollEFR* 19 (1974).

Gli architetti francesi dell' ottocento (Paris/Rome 1981). Catalogue of an exhibition.

P. von Blanckenhagen, C. Alexander, "Paintings from Boscotrecase," *RM* Suppl. 6 (1962).

O. J. Brendel, "Der grosse Fries," *JDAI* 81 (1966) 206–60. Interpretation of Villa of Mysteries painting.

R. C. Carrington, *Pompeii* (Oxford 1936).

E. C. Corti, *The Destruction and Resurrection of Pompeii and Herculaneum* (London 1951, unaltered from original German of 1940).

J. Crook, "Working Notes on Some of the New Pompeii Tablets," *Zeitschrift für Papyrologie und Epigraphie* 29 (1978) 229–39.

M. Della Corte, *Case ed abitanti di Pompeii²* (Pompeii 1954).

M. De Vos, "Casa di Cerere: scavi nuovi sconosciuti, pitture e pavimenti," *Mededelingen van het Nederlands Instituut te Rom* 38 (1976) 37–75.

S. Di Caro, "Sculpture della villa di Poppaea in Oplontis," *CronPomp* 2 (1976) 184–225.

E. Diehl, *Pompeianische Wandinschriften²* (Bonn 1930).

H. Eschebach, *Stadtebauliche Entwicklung des antiken Pompeii* (Heidelberg 1970).

———, *Pompeii: erlebte antike Welt* (Leipzig 1978).

———, "Die stabianer Thermen in Pompeii," *Denkmäler antiker Achitektur* 13 (1979).

R. Etienne, *La vie quotidienne à Pompeii*[2] (Paris 1977).

S. Ferraio, *Stabiae: le ville e l'antiquarium* (Castellamare di Stabia 1981).

A. Di Franciscis, "Villa rustica di Oplontis," *PdP*, no. 123 (1973) 453–76.

J. L. Franklin, Jr., "Pompeii: the Electoral Progammata, Campaigns and Politics A.D. 71–9," *Papers and Monographs of the American Academy in Rome* 28 (1980) 17–137.

M. Gigante, *Civiltà delle forme litterarie nell'antico Pompeii* (Naples 1979).

C. Giordano, "Su alcune tavolette cerate dell'agro Murécine," RendNap n.s. 41 (1966) 107–21; *id., ib.* 45 (1970) 211–32; *id., ib.* 47 (1972) 311–18.

W. F. Jashemski, *The Gardens of Pompeii, Herculaneum, and the Villas Destroyed by Vesuvius* (New Rochelle, N.Y. 1980).

Th. Kraus, L. von Matt, *Pompeii and Herculaneum: Living Cities of the Dead* (New York 1975; German original 1973).

A. Laidlaw, "Reconstruction of the First Style Decorations in the House of Sallust in Pompeii," in L. Bonfante Warren, ed., *In Memoriam O. J. Brendel: Essays in Archaeology and the Humanities* (Mainz 1976) 105–14.

E. La Rocca, M. and A. De Vos, *Guida archeologica di Pompeii* (Verona 1978). Exemplary.

A. Maiuri, *La Casa del Menandro* (Rome 1933).

———, *La Villa dei Misteri*,[2] 2 vols. (Rome 1947).

———, *Ercolano*[4] (MPI *Guides*, Rome 1954).

———, *Ercolano: I nuovi scavi (1927–1958)* I (Rome 1958).

———, *Pompeii*[8] (MPI *Guides*, Rome 1956).

———, "Pompei et la guerra," in *Pompei ed Ercolano fra case ed abitanti* (Milan 1958) 263–74.

B. Maiuri, *Museo Nazionale di Napoli* (Novara 1957). Recommended. Good photos, including color; intelligent comments.

Neil McKendrick, "Pompeii," *Horizon* 4.4 (1962) 42–69. On history of excavations, with special reference to Sir William and Lady Hamilton. Good color photos.

D. Mustilli, "La villa pseudourbana ercolanese," *RendNap* n.s. 31 (1956) 77–98. On the Villa of the Papyri.

G. O. Onorato, *Iscrizioni Pompeiane: la vita pubblica* (Florence 1957). One hundred and forty-seven inscriptions, translated into Italian.

Pompei: i tempi della documentazione (Rome 1981). Exhibition catalogue: photos, drawings, paintings from archives.

L. Richardson, Jr., "The Archaic Doric Temple of Pompeii," *PdP*, no. 157 (1974) 281–90.

———, "The Libraries of Pompeii," *Archy* 30 (1977) 394–402. "Santuari dei Lari" may be library.

———, "Pompeii: the Casa dei Dioscuri and its Painters," *MAAR* 23 (1955).

F. Sbordone, *Ricerche sui papiri ercolanesi* 3 vols. (Naples 1969–79).

K. Schefold, *Vergessenes Pompeii* (Bern 1962). Rich illustration, dubious iconography.

———, "La peinture pompeienne: l'évolution de sa signification," *CollLat* 108 (1972). Previous remark applies.

V. Spinazzola, *Pompeii alla luce degli scavi nuovi di Via dell'Abbondanza (Anni 1910–1923)* 2 vols. and vol. of plates (Rome 1953).

"Splendors of a Newly Discovered Roman Villa," *Horizon* 16.4 (1974) 22–25. Oplontis. Good color photos.

Patrizia S. Tumolesi, *Gladiatorum Paria: annunci di spettacoli gladiatori a Pompei* (Rome 1980).

A. W. Van Buren, "Pompeii," in *RE* (1952) cols. 1999–2038.

J. B. Ward Perkins, Amanda Claridge, *Pompeii AD 79* (London 1979). Catalogue of an exhibition on 2,000th anniversary of eruption.

F. Zevi, "La casa Reg. IX.5.18–21 a Pompei e le sue pitture," *StudMisc* 5 (1964) 6–73. On House of Jason. Disagrees with Schefold's symbolic interpretation of paintings.

CHAPTER 9: *Flavian Rome*

H. Bauer, "Il Foro Transitorio e il Tempio di Giano," *Rend PontAcc* 49 (1976/7) 117–50,

M. Bergmann, P. Zanker, "Damnatio Memoriae: umgear-
beitete Nero- und Domitians-Porträts," *JDAI* 96
(1981) 317–412.

P. H. von Blanckenhagen, *Flavische Architektur* (Berlin
1940).

G. Wataghin Cantino, *La Domus Augustana* (Turin 1960).

A. Chastagnol, "Le senat romain sous le règne d'Odoacre,"
Antiquitas 3 (Mainz 1966). Inscriptions reserve Colosseum seats for senators.

F. Coarelli, "Il Campo Marzio occidentale: Storia e topografia," *MEFR* 89 (1977) 807–46.

A. M. Colini, "Forum Pacis," *BullComm* 65 (1938) 7–40.

———, *Stadium Domitiani* (Rome 1943).

G. Cozzo, *Ingegneria Romana* (Rome 1928).

H. Finsen, "Domus Flavia," *AnalRomInstDan,* Suppl. 2
(Copenhagen 1962).

———, "La residence de Domitian sur le Palatin," *ib.*, Suppl.
5 (Rome 1969).

G. Lugli, *Roma antica* (Rome 1946) 269–76 (Forum
Pacis, Forum Transitorium); 319–48 (Colosseum);
486–93, 509–16 (Palace of Domitian).

W. L. MacDonald, *The Architecture of the Roman Empire*
I[2] (New Haven 1982) 47–74. Domus Flavia.

F. Magi, *I Rilievi Flavi del Palazzo della Cancelleria*
(Rome 1945).

M. Scherer, *op. cit.* in ch. 3, 49–62 (Palatine); 75–76
(Arch of Titus), 80–89 (Colosseum), 101–2 (Forum
"of Nerva").

E. Simon, "Zu den flavischen Reliefs von der Cancelleria,"
JDAI 75 (1961) 134–56. Interprets frieze Fig. 9.12
as *adventus* in Rome, date A.D. 93.

B. Tamm, *Auditorium et Palatium* (Lund 1963). In English.

J. M. C. Toynbee, *The Flavian Reliefs from the Palazzo
della Cancelleria in Rome* (Oxford 1957).

CHAPTER 10: *Trajan: Port, Forum, Market, Baths, and Column.*

G. Becatti, *Scavi di Ostia* 2 (Rome 1954). Mithraea.

———, *Scavi di Ostia 6: Edifizio con opus sectile fuori Porta
Marina* (Rome 1969).

G. Boni, "Roma—Esplorazione del Forum Ulpium," *NSc* (1907) 361–427.

J. Bradford, *Ancient Landscapes* 248–56. Claudius's and Trajan's harbors.

G. Calza, *Scavi di Ostia* 1 (Rome 1953).

——— and G. Becatti, *Ostia*¹ (MPI *Guides,* Rome 1957).

———, *La necropoli del Porto di Roma nell' Isola Sacra* (Rome 1940).

R. Calza, "Sui ritratti ostiensi del supposto Plotino," *BdA* 38 (1953) 203–10.

———, E. Nash, *Ostia* (Florence 1959). In Italian. Superb photos.

A. Carandini, "Le Terme del Nuotatore I–III.2," *StudMisc* 13 (1968); 16 (1970); 21, 2 vols. (1974).

J. Carcopino, *Daily Life in Ancient Rome* (New Haven, 1940) 173–84. Businessmen and manual laborers.

K. De Fine Licht, "Untersuchungen an der Trajansthermen zu Rom," *AnalRomInstDan,* Suppl. 7 (1974).

Dossiers d'Archéologie 17 (July-Aug. 1976). Devotes entire issue to Trajan's Column: new photos, maps, copious panel-by-panel description.

P. Ducati, *L'arte classica*³ (Turin 1948), 619–28 (Trajan's Forum and Column).

B. M. Felletti-Mai, "Ostia: Casa delle Volte Depinti e Pareti Gialli," *Monumenti di pittura antica scoperti in Italia* 3.1 and 2 (Rome 1961); *id. ib.,* fasc. 3.3 (1967) is on House of Muses, Ostia.

F. Bobo Florescu, *Tropaeum Traiani: das Siegesdenkmal von Adamklissi* (Bucharest-Bonn 1965).

———, *Die Trajanssäule* (Bucharest 1969).

K. Lehmann-Hartleben, "Die antiken Hafenanlagen des Mittelmeeres," *Klio,* Beiheft 14 (1923) 182–98. Claudius's and Trajan's harbors.

P. Buccini Leotardi, *Scavi di Ostia 10: Marmo di cava* (Rome 1979).

G. Lugli, *Roma antica* (Rome 1946) 278–307. Trajan's Forum and Market.

———, and G. Filibeck, *Il Porto di Roma imperiale e l'agro Portuense* (Rome 1935).

W. L. MacDonald, *op. cit.* in ch. 9, pp. 75–93. Trajan's Market.

P. MacKendrick, *The Dacian Stones Speak* (Chapel Hill 1975).

R. Meiggs, art. "Ostia," in *Oxf. Class. Dict.*[2] (Oxford 1970).

———, *Roman Ostia*[2] (Oxford 1973). Exemplary.

P. M. Monti, *La Colonna Traiana* (Rome 1980). Good photos.

J. E. Packer, "The Insulae of Imperial Ostia," *MAAR* 31 (1971).

A. Pascolini, *Return to an Ancient City: Ostia* (Rome 1978). One hundred and thirty drawings, mostly reconstructions. Good elementary introduction to the site.

A. L. Pietrogrande, *Scavi di Ostia 8: le fulloniche* (Rome 1976).

P. Romanelli, *La colonna traiana: relieve fotografici eseguiti in occasione dei lavori di protezione antiaerea* (Rome 1942).

P. L. Romeo, "Ristauro delle Terme di Traiano," *Bull Comm* 84 (1977) 249–59.

M. Floriani Squarciapino, "The Synagogue at Ostia," *Archy* 16 (1963) 195–203.

M. Steinby, "Ziegelstempel: Rom und Umgebung," *RE* Supplbd. 15 (1978) cols. 1489–531. Stamps show Ostia at its architectural peak under Hadrian.

O. Testaguzza, *Portus* (Rome 1970). See also his article, "The Port of Rome," *Archy* 17 (1964) 173–79.

E. D. Thatcher, "The Open Rooms of the Terme del Foro at Ostia," MAAR 24 (1956) 167–264.

P. Zanker, ed., "Hellenismus in Mittelitalien," 2 vols., *Abhandlungen der Akademie der Wissenschaften in Göttingen,* ph.-hist. Kl. 97 (1976). A colloquium on Hellenistic influences.

CHAPTER 11: *An Emperor-Architect: Hadrian*

S. Aurigemma, *Villa Adriana* (Rome 1961).

———, *Villa Adriana*[3] (Tivoli 1955).

A. Barattolo, "Sulle decorazioni della cella del Tempio di Venere e di Roma all'epoca di Adriano," *BullComm* 84 (1975) 133–48. Believes apses are Maxentian.

M. E. Blake, D. T. Bishop, *Roman Construction in Italy III: Nerva through Antonines* (Philadelphia 1973).

H. Bloch, "I bolli laterizi e la storia edilizia romana," *Bull Comm* 65 (1937) 115–87.

F. E. Brown, "Hadrianic Architecture," *Essays in Memory of Karl Lehmann* (Locust Valley, N.Y. 1964) 55–58.

E. Clark, *Rome and a Villa* (New York 1952), 141–94.

K. De Fine Licht, *The Rotunda in Rome* (Copenhagen 1968). On the Pantheon.

A. Hoffman, "Das Stadion in der Villa Hadriani, *Sonderschriften DAI Rom,* 4 (1980).

H. Kähler, *Hadrian und seine Villa bei Tivoli* (Berlin 1950).

D. Kienast, "Zur Baupolitik Hadrians in Rom," *Chiron* 10 (1980) 391–412.

G. Lugli, *I monumenti antichi,* 3 (Roma 1938) 123–50 (Pantheon) 693–708 (Hadrian's mausoleum).

———, *Roma antica* (Rome 1946) 234–40 (Temple of Venus and Rome).

W. L. MacDonald, *op. cit.* in ch. 9, pp. 94–121. Pantheon.

———, *The Pantheon: Design, Meaning, Progeny* (Cambridge, Mass. 1976).

———, B. Boyle, "The Small Baths at Hadrian's Villa," *JSAH* 39 (1980) 5–27.

C. L. V. Meeks, "Pantheon Paradigm," *ib.* 19 (1960) 135–44.

E. S. P. Ricotti, "Criptoportici e gallerie sotteranee di Villa Adriana: topologia e funzione," *CollEFR* 14 (1973) 214–48 and plates.

D. S. Robertson, *A Handbook of Greek and Roman Architecture*[2] (Cambridge 1954), 246–51 (Pantheon), 252–54, 316 (Piazza d'Oro).

R. Syme, "Hadrian the Intellectual," *Les empereurs romains d'Espagne* (Paris 1965) 243–49.

A. W. Van Buren, "Recent Finds at Hadrian's Tiburtine Villa," *AJA* 59 (1955) 215–17 (Canopus).

P. Verduchi, "Le terme con cosidetto Heliocaminus," *Quaderni dell'Istituto di Topografia Antica, U. di Roma* 8 (1975) 55–95.

J. B. Ward Perkins, "Taste, Tradition, and Technology," *Studies in Classical Art and Archaeology: A Tribute to P. H. von Blanckenhagen* (Locust Valley, N.Y. 1979). On originality of Roman architecture.

M. Yourcenar, *Memoires d'Hadrien* (Paris 1951; Engl. trans., New York 1954).

L. Ziehen, art. "Pantheion," in *RE* 18 (1949) cols. 729–41.

CHAPTER 12: *Antonines through Constantine*

W. J. Anderson, R. P. Spiers, and T. Ashby, *The Architecture of Ancient Rome* (London 1927) 99–113 (Baths).

T. Ashby, *Aqueducts of Ancient Rome* (Oxford 1935).

T. Ashby, "The Classical Topography of the Roman Campagna 3," *PBSR* 4 (1907) 97–112. On Sette Bassi villa.

A. Bartoli, *Curia Senatus* (Rome 1963).

H. W. Benario, "Rome of the Severi," *Lat* 17 (1958) 712–22. Chronological table of buildings of the dynasty.

B. Berenson, *The Arch of Constantine or the Decline of Form* (London 1954).

R. Bianchi Bandinelli, *Rome: The Late Empire* (see under *General*).

M. E. Blake, *op. cit.* in ch. 11.

O. J. Brendel, *op. cit.* under *General*.

R. Brilliant, "The Arch of Severus in the Roman Forum," *MAAR* 29 (Rome 1967).

E. Brödner, *Untersuchungen an der Caracallathermen* (Berlin 1951). On bath-basilicas.

C. Caprino *et al.*, *La colonna di M. Aurelio* (Rome 1955).

C. D'Onofrio, *Castel Sant' Angelo* (Rome 1971). A coffee-table book.

Dossiers d'archeologie 41 (Feb.-Mar. 1980). Entire issue devoted to portraits of emperors.

R. J. Forbes, *Notes on the History of Ancient Roads and their Construction* (Amsterdam 1934) 115–68.

L. Franchi, "Ricerche sull'Arte di Età Severiana in Roma," *StudMisc* 4 (1964) 1–48 and plates. It orientalizes, militarizes, popularizes.

A. Frazer, "Iconography of Emperor Maxentius' Buildings in the Via Appia," *Art Bulletin* 48 (1966) 385–92. Notes palaces regularly had hippodromes attached.

A. Giuliano, *L'Arco di Costantino* (Rome 1955).

G. M. A. Hanfmann, *Roman Art* (New York 1964). Good on late period.

L. A. and L. B. Holland, "Down the Tiber on a Raft," *Archy* 3 (1950) 87–89.

H. S. Jones, *Companion to Roman History* (Oxford 1912), 40–49 (roads).

R. Krautheimer, *Rome: Profile of a City, 312–1308* (Princeton 1980).

J. G. Landels, *Engineering in the Ancient World* (London 1978). Figs. 31–33, 38–40, 56, 82–83, 94, 118, 122–29, 140, with accompanying text, illustrate this chapter.

G. Lugli, *Monumenti minori del Foro romano* (Rome 1947) 122–38. Temple of Antoninus and Faustina.

E. Nash, "Secretarium Senatus," *In Memoriam O. J. Brendel* (Mainz 1976) 191–204.

J. H. Oliver, "The Ruling Power," *Transactions of the American Philosophical Society,* n.s., 43.4 (Philadelphia 1953). On Aelius Aristides's panegyric on Antonine Rome.

J. Packer, "La casa di Via Giulio Romano," *BullComm* 81 (1968/9) 127–48. On apartment house at foot of Capitoline Hill.

K. S. Painter, "Roman Villas in Italy: Recent Excavation and Research," *Occasional Papers, Dep't of Greek and Roman Antiquities, British Museum* 24 (1980).

H. Plommer, *Ancient and Classical Architecture* (London, 1956), 338–44 (Baths).

G. Radke, "Viae Publicae Romanae," *RE* Supplbd. 13 (1973) cols. 1417–686.

L. Richardson, Jr., "The Date and Program of the Arch of Constantine," *ArchClass* 25 (1975) 72–78. Dates it late: 326; it parades C.'s virtues.

I. A. Richmond, *The City Wall of Imperial Rome* (Oxford 1930).

I. S. Ryberg, "Panel Reliefs of Marcus Aurelius," *AIA/CAA Monographs* 14 (1967).

G. Pisani Sartorio, R. Calza, *La Villa di Massenzio* (Rome 1976).

G. H. Stevenson, "Communications and Commerce," in *The Legacy of Rome* (ed. C. Bailey, Oxford 1923) 141–72.

M. Todd, *The Walls of Rome* (London 1977).

J. M. C. Toynbee, *The Hadrianic School* (Cambridge 1934). Magisterial treatment of art, on numismatic evidence.

E. B. Van Deman, *The Building of the Roman Aqueducts* (Washington 1934).

L. Vogel, *The Column of Antoninus Pius* (Cambridge, Mass. 1973).

M. J. Vermaseren, C. C. Van Essen, *The Excavations in the Mithraeum of Santa Prisca in Rome* (Leiden 1965).

J. B. Ward Perkins (see under Boëthius, above, *General*). Pp. 332–33 (Sette Bassi); 509–11 ("Minerva Medica").

T. P. Wiseman, "Roman Republican Road-Building," *PBSR* 38 (1970) 122–52.

CHAPTER 13: *Caesar and Christ*

C. Ampolo *et al.*, "La villa del Casale a Pza. Armerina: problemi, saggi stratigrafici, ed altre ricerche," *MEFR* 83 (1971) 141–281. Mosaic dated 320–40.

B. M. Apollonj-Ghetti, A. Ferrua, E. Josi, E. Kirschbaum, *Esplorazioni sotto la confessione di San Pietro in Vaticano eseguite negli anni 1940–1949* 2 vols. (Rome 1951).

A. Carandini, "Ricerche sullo stile e la cronologia dei mosaici della villa di Pza. Armerina," *StudMisc* 7 (1961/2).

———, "La villa di Pza. Armerina, la circolazione della cultura figurativa africana nel tardo impero, ed altre precisazioni," *DialArch* 1 (1967) 93–120. Late date.

———, "Appunti sulla composizione dell mosaico detto 'grande caccia' della villa del Casale a Pza. Armerina," *ib.* 4/5 (1971) 120–34. Motifs repeated, but not symmetrically.

F. Castagnoli, "Il circo di Nerone in Vaticano," *RendPont Acc* 31 (1959–61) 97–122.

C. Castelli, ed., "Le iscrizioni della necropoli dell' Autoparco Vaticano," *Acta Instituti Romani Finlandiae* 6 (1973).

A. Ferrua, *Le pitture della nuova catacomba di Via Latina*

(Vatican City 1960).

G. V. Gentili, "Piazza Armerina: grandiosa villa romana in contrada Casale," *NSc* (1951) 291–335.

———, *The Imperial Villa of Piazza Armerina* (MPI *Guides*, Rome 1956).

M. Guarducci, *La tomba di Pietro* (Rome 1959). There is also an English translation.

H. Kähler, "Die villa des Maxentius bei Pza. Armerina," *MonArtRom* 12 (1973).

E. Kirschbaum, *The Tombs of Peter and Paul* (New York 1959).

H. P. L'Orange and E. Dyggve, "Is it a Palace of Maximian Herculeus that the excavations of Piazza Armerina bring to light?," *Symbolae Osloenses* 29 (1952) 114–28.

G. Lugli, "Contributi alla storia edilizia della villa romana di Pza. Armerina," *Rivista Nazionale di Archeologia e Storia dell' Arte* 11–12 (1963) 28–52. Thinks Labors of Hercules mosaic oldest, dates it 350–70.

B. Pace, *I mosaici di Piazza Armerina* (Rome 1955).

A. Prandi, "La tomba di San Pietro nei pellegrinaggi dell' eta medioevale," *Atti del 4° Congresso sul tema pellegrinaggi e culto dei santi in Europa fino all prima crociata* (Todi 1963) 285–447, 159 plates.

S. Settis, "Per l'interpretazione di Pza. Armerina," *MEFR* 87.2 (1975) 873–994. Dates villa 300–20, and ascribes it to Maxentius.

J. Stevenson, "The Catacombs," in series *Ancient Peoples and Places* (London 1978).

J. M. C. Toynbee and J. B. Ward Perkins, *The Shrine of St. Peter and the Vatican Excavations* (London 1956).

Index

Abgar, King, 396
Absolutism, 313, 374, 413
Achaea, 378
Achelóüs, 323
Achílles, 41, 220, 239
Acília, 75
Acqua Acetósa, 76
Acquaróssa, 75, 89
Actaéon, 277
Áctium, 179, 181, 194
Adamklísi, 298
Addaúra, 26
Admiralty, 227
Adriatic, 36, 117, 137
Aélius Aristídes, 380
Aemílius Paulus, L., 191
Aemilius Scaurus, M., 171
Aenéas, 74, 77, 83, 95, 114, 169, 191, 197, 211–12, 222, 275, 387
Aenéid, 192, 194, 197
Aéschylus, 434
Aesculápius, 298. See also Asclépius
Africa, 277, 295, 356, 387, 430
Agávē, 235
Agger, 40, 106
Agríppa, M. Vipsánius, 182, 183, 198, 210, 358
Aion, 380
Ajax, 220
Akkadians, 8
Alabaster, 36, 326
Álaric, 409
Alba Fucens, 113, 197–220, 130, 134, 332

Alba Longa, 74, 75, 77, 191, 309
Alban Hills, 72, 74, 77, 78, 85, 86, 309–10
Albénga, 127n
Albínius, L., 191
Alcaéus, 277
Alexander the Great, 60, 186, 189, 276, 433
Alexander Sevérus, 389
Alexandria, 142, 143, 273, 345, 356, 368, 370, 372
Algiers, 193
Állia, R., 76
Alps, 30
Altheim, 5
Ámazon, female warrior, 372
Amber, Baltic, 10, 17, 36
Ambrósia, nymph, 433
American excavations, 98, 113, 241
Ammon, 273
Amphitheatrum Flávium, 240
Ámphoras, Phoenician, 77
Anaclétus, Pope, 441
Anatomy lesson, 443
Ancestor worship, 275
Anchíses, 169
Ancóna, 339
Ancus Mártius, King, 75, 114
Andrén, A., 102
Andrómachē, 239
Anicétus, Pope, 441
Ánio, R., 75, 392; tufa, 91, 106, 111; valley, 391

Annóna, 335
Ántefix, 35, 62
Antémnae, 75
Antígonus Gonátas, King, 276
Antínous, 349, 356, 364–67, 370, 378
Antíochus III, King, 92
Antónia Maior, 211; Minor, 210
Ántonine dynasty, 320–22, 322, 375, 377, 385, 400
Antonínus Pius, 374, 377, 438
Antónius, M., 173, 181, 194, 195, 198, 300
Ańzio (Ántium), 40, 106, 115, 137
Ápennine(s), 15, 72, 402
Aphrodíte, 184. *See also* Venus
Apis, 216, 273, 277
Apollo, 32, 60, 103, 180, 188, 206, 233, 235, 240, 298, 323, 367, 413, 438
Apollodórus of Damascus, 331, 336, 339, 340, 343, 353
Aqueducts, 389–95, 425
Aquileía, 402n
Aráchne, 305
Árdea, 40, 76, 106
Aréne Cándide, 7, 8
Áres, 372. *See also* Mars
Arézzo (Arrétium), 58, 191, 402n
Argo, 222
Argonauts, 58
Ariádne, 276, 277, 278, 279
Áries, 380
Aríminum, 402. *See also* Rímini
Aríōn, 429, 432
Armenia, 188n, 378
Arnaz, dwarf, 41
Arno, R., 28
Arnoáldi, 21, 23, 24
Árretine, 131, 333
Arrétium, 191, 402n. *See also* Arezzo
Arringatóre, 58
Árrius Crescens, C., 254
Art, aulic, 416; plebeian, 416
Ártemis, 232, 235, 277, 365. *See also* Diana
Ascánius (Iulus), 210
Ascháffenburg, 245
Asclépius, 155. *See also* Aesculápius
Ashby, Thomas, 389, 391, 393, 394, 395
Asia, province, 394

Asia Minor, 30, 216
Astárte, 47, 48
Athéna, 60, 179, 233, 353
Athens, 72, 189, 206, 351, 352, 361, 368, 371, 380, 434
Atlantic liners, 224
Átrium, 7, 252
Átticus, T. Pomponius, 173
Attiké, prostitute, 264
Áttis, 111
Audebert, N., 406
Augean Stables, 300, 433
Augustan Age, 214
Augustan compromise, 189, 206, 279
Augustan propaganda, ch. 6, *passim*
Augustine, 330
Augustus, 71, 83, 99, 296, 353; builds Ostia theater, 117; birthday (23 Sept.) 179; civic crown, 182; builder, 182, 300; of Prima Porta, 186; as Prince of Peace, 194; propagandist, 194; as Jupiter, 199; bimillennary, 204, 420; on Ara Pacis, 208; pretensions mocked, 272; on Boscoréale silver, 277; and Hadrian, 358; in Pántheon, 358; aqueduct, 395; glorified, 397
Aulic art, 381, 385
Avele Feluske, 30, 40, 93
Avile Vipina, 41
Avle Metele, 58
Axial symmetry, 286, 289, 331, 336, 399

Babylónia, 50
Bacchánte, 279
Bacchic frenzy, 235; initiation, 183; symbols, 298
Bacchus, 131, 276, 279, 309. *See also* Dionýsus
Bacon, Sir Francis, 281
Baiae, 358
Balkans, 6, 24
Balzi Rossi, 7
Barberíni tomb, 68; Palace, 142, 147, 152; mosaic, 143, 432; family, 362
Baroque, 306, 344, 367, 368
Bazaars, Near Eastern, 336
Belgians, 113, 117

Belisárius, 410
Bellóna, 302
Belvérde, 9, 10
Benácci, 21, 24
Benevénto, 137, 214
Berenson, B., 413
Bernadíni tomb, Praeneste, 68
Berníni, G.L., 161, 189, 362
Biánchi Bandinélli, R., 426
Bibulus, C. Publícius, tomb of, 92
Birnam Wood, 430
Biscéglie, 10
Bismántova, 16
Bithýnia, 356, 378
Bitúitus, 120
Black-figure ware, 23, 36, 53
Blera (Biéda), 57
Bloch, H., 315, 335, 342, 370
Bocchóris, Pharaoh, 143, 185
Bologna (Bononia), 20, 137
Bolséna (Volsinii), 32, 38, 40
Bonaparte, Lucien, 66
Boni, G., 77, 83, 85, 87, 90, 105, 333
Boniface VIII, Pope, 362
Boscoreále, villa, 262–63, 276, 277
Boscotrecáse, villa, 272
Boston, Museum of Fine Arts, 174,
    220; Public Library, 327
Bovíllae, 403
Brácciano, L., 395
Bracciolíni, Poggio, 406
Bradford, J., 1, 2, 4, 6, 10, 13, 27,
    64, 136, 137
Brahminism, 242
Bramánte, D., 161, 308
Brendel, O., 102
Bridges: Pons Aélius, 368; Fabrícius,
    171; Mílvius, 92, 171, 413; Sub-
    lícius, 13
Bríndisi, 137, 339
Britain, pearls, 169; Hadrian's Wall,
    409
Britannia, 212
British School at Rome, 2, 389
Brízio, E., 35
Bronze Age, 9, 10, 11, 13, 14, 15,
    83, 114
Brothels, 83, 313
Brown, F.E., 89, 132, 134, 195, 373
Bruno, G., 370
Brussels, 276

Brutus, L. Junius, 58
Búcchero ware, 41, 81, 82, 85, 101
Bucránia, 65, 206
Bulwer-Lytton, E., 251
Building materials, alabaster, 332;
    concrete, 154, 308, 358, 361,
    404; granite, 290; marble: Afri-
    can, 287, 289; Carrára, 189;
    cipollíno, 332, 377; giállo an-
    tíco, 332; Parian, 332; Pentélic,
    172, 332; portasánta, 332; pór-
    phyry, 332, rosso antíco, 332;
    onyx, 332; selce, 403, 405;
    speróne, 188; trávertine, 177,
    291, 296, 327; tufa, 327; Anio,
    106, 111; cappelláccio, 102, 105,
    106; Fidénae, 91, 106, 115;
    Grotta Oscúra, 91, 105, 108;
    Montevérde, 106, 111; pe-
    períno, 169, 287, 289, 377; Veii,
    171
Byzantine(s), 374, 410, 428, 432

Caecília Metella, 174
Caecílius Jucúndus, L., 228, 266
Cáelius Vibénna, 41
Caere. See Cerveteri
Caesar, C. Julius, 99, 101, 110, 166,
    169, 174, 177, 191, 193, 214,
    300, 304
Cágliari, 157
Caile Vipinas, 41
Calígula, 199, 216, 217, 225, 374
Calpúrnia, 260
Calpúrnius Piso, L., 260
Caltagiróne, 27
Calza, G., 114, 115, 117, 314
Camíllus, M., 41, 382
Camitlnas, Marce, 41
Campágna, Roman, 72, 392
Campánia, 136
Campo di Serviróla, 15
Campus Mártius, personified, 381
Canále, 23, 26
Caníno, Princess, 66
Capannelle, 393
Capestráno, warrior, 23, 26
Cappelláccio, 91, 102, 105, 106
Cápri, 216, 219, 222
Capricorn, 199
Cápua, 47, 57, 174, 402

Caracálla, Emperor, 310, 393, 396, 397, 399
Carandíni, A., 426
Caravággio, 237
Carbon-14, 9, 16
Carcopíno, J., 232
Cardo, 50
Carrára marble, 189, 332
Carrhae, 197, 396
Carthage, 17, 18, 23, 47, 113, 394, 425
Cartílius Poplícola, C., 319
Caryátids, 189, 332, 371
Casanóva, brother of the notorious, 245
Castagnóli, F., 95, 134
Castel d'Asso (Axia), 38, 55, 57
Castel Gandólfo, 72, 309
Castél Sant'Angelo, 368
Castellázzo di Fontanelláto, 10, 13
Castor, 95, 189
Cátacombs, 442, 443
Catánia, 220
Catilinárians, 111, 134
Cato, the Elder, 124; Younger, 174
Censors, 120
Centocélle, 298
Centuriation, 114, 134–37
Cérberus, 64, 69
Céres, 327, 416. See also Demeter
Certósa situla, 24
Cervéteri, 32, 47, 64, 68, 78, 106, 174, 191. See also Caere
Cerýneia, 60
Chalcolithic Age, 8
Chariot races, 300
Chartres, 361, 385
Charun, 36, 41, 54, 57, 64
Chatti, 304
Chicago, Pit, 336
Chiéti, museum, 120
Chippendale, Thomas, 335
Chorobátes, 403
Chiron, 277
Chiúsi (Clusium), 32
Christ, 338; at Ostia, 330; as Fisher of Men, Good Shepherd, and Sun, 436
Christianity, Christians, 242, 273, 387, 389; martyrs, 290, 435; at Ostia, 316; archaeology, 374; on

Column of Marcus Aurélius, 385; in Empire, 410; God, 413; persecution, 434; church fathers, 434; cross, 436, 438; as state religion, 443
Cícero, M. Tullius, 98, 161, 173, 309
Cincári, 387
Cipollíno, 326, 332
Circus factions, 418, 426
Civic crown, 193
Civil War, Roman, 157
Cívita Castellána, 60
Clans, 42, 75, 92, 189
Clark, Eleanor, 357
Claudius, Emperor, 193, 199, 216, 217, 226, 236, 277; port, Ostia, 117, 323; L. Nemi outlet, 224; aqueduct, 395
Claudius Caecus, Ap., 189
Claudius Marcéllus, M., 191
Claudius Pompeiánus, T., 382
Clemency, 382
Cleopatra VII, 169, 181, 194, 361, 443
Clódius, P., 309
Clúsium (Chiusi), 45
Clustumína, voting district, 76
Coarelli, F., 338
Coin hoard, Cosa, 133
Colini, A.M., 197, 287, 289, 310
Collátia, 75
Collégia, 408
Colonies, Roman, 106; Latin, 98, 106, 107, 108, 113; colonization, ch. 4, passim
Columbus, C., 224
Cómmodus, Emperor, 374, 387
Compósite capitals, 296
Concord, Temple, 131
Concrete, 308, 358, 361, 404
Confessions (of Augustine), 330
Conspicuous consumption, 287; waste, 434
Constantine, Emperor, 364, 374, 382, 383, 406n, 409, 413, 416, 426, 434
Constantinople, 361, 374, 409, 418, 426
Constántius Chlorus, 429
Constantius II, Emperor, 331, 426
Continuity, 445

Copper, German, 15
Cora, temple, 141
Corinth, 72, 394; Corinthian capitals, 180, 186; columns, 179, 193, 284, 313, 377; half-columns, 406n; order, 145
Corsica, 92
Cosa, 113, 132; comitium, 98, 131; excavation technique, 121–24; walls, 121, 124; Capitólium and Arx, 122, 124; pottery, 123, 126n; Temple X, Via Sacra, cisterns, 124, 133; terracotta warrior, 124, 128; temple of Mater Matuta, 128; Forum, arch, basilia, curia, atrium publicum, Temple of Concord, Bacchic shrine, 131; site museum, coin hoard, 133
Cozza, L., 95
Cozzo, G., 291, 292, 293, 294
Cozzo Pantáno, 27
Crassus, 186, 197; the Younger, 174
Crawford, O.G.S., 1
Cremation, 16, 21, 75, 83, 85, 86, 92
Cremóna, 137
Crete, 15, 356
Crucifixion, parody (?), 430
Crustumérium, 76
Ctésiphon, city, 396
Cumae, 54, 95
Cupid, 184, 186, 199, 216, 222, 233, 239, 279, 298, 300, 316, 319, 322, 364, 425
Cursus honórum, 42, 189
Cýbele, 111, 387. See also Magna Mater
Cyparíssus, 433
Cyprus, 17, 68
Cyréne, 356

Dacia(ns), 331, 332, 333, 338, 339, 340, 378, 380, 413
Dáedalus, 277
Dalmátia, 137, 188
Damnátio memóriae, 195, 302, 304, 389, 397
Dánaids, 235
Daniel and lions, 443
Dante, Purgatorio, 339
Danube, R., 338, 339

Dáphnē, nymph, 277, 433
Décima, Castel di, 74, 75, 76, 77, 81
Decumánus, 50
Dedúctio, 139
Degrássi, A., 155, 189, 194
Deianeíra, 277
Deméter, 235. See also Ceres
Democracy, 380
Dennis, G., 28–29, 45, 55, 65, 66
Dessuéri, 27
Diana, 188, 222, 252, 275, 429
Dimíni, 5
Dio Cassius, 343
Dioclétian, Emperor, 162, 313, 374, 393, 402, 410, 424, 433
Diomédes, 220, 433
Dionysíus I (Syracuse), 107
Dionýsus, god, 276, 367, 433, 438. See also Bacchus
Dirce, 278
Dogs, 15
Dolia, 74, 85, 323
Domítia, 211
Domitian, Emperor, 87, 120, 169, 206n, 217, 222, 281, 282, 284, 295, 296, 298, 300, 301, 303, 305, 319, 342, 374, 382
Domítii Ahenobárbi, 134
Domitíus Ahenobárbus, (cos. 59), alleged bust of, 174; Cn., father of Nero, 211
Doric order, 145, 313
Doryphoros, 186
Drusus, stepson of Augustus, 198, 208, 210; grandnephew of Tiberius, 182
Ducáti, P., 21, 27
Dumas, Alexandre, 245
Dunsinane, 430
Dutch, excavation, 76, 240; art, 281

Earthquake of 62 B.C., Pompeii, 273
Edéssa, 396
Egypt(ians), 8, 36, 68, 143, 216, 217, 380, 438; hieroglyphs, 47; scarab, at Décima, 74; grain, Ostia, 115; pyramids, 197, influence, Pompeii, 273, 277; Hadrian in, 368
Elagábalus, Emperor, 387, 406n
Elba, 54

Elephants, 163, 242, 353, 383
Eleusínian mysteries, 235
Elógia, 189
Emperor worship, 306
Endýmion, 278
Énnius, Q., 140
Entremont, 26
Éphesus, Library of Celsus, 250
Epicúrus, garden of, 260
Epidaúrus, 111
Este, 21, 74
Etrúria, Etruscans, 18, 21, 24, 78;
    ch. 2 passim; origin, 30–32;
    League, 32, 44; cities, 32–40;
    political organization, 40–45;
    language, 45–48; religion, 48–
    57; art, 57–64; daily life, 64–
    69; orientation, 102; temple
    types, 103, 128, 131; at Vulci,
    121; -Campanian pottery, 124;
    tumuli, 197, 368; triplicity, 317;
    idea of heaven, 438
Eurípides, 139, 434
Európa, 277
Eurýdicē, 233
Eurýsacēs, tomb of, 228, 230, 330
Evánder, King, 77, 83

Fabius Rulliánus, Q., 79
Fabrícius, L., 171
Fabúllus, painter, 239
Factions, circus, 417–18, 432
Faésulae (Fiésole), theater, 141
Falérii Véteres (Cívita Castellána),
    60, 75
Fancíulla di Anzio, 241
Fánnius, Samnite, 79; —Synistor, 276
Fasces, 40, 208
Fascists, 71, 178, 188, 197, 201, 339
Fasolo, F., 145, 147, 148, 149, 150,
    154, 155
Fasti, 90, 194–95, 331
Faustína, Empress, 377, 380
Faustinus, 222
Ferentíno, market hall, 336
Ferónia, 108
Ferrára, museum, 36
Fíbulae (safety pins), 10, 20, 21,
    24, 74, 78, 79, 82, 85
Ficána, 75
Ficoróni cista, 58

Fidénae tufa, 91, 106, 115
Fiorélli, G., 245
First Punic War, 72
Fiumicíno, airport, 323
Flamen; Dialis, 92, 208, 382; of
    Mars, 208
Flavian dynasty, 236, 242, 281, 300,
    302, 304, 313
Florence, Archaeological Museum,
    28, 57, 58, 204
Foggia, 1, 2
Fontana, Carlo, 368
Forma Urbis. See Rome, Marble
    Plan
Fórmiae, Cicero's villa, 173
Forster, E.M., 58
Fortúna, 108; at Praeneste, 142–55
Francis I, King, 337
Françoís, A., 41
Francolíse, 174
Frangipáni, 296
Frank, Tenney, 91, 105, 106
Freemasons, 235
French, excavations, 38, 331, 406
Frontínus, 388, 391, 393, 394
Fúlvius Flaccus, M., 72
Furies, 233

Gábii, 74, 75, 92, 157
Gaius Caesar, 181, 182, 186, 198, 210
Galátia, 188n
Galba, Emperor, 282
Gallicáno, 392
Gamberíni, R., 194
Garibáldi, G., 245, 410
Gánymede, 222, 232, 233, 296
Gardens, Pompeii, 277
Gauls, 36, 104, 108, 113, 188, 327,
    378; invaders, 38, 76, 99, 101;
    Vercingétorix, 111; Bitúitus,
    120; at Telamóne, 128; feared
    at Cosa, 128
Gemma Augustéa, 199
Genius (guardian spirit), 275; of
    Senate, 301, 382; of Roman
    people, 301
Gens, Tongília, 134; Volúsia, 139;
    Julia, 169. See also clans
Gentíli, G.V., 426, 428, 434
Genua, 402n
Geometric pottery, 23, 26

Geórgics, 197, 212
Germania, personified, 378
Germánicus, 199, 210
Germans, 127, 227, 252, 278, 304, 385
Germany, copper from, 15
Géryon, 433
Geta, 395, 396
Getty, J. Paul, 260
Giállo antíco, 326, 332, 361
Giannútri, Is., 127
Gibbon, E., 377, 418
Gigliόli, G.A., 197
Gjerstad, E., 72, 87, 90
Gladiators, 69, 250
Goethe, 245
Golasécca, 24
Golden Fleece, 233
Gomorrah, 273
Gorgon, 381
Goths, 391, 410, 444
Gracchi, 137
Gracchus. *See* Semprónius
Graces, 276
Granite, 290
Greek forms, 206; Domítian and the, 284, 308–10; Roman adverse view of, 313; inscription, Ostia synagogue, 328; names, 438, 440
Grimáldi, 7
Groma, 403
Grotesques, 237
Grotta Oscúra tufa, 91, 105, 108
Gugliélmi, Marchese, 53
Gullíni, G., 145, 147, 148, 149, 150, 154, 155
Gustav VI, King, 21

Hades, 233
Hadrian, Emperor, 152, 189, 239, 242, 320, 322, 331, 377, 425, 440; ch. 11, *passim;* architect, 308, 346, 358; philhellene, 310, 352; buildings in Ostia, 317, 327; consolidates Dacia, 341; villa nr. Tívoli, 342–52, 362–69; poet, 348; personality, 349, 372–73; restores Olympieíon, Athens, 353; wall (Britain),

356; pacifier, 380; repairs aqueduct, 395
Halicarnássus, mausoleum, 197
Hamilton, Emma, Lady, 245
Hánnibal, 32, 106
Harvard, Stadium, 291; University, 315
Hébē, 382
Hector, 239
Helen, 232, 233, 239
Hélena, mother of Constantine, 406n
Hellenic culture, 133, 193
Hellenistic culture, 143, 155, 157, 179, 222, 234, 279, 333
Hemingway, E., 291
Hepatóscopy, 48
Herculáneum, 243, 244, 245, 251, 260, 263
Hercules, 69, 232, 233, 298, 300, 339, 365, 382, 428, 438; Forum Boárium, 95n; Alba Fucens, 119–20; Lucus Feróniae, 139; revetment, Palatine temple, 180–81; Pompeii, 277–78; Achelóüs, 323; labors of, 377, 432–33, 443; Severan arch, 396; apotheόsis, 433
Hercúlius, 433
Hermes, 57, 367, 372, 438
Heródotus, 30
Hesíone, 232, 233
Hippo Regius, 425
Hippócrates, 316
Hippodromes, 310
Hippólytus, 235, 239, 278
Hírtius, A., 300, 303
Hispánia, personified, 378
Homestead Act, 139
Honórius, Emperor, 409
Horace, 103, 194, 197
Horus, 438
Housing, government, at Cosa, 133
Humbert I, King, 362

Iácopi, G., 217, 218, 219
Ícarus, 277
Illýricum, 6, 339
Imitation of Rome, 339
Impasto, pottery, 78, 82, 85

Inhumation, 20, 75, 79, 83, 85, 86, 92
Ionic-Italic capitals, 149
Iphigenía, 232, 277, 278
Iron Age, 13, 15, 18, 20, 24, 26, 79, 81, 82, 83
Íschia, Is., 72, 95n
Isis, 216, 273, 276, 438
Isles of the Blest, 235
Istacídius Zósimus, L., 257
Istituto Geografico Militare, 110
Italia, personified, 199
Italians, excavations, 113, 114
Italic tribes, 113; temples, 169, 193
Iulus, 169. See also Ascanius
Iwo Jima, 199

Janus, 72, 416
Japanese, 275
Jason, 233
Jefferson, Thomas, 10, 364
Jerusalem, 284, 303
Jewish War, 298
Jews, Roman names taken by, 328
Jonah, 436, 443
Jordan, R., 296
Joseph and his brethren, 436
Jove. See Jupiter
Jovius, 433
Jugúrtha, 111
Julia, 183–84, 210
Julia Domna, Empress, 199, 389, 397
Julio-Claudians, 192, 215, 216, 228, 240, 255, 282, 304, 320
Juno, 35, 327, 380, 382, 416; Sospita, 72; of Gabii, 75; Curritus, 108, 110
Jupiter, 35, 92, 380, 382, 387, 433; Anxoránus, 157–58; Ammon, 189; Justinian, 418
Júvenal, 374, 383
Juvéntus, 382

Kähler, H., 161, 304, 347, 426, 433
Kings, Roman. See table, p. 73
Kos, 155–57
Kouros, Marzabótto, 36

Lambóglia, N., 127n
Lanciáni, R., 105, 286, 289

Laócoön, 219, 241, 433
Láres, 389; Permaríni, 108
Lars Porsénna, 45
Last Days of Pompeii, 245, 251
Last Supper, 443
La Tène, 23
Latin(s), 86; colony, 98; League, 108, 402; language, in Mass, 445
Látium, 26, 71, 72, 77
Lauréntum, 74
Lavínium, 95n
Lays of Ancient Rome, 45, 197
League, Etruscan, 32, 44; Latin, 108
Lehmann, Phyllis W., 157
Lemnos, Is., 30, 32
Lepcis Magna, 425
Lérici, C.M., 52
Levánzo, Is., 26
Lex Licínia Séxtia, 108
Libby, W.F., 18
Libraries, Rome, Palatine, 180; Trajan's Forum, 332; Pompeii, Timgad, Éphesus, 250; Tivoli, Hadrian's villa, 344, 348
Libya(ns), 183, 378
Licinio–Sextian law, 108
Lictors, 40
Ligório, Pirro, 161
Ligúria, 15
Lilliu, G., 16, 18, 27
Lipari, Islands, 26
Liris Valley, 117
Lists, 195
Litérnum, 92
Lithostroton, 147, 149–50, 151, 158
Lítuus, 65
Livia, Empress, 76; villa of, 185; On Ara Pacis, 210; statue, Pompeii, 257
Livy, 83, 102, 105, 126, 194, 197
Logic, Roman, 292
London, Houses of Parliament, 397
L'Orange, H.P., 426
Lorraine, Claude, 85
Lo Scasáto, 60
Louvre, Ara Pacis slab in, 204; Borghese gladiator, 240; Bosco-reále treasure, 263
Lucílius, C., 140
Lucius Caesar, 181, 182, 198, 210

Lucrétia, 75, 104
Lucretius, T., 83
Lucúlli, 155
Lucullus, L. Licínius, 143, 145, 191
Lucullus, M. Licínius, 143, 145, 155
Lucumo, 44, 45
Lucus Feróniae, 139
Ludi Megalénses, 111
Ludwig, K. of Bavaria, 245
Lugli, G., 426
Lunghézza, 75
Luni sul Mignóne, 21
Lutátius Catuls, Q., 158
Lycúrgus, King of Thrace, 433

MacDonald, W.L., 361
Macedonia, personified, 276
Macólnia, Dindia, 58
Macro, Q. Naévius, 120
Macstrna (Servius Tullius), 41
Madison, WI, 319
Maecénas, on Ara Pacis(?), 211
Maenad, 323
Magi, the three, 436
Magi, F., 301, 304, 439
Magíster pópuli, 42
Magna Graecia, 74
Magna Mater, 298
Maiúri, A., 255
Malalás, John, 428
Malibu Beach, CA, Getty Museum, 260
Mandéla, 391
Manifest Destiny, 108, 137
Marble, Pentelic, 172; Carrára, 189, 332; African, 287, 289; depository, Ostia, 326; Parian, 332; Greek island, 377
Marble Plan. *See* Rome, Marble Plan; Rome, *Forma Urbis*
Marcéllus, M. Claudius (died 23 B.C.), 182, 183, 191, 198
Marcus Aurélius, Emperor, 374, 380, 381, 382, 385
Marémma, Tuscan, 121
Maríno, 92
Márius, C., 106, 127, 141, 155, 191
Mars, 76, 193, 239, 301, 303, 387; in Regia, 89, 101; on Ara Pacis, 212; in Pompeii, 277; on Cancellería relief, 303; in Forum

of Augustus, 305; on Severan arch, 396
Marsyas, 131, 235, 277
Martial, 222, 383, 434
Marxists, 71
Marzabótto, 23, 34–36, 50, 101, 103, 115, 124
Massería Fongo, 4
Mater Matúta, 72, 76, 128
Matéra, 6
Mauretánia, 378
Maxéntius, Emperor, 353, 409, 410, 416, 428, 429, 432
Maxímian Herculius, 426, 428, 429, 432, 433
Maximílian, Emperor of Mexico, 281
McCann, Anna M., 127
McKim, C. F., 291; McKim, Mead and White, 327
Medea, 233, 235, 277, 309
Medúsa, 224, 277
Meiggs, R., 319
Melaníppus, 60
Menánder, 139, 263
Menedémus, philosopher, 276
Meneláus, 220
Menérva, 35. *See also* Minerva
Mengarélli, R., 52
Mercury, 60, 269, 275, 377, 387. *See also* Hermes
Mesopotámia, 8
Metéllus Créticus, Q. Caecílius, 174
Michael, archangel, 370
Michelangelo, 161, 195, 237, 383, 411, 433
Middle Ages, 292, 296, 333, 385, 394
Milan, 416
Millennium of Rome, 295
Milócca, 27
Minérva, 35, 95, 275, 301, 305, 377, 381, 382, 387, 416, 438
Mínotaur, 89
Mithraéa, 3, 16, 380, 399, 399n
Mithridátes, King, 163
Módena (Mútina), 137
Moésia, 339, 378
Molfétta, 6
Molína di Ledro, 13
Mónica, 330
Monte Circeío, 9
Montevérde tufa, 91, 106, 111

Moon, planet, 387
Morávia, 385
Morétti, G., 201, 202, 204
Mozart, W.A., 364
Murat, Joachim, 245
Muses, 235, 305, 306, 309, 323
Museums. See Boston, Chiéti, Ferrara, Florence, Louvre, Malibu, Naples; New York, Metropolitan; Palestrína (Praeneste), Pompeii, Pyrgi, Rabat; Rome, Capitoline, Conservatóri, Forum Antiquarium, Palatine Antiquarium, Pigorini, Terme, Vatican, Villa Giúlia; Tarquínia, Zágreb
Mussolini, Benito, 167, 178, 188, 224, 277, 287, 290, 305–306, 310, 314, 420
Mycenáe(an), 10, 15, 21, 89

Naples, earthquake of 1980, 263n; Kingdom of, 245, 249; National Museum, 143, 252, 260, 263, 275, 276, 378
Narcíssus, freedman, 277
Neánderthal man, 9
Némean Lion, 377, 433
Némesis, 279
Nemi, L., 127n, 217; houseboats, 222–27; temple of Diana, 227
Neolithic, 7, 26
Neo-Pythagoréans, 234, 235
Neptune, 320, 377, 382
Néreids, 434
Nero, grandnephew of Tiberius, 182
Nero, Emperor, 110, 134, 216, 217, 227, 236, 237, 239, 240, 242, 282, 283, 284, 291, 293, 306, 344, 356, 374, 417, 424, 435, 439, 441
Nero Claudius Drusus, Augustus's stepson, 192
Nerva, Emperor, 199, 302, 377, 382
Nessus, centaur, 433
New England, 128
New York, Metropolitan Museum, 276
Nigídius Figulus, P., 234
Nile, R., 143; personified, 372; holy water, 277
Níobe, 57

Nísibis, 396
Noah, drunk, 443
Nórchia, 55
North Africa, 320, 327, 425, 430
Norwegians, 426
Notízie degli Scavi, 420
Novilára, 10
Nucleus (of Roman road), 404
Numa, King, 82, 86, 90, 101
Nurághi, Sardinian, 16–18, 26
Nymphaéa, 217, 240, 309, 372, 412, 416
Nymphs, 240, 277

Obelisk, Rome, Pza. S. Pietro, 323; on Antoninus Pius column, 381; in Circus of Maxentius, 413; in Circus Maximus, 417, 426; in child's circus mosaic, Pza. Armerína, 432
Ocean, personified, 199
Octávia, sister of Augustus, 198, 208, 211
Octávian, 177, 178, 179, 181, 194, 195, 197, 228, 234. See also Augustus
October horse, 90
Odoacer, King, 295
Odýsseus, 220, 278, 429. See also Ulysses
Ódyssey, 220
Oédipus, 277
Olympic victors, 195
Olýnthus, 35
Omphálē, 278
Onyx, 326
Oplontis, villa, 261
Ops, goddess, 89
Opus, incértum, Sullan, 145, 147, 148, 149, 153, 160, 162; reticulátum, 165, 317; sectíle, 316; signínum, 128; vittátum, 375, 412
Orbetéllo, 124
Orders of architecture. See Composite, Corinthian, Doric, Ionic, Tuscan
Oréstes, 233
Orientalizing pottery, 23
Órpheus, 233, 429
Orsi, P., 21, 26, 27, 420
Orte (Úmbria), 402

Orviéto, 32, 40, 55, 57. *See also* Volsinii
Oscan language, 248, 257
Òsimo (Aúximum), 137
Osíris, 277, 367
Osrhoení (Mesopotamian people), 396
Ostería dell'Osa, 74
Ostia:
history: Italian excavation, 113, unfinished, 139; Ancus Martius, 114; castrum, 91; pre-Sullan, 327; Trajan, 314–31; Hadrian, 316, 322–23; Antonine & Sevéran, 316; post-Severan, 322; decline, 330–31
plan, 317; gates, Marina & Romana, 319, Laurentína, 328
Municipal life: 319–22; Forum, 317, 319, 327, 331; *duovíri,* 319; cúria, 319–331; Imperial Palace, 322, *Fasti,* 331
public amenities: aqueduct (Calígulan), 216; Baths: of the Seven Sages, 316, 320; of Neptune, 316, 320; Forum, 321, 352, 367; del Invidióso & Nuotatóre, 320; firemen's barracks, 322; theater, 117, 320; thermopólia, 327; safari park, 326
housing & daily life: garden apartments, 117; comparison with Pompeii, 264; contrast with Pompeii, 315; apartment houses, 322–23, *dolia,* 323; House of Cupid and Psýchē, 316
trade & industry: Claudian harbor, 117, 315, 323–326; Trajan's harbor, 315, 326–27; lighthouse, 323, 326; shops, 323, warehouses, 117, 319, 327; Piazzále delle Corporazióni, 316, 320, 326–27; *scholae* (guildhalls), 327; Portus, 330
religion, afterlife: Capitólium, 317, 327; half-scale Pántheon, 327; Domitiánic temple, 320; temple of Rome & Augustus, 327; temples of Ceres, Fortuna, Venus, & Spes, 327; of Hercules, 327; of Magna Mater, 328; of

Serápis, 328; Mithráea: 322, 328, 330; of Felicíssimus, 328; synagogue, 328; Christian building, 316; basilica & House of the Fish, 330; Christianity in, 331; Ísola Sacra cemetery, 330, 439
art & architecture: dating, 316; imitates Rome, 319; House of the Yellow Walls, 322; of the Muses, 322–23; dei Depínti, 323; of the Painted Vaults, 322; marble depository, 326
Ostia Antica, village, 320, 330
Ostia Lido, 315
Otho, Emperor, 282
Oubliettes, 120
Ovid, 266
Oxford University, 405
Ozymándias, 201

Páce, B., 426, 434
Pacúvius, M., 140
Paestum, 137, 141
Palaeolithic, 5
Palestrina, Barberini museum, 141, 142, 152. *See also* Praeneste
Palládio, A., 161, 364
Palladium, 220, 222, 232, 387
Pan, 278, 428
Pantálica, 23, 27
Papacy, 419. *See also* Pope
Paris, 233, 239
Parma, 137
Parthia(ns), 186, 197, 206, 380, 396, 408
Pascoláre di Castello, 72
Pasíphaë, 235
Passo di Corvo, 4, 5, 7, 8
Patróclus, 57, 220
Paviméntum, 403
Pavonazzétto, marble, 326, 332
Pax Romana, 380
Pega valley, 36
Pégasus, 392
Penátes, 412
Penélopē, 278
Péntheus, King, 235
Peperíno, 92, 169, 287, 289, 377
Pérgamum, 188n, 222, 433
Pérseus, 120, 278

Persia, personified, 276
Persuasion, personified, 185
Perugíno, Pietro, 237
Pèsaro (Písaurum), 137
Peschiéra, 14
Pesco Montano, 403
Petrónius, 272
Phaedra, 235, 239, 277, 278
Phaéthon, 183, 277
Phaon, 233–34
Philhellenism, Hadrian's, 310, 353
Philippi, battle of, 193
Philodémus, Epicurean, 260
Phocas, Emperor, 362
Phoenicia(ns), 18, 47, 77
Phoenix, Achilles's tutor, 277
Phrýgia, 32, 328, 330
Piacénza (Placéntia), 48, 137
Pianéllo, 15–16
Piázza Armeriña, hunting lodge,
    375, 419, 420–34; aqueduct,
    425; dating, 426–29; "Bikini
    girls," 420, 433–34; basilica,
    420, 433–34; atrium, 424; elliptical
    court, 425; large hunt mosaic,
    425, 430–32; nursery, 425; peri-
    style, 425; Circus Maximus
    mosaic, 426, 428; small hunt
    mosaic, 428, 429–30; griffin,
    430; child's circus mosaic, 432;
    triclinium, 432; labors of Her-
    cules, 432–33
Picasso, P., 433
Picénum, 24
Pietas, 174, 381, 382
Pietrabbondánte, theater, 141
Pietro da Cortóna, 161
Pigoríni, L., 10–13, 35, 74, 79
Pintadéra, 15
Piranési, G.B., 28, 85, 161
Pirélli, tire manufacturer, 347
Pisces, zodiacal sign, 380
Pius XI; pope, 434; – XII, 435
Placéntia, 402. See also Piacénza
Plato, Republic, 174
Plautiánus, C. Fúlvius, 397
Plautílla, 397, 399
Plaútios, Novios, 58
Plautus, 111, 272
Plebeian art, 381
Plemmírio, 27

Pliny the Elder, 219, 233, 284, 357,
    395
Plotínus, (?) at Ostia, 316
Po valley, 16, 137, 402
Politórium, 74
Pollux, 95, 189
Polýbius, 115
Polyclítus, 186
Polyphémus, 120, 220, 237, 429
Pompeii, 36, 131, 139; ch. 8, passim
  history: Oscan (Samnite), 248,
    249, 257; Sullan, 208, 255;
    Colónia Venéria Cornélia, 248;
    Julio-Claudian, 255; earthquake
    of A.D. 62, 273; damage, World
    War II, 252; earthquake of
    1980, 263n
  plan: insulae, 248, 250; Via dell'
    Abbondánza, 251; gates:
    Nócera, 245; Herculáneum,
    255; Marine, 264, 277; Vesu-
    vius, 273
  municipal & private life: Foro
    Triangoláre, 246; comítium,
    249; basílica, 249, 266; House
    of C. Julius Polýbius, 249; graf-
    fiti, 264, 266, 272, 273, 275
  public amenities: theaters, 141,
    250; stepping stones, 249;
    amphitheater, 250; library, 250;
    Stabian Baths, 250, 263n; inns,
    264; thermopolia, 264
  housing: gardens, 271–72; House
    of Fabius Rufus, 245–264; of
    Tragic Poet, 251; Moralist,
    251–54; Octávius Quártio, 269–
    70, 352; Faun, 252, 276; Sallust,
    252, 276; Pinárius Cereális, 268;
    Surgeon, 268; Cryptopórticus,
    269, 275; Fabia, 272; Caecílius
    Jucúndus, 273; Ceres, 276;
    Floral Bedchambers, 276; Jason,
    277; Villa Imperiále, 277; Villa
    of Mysteries, 276, 278–81, 304
  trade: Euxínus's wineshop, 264;
    shipowners' club, 267; Stépha-
    nus's fullonica, 268; shop of
    Verecúndus, 268–69; Caecílius
    Jucúndus, 228, 266–67; House
    of the Ship Europa, 270–72
  religious life: Doric temple, 248;

Villa of Mysteries, 255, 276, 278–81; Livia, statue, 257; Mercury, 269; Isis, 273, ancestor worship, 275
art, literature: Second Style, 143, 172, 173, 276; First Style, 147, 276; tags from poets, 264, 266; House of Véttii, 267–68; Alexander mosaic, 276; Third Style, 276–78, 305; Fourth Style, 278, 305; Pompeian red, 278; pattern books, 432
Pompeíus Magnus, 163, 174, 177, 214, 309
Pómptine Marshes, 76, 402
Ponte Lupo, 392
Póntifex Máximus, 101, 103, 210, 306, 317, 445
Pope (bishop of Rome), 301. See also Papacy
Poppaéa, Empress, 237, 261
Populónia, 32, 54, 57
Pórphyry, 326, 361
Portasánta (Chian marble), 326
Portugal, 54
Portus (Ostia), 330
Posto, working villa, 174
Postúmius Regillénsis, A., 189
Postumius Albínus, A. (cos. 180), 110
Pozzolána, volcanic sand, 154
Pozzuóli (Puteóli), 137, 267
Pottery: orientalizing, 22; black-figure, 22, 36, 53; red-figure, 22, 36; geometric, 26; Attic, 36; proto-Villanóvan, 75, 114, 320; impasto, 78, 82, 85; sub-Geometric, 82; búcchero, 85, 101; proto-Corínthian, 95; Etrusco-Campanian, 124; plain black glaze, 126; Árretine, 131, 333; N. African, 320; terra sigilláta D, 426
Praeféctus annónae, 336
Praenéste, 58, 189, 291, 334, 335, 358, 425; Barberíni & Bernadíni tombs, 68; Sanctuary of Fortune, 141–55; date, 155; propylaéa, 142; Antro delle Sorti, 142; basilica & lower sanctuary, 145; upper sanctuary, 147;

ramp, 148; wellhouse, 150; shops, 151; Cortina terrace, 151; exedra, 155; tholos, 153, 166; Barberíni mosaic, 432; use of concrete, 153–54. See also Palestrína
Praetor Etrúriae, 42
Praetórian guard, 217, 381
Prática di Mare (Lavinium), 95
Prima Porta, villa of Livia, 76, 185
Proféctio, 301
Propaganda, Augustan, ch. 6, passim
Propértius, 266
Proto-Corinthian ware, 53, 95
Proto-Villanóvan ware, 16, 23, 72, 75, 114, 320
Provinces, personified, 188, 378
Prýtanis, 45
Psýchē, 316
Ptólemies, 143, 145
Púglia (Apulia), 1, 6, 137
Puglísi, S.M., 79, 81, 85
Pygmies, 322
Pyramid, Great, 8, 18, 197
Pyrgi, 47, 60
Pythágoras, 234

Quadi, 385
Quislings, 339, 385

Rabat, museum, 174
Rabírius, architect, 169, 305, 306, 311
Radiant heating, 225
Randall-MacIver, D., 18
Raphael Sanzio, 161, 237, 362
Ravenna, 426
Red-figure ware, 23, 36
Réggio Emília (Rhegium), 15
Regíllus, L., 95, 189
Remedéllo, 8
Remus, 58, 95, 212
Renaissance, 28, 177, 208, 236, 290, 370, 406, 411, 434, 444
Renan, E., 387
Revetments, 35, 101, 103, 108, 115, 117, 180, 193, 336, 377
Rex sacrorum, 45
Rhodes, 219; marble, 147; sculptors, 219

Ricci, Corrádo, 167–68, 188, 191, 333
Richardson, L., Jr., 132, 413
Richmond, I.A., 405, 408, 409
Rímini (Aríminum), 21, 137
Roads, Roman, 402–406
Róbbia, Luca della, 210
Roma, goddess, 199, 212, 296, 301, 381, 416, 430
Roman, army, 338; attitude to war, 333; Campágna, 391, 393; conspicuous waste, 434; historicism, 333; intelligence, 309, 310; logic, 292; navy, 338; Peace, 380; roads, 402–5; puritanism, 165, 166; unsporting, 429
Romania(ns), 333
Romantics, 309
Rome:
  history: Roma Quadrata, 13; archaic, 71; Forum necrópolis, 74, 75, 77, 78, 79, 86; Pálatine hut village, 78, 86; equus Domítiani levels, 98; Augustan, ch. 6; Circus Maximus obelisk, 417, 426; millennium, 295
  topography: Campus Martius, 201, 284, 300, 380; Clivus Argentárius, 169; Forum of Nerva, 188; Hills: Áventine, 106, 112, 400, 417; Caélian, 283; Cápitoline, 89, 158, 333; Ésquiline, 86, 104, 105, 333; Janículum, 287; Pálatine, 72, 77, 95, 417; Quírinal, 78, 86, 95, 106, 333; Largo Argentína, Sevéran portico, 110; Marble Plan, 110, 167, 283, 284, 287, 289. See also Forma Urbis. Porte: Maggióre, 229, 393; Asinária, 409; Appia, 409; Septimóntium, 89; Súbura, 188, 305; Tarpeían Rock, 103; Tomb of Hatérii, landmarks on, 298–300; Velábrum, 397, 416; Via Flamínia, 171; walls: agger, 40, 106; "Servian," 91, 92, 104, 106, 108; Aurelian's, 375, 405–10
  politics, propaganda: arches: of Argentárii, 396–97; of Augustus, 181, 194–97; Constantine,

214, 296, 331–32, 364, 375, 382, 413–16; of Janus, 416; Lucius & Gaius, 181; M. Aurelius, 382; Septímius Sevérus, 85, 214, 296, 375, 396, 416; of Tibérius, 416; of Titus, 214, 242, 294, 296. Altar of Peace (Ara Pacis), 179, 183, 188, 191, 201–14, 217, 296, 301, 304, 396, 435. Basilicas: Aemília, 166–67; Júlia, 92, 166, 332, 416; of Maxéntius, 162, 289, 375, 409, 413; of Trajan, 331–32. Calendar-sundial, 206n. Cancellería relief, 214, 284, 301–304, 305, 382. Castra Praetória, 217. Columns: of Antonínus Pius, 375, 380; of M. Aurelius, 214, 375, 385, 396, 413; of Trajan, 214, 296, 331, 332–40, 380, 383, 385, 396, 413, 433. Comítium, 91, 98, 99. Cúria, 412. Domus Transitória, 241; Equestrian statue of M. Aurelius, 383. Fora: of Augustus, 188–94, 305, 331, 332; of Caesar, 166–69, 189, 305, 331; of Peace, 165, 282, 284, 286–90, 305, 364; of Trajan, 188, 314, 331–33; Transitórium, 282, 284, 287, 304, 331. Mausoléa: of Augustus, 174, 192, 197–200, 368; of Hadrian, 174, 342, 368; of Rómulus, 412. Nero, colossus, 243. Rostra, 95, 98, 99, 108. Secretárium Senátus, 412. Tabulárium, 141, 158–61, 284, 291. Tombs: of Bíbulus, 92; of Scípios, 92 & n; Caecília Metélla, 74. Tulliánum, 91, 112
Housing: Cápitoline ínsula, 383: Casa dei Grifi, 82, 172; Domus Flavia, 78, 81, 143, 217, 284, 306–9, 353; — Tiberiána, 216; Hut "of Romulus," 83, 183, 308: Golden House (Domus Aúrea) of Nero, 215, 235, 236–42, 282, 284, 291, 292, 344, 353, 424; House of Augustus, 182, 183; of Lívia, 183; octagon under T. of Venus & Rome, 240, 353; House of Scipio Africánus

(?)167; Villa under Farnesína, 143, 183; of Maxéntius, 377; Sette Bassi, 375; Severán palace, 387; "Minerva Médica," 417

public amenities: amphitheaters: Castrénse, 406n; Colosséum, 167, 182, 240, 242, 283, 287, 290–95, 298, 300, 313, 352, 353, 430; Vatican, 435, 441. Aqueducts, 389–95; Severán, 387; Alsietína, 395; Ánio Novus, 391, 394; — Vetus, 391, 394; Appia, 189, 389; Claudia, 391, 393, 394; Julia, 393, 395; Márcia, 389, 391, 393, 394, 399; Tépula, 394; Virgo, 395. Baths: of Caracálla, 326, 375, 397–400, 411; Cónstantine, 333; Dioclétian, 162, 336, 375, 410–11; Titus, 242; Trajan, 236, 336–37. Circuses: of Flamínius, 112, 165; Maxéntius, 409, 412; Máximus, 387, 406n, 413, 417–19; Variánus, 406n. Cloáca Máxima, 104, 105, 305, 416. Libraries: Palatine, 180; Trajan's Forum, 331, 332, 333, 411. Ludus Dácicus, 295. Lupánar, 83, 313. Odéum of Domitian, 313. Pons: Aélius, 368, Fabrícius, 171; Mílvius, 92, 171, 416; Sublícius, 13. Stadium of Domítian, 284, 308, 310–13. Theaters: of Balbus, 165, 183; Marcéllus, 112, 313; Pompey, 108, 110, 161, 163, 166, 364

trade: Empórium, 112; Eurýsaces, baker, tomb of, 229, 298; Forum Boárium, 171, 317, 417; — Holitórium, 72; Pórticus Aemília, 112; Minúcia (frumentária), 110; Trajan's Market, 162, 333–36, 383; Via Biberática, 335

religion: Aula Isíaca, 143, 216; Ara Pietátis, 193; Christianity: basilicas, 332; bishop, 444; catacombs, 443; Mocking Crucifix, 387; Old St. Peter's, 332, 434, 435; St. Peter's, cemetery under, 330, 435–42; Campo P, 438–43; Aedicula, 439, 441, 444;

niche of pallia, 444; San Sebastiáno (Via Appia), 442. Lapis Niger stele, 91, 93, 99. Mithraéa: under baths of Caracálla, 399; Ostia, 328; Santa Prisca, 400n. Régia, 44, 75, 89, 95, 101, 102; subterranean basilica, 217, 228–36, 436. Temples: Aesculápius, 111; Antonínus & Faustína, 79, 240, 374, 377; Apollo in circo (Sosiánus), 178–79, 180, 181, 182; —Palatínus, 179; in Largo Argentína, 91, 92, 108, 166; Castor, 182; Claudius, 283; Concord, 182; Divus Julius, 181, 182; Fortúna, 72;—Redux, 304, 382, 383; Hadrianéum, 377; Hercules Victor (Forum Boárium round temple), 171, 172; Janus, 72; Juno Sóspita, 72; Jupiter Capitolínus, 35, 60, 91, 102, 103, 298, 382;—Tonans, 298; Magna Mater, 111; Mars Ultor, 193; Mater Matúta, 72; Minérva, 287; Pántheon, Agrippa's, 182; Domítian's (?), 304; Hadrian's, 154, 239, 342, 349, 357–63, 364, 367; Romulus, 412; Spes, 72; Sun, 387; Trajan, 331, 350; Veióvis, 158; Venus & Rome, 239, 242, 342, 343, 352–56, 358; Venus Génetrix, 169; — Víctrix, 166. Vatican parking lot, pagan cemetery under, 440. Vesta, shrine, 82, 90, 101, 183, 387; Átrium Vestae, 242, 389

Museums, art: Civiltà Romana, 290; Capitoline, 58; Conservatóri, 79, 102, 378; Brutus in, 58; Wolf, 58; Ésquiline fresco, 78, 79, Apollo in circo frieze, 179; Fasti, 195; Arch of M. Aurélius panels, 382; colossal Cónstantine, 413. Forum Antiquárium, 78, 83, 167; Palatine, 81, 172, 387; Pigoríni, 10; Terme: 143, 183, 378, 389, 411; Farnesína frescoes & stuccoes in, 183; villa of Livia garden fresco, 185–86; Fanciúlla di Ánzio, 240; Ara Pacis slab, 204;

Rome (*continued*)
Vatican, 28, 58, 66, 92, 191, 241, 301, 308, 378, 380; Belvedére torso in, 166; Prima Porta Augustus, 186; Ara Pacis slabs, 204; Hatérii tomb, 298; Cancellería relief, 300; Ostia mosaic, 322; Laócoön, 219, 220, 240; athletes mosaic, 400. Villa Giúlia, 28, 60, 75, 76
post-classical: Aqua Felíce, 406n; — Paolo, 287; airport (Fiumicíno), 323; American Academy, 2, 391, 395; anti-pollution measures, 296, 337, 383, 396; Bourse, 377; British School at, 2; Castel Sant' Ángelo, 362, 370, 372. Churches: Gesù, 204; San Bernárdo, 411; — Gíorgio in Velábro, 397; — Giovanni in Lateráno, 332, 383, 412; San Lorénzo fuori le Mura, 332; — Lorenzo in Miránda, 377; — Martíno, 412; — Nicóla in Cárcere, 72; — Páolo fuori le Mura, 332; — Piétro in Vaticáno, 177, 189, 323, 419; — Sebastiáno (on Palatine), 387; Sant'Adriáno, 412; — Agnése in Agóne, 311; — Omobóno, 72; Santa Croce in Gerusalémme, 406n; — Francésca Romana, 167; Maria ad Mártyres (Pántheon), 362; — Maria Maggióre, 387; Prisca, 399n; — Sabína, 332; Sistine Chapel, 433; Farnése gardens, 78; French Academy, 111, 204, — School of Archaeology, 389; Grand Hotel, 411. Palazzi: Braschi, 220; Caffarelli, 102; Farnese, 300; Fiáno, 201; del Senatóre, 161; Venézia, 167. Pasquíno, 220. Piazze: Campidóglio, 383; Colónna, 385; Esédra, 410, 411; Navóna, 310, 412; di Pietra, 377; del Pópolo, 191; San Giovánni in Lateráno, 417; Venézia, 287. Ponte Sant'Ángelo, 368. Porte: San Lorénzo, 408. San Pancrázio, 410. St. Peter, on Trajan's Column, 332. Swedish Archaeological Institute, 2. Términi, 106, 411. Trastévere, 183, 383, 395. Villa Médici, 111, 204.
Vie: Corsía Agonále, 310; Corso del Rinasciménto, 310; Eleniána, 406n; dei Fori Imperiáli, 413 (*See also* Via del Impèro, below); G. Giolítti, 416; di Grotta Pinta, 165; dell'Impèro, 167, 188, 287; Viminále, 412
Rómulus, King, 95, 174, 188n, 189, 194–95, 210, 212, 308
Rosélle, 32. *See also* Ruséllae
Rosétta Stone, 47
Rosso antíco, 326
Rothschild, Edward, de, 263
Royal Air Force, British, 1
Rudus, in Roman roads, 404
Ruséllae, 38. *See also* Rosélle
Rúspoli, Prince & Princess, 53

Sabaúdia, Domitian's villa at, 352
Sabína, Empress, 139, 366
Sabine(s): women, 76, 79, 167; inhumed dead, 86; Numa, 101; hills, 39
Säflund, G., 15, 105, 106, 107
St. Peter: in Tulliánum, 111; basilica of, 291; alleged bones of, 441
Salérno, 137
Samnites, 24, 113, 117; Second S— War, 79; at Pompeii, 257. *See also* Oscan
San Fuóco d'Angelóne, 4, 6
San Giovenále, 20
Santa Sevéra, 47
Sappho, 233–34, 277
Sardinia, Is., 15, 16, 327
Sargent, J.S., 239
Sarmátians, 339
Sassi Cadúti, temple, 60
Sátricum, antefixes, 62; T. of Mater Matuta, 76
Saturn, 387
Satúrnia, 402n
Satyrs, 239
Scasáto, Lo, 60
Scherer, M., 309
Scipios, 92
Scóglio del Tonno (Tàranto), 10

Scorpio, zodiacal sign, 199
Scýthia, 380
Seasons, 298
Sejánus, L. Aelius, 120, 219
Selce (in Roman roads) 403, 405
Seleúcia-on-Tigris, 396
Semprónius Gracchus, Ti., 103; C. 137; Ti. senior, 191
Senate, Roman, 302
Serápis, 216
Sérvius Túllius, King, 45, 72, 82, 104
Sesklo, 6
Sesto Fiorentíno, 136
Sette Finéstre, villa, 133
Settis, S., 428n, 432
Seven against Thebes, 60
Sevéran dynasty, 110, 201, 222, 357, 374, 387, 406n
Sevérus, Septímius, Emperor, 165, 389, 399; arch of, 395–97
Síbylline Books, 180
Sicily, 16, 19, 21, 117, 420
Sículan culture, 22, 26, 27
Siléni(us), 278, 279, 323, 372
Sílius Itálicus, poet, 40
Silvánus, 364, 367
Simon, Erika, 304
Sítule, 21, 24, 382
Sixtus V, Pope, 332, 387
Sodom, 273
Sóphocles, 434
Sósius, C., 179, 180
Spain, 313, 327, 346
Spálato, 162, 424
Sparta, 72
Spelúnca (Sperlónga), 217
Sperlónga, 120; villa, 217–22, 308
Speróne, building stone, 92, 188
Spes, Temple of, 72, 327
Sphinx, Augustus's signet, 193, 212
Spina, 34, 36–38, 50
Spinazzóla, V., 251–52, 314
Spoléto (Spoletium), 137
Stábiae (Castellammare di Stabia), 277
Statílius Taurus, T., 236
Statúmen, in Roman roads, 403
Stentinéllo, 26
Stone-robbing, 300
Strategic Air Command, American, 2; British, 2

Strong, D.E., 227
Stucco, 183, 216, 230
Stúdius, painter, 185
Sub-Geometric ware, 82
Subiáco (Subláqueum), 391
Sudan, 143
Suetónius, 219n
Su Naráxi, 16–18
Sulla, L. Cornélius, 106, 148, 149, 155, 158, 163, 174, 177, 191, 214; Sullan phases: Ostia, 117, Alba Fucens, 118, 120, Cosa, 134; Praenéste, 141; building activity at Rome, Ostia, Pompeii, Pietrabbondánte, Faesulae, 141
Sulla, nephew of above, 276
Sulpícius Cinnamus, C., 267
Summum dorsum, in Roman roads, 404
Sun, as god, 387; Christ as, 436
Swastika, 26, 78
Swedes, 105
Syphax, 120
Syracuse, 23, 28; Eurýalus wall, 107; navy, 113
Syria, 68, 331, 368

Tábulae pontíficum, 102
Tácitus, historian, 217, 236, 380, 435
Tarchúnies Rumach, Cneve, 41. See also Cn. Tarquinius Romanus
Tarquínia, 46, 47, 52, 78, 95; painted tombs, 28; Villanóvan phases, 32; cursus honórum, at, 42; Tomb of Orcus, 42, 44, 48; of Hunting & Fishing, 53; Ara della Regína, 62; of Leopards, 68; of Shields, Chariots, Olympic victors, Augur, 69
Tarquins, Kings: I, 41, 82, 87, 98, 102, 417; — the Proud, 41, 75, 82, 102, 103; dynasty, 103, 104, 418
Tarquínius Romanus, Cn., 41
Tarracína. See Terracina
Tauris, 232
Tavoliére, 2, 4, 5, 7, 13, 15, 24
Taylor, Doris M., 126
Telámon, battle of, 128
Temples, Tuscan, 30

Térence, 111
Terra sigilláta D, 426
Terracína, 141, 158, 402, 403
Terremáre, 11–13, 15, 24, 26, 35, 79
Thapsos, 27
Thatcher, E.D., 321
Theaters. *See* Alba Fucens, Faésulae, Herculáneum, Minúrnae, Óstia, Pietrabbondánte, Pómpeii; Rome, Balbus, Marcéllus, Pompey; Tivoli, Hadrian's villa; Túsculum
Thebes, 60
Themístocles, 316
Théseus, 179, 277, 278
Thetis, 239
Thoas, King, 232
Thrace, 378, 433
Tiber, Is., 114, 171; R., 13, 28, 106, 171, 315, 368, 412; Fiumicíno branch, 326; personified, 372
Tiberius, Emperor, 120, 181, 182, 198, 216, 217; as Mars, 186; on Gemma Augustéa, 200; on Boscoreále silver, 277; fast journey, 405
Tibur, Sullan temples, 141
Tigris, 396
Tilly, Bertha M., 74
Timgad, library, 250
Tin(ia), 35, 48
Titus, Emperor, 281, 282, 300, 301
Tivoli, 177; T. of Hercules Victor, 161; Villa d'Este, 161; trávertine, 177; aqueducts in area, 391, 392. *See also* Tibur
Tivoli, Hadrian's villa, 162, 341, 342, 343, 344–52, 362–72, 424: Poecíle, 308, 345; Small Baths, 342; Teátro Maríttimo, 342, 347–49, 358, 364, 366; "Stadium," 342, 349–52, 367; Canópus, 342, 343, 346, 370–72; Piázza d'Oro, 342, 343, 362–67; Serapéum, 343; triclínia, guest quarters, palaces, baths, library, pools, porticoes, slave quarters, T. of Serapis, 344; cryptoporticus, 344; 346; firemen's barracks, 344, 352; Praetorium, comparison with Versailles, 345; Academy, "Hell,"

346; Piázza d'Oro, 352, 364–67; Large Baths, Heliocamínus, 352; Small Baths, 356; 367; Caryátids, 370; sculpture, 370
Todi, "Mars" of, 58
Tongília, gens, 134
Torre Galli, 23, 26
Toynbee, J.M.C., 304, 436
Trajan, Emperor, 236, 295, 298, 313, 440, ch. 10, *passim*, 377, 403; & Ostia, 117, 314–31; *óptimus princeps*, 314, 332, 337; head, Ostia, 316; building activity, 342; aqueduct, 395
Trávertine, 177, 290, 296, 325, 327
Tribes: Italic, 113; Germanic, 127
Triéste (Tergéste), 137
Trimálchio, 272
Triptólemus, 235
Tritons, 233
Trojan War, 41, 72, 239, 245
Troy, 232, 387; Troy VIII & IX, 23
Tuchúlcha, 57
Tufas, 91–92, 327
Tunísia, 137
Turin (Augusta Taurinórum), 137
Turner, F,J., 139
Tuscan, order of architecture, 163; temple, 30
Týdeus, 60
Tyrrhénian Sea, 121

Ulýsses, 232. *See also* Odysseus
Underwater archaeology, 127 & n
Uni, 35, 48
Útica, 174

Vagliéri, D., 79, 81
Val Camónica, 9
Valadiér, G., 161
Valérian, Emperor, 443
Valérius: Ántias, 76; Maximus, M', 191; Poplícola, 76
Vandals, 444
Van Deman, E.B., 249, 389, 391, 393, 394, 395
Van Essen, C.C., 240
Vanth, 41, 279
Varro, M. Teréntius, 180
Vases, Attic, 36
Veii, Apollo of, 32, 60, 103; Vulca, 60; Portonaccio temple, 95;